THE
AFRICAN
GIANT

The Story of a Journey

BOOKS BY STUART CLOETE

Novels of South Africa

WATCH FOR THE DAWN
THE TURNING WHEELS
THE HILL OF DOVES
CONGO SONG
THE CURVE AND THE TUSK

Non-Fiction

YESTERDAY IS DEAD
AGAINST THESE THREE
THE THIRD WAY
THE AFRICAN GIANT

Poetry

THE YOUNG MEN AND THE OLD

●

THE
AFRICAN
GIANT

The Story of a Journey

BY STUART CLOETE

*Illustrated with photographs and maps
by Rehna Cloete*

•

HOUGHTON MIFFLIN COMPANY BOSTON

The Riverside Press Cambridge

Dedicated ...

• To TINY, my companion, friend, wife and photographer who never failed me in any of her capacities, and to all those who helped us on our way by putting us up, giving us meals, information and friendship. Most of them are mentioned by name and I apologise for any that I have omitted to thank through an oversight, lack of space, or loss of my notes.

There are certainly some errors in the book. Ordinary errors, careless errors and accidental errors due to tiredness when I redrafted my notes or tried to remember everything after an exhausting day. Bits of paper have been lost, have been dissolved in sweat and rain. They have been eaten by rodents and insects. It has been a long job, almost a year of travel and a year of writing. I have told the truth as I saw it. Others might see it differently, but what I present is one facet of the transition of a continent from the iron age into the present.

Above all I dedicate *The African Giant* to the white men who have given their lives to Africa and the African. And to those Africans who are devoting themselves to the service of their people in this difficult time.

Acknowledgments

● I wish to express our thanks to everyone who was so kind and helpful to us in every way, and to whom we are indebted for hospitality, advice, information — even friendship to passing strangers. Among them were:

Kimberley

The De Beers Company
Mr. Harry Beck
Mr. Warren
Mr. and Mrs. Alex Hall

Mr. and Mrs. Gallagher
Miss Olive McIntyre
Mr. and Mrs. Sneeman
Dr. Stuart

Rhodesia

Their Excellencies Sir John and
  Lady Kennedy
Brigadier and Mrs. L. Deedes

Mr. William Gale
Mr. T. C. Tebbit

Nigeria

Their Excellencies Sir John and
  Lady MacPherson
Mr. E. A. T. Benson
Mr. and Mrs. D. Potts
Mr. H. R. E. Browne
Mr. and Mrs. Conrad Williams
Mr. and Mrs. Rex Niven
Mr. and Mrs. Ian Gunn
Mr. R. G. D. Horsley
Captain Wally Shaw
Mr. Gordon Rogers

Dr. Adeniyi Jones
Mr. and Mrs. W. Keeler
Mr. Tony McClellan
Mr. John Stocker
Mr. and Mrs. L. Gobels
Colonel Macray
Colonel Thorn
Mr. and Mrs. McInnes
Mr. Cecil Iles
Colonel and Mrs. Andrews
Dr. Kenneth Mellanby

Nigeria (*continued*)

Mr. and Mrs. K. Munro
Mr. Butcher
Mr. C. Crowsdale
Captain and Mrs. P. Conroy
Mr. R. H. Ambler
Mr. D. Smith
Mr. James
Mr. Allen
Mr. A. D. Walter
Mr. Cuthbert Mayne

Colonel and Mrs. Davies
Mr. Counsell
Captain Bowler
Colonel Marshall
Colonel Milligan
Mr. Rakar
Their Excellencies the Emirs of
    Kano, Bida, Zaria
The Oba of Benin
The Oni of Ife

The Gold Coast

Their Excellencies Sir Charles
    and Lady Arden-Clarke
The Prime Minister, Dr. Kwame
    Nkrumah
Nana Sir Osei Agyeman Prem-
    peh II
Nana Amonoo Aferi
Nana Aduku Abakio
Nana Mbro V
Commander and Mrs. Jackson
Mr. James Moxon
Mr. Sean Graham
Mr. and Mrs. H. Sparkes
Mr. John Matson
Captain and Mrs. Barry Lane
Mr. J. T. Alexander
Mr. and Mrs. A. S. Jones

Mr. R. A. Raymond
Mr. and Mrs. D. M. Allen
Raja Rameshwar Rao
Dr. T. M. Wilson
Dr. and Mrs. Odamatten-Easmon
Dr. Oku Ampofo
Miss Gloria Addae
Mr. Hughes
Mr. H. Peters
Mr. Arkhurst
Mr. W. H. Beeton
Mr. Grieve
Miss McInnes
Mr. B. C. B. Nutsugah
Mr. Crepi
Dr. Stewart Simpson

Liberia

President V. S. Tubman
The Honorable G. A. Padmore
The Honorable W. R. Tolbert
The Honorable R. A. Herries
The Honorable James Morgan
Mr. W. Ajassiz Knuckles

Mr. Simpson
Miss Simson
Mr. Lloyd Whisnant
The Firestone Company
Mr. and Mrs. Lotz
Mr. and Mrs. David Soper

The Congo

His Excellency Monsieur Pétillon
Their Excellencies Monsieur and Madame Rik Cornelis
Monsieur A. Samuel
Monsieur André Scohy
The United Africa Company and Huileries du Congo Belge
Mr. B. Tollinton
Monsieur T. Jonniaux
Monsieur and Madame Lorent
Monsieur and Madame Roger de Gaulle
Monsieur Renders
Monsieur Delbeke
Monsieur Flamez
Monsieur and Madame Fosseprez
Monsieur and Madame F. Maisse
Monsieur and Madame G. Drousie
Mr. Le Blanck
Mr. and Mrs. H. R. Lancaster
Monsieur and Madame P. Fauconnier
Monsieur Jean Labrique
Monsieur Caps
Monsieur Bernier
Monsieur and Madame Siquet
Monsieur and Madame Fogenne
Monsieur Vin
Monsieur and Madame Copain
Monsieur Gillon
Monsieur Charles Met en Ancxt
Monsieur de Castellaire
Doctor and Madame d'Hooghe
Captain de Medina
Baron Alec Jolly
Monsieur and Madame Mailland of Brazzaville

Uganda

Their Excellencies Sir Andrew and Lady Cohen

Kenya

Their Excellencies Sir Evelyn and Lady Baring
Lord and Lady Delamere
Colonel Ewart Grogan
Mr. Jack Block
Mr. and Mrs. John Lambert
Mr. Stanley Lawrence Brown
Mr. David Lunan
Mr. Mervin Cowie
Mr. Walter Shapley
Mr. Rodney Chilton
Mr. Alastair Mathews
Dr. Christopher Wilson
Mr. Michael Durnford
Miss M. Tighe
Dr. L. S. B. Leakey

Contents

Illustrations

Following p. 160

1. The Big Hole, Kimberley
2. Digger shaking out first wash
3. Ruins of Zimbabwe
4. Desert horseman
5. Kuri ox from Lake Chad
6. Kano shop
7. Kano house
8. Fulani girls, near Kano
9. Mounted Bida spearman
10. Emir of Bida
11. Emir's trumpeters
12. Medicine stall, Lagos market
13. Ju-ju house, Badagri
14. Altar at Benin

Following p. 288

15. Monuments of the Asafo
16. Methodist ladies dancing at Abori
17. King in palanquin
18. Chiefs' umbrellas and drums
19. Fishing canoes at Senya Beraku
20. Woman chewing newly severed goat's leg
21. Old castle
22. Christiansburg Castle
23. The Right Honorable Kwame Nkrumah
24. Witch doctor assistants
25. Drummer in hysteria
26. Bapende chief
27. Bapende hairdos

THE
AFRICAN
GIANT

The Story of a Journey

• *North and South Rhodesia*

1

Diamonds in the Streets...Kimberley, South Africa

● A JOURNEY must have a starting point, and a cause, there must be some reason for it. Fundamentally, a journey of any kind is abnormal. Both men and animals tend to stay where they are born unless they are driven to move in search of food or mates, or forced away by the pressure of war or disaster.

Our aim was a trip, a change, a search for adventure — for something different — and the desire to clarify our minds about the racial ferment of Africa. How capable was the black man? What had the white man achieved? What was the picture today? What would the picture be tomorrow?

The trip started where colonial Africa began. At the Cape of Good Hope, the garden established by the Dutch East India Company in 1652, as a halfway house to the riches of the East. Where my ancestor landed with Van Riebeeck and, in 1656, received the first grant of land ever given to a white man in Africa. The Peninsula, with its lushness, its mediterranean climate and flora, ends with the Hex River Pass. Where Africa begins. The Karoo with its succulents, its aloes, its strangely shaped hills, is the first sample of the continent.

Fortunes are now being made by sheep farmers in this curious country which, to a man who is not a sheep farmer, looks like a desert. From the train one can see an occasional homestead, an occasional patch of emerald alfalfa under irrigation, an occasional weeping willow by an occasional dam. This is the country of the occasional. Sheep country in which one sees no sheep, inhabited country in which one sees few men or houses, a country with rivers every few miles, but with watercourses empty of water, as the sky is empty of birds and the veld empty of game. There was nothing to look at but sandy soil, rocky outcrops, strangely shaped hills which, in the mauve shadows of the desert evening, seemed to resemble rows of dead elephants lying side by side with extended trunks.

In the dining saloon a woman spoke to us. She remembered Tiny's big, heart-shaped aquamarine ring. It was an interesting encounter and amusing to be recognized by a bit of jewellery. We had met her seven years ago in Pretoria. Where were we going? What were we going to do?

"We're going on a trip," we said.

"A holiday?"

"Not exactly. A trip to see what we can see."

It was not easy to explain. We scarcely knew ourselves — only that we must go. Driven to travel like lemmings by some hidden urgency.

We reached Kimberley in a singularly shivery cold dawn and went to the Grand Hotel. We were fortunate enough to get a big corner room with a fireplace in it on the second floor. Number 35 was a queer shape. The corner facing the street was cut off diagonally — this was the result of the Boer "Long Tom" shell that had killed George Labram on the ninth of February, 1900, while he was dressing to go out to dinner with Mr. Rhodes. "Long Cecil" was the British reply to the Boers' "Long Tom." It was built by Labram, the American chief engineer to De Beers, with the help of Mr. E. Goffe, their chief draftsman. It was made out of a solid piece of hammered steel, ten feet long and ten and a half inches in diameter, weighing two thousand, eight hundred pounds. Its construction took only twenty-four days and most of the tools used had to be manufactured in the mine machine shops before it could be begun. It was capable of throwing a twenty-eight-pound projectile a distance of five miles, and Mortimer Menpes, the famous war correspondent of the period, said "that of all the things I have personally seen and read of in the annals of war, the most remarkable is the making of this gun in a mining workshop in the centre of Africa."

So our trip had begun well, with romance and history. But how curiously that history reads now with its tales of bombardments that today would scarcely be mentioned in the press, and of hardships and horrors that sound more like the description of a picnic than a war to our more sophisticated ears.

As far as I was concerned, the Big Hole dominated Kimberley. This abandoned mine was the womb of modern Africa. It was here that Johannesburg was born, that Rhodesia was born. Here that modern industry first appeared in Africa. Here that the first wheels turned that were not wagon wheels. It was only when diamonds were discovered that the great scramble for Africa began and all the nations of Europe rushed into the vacuum of the continent, claiming everything that was still unclaimed. Everyone must have a share. Everyone who had a share must increase his holding. Africa was carved up like a sirloin.

Kimberley was the beginning. Kimberley is De Beers and De Beers is Rhodes. He is the father. The great man who died young, childless, exhausted, having given birth to a nation and an idea. Mr. Rhodes still lives here. In the Kimberley Club, in his house, in the big kameeldoorn under whose shade he sorted his parcels of diamonds, in the flat rocks he used as a mounting block, in the hitching post to which he tied his horse.

The streets, running "every which way," began as tracks dividing the claims. The ghosts of the diggers would not lose themselves if they chose to return. The Big Hole is beyond destruction and there are still some wood and iron shanties standing that once housed the men who became South Africa's first millionaires. Kimberley, with the possible exception of Stellenbosch, alone remains authentic in South Africa. Table Mountain has been desecrated with a cable way, the old buildings of the town torn down, and the sea itself pushed back to form an industrial foreshore. Pretoria is a suburban collection of villas dominated by the Union Buildings. Johannesburg, a microcosm of New York, a tawdry copy, is ashamed of the mine dumps that produce its riches. They have grown away from history. Oom Paul Kruger, the old President, is no longer there. But Mr. Rhodes is still in Kimberley.

That was what they called him. Mr. Rhodes, or the Old Man. No one called him C. J., or John or Cecil. No one plain Rhodes. In his time he was a giant and his shadow still hovers over Africa. His words are not yet forgotten. When Sir Ernest Oppenheimer heard they had started plastering the De Beers offices in Kimberley — they are built of beautiful red brick with white woodwork — he rushed down and said: "You can't do that. Mr. Rhodes would not like it." The brickwork that had been covered was stripped at once. Rhodes may not have been an entirely admirable figure. But he was great. He was beloved and hated. He belonged among those semi-mythical English figures, of whom Sir Winston Churchill seems to be the last example. It is probable that such men still exist but their style is cramped by bureaucracy, by swift communications.

We dined at the Kimberley Club several times, and I was made an honorary member and often went in for a drink in the evening. In the Boer War Colonel Kekewich planned the defence of Kimberley here, and Lord Kitchener and General Freude who later commanded the British expeditionary force in 1914 both lived here. The Duke of Windsor stayed here, and the King and Queen used the Club as their headquarters. Victorian in furnishings and feeling, it exuded an atmosphere of wealth, security, cosiness and history, with its portraits, its mounted horns, trophies and curious souvenirs of war and peace. Its bronzes, leather-bound books, brass bar rail, open coal fire and mahogany tables, and the weighing chair that Mr. Rhodes must have used with its scale on the left arm. Nothing was meretricious. Everything — even the drinking men — had been built to last. Some were old-timers who remembered Mr. Rhodes when they were boys.

So did some of the coloured people. Moses, the chauffeur of the car De Beers had put at our disposal, remembered him during the siege. As a small boy he had had the job of lying on his back at the bottom of the Big Hole, watching for falls. He told us about some of the disasters he had seen, of men cooked in rushes of boiling mud so that no one could tell whether they were white or black, about land falls, about the horses and mealie meal they had lived on in the war. He received an engraved gold watch from the company for fifty years' service, while we were here.

There are many long service men on the mines and many come back year after year. De Beers do not have to do any recruiting. The conditions in their compounds are good enough to attract all the labour they want. The workers are well paid and well looked after, and leave at the end of their time with their pockets full of money, having been unable to get out and spend it. The Zulus have an interesting habit of forming small parties, calling one of their number the banker, giving him all their money to carry, and then forming a guard round him to protect him from danger or temptation till they get home. Lone mine workers are often held up and robbed, made drunk and rolled, or stripped by prostitutes who catch them, woman hungry, when they come out.

The men who were not working were resting on the lawn in the compound when we visited it. Some were sewing, some cooking. They have a swimming bath which they seldom use in spite of the heat in summer. They prefer cooking their own food and only about half of them take the hot soup that is issued to the early morning shift. They have recreation and game rooms. Many of them learn to read and write at the adult education classes, and some take courses in first aid. All boss boys are fully trained and since this has been done there has been no sepsis from minor accidents. The boys could also obtain vocational training and learn carpentry, tailoring and shoemaking.

Dr. Stuart told me it was possible to do any operation in the hospital, which is superbly equipped, but that their aim was to keep it empty. According to the law they must have a hundred beds for every four thousand workers, but almost all of them were empty — so many, in fact, that facilities had been offered to the municipality. At the moment there was a daily average of eight patients of all kinds. There was sixty per cent less sickness here than on the Rand gold mines and accidents had been cut from seventy-seven in 1947 to five in 1951 by Mr. Howard Taylor's new safety programme.

The hospital was the ordinary cottage kind, consisting of long, low bungalows set round open squares of lawn. Much cheaper to build, and more economical to run, than the great multi-storey buildings to which we have become accustomed in our cities.

Our friend Mr. Warren, manager of the Wesselton mine, told us some interesting things about the Africans who work for him. He can never keep an office cat. As soon as it gets fat, it disappears, the Basutos being so fond of them to eat. He had even been offered ten shillings for a big tabby. The men refuse to keep their rooms clean — this is woman's work — and a special squad has to be employed to do it. They have had much difficulty in getting the men to eat vegetables — because they said "they were neither women nor rabbits." Among Africans only women eat greens. They have to do their own laundry but, as this too is woman's work, new methods had to be devised as they refused to do it with their hands, like women. So troughs were built and they wash their clothes by tramping them with their feet. Only fifty per cent of them go to the cinema, which is laid on free. They take no interest whatsoever in the beauty or cleanliness of their surroundings, walk across flower beds and never notice if a building is freshly painted. They are very fond of chequers but the boards, which are fixed to the tables, have to be covered with thick glass, as they bang the men down so hard that they wear them out. Their great amusements are the concerts, which they get up for themselves and which are very profitable as they get paid both for singing and not singing. If a boy does not like the song someone is singing, he offers him half a crown to stop. The man who wanted it now ups his bid, and so it goes on, the for and against bidding against each other. There are few quarrels as gambling is not allowed, and there are no women or drink. They brew a kind of weak kaffir beer of fermented mealie meal which, although it is forbidden, is winked at, and sometimes they manage, in spite of being searched, to bring up sticks of dynamite to spike it. Since dynamite is insoluble its effect is purely psychological, but as the African is very susceptible to suggestion the result is often explosive. Carbide is also added to the beer which is drunk as it fizzes. Fuses, often with the detonators still attached, are smuggled up from the mine. After removing the detonators the fuses are used for bootlaces.

The minimum pay is 4s. 9d. per shift, rising to 8s. 6d. and going up to 10s. or 11s. on piecework. Out of this they must buy their own food from the compound store, which, except for meat which is subsidized at 9d. per pound, almost a shilling under market price, is sold at cost.

When the boys do fight the results are serious as they use knobkerries and knives. They are never grateful for anything done for them, but resentful if something they have become accustomed to is taken away from them, the exception being when they were given a church. On this occasion they wrote a letter of thanks to the compound manager.

This was a general picture of labour conditions, and the operation of the mind of the more or less raw African in the process of transition. I found nothing to surprise me much, nor saw any great cause for grievance on their part. At the end of their contract they would go home with from fifty to a hundred pounds in their pockets, on which they could live for several months in their own territory without doing anything. The time must come when they must choose between town and country; between working for a master, or for themselves as tradesmen all the time, or farming all the time. But that time has not yet come. Today no African will stay on and work, however much you offer him, if he wants to go home and rest. And no African will leave home and come to work until hunger begins to drive him. Socio-economics, as we know them, cannot at present be applied to the ordinary unskilled or semi-skilled African worker.

The company issues redeemable tokens for use in the store because money, particularly in the resemblance of the half crown to the florin, often confuses the natives. Some boys, in the early days, had never even seen money. The company also keeps their money if they want it banked, and though there is usually an estimated thousand pounds hidden in the compound there is very little theft.

We went underground with Mr. Warren. We were not very keen on it but felt that having done so much we might as well do the rest, and equipped with helmets and overalls, we went down. I was much relieved at the slow descent.

We went down to the sixteen-hundred-foot level and watched the work going on. The whole place was well lit and whitewashed but I would not care to work underground. I could not stand upright anywhere, suffered from claustrophobia and was very glad to get back to the surface, which is where a man belongs. The work of running the skips is most complex and exhausting, as a mistake could cause much loss of life, and the shifts are short. We went into the engine rooms and watched the great wheels turning as the cables unwound like the reels of giant fishing rods. We saw the compressors that were the lungs of the mine and the pumps that sucked away the water.

Mining was the first paid work, other than farming, which the African had ever done. This was his introduction to industry, his first contact with money and machinery. The point where the old Africa of the Boer hunter and farmer ended; where the new, with the discovery of diamonds and gold, began.

Less than a hundred years ago much of this treeless plain had been heavily bushed. In a few places it had been preserved. The veld at De Beers' shooting box was much as it had always been and still carried plenty of game — springbok, hartebeeste and wildebeeste. Mr. Rhodes had had zebra reintroduced but they had been eaten during the meat shortage of the war. There had been fighting here, too, in the early, pre-diamond days when the kaffirs, the Matabele, had swept over the land. I met a Mr. Thompson whose grandfather, one of the old-timers, had been tortured to death on the farm where his descendants lived, less than fifty miles away.

We went to see the Bushman carvings near the Vaal River. Here, on big, flat outcrops of a kind of polished iron stone, the little hunters had drawn warthog, eland and giraffe most realistically. Some were completely incised, others were outlined by a series of dots. The rock was so hard that I could not even scratch it with my knife.

On the Fourth of July we had dinner with the Morrisons. Mrs. Morrison, a very beautiful American brunette, had staged a party. Everything was decorated with the stars and stripes. It was most touching to think that all over the world other expatriate Americans were doing the same thing. The women wore beautiful diamonds.

And why not? This was where diamonds were wholesale.

I arranged to meet some coloured people and saw the result of the new government's Group Areas Act. A slum of corrugated iron and huts, called the Malay Camp, was being levelled and its inhabitants, most of them gamblers, thieves and prostitutes, were being moved to new cottages that were a vast improvement on anything they had had before. But on the other hand, very respectable coloured families, who had had quite large houses in white areas and who had lived exemplary lives there, were also being moved into the same area, which created much hardship and gave them a grievance. They did not want their children to mix with the slum children who would be their neighbours. The cottages were much too small for their big Victorian furniture. The houses had no garages for their cars. The mistake in this type of legislation would appear to be its blanket quality. The social grades and snobbery among the coloured people are as great as those among white people, and they have not been taken into consideration. This also applies to the Africans, though to a lesser degree, as few of them have risen so high, and the worst not sunk so low. I visited some coloured homes and was entertained by coloured people under conditions which compared most favourably with those of some white people. I would have been happy to have slept in their houses, which is more than can be said of many white homes that I have seen. This is the crux of one phase of the colour problem. Such people know themselves to be superior in education, and as citizens, to many of the lower class and more degraded white men. This is an incontrovertible fact, yet they are officially regarded as inferior to them.

The legal definition of colour is curiously elastic and without precision. A coloured person is one who appears to be coloured and associates with coloured people. But the coloured people are well aware that many people who are considered white have a great deal of coloured blood in them. They know, too, that coloured people are passing over into the white orbit every day — plenty of them are blondes with blue eyes — and if they are prepared to give up their families and friends and move to an area where they are unknown, they find no difficulties. The shortage of skilled labour makes the industrialists ready to welcome anyone who appears to be white.

Among both coloured and Africans I found the young men less and less prepared to co-operate with the white man, and in disagreement with their parents who believe in going slow. They want direct action — a euphemism for violence. Actually, a great deal has happened in the last fifty years, particularly in the last twenty-five, and time, patience and education would solve the problem eventually. But their patience is exhausted, and they have lost, not without some reason, all confidence in the white man. Even among coloured people I heard sympathy for the Mau Mau. At the time I did not know enough about the movement to be able to refute their arguments.

A year ago there were riots here and the Africans burnt the police station, their own beer hall and crèche. There is always this tendency among Africans to destroy their own facilities because they are symbolic of the white man's buildings, and attainable. The difficulty is to find a means of dealing with people whose scales of civilisation, education and culture are so varied, with a coloured man who has university degrees but who may have relatives who are drunken criminals, or an African doctor whose family is still living in an early iron-age tribal culture. The coloured people really belong on the white side of the fence, since it was the white man who produced them. The Africans must sort themselves out into civilised and tribal, into those who wish to acquire a Western standard, and those who repudiate it. Already the pattern of the African mind in transition is becoming apparent. The Mau Mau is a violent manifestation of a desire to go back into the past, before the white man came, where though the African had no physical or material security, he had the psychological certainties of native law and custom, of precedent, to direct him.

The great difference between the African and the coloured man, that is, the Negro and the mulatto, is that for the black man the white can be totally irrelevant, someone he can take or leave, can live with or without. He can work among white men, with white men, for white men, and then go back to his blackness which is as complete for him as is the whiteness of the white man. The black can live alone or in symbiotic association with the white and each remain himself in essentials, each choose what he wants from the other's culture. But the coloured man can never get away from the whiteness that is part of his dual heritage. Every time he looks in a mirror, every time he meets a black man or a white, he thinks of it. If he meets another man of colour he thinks: Is he darker than I am? Is he lighter? Pride, envy, hatred, shame, gratitude, all assume an exaggerated emotive importance. There is a tendency for everything to be subjected to the litmus paper of his prejudice. An unintentional slight is a rudeness due to his colour. A kindness is the patronage of someone who dares to be sorry for him. A white man can forget he is white, a black man forget he is black, but it is difficult for the coloured man, a blend of the two races, with a mixed and tortured psychology, ever to forget himself.

The country outside the town was flat and bare, the sun-dried grass almost white. The great plains ran on into the horizon with here and there a low ridge, like a roller in a sea of veld. There was some mimosa scrub, vaalbos and clumps of tall, flat-topped thorns. Small red anthills were scattered as if they had been sown by some giant hand. The cattle were fat with heavy winter coats. Here and there a steel windmill cut into the horizon. A pair of secretary birds walked along a wire fence, a flock of tall grey cranes hunted locusts and in the pale sky a great flock of sea gulls circled. Sea gulls here, four hundred miles from the sea. The first ones had been brought as pets by some Air Force officers in the war, and they had established themselves on the pans and dams.

This plain was once covered with moving herds of game, in such thousands that they were uncountable. Now it was not a desert but the threat of it was here.

We were taken to see the dogs that guarded the mines. They were wonderfully trained Alsatians bred from imported field-trial dogs. Scientists deny the possibility of acquired characteristics being inherited, but no dog trainer or farmer will agree with them. Police dogs, gun dogs, sheep and cattle dogs have all been developed as fixed breeds with special mental characteristics by breeding from selected parents. Such characteristics are transferable — half-bred dogs often show these special qualities of retrieving, herding or pointing, and such racial characteristics as running through water with an open mouth scooping it up as they go if one parent is an Alsatian.

Among other amenities in Kimberley were the very remarkable library with one of the best collections of Africana in the world, the McGregor Museum, and the Duggan-Cronin Bantu gallery with a collection of native photographs and artifacts that is probably unique. We spent a lot of time in all of them. There was nothing we did not enjoy, except the cold. It was a bitterly cold winter.

But I had made an error in my timing. Kimberley was no place to visit on one's wife's birthday. After all, what can one give one's wife under such conditions? The choice boils down to how big a diamond can one get for how little money? And here we had a bit of luck. We found a very pretty stone of quite a nice size set in a man's ring — part of an estate which a jeweller had for sale. I asked Tiny if she minded a secondhand diamond. She did not. So I said we would take it if it could be valued by De Beers. The jeweller agreed and it was sent over to a friend — Mr. Alex Hall — who passed it on and received the following answer:

Dear Alex,
The stone is of old-fashioned cut and badly cut at that. As you can see, it has no shape, being neither round nor square. The colour is good but it is badly spotted. I should put the value at £30 per ct., which means that the price of the ring is a fair one. Personally, I don't like the stone.

It was also suggested that I could buy a really flawless diamond from De Beers at a more or less wholesale price (of eighty pounds a carat, I think it was). But we were against having a perfect but almost invisible stone for eighty pounds when we could have a nice, very showy one, even if it had spots (that were invisible except to an expert with a glass) and was badly cut, for sixty.

"After all," I said, "it's the idea that counts, and it's a very good safari diamond, don't you think?" And she did.

2

Mr. Rhodes ... Kimberley

● THE STORY of diamonds is a strange tale of love and lust; of
murder and sudden death; of accidents, hope and despair, though
I did not realise it till I came to Kimberley, the diamond city, and
saw the Big Hole where hundreds, if not thousands, have died in one
way or another. By rock falls and mud rushes, by being crushed
beneath overturned carts or killed in quarrels about money or
women, by rotgut drink, exposure and disease. Deserted now, surrounded by high wire, it is quiet, still, save for the scream of the
swifts and the cooing of the rock doves that nest in its man-made
cliffs. The biggest hole in the world, a mile around and 1335 feet
deep, in which at one time as many as fourteen thousand men
sweated in temperatures so high that the oily shale of its walls have,
at times, begun to smoulder, ignited by the sun's rays striking a
discarded gin bottle. But death has not finished with it yet. Suicides
are still found floating in the water. Small, unwanted children are
still thrown into it.

Every girl in the world wants a diamond. Every woman who has
one wants more, and the diamond industry is dependent on their
wants. Dependent on the rings, on the bracelets, the brooches and
clips that flash across a restaurant as they catch the light. Dependent
on engagement rings, on love, licit and illicit, on sex.

There are still diamonds in the streets of Kimberley. When new
buildings go up, the soil is washed and diamonds are recovered. I
met Mr. Cameron Kiddie, who had found a parcel of thirty-seven
carats when he enlarged his house. The biggest, which he showed
me, was a fine, blue/white six-carat stone.

Between the first diamond found in 1866 and today, an enormous
industry, employing thousands of men, and millions of dollars' worth
of equipment, has sprung up. But the gamble, except for the alluvial
digger, has been taken out of mining. The needles remain in the
haystack, but the haystack is dealt with with such mechanical

efficiency that none of them are lost. This was the first thing that struck me when I was told about it — the incredible ratio of 35,000,000 to 1. Thirty-five million pounds of ground to be processed to recover one pound in weight of diamonds, of which three quarters are industrial stones. The remaining quarter are the most beautiful and portable form of wealth in the world. The only form in which a fortune, negotiable anywhere, can be carried in a pocket.

And it all began when in 1866 a child, the son of Daniel Jacobs, a Dutch farmer near Hopetown, brought home a handful of pebbles he had picked up on the banks of the Orange River, and dumped his collection on the dung-smeared floor. More mess, his mother said. More to sweep onto the veld where such things belong. But a neighbour, Van Niekerk, happened to be visiting at the time and seeing one stone much prettier than the others, offered to buy it. Take it if you like, the child's mother said. It's just a *blink klippie* — a shiny stone.

The shiny stone passed through several hands before it was identified and sold for £500. Then another was found at the junction of the Vaal and Orange rivers. This superb white stone of eighty-three and a half carats was picked up by a shepherd, and an expert was sent from England by Harry Emanuel, a diamond merchant, to look the place over. He found nothing. He said he did not think diamonds would ever be found at the Cape and that those which had been found were accidental and must have been brought from a great distance and dropped by ostriches which swallow pebbles to aid their digestion. So much for the expert.

And then, suddenly, diamonds were found in quantity, and the rush began. By 1871 ten thousand diggers were shaking the sand of the river soils through their sieves in a frantic search for wealth. There was no thought of pipes then. No worry about how diamonds were formed, or how they came to be where they were. They were there and that was enough. Among the early birds were Cecil John Rhodes, J. B. Robinson, Alfred Beit, Barny Barnato — men who were to become mining magnates. Fabulous figures that decorated the late Victorian period.

And with the diggers came the riffraff of the world — the crooks, criminals, confidence men, prostitutes, publicans. The human vultures who follow the prospector from continent to continent as soon as success is certain. Seldom has a more curious mixture of men been found in an upland prairie soon to be a desert. There was no railroad. The men came by ox wagon, by coach, by Cape cart, on horseback and on foot. They lived in anything they could find or rig up. In tents, in corrugated iron huts, and under the open sky. Water was the problem. At times it went up to two shillings and sixpence a gallon. When my father was here in the early days he found it cheaper to wash in soda water. It was colourful all right, if by colour one means fighting and drinking and whoring. There was rape, robbery, murder and incest. Romantic — if one means squalor, with the down-and-outs starving while the successful drove out with four blood horses and postillions, their barmaid mistresses at their sides. But that was the way it was. The mining camp way, with the money easily won and quickly spent. With the diggings spread out over sixty miles from Hebron to Sefonels.

At first it was all alluvial, all dry sorting, so that the miners missed many stones that were dirt coated, because dust got in their eyes. The centre of all this activity was Kimberley, then known as Vooruit-zicht, the farm belonging to the two De Beers brothers. It was bought for £6000 and long afterwards one of them complained about the price he had received, saying he understood it was worth more millions than he had received thousands. "And what would you have done with six million pounds if you had had them?" he was asked. "Me?" he said. "Magtig, I would have bought a brand new wagon, new yokes and a wire trek touw (central rawhide rope or chain on to which the ox yokes are fastened)!" This was the limit of his imagination.

His house still stands. We saw it. It had three main rooms with various additions. It is built of mud bricks. The thatched roof has been replaced by corrugated iron. The home of a man who had farmed and hunted with millions under his horses' unshod hoofs.

Gradually the ground where Kimberley now stands was worked out. The first Stock Exchange in South Africa was built, and in the middle of it all, its central vortex, was the Kimberley Mine. The BIG HOLE of today. The claims went down and down. Looking up from the bottom the whole sky was cut into sections by the maze of cables, the spiderweb of haulage ropes that led out of this vast amphitheatre. As the ground on the edge ceased to be productive the claim holders either threw up the sponge or tried to buy new claims nearer the centre. Costs went up. Men amalgamated. The amalgamations amalgamated. Then the blue ground was struck, and many, believing this was the end of the diamonds, covered it up with yellow top soil and sold up. Then it was discovered that there were diamonds in the blue ground, that the yellow clay was merely an oxydised form of the blue and that the volcanic funnel — the pipe as it is now called — went down to unsuspected depths.

Claims fell in or were flooded. Titles were insecure. Pegs were lost. Surveying became impossible in the chaos of a crater which looked as if some mad giant had spooned great cubes out of it and spread them out on the veld above. This was the point where Cecil John Rhodes began to operate, to plan order. He found that the diamonds sold by the diggers every Friday, to obtain the working capital they needed for the following week, were sometimes almost given away. He saw that to save the industry the output of all the claims must be co-ordinated into one vast undertaking. Only by this means could the price of diamonds be regulated. The output must be keyed to the world demand.

But there were other ideas in his mind as well. Of wealth that could be used politically and of the power that went with wealth. There was his dream of Empire. Looking into the seething hole, watching the human ants at their work, he saw that a new South Africa was being formed. But it was one thing to have the dream and another to carry it out. Though, when nearing his end, he complained: "So little done, so much to do," he had accomplished the almost impossible. Had created Rhodesia and the De Beers Company, had produced the capital that developed the gold mines of the Rand, and started an almost bankrupt country on a wave of prosperity which has not yet reached its climax. This was the first great industry in Africa. This was the first time that kaffirs had had money to spend. The mines were the door through which they passed from an early iron age, where they possessed nothing, into the Aladdin's Cave world of today, where everything is possible.

The skips that dropped the naked kaffirs into the bowels of the earth were, by a strange paradox, the means that would finally enable them to rise out of their savage environment.

The process of final amalgamation was slow; Barny Barnato's group was the last to hold out against it. But in the end, even he gave in. Curiously enough, not for financial reasons, but for the snob appeal of being made a member of the Kimberley Club after he had been black-balled three times.

Many years later, Barny committed suicide by jumping into the Atlantic Ocean on the way to England from the deck of a Union Castle liner. He was in good health and his affairs in good order. No one could explain his suicide. But there is a story in Kimberley that it was due to a curse put on him by a digger called Schwab who had been given a long sentence for I.D.B. Barny is supposed to have been mixed up in the business, and when Schwab was caught, to have promised to take care of his family — this was the tradition on the fields, the unwritten law of Illicit Diamond Buying. However, when he came out of prison, Schwab, his own health broken by seven years hard labour on the breakwater, found his wife and children living in penury, nothing having been done for them. He went to see Barny and cursed him. He said: "I will never leave you. Wherever you look you will see my face, and when I die you will die too." According to the legend, Schwab died at approximately the same time that Barny leapt over the ship's rail.

I.D.B. — Illicit Diamond Buying — was a great problem, more than half the stones found being said to disappear in this way. The penalties were severe but the rewards so great that the risk seemed worth while. Diamonds were hidden in the veld to be picked up later; were swallowed, were forced into incisions in the body and hidden in the mouth, ears and nostrils. These losses led to the Compound system, and natives employed on the mine were not allowed to leave until their contract had expired. A few days before leaving they were incarcerated, dosed with laxatives, and given detention gloves — enormous, perforated, heavy leather mittens that were padlocked onto their wrists. While wearing these gloves they could not pick up any small object. They could not even hold a spoon, so the right-hand glove had a slit in it into which the handle could be stuck. Many diamonds were recovered by this system, which has now been abandoned as all the boys are X-rayed before they go. Many boys try to take something away with them, bits of crystal or glass known as schlenters. I saw a number of them that had just been collected. This seems to be done just to tease the white man and see if he can really find them. The fact that he does is, in itself, a great deterrent to theft.

Diamonds, however, still do find their way out of the mines through the white foremen, not all of whom, however carefully they are screened, are necessarily honest. The white employees go home every night and are not searched, so the temptation is very great. They give the natives dagga (hemp) which they are mad about, many of them being addicts, and brandy, which is forbidden by law, in exchange for stones.

Still more are stolen on the alluvial diggings where the native workers live in open villages — locations — without supervision, with their families, and work for a wage of 25s. to 30s. a week on which they can scarcely live.

Here both theft and disposal are made easier. The usual plan is to pass the stolen stone to another digger — coloured, native or white — who has a claim. The stone is sold the following week as one of his own parcel, with almost no danger of detection.

A diamond cannot be broken by pressure — only by a sharp blow. In De Beers' head office they showed me a small one-carat diamond that has been pressed into a steel plate and is embedded in it. A rough and ready test is to squeeze the stone in a pair of pliers. A crystal or piece of glass will break at once. Another test is to drop it into a glass of water where, if it is real, it is invisible, and of course there remains the simplest test of all — to see if the stone will scratch glass.

Some natives take a great deal of trouble making schlenters, shaping them carefully, and even boiling them in condensed milk to give them the oily feel that is peculiar to a diamond. A parcel of diamonds placed in an envelope and X-rayed will show nothing, whereas the simulated stones show up quite clearly. They do show, however, if swallowed, but they cannot be differentiated from gall stones or similar foreign bodies. In this case the native is held and X-rayed every day to see if the object moves in his body. A diamond, owing to its great specific gravity, will always work its way downwards through the bowels, moving a little day by day.

After amalgamation the method of mining began to change. Open mining was abandoned. Deep shafts were sunk away from the pipe, and into them galleries were driven which ended in working chambers where the blue ground was quarried and carried to the surface, where it was spread on what were called floors — large, flat areas of ground. It was left here to weather and was slowly broken up under exposure to sun, air and rain. The process was accelerated by watering and harrowing the ground. To protect the floors from thieves they were not only fenced with double, high barbed fences but also patrolled with German shepherd dogs and cross-bred mastiffs. The floors are no longer used, since the new method of recovery by means of greased tables has been discovered. But all De Beers property is still guarded by German shepherd dogs whose chains are fastened to long wires so that they can patrol the periphery of the whole area. In addition, each section has a watchman with a free dog that is trained to attack.

Alluvial digging still goes on in much the same way as it did in the early days, though everything is more orderly now that the fields are under the supervision of the De Beers Company.

Forty-five foot square claims are staked and the top soil, which varies from six to thirty feet in depth, is cleared away. None of this may lie on a neighbouring claim so it must all be moved again later when the ground below it is worked. Under this top soil comes the gravel which, if it is diamondiferous, will carry bantams (from the Dutch *Bandan*, a banded pebble) and other small rounded and almond-shaped stones, among which will be found tiny garnets, olivines, agates, crystals and carbon which are all associated with diamonds. This layer, which varies in depth, is handled most carefully and is passed over the "baby," a long cradlelike sieve hanging by its four corners to a heavy wooden frame which is rocked back and forth by a native boy. The largest stones are removed by hand. The remainder are freed of most of the light dirt and sand with which they are mixed by friction against each other, but even at the end of the process they are far from clean. They are next put into the rotary, a large iron tambourine-shaped pan in which harrowlike teeth are revolved by man power. Water is continually added in order to keep the mixture to the creamlike consistency which will float off the lighter matter — mud and light stones — and drive the heavier to the sides where it is collected. Now comes the final process, the washing. The heavy residue of more or less clean pebbles is put into a sieve with a medium-sized mesh, which is shaken by a boy holding it under water as he works. The heavier stuff works its way to the bottom so that, if he is a skilled operator, when the sieve is inverted on the sorting table the diamonds and carbon will appear right in the centre on the top of the heap.

Few diamonds are found in the first sieve, for here the pebbles are about the size of a filbert nut. The second sieve has a finer mesh and holds everything bigger than a split pea.

Then comes the last sieve. Nothing bigger than a grain of sand will pass through this mesh. Here the search becomes really careful. Layer by layer the digger goes through the heap with his sorting plate. While we were watching, one digger — a lady in this case — found a small stone, which gave us an idea of the excitement there must be if a big one is discovered.

I was told that few diggers were independent. Most are staked by a diamond buyer or storekeeper on a fifty-fifty basis, the debt sometimes running up into hundreds of pounds.

Each Friday De Beers send down their representatives and the diggers — white, brown and black, male and female file in with their parcels. They carry them in twists of paper, in little screw-top containers, in aspirin bottles. Each stone is weighed, examined for flaws and valued. De Beers will buy everything at their own valuation if the digger cannot get a better offer from the independent buyers who come on the same day. In this way there is no danger of a digger being swindled.

The life the diggers lead is strange — it is hard but filled with glittering hopes. They are all gamblers, and anyone bitten by the diamond bug is infected for life. Every retired digger I met wanted to go back. No one on the diggings wanted to leave. Every tomorrow is an adventure, each upturned sieve may hold a fortune. And they are free. Free to live hard, uncomfortable lives in a climate that is icy cold in winter and a hell of heat in summer. But they have no master, no god but luck. And it is out of this hand-to-mouth existence that the great diamond industry has grown, where huge skips carry the diamondiferous soil up from the bowels of the earth at a rate of more than ten tons a minute, and the giant rotaries are the size of a small room.

The blue ground is mined from as much as sixteen hundred feet below the surface, carried along miniature railroad tracks in coco pans by natives who are paid by piecework (3d. a truck) tipped down chutes, lifted to the surface, dumped into the crusher, washed in thousands of gallons of water, passed through screens and jigs, graded, and the final residue shot into the crystal-clear waterfalls that tumble onto the grease tables that are the end of the journey.

The tables are a series of three long shelves covered with thick Vaseline to which the diamonds stick and the other pebbles — now reduced to a minimum — pass over. While the water is running the diamonds are almost invisible, but as soon as it is turned off they can be seen lying like white plums in a yellow cake.

At intervals the tables are scraped and the mixture of Vaseline and diamonds, varying in size from a nut to a pin's head, is transferred to an iron pot with a lid. When full this pot is placed in boiling water. When the Vaseline has melted the stones are strained out of it and it is cooled and used again.

The diamonds are now soaked in acid and then, to remove the last vestige of grease, fried in a cheap iron frying pan — the sort that can be bought in any Ten Cent store. This was the final paradox, to see the day's recovery in two little piles worth approximately $50,000 glittering in the sun on the sorting table, and beside them, standing upright against the wall, a common frying pan. This, and the fact that those little heaps represented the day's total take from two immense mines. Together they would not have filled the pocket of my jacket.

Hundreds of white men, thousands of half-naked Africans, had sweated to this glittering end. Millions of pounds of ground had been processed. Thousands of women would be made happy by the final product, and the machine tools of industry would, tipped by the industrial stones, manufacture the weapons and gadgets that characterise our enlightened age.

The definition of an industrial stone is anything that does not refract light. That has no glitter. The spots that are cut out of gems, if large enough, are used for tools, or if too small are ground into powder for polishing other diamonds. Some industrial stones do not look like diamonds at all, but resemble pieces of stone, something between a small black meteorite and a bit of anthracite. In the old days no one was interested in them. In fact, it would appear that no one bothered much with anything smaller that a split pea. The tailings of some of the older mines are now being rewashed and a great deal of valuable material recovered.

The blue ground is a soft grey conglomerate rock, or hard clay that is water-soluble. It is in this stuff that the diamonds originated under the heat and terrific compression of volcanic disturbances. A perfect diamond is a crystal of octahedral form, resembling two four-sided pyramids set one above the other. Diamonds vary in size from minute stones to the incomplete Cullinan of 3025 carats (a carat equals 200 milligrams). They are classed into more than a hundred grades by sorters sitting at long tables covered with white paper fastened down with thumbtacks. Wearing magnifying-glass head pieces and using forceps, they pick them up one at a time and arrange them in little heaps that look, when the stones are small, like little piles of glittering sugar.

The diamonds are then sold to buyers, who cannot buy big stones without taking a parcel of small ones as well. The cutting is done by means of a thin disk of bronze alloy whose edge is treated with a mixture of diamond dust and oil, revolving at five thousand revolutions a minute. Even at this speed a medium-sized stone may take a day to cut in half. When finished, a diamond may have, if it is a perfect stone, as many as fifty-eight facets, including the table or top. After being cut it is polished — again with diamond dust — and then set and ready, after all its adventures, for the finger of some eager girl, the breast of a matron, the crown of a Queen, or the wrist of a courtesan.

This is the story of Kimberley; think of it when you see the light catch on a ring. It is history you are looking at. Ancient geological history of eruptions, a later history of love and passion, and a future history, since diamonds can hardly be destroyed. It is all there, the very symbol of riches and romance.

It was now time to leave Kimberley for the North, for Rhodes's Hinterland. The jewelled interlude was over.

3

The Place of Killing ... Southern Rhodesia

● NOTHING CAN BE SOLD without a pretty girl. Every advertisement portrays a lady standing beside a motorcar, opening a fridge or smoking a cigarette. Every man who buys a new shirt is led to believe that as soon as he has it on a beautiful girl will fling herself into his arms. To this I have built up the necessary sales resistance. But I am not ready for pretty customs officers.

There was a knock on the door of the compartment and in came a willowy blonde in a pale blue uniform with dark blue facings and gold buttons. A blue forage cap was perched on her golden curls. She held my passport in long fingers with beautiful red-painted filbert nails and asked if I had anything to declare. I hadn't, but could hardly reply in my astonishment at this wonderful public relations device. It could be carried much further — why not beautiful tax collectors, beautiful everything. Beauty should be the criterion in a bureaucracy. It would make it almost painless. Another pretty girl dealt with our plane tickets and the last girl I saw in Salisbury, Bill Gale's daughter, was as pretty as they come. So the beginning, the middle and the end of Rhodesia were good — and blond. This experience certainly biased me in favour of the country.

It was very different from our country, South Africa. There were more trees and bigger trees. The farms were tidier and more neatly laid out and everywhere there were signs of conservation. The dongas were dammed, the lands contoured and all the cattle and natives I saw looked fat. It seemed a fatter land, richer and younger. The guts had not yet been ripped out of it. I now saw for the first time the granite kopjes so typical of the North, rising out of the plain like great piled castles. Big heaps of rock with smaller rocks on top of them supporting still smaller ones, that looked from the passing train no bigger than a man's hand, but which must have been enormous when one got up to them. There is no scale to measure things in Rhodesia — everything is more than life size, and here one could see the age of the continent. These rocks had not been piled up. The soil had been washed away from them for hundreds of centuries. Erosion is no new thing. What is new in Africa is the way we have accelerated it. Our greatest problem is not the native question, but the measures we take to arrest it. And the ratio of increasing population to decreasing arable land.

The train was following the path of history. Rhodes and Jameson had come this way; so had Selous and Thompson, both of whom I had met as a boy. This was the way the pioneers had come. It was the northern hinterland that had called to adventure. We passed the little isolated graves of the adventurous. We saw oxen pulling sledges made of big tree forks, we saw blue jays, hornbills, go-away birds and hoopoes.

We were met in Bulawayo by Brigadier John Deedes.

Next day we went to the Matopos, the piled masses of rock that is the Rhodesian Westminister Abbey, where Rhodes lies buried, guarded by the spirits of *"the brave men"* of Wilson's Shangani Patrol, and other heroes. *"For here lie all men who deserve well of their country."* Here, in this playground of gigantic gods who had thrown the great hills about like toys and bombarded them with rocks as big as houses. Rhodes's grave is marked by a plain bronze plaque with the words "Here Lies Cecil John Rhodes." There is no date of birth or death. The rocks are daubed with brilliant lichens — orange, green, and some are grey, spotted with white, like the wing of a guinea fowl.

On and on into the distance rolled this tumbled land. On a high cliff two bataleur eagles sat perched. Descendants perhaps of the eagles who had seen Moselekatse's exhausted impis come in from the South after their defeat by the Boers. These Zulus were the Matabele who, having fled Chaka's despotism, set up one of their own and here continued the raids which were their only pleasure.

These master races that appear on every African panorama are interesting. Zulus in the South, Fulanis in the North, Ashanti in the West, Somalis and Masai in the East. These were the masters in Africa till the white man broke their tyranny.

Somewhere in a hidden cave here Moselekatse, the father of Lobengula, the last king of the Matabele, lies buried, sewn into the hide of a black ox.

It was here in Bulawayo that the Matabele had their capital. This was the infamous "place of killing" where thousands had been smelt out and died. Where men and women had been thrown over the cliffs for the vultures, and into water for the crocodiles. Here that Lobengula tried out his new rifle on his subjects. Here that the diamonds, stolen by the Matabele workers on the Kimberley mines, finally came to rest in the king's own money box — a four-gallon kerosene tin which has not yet been found. Here that M'limo, the witch doctor, was killed by Major Frederick Russell Burnham, the famous American Indian scout and fighter. Here that Rhodes, alone and unarmed, met the indunas who had led the Matabele rebellion, and made peace with them.

On the drive home we passed native kraals surrounded by high hedges of a fine kind of euphorbia. I found it was called rubber hedge and contained a poisonous white latex which nothing, not even goats, would eat.

We visited the Centenary Exhibition, which gave us a preview of what we would see later on our trip. The Kenya pavilion was decorated with enormous murals of animals, and had some magnificent hunting trophies, including a ten-foot leopard skin which had unquestionably been stretched, but must nevertheless have been a near record. There was also a black leopard, much rarer in Africa than in India, and always considered more savage than its spotted brother. These dark animals are simply melanistic sports, not a different variety, and some people believe their bad temper is due to loneliness as their own kind avoid them because of their colour. In the Uganda pavilion there was a very nice tame baby leopard. The Congo exhibits of sculpture and painting were in charge of Monsieur P. Vin, whom we met again some months later in Bukavu. The Angola people had achieved the impossible. They had, by an amazing presentation, made statistics both interesting and decorative. There was a great deal of very rare Africana material in the Rhodesian hall, which was very large and built round the enormous artificial bole of a baobab. There were historic trophies of all kinds, and models of Matabele warriors in all their panoply of weapons, ostrich plumes and white cow-tail kneelets. There was a section cut from the tree at whose foot Major Wilson and his men, after their desperate attempt to capture Lobengula, fought to the death with such gallantry that the Matabele honoured their bodies. Having exhausted their ammunition they stood up, shook hands with each other, and waited the final charge of the warriors to sweep over them in a black wave of feathers and stabbing spears.

The streets in Bulawayo must be the widest in the world. That was Mr. Rhodes's idea. They must be wide enough for a wagon with a full span of sixteen oxen to turn in. There are no oxen now, and they are very hard to get over and when driving down them one has to watch for the storm water sluits that cross the streets at right angles every hundred yards or so. It is a fine and vigorous city.

That night we were asked to a reception and dance at Government House to meet the Governor General of Mozambique. For this function I put on the £12 ($36) Tuxedo that I had bought in Kimberley. It was thin and light. I looked rather like a headwaiter. But I certainly was not going to take my good dinner jacket on a trip where everything would be written off before we got back, apart from it being too heavy to take by air and too thick for the tropics. We were introduced to Their Excellencies Flag Captain Gabriel and Senhora Teixeira. He was a handsome soldierly looking man of fifty-odd and his wife was a perfectly beautiful and most soignée woman. Her hair was grey; she was no longer slim but had magnificent dark, flashing eyes, and wore a very lovely dress of oyster-grey satin decorated with diamanté and opalescent iridescent embroidery.

I talked to the Governor about Portuguese East Africa which I had visited, elephant hunting, some years ago. He told me three fifths of the country was infested with tsetse fly and that he was beginning some experiments with African buffaloes to see if they could be bred in captivity as they were immune to 'ngana. He was having them caught young, raised with cattle and dehorned. This should be an interesting experiment to watch.

The Governor, Sir John, and Lady Kennedy were most charming. I talked to him about the progress of the Africans, and his idea was that it was a mistake to go too fast but on the other hand they must not be allowed to become disgruntled. This was certainly a counsel of perfection with which no one, except perhaps an already disgruntled African, could disagree. I then met Major Sharp, D.S.O., M.C., one of the old pioneers who had discovered radium and uranium in the Congo. He said what I had heard before, and would hear so often in the future again: that the Africans had never done anything for themselves. They had tamed no wild animals, brought no wild plants on into cultivation. He talked about the taming of elephants by the Belgians in the Congo and he told me they had tried to form a regiment of cavalry mounted on zebras. They had captured them by driving several thousand head of game, including lions, into a big kraal, and then cutting them out. It had not been a success.

The Rhodesian African Rifles band played dance tunes with more verve than accuracy. Their dark rifle-green tarbooshes and uniforms looked very smart. I was told that the regiment was not up to strength and that they were not really natural soldiers. I wondered where the Matabele blood had gone.

We saw the old indaba tree, under which Lobengula sat when he gave judgments, in the garden here. How strange to think of it all ending only sixty-odd years ago. How much horror had this tree seen, how much blood had been spilt on the ground at our feet? How many white men had come here as mendicants, craving concessions for gold, for ivory, asking for black maiden-flesh? A beautiful dark girl in a cream and gold dress with a wide golden belt rustled by. Another girl in white, with long, smooth pale gold hair passed on the arm of a soldier in mess kit. Here, where not so long ago naked girls had been carrying pots of beer and baskets of meat balanced on their heads, where naked warriors, secure in the arrogance of their numbers, had leant up on their spears watching them swing past.

In the evening the Deedeses gave a very nice cocktail party where Tiny read palms with her usual skill: palmistry, which is impossible to believe in on logical grounds, but which is so often right that one almost ceases to believe in logic. She told one woman she would have difficulty bearing children. The woman said she had had one child born dead and a Caesarean for the other. She told a doctor that he was a doctor and suffered from heart trouble. He said he was and did, but he had not even told his wife. At another place she told me that a child of five, a dear little blond girl, would be a drunk, but of course she could not tell her mother and she must have made a mistake. But the next evening the child stole two of the drinks that had been poured out and got plastered. Palmistry was known in India in 2000 B.C. It was known in ancient China and Egypt. There are ancient books on it and many modern ones, but none of them can explain it.

It was at this party that we met Bill Gale, later to become a close friend, who was to pick us up at 9 A.M. next day and take us round the country. He was head of the Public Relations Office and the author of several books about Rhodesia. He was a smallish, quick moving and thinking man, with a combination of those qualities which seem to lead to success — drive, energy, health, luck and a capacity for judging men and delegating authority. We met a lot of top brass on our trip and sometimes I wondered if things might not be better if they were left to run them. An undemocratic thought which I immediately thrust behind me. The mass which knows nothing must, in the long run, know better than the technicians and experts who have devoted their lives to a job, and have reached the top of their respective trees.

We lunched at Shangani, a biggish and prosperous asbestos town, very neat and tidy with new little suburban villas, geometrical gardens ablaze with tropical flowers and a company swimming pool and tennis courts, all rigged with floodlighting so that the cool nights could be used for sport as well as love. Wherever there are people there is bound to be love, and there were some nice tropical backgrounds for it here. Wherever there are Englishmen or Americans there are bound to be sports. Games intrigue the African as a form of white man's madness. Tennis in some parts is called "work with a ball."

We passed small private mines in the bush with Romantic Lone Star, Little Nugget and Dead-Man sort of names that might have come out of a Western film. We passed enormous isolated transformers that looked very odd among the trees. Another of the African paradoxes that are so fascinating. But Rhodesia is very highly electrified, and still more power is being developed in several new projects.

Bill told us a story about a propaganda film which had been made by the tea manufacturers to encourage Africans to drink more tea. The story was about two brothers. One drank only tea and prospered. The other drank beer. He had a lot of fun but never got anywhere. At last he was persuaded to go to Johannesburg to make money. He got into more trouble with evil companions there and finally was robbed of all his earnings. The moral was, of course, that if he had drunk tea none of these troubles would have overtaken him.

I said: "And what effect did it have?"

"None," Bill said, "except to discourage people from going to Johannesburg and drinking tea. They said it was better to stay at home and drink beer." The African is very logical — only his logic does not always work the way the white man thinks it will.

We reached The Great Zimbabwe Hotel in time for tea and went down to see the ruins that are one of the most impressive sights in Africa and one of its greatest mysteries. Here, in a flat saucer set among the mountains, is a big stone castle — a monument to some past, forgotten culture. There are no native legends about it, no stories. There are no natives who can build in stone like this today. So Zimbabwe stands, set like a gigantic asterisk in the blank page of African history.

There are some beautiful trees between the hotel and the ruins, and a feathery, mauve spirea-like shrub, a creeper — a pink bignonia — that is named after the place, Zimbabwe creeper.

The layout of the temple, or elliptical building, is curious and apparently without design. There are near-circles, circles, inter-secting walls of tall, mortarless stone and narrow passages. There is a gigantic monument that is certainly a phallus; hundreds of small, pocket-sized phalli have been found in the ruins. The top of the high walls are decorated with monoliths set vertically. Did they ever have the heads of enemies impaled upon them?

Estimates of the age of Zimbabwe vary. Some experts think it may have been begun three thousand years ago by some Eastern or Near Eastern people, who colonised Africa and used these buildings as a central depot for gold, ivory, gums, skins and slaves before exporting them. Other experts consider them to date from the fourteenth or fifteenth century and see no resemblance in their architecture to any Oriental or European style. These experts have evidently never seen Kano, where the high-walled compounds, the monoliths, the decorations in mud and general layout all recall Zimbabwe.

The latest estimates, based on the new methods of radio carbon dating, put the date at about A.D. 500. This would make the theory of its being pre-Islamic Arab a possibility. There is no doubt about Africa being explored in the distant past. Arab, Persian, Indian and Chinese ships have certainly visited the coast for thousands of years, and expeditions must have penetrated far into the interior in search of gold, tin, ivory, precious stones, skins, feathers, wild animals and slaves. They were men like ourselves, and the next range must have called to them as it calls to us. One can never be first in Africa. Some very strange Kilroys have always been here before, and a long time before too.

I had a feeling of things having happened here when I stood under the walls of Zimbabwe, of blood and cruelty, of strange rites and sacrifices, of lust. This was a haunted place, though not by ghosts that one could feel. Not that I believe in ghosts. I am merely nervous of them. In the moonlight the walls were almost white, the shadows more than black. The big trees, that had been left when the bush, which had once wrapped the ruins in a secret cloak, was cleared, threw fantastic shadows. The monoliths pointed like fingers to the stars. The night was crisp and cold. A hunting jackal called and was answered by its mate. Some plover, always active in the moonlight, screamed when something put them up. I felt isolated here, suspended in time and space, utterly detached. We knew we had experienced something that was unforgettable, that we had made, as it were, with the hands of our minds a memory that would endure. Something solid, an object, as real as a ball moulded out of clay.

In the morning, with the warden to guide us, we climbed the Acropolis. This was the stronghold that guarded the temple and is a steep hill of immense piled rocks which have been turned into fortifications by walling up the spaces between and burrowing in behind them to create caves. It was a very strong defensive position which even today, with modern weapons, would present a formidable obstacle. At the bottom of the hill there are the spring-fed waterholes which supplied the garrison with water. I do not know if their vicinity has ever been excavated, but interesting remains are often found near water where ladies sit and gossip. They tend to drop things, to lose an earring, to break a necklace, to smash a water pot. Springs in Africa are so rare that the use of each must go back into pre-history. At each, one can visualise a never ending string of women passing through time as if it were an arch.

One of the most interesting things in the Acropolis was the gold furnace enclosure, a kind of open-sided cave where, owing to its height above the plain, and exposure, a strong wind blows continu- ously, creating a natural blast furnace. Early explorers found traces of early gold-smelting operations and some evidence of ironwork being carried out at a later date.

We ended the morning with a visit to the small museum at the office to see some of the objects recovered from the ruins. Among them were two small phalli, one circumcised and the other not, euphemistically labelled CHARMS. There were some pieces of ham- mered gold foil used for plating wooden objects and golden tacks for holding the foil, which I thought of when on the Gold Coast I saw the linguists' sticks whose carved heads were gold plated, some of them even resembling the vulturine birds in local soapstone which are so typical of Zimbabwe. Right through Africa the resemblances in custom and artifact appear to me to be much greater than the differences, and point to common and forgotten sources. Among other things found here were fragments of Ming and Celadon por- celain, Persian pottery and Arab glass.

Natives were inhabiting the ruins when they were first described in 1873 by Karl Mauch, the German explorer. The Portuguese knew about these African ruins — there are a number of them in this area

— and believed Zimbabwe, the biggest of them all, to be a distribution centre and storehouse for goods waiting for export from Sofala, the old Arab port two hundred and thirty miles away. Immense quantities of gold have been mined from what is now Rhodesia. The gold for King Solomon's temple may have come from here, and almost every mine that is operating today is on the site of an ancient working, which shows how carefully the country must have been prospected. Ancient workings have also been found in the Transvaal and elsewhere.

The Sandses' house was charming, with a wonderful view. We talked about storms. Mrs. Sands's cocker was almost hairless, having been struck by lightning when he was sitting under the kitchen stove. Mr. Sands told me that there is a mountain that the natives say can speak. He has heard it three times. It is supposed to be the voice of the gods and this may have been the reason for establishing a temple here. He told us that there were barbel in the ponds and that they were excellent eating, and that if skinned and soaked in salt water for forty-eight hours they lost all their muddy flavour. I told him about the mudfish we had seen in the sludge dams at Kimberley where the water was as thick as pea soup from having been used so often in washing the ground brought up from the mines. He told us about honey from the Mopani flowers, which burns the mouth. He had been a policeman and knew the desert country. He showed us a map made by Sanson in Abbeville in 1656 which showed the interior of Africa with great accuracy considering it was supposed to be entirely unexplored.

It was now time to say goodbye to Zimbabwe. We had seen a marvel, one of the wonders of the world. Here, in what was until recent years the unknown interior of Africa, was the evidence of a race of people who, whether they were immigrants or indigenous natives, had disappeared as a cultural unit. They had left hundreds of ruins, of which Zimbabwe was the noblest, which displayed great imagination and energy but no clue as to who they were, whence they came, or where they went.

Zimbabwe is not merely an archaeological problem. It is also a psychological problem. How is it that there are no memories or legends about so notable a place? We may one day learn more but it is tragic to think of the thousand ounces of gold artifacts that the Ancient Ruins Company, which raped it, melted down without regard for their historic importance. It is believed that when he heard of what had been done, Mr. Rhodes lost his temper, for the only time in his life, with Dr. Jameson whom he regarded as responsible for the company's formation.

We came to the Bakita Reserve where the natives have wonderful gardens. But it took thirteen years to reach its present stage. At first when a specially trained native grew tall mealies, and his neighbours' failed to prosper, it was attributed to witchcraft and his crop was destroyed. Only witchcraft could produce this astounding difference. And obviously these tall mealies were sucking nourishment from their neighbours.

The Rhodesians have a system of training Africans and then setting them up as student teachers in various localities which seems to be most successful. Certainly everyone here looked very happy and prosperous. They were all fat, and smiled as they raised their hands in greeting as we went by. They were, in fact, on a better wicket, as far as happiness was concerned, than many European peasants.

We now dropped down into the low veld, a monotonous area of solid mopani bush only broken by baobabs of all sizes and ages. There were even giants, probably several thousand years old, that had died and were disintegrating into a strange pulpy mess. They have never been wood. They were just tissue held together through the centuries by the quality of life that had swelled their trunks with the sap of a vegetal elephantiasis, enlarging them progressively, grotesquely, till they became monstrous, and curiously beautiful in a foul, voluptuous manner. Of all the trees I have ever seen, the baobab fascinates me the most.

A few hours later we drove into Umtali, the most charming little town in Rhodesia. It consists of a single main street which runs along a hog's back. We came in past the native location, one of the best in the country and remarkable for its low crime rate, or perhaps not remarkable, for housing is related to crime. The police were very neat and clean in long, well-pressed khaki tunics and shorts. They were unarmed. There were plenty of trees in the streets and gardens. All looked magnificently healthy.

We stayed at the Hotel Cecil, a very fine, completely modern hotel. While we were sitting in the drawing room having tea a little brindle, tailless bitch, that looked as if she was part griffon and part peke, ran in. I called to her. She jumped on to my knee and licked my face. I put her down. She sat up and begged for cake and danced on her hind legs in a most endearing fashion. No one knew anything about her. If I had been on my own and had a home I would have stolen her. At last I took her over to the charge officer at the police station.

I said: "I have come in to report a dog I have found."

They said I must describe the dog. I did so.

"Why," the constable said, "we've got her. She's here."

"No, she isn't," I said, popping her on to the desk.

"Where's that dog that was brought in this morning?" he asked someone standing behind him.

"Gone!" he said. "Got out."

"Well, she's back," I said.

I certainly hope she was found, claimed by her owners or got a good home. I have seldom met a dog with greater charm or personality, a dog that was sweeter, or uglier. A veritable *jolie laide* among pet dogs.

4

The Smoke That Thunders...Northern Rhodesia
and Victoria Falls

● NEXT MORNING, still thinking about our little dog, we moved
on to the Leopard Rock Hotel, which was set on one of the most
beautiful sites in the world, perched up in the mountain forests
with a view across the low veld into the bush of Portuguese East
Africa.

We had followed the route of the royal tour and now slept in
the room that Princess Margaret had used. The room was very de
luxe with brand-new pale golden bird's-eye maple furniture that had
been put in for the Royal Visit. The draperies and counterpanes
were green silk brocade and the over-all carpet green to match.

Leaving Tiny to unpack I went down to the lounge and ordered
a drink. A few minutes later I was surprised to see her rush in in a
great state of excitement. "Guess what!" she said.

"What?" I said.

"I've got white satin-lined drawers," she said. "I've never had
white satin-lined drawers before!"

A deep silence fell in the room. Our fellow guests were of the
rather stuffed-shirt-county-English type. At first I did not understand. But I got it in the end. All the drawers in the Princess's
room were lined with quilted white satin.

In front of the hotel we picked up some little red seeds from a
creeper, found some bushes of dombeya and a mauve flowering
shrub that I had had in my garden, both of which seemed to grow
wild here. It is always interesting to find flowers that one knows
in gardens growing wild.

After breakfast we went on again, away from the forest and bush
and into the bare, open veld of Mashonaland, that was only relieved by patches of scrubby thorn trees and the usual great piles of
rock among which the Mashonas hid their huts as if they were still
afraid of the raiding Matabele. By teatime we were in Salisbury.

A woman passed us with a grey monkey running on a lead. A

few minutes later a gentleman in a cowboy hat, top boots, riding a Palomino horse came past. Many men wore no coats, and their shirt collars were undone. We had reached the wide open spaces, where men were men, at last.

The first thing we were shown was the tobacco floor. Tobacco is the life blood of Rhodesian agriculture. The auctioneers were American and spent half their time here and half in the southern tobacco states. The two-hundred-pound bales were arranged in long rows. The auctioneers walked down the aisles preceded by the starters who gave the opening price. The buyers followed the auctioneers. The bids were in pennies per pound. There are fifty-odd grades of tobacco. An average price seemed to be about £50 a bale and the duty paid in the United Kingdom £3 17s. 8d. per pound, almost £800 per bale.

My next visit was to Mr. Paver of the African Newspapers Limited. He told me that some Africans in the newspaper world make £50 a month and that a number make more than £1000 a year in business, running native buses or in other ways. But many of them go broke and only about one in five hundred storekeepers succeeds. He had six hundred African correspondents sending in news from all over the country. "News, not views," he said. He did not want to know what they thought. He had African leader writers. He said there was a need for a native vehicular language. Kitchen kaffir, a debased Zulu, was useless. Chinyanza, a Nyasa language, would probably be the best. Too many languages were taught in the schools. Various missionaries had specialised in subsidiary dialects, making dictionaries and translating the Gospels, and were loath to give them up, which was a pity. I agreed with him but went further. I said all white men should know a major native language. Mr. Paver said the Africans were quite efficient but did not like responsibility. They did not like being left to run the paper by themselves if he went away for a few days. He said they were mistrustful of each other, because if anyone knew too much about you there was always the danger of them employing their knowledge against you. He introduced me to Mr. T. S. Savanhu, the African journalist who had accompanied the Queen on her tour. A very nice and intelligent young man who, I believe, has now been made a member of the Journalists' Association of Rhodesia. He said what was needed was an African middle class with an earning capacity of £500 to £1000 a year. This would provide a stable social factor. Polygamy was disappearing among educated Africans, as they found that one wife was expensive enough.

He said there was some danger of educated natives taking advantage of the less well educated. We talked about equal pay for equal work and I said this was not only a black-white argument, it was also a sexual argument among white people which had not yet been solved. We discussed the manners of Africans which, he said, were often misunderstood by white people. For the African, it was good manners to sit on the floor in the presence of the Queen, not to get up or greet first. It was good manners to go into a room before your guest, thus proving there was no trap in it, and exposing your defenceless back to him as a sign of trust.

Where can Africans go here? How far? The sky is the limit in Rhodesia if they have brains and integrity. This was the moment of federation. It had not yet been confirmed, and it appeared that some of the Nyasa people were against it. It was the same old problem. They wanted to live their own lives undisturbed, in peace in their huts, but they also wanted a motorcar and a radio. So does everyone, but it is difficult to persuade the African that he cannot have his cake and eat it too.

In the afternoon I went into native affairs with Colonel G. H. Hartley, which confirmed my feeling that things were being done very sensibly here. I still had to see the Congo, but when I had my opinion remained unchanged. The African was well taken care of in Rhodesia, had every chance of advancement, but was not over-babied.

We visited bachelor barracks which were more than adequate and were inhabited by the migrant male labour which comes into town to work for a few months and then returns to rest in the reserves. By the time they come back, most of these Africans have forgotten what they have learnt and have to start all over again, usually at some other job. This makes the building up of an efficient labour force very difficult. We visited the houses in the townships. They had up to five rooms, a proper lavatory, water and light laid on, and one shower to two houses. The rents of 15s. per month were paid by the employer if the wages were under £8, were split between £8 and £9 10s., after which the tenant paid it all. Revenues from the beer halls were used to help pay rent. There are separate beer halls for men and women to prevent what the West Africans call "woman palaver" which would certainly end in fights. On the other hand the

Africans have a grievance about not being able to drink at home in family groups.

We visited the bazaars which were very well arranged; the shops, all African owned and run, being grouped round a big square-walled enclosure, with a gate that was closed when business was over.

I went into the question of miscegenation, which was not a criminal offence if the man was white and the woman African. But if the woman was white she was deported if not a national, or put into a house of correction if she was. There had been a few cases of young girls having affairs with houseboys. Decadence exists everywhere but sex delinquency gains in importance where colour enters into it.

We discussed the actual problem of labour, of what must eventually happen in Africa. Grown men cannot go on forever making toast, changing sheets and baking cakes in white people's kitchens as houseboys. Women must eventually be brought into domestic service, and trained for light factory work. This will necessitate a vast propaganda campaign, instruction in the use of contraceptives and the creation of crèches where children can be left. At the moment, only the exceptional African woman can be used as they are always either pregnant or carrying an unweaned child.

The next day we visited the Domboshawa training school and met Mr. Hampton, the principal. This was the best thing of its kind I have seen anywhere — a disciplined Christianity which produced a very happy and efficient atmosphere. Everything was very well run and beautifully clean. It was here that I saw a pen of very attractive black, hornless native Sanga cattle for the first time. There is very little doubt that for ranching purposes native breeds should be improved by selection, rather than by using exotic bulls to grade up the stock.

All the young Africans working here greeted us most politely. I was astonished to be told that some white people did not reply to their greetings, which made it very difficult to insist on good manners.

From here we went on to the Chindamora Reserve where they were having an agricultural show. The show was very good with many varieties of so-called bird and insect-proof millet, some of which grew along the stem like a furry animal's tail. There must have been a hundred kinds of cow peas and beans, several varieties of groundnuts — among them a pale pink and a pure white were new to me. There was also a coarse sugar cane which was very interesting as it is much too cold here for the ordinary varieties to grow. I wondered how many odd things were growing in various parts of the world which have not been investigated. Fruits, cereals, tubers, whose cultivation could be spread over a much wider area if they were known. West and East Indian plants which would grow in Africa. African plants, such as the oil palm and certain gourds, which could be grown in other tropical countries.

There were exhibits of needlework, wood carving and ironwork (assegais, knives) and quite a large stall of cooked foods, including jams and preserves, though how these were made over an open fire was a puzzle and a great credit to their makers. There were cakes, bread and scones of various kinds, cooked meats and fried eggs. All foods were judged by Africans as African and European tastes differ. No white person would give a prize to an egg fried till it was dry and flat, and no African would tolerate a nice lightly fried egg whose yolk would break at a touch.

There were five thousand people here — some had come from fifteen miles away. All were very clean, all well dressed. The girls from the various schools wore different coloured uniforms and berets to match. Twenty years ago these people had been naked and filthy. Cleanliness, as Mr. Beck, the district officer, pointed out, is often a matter of economics. Soap costs money and washing wears out clothes. But in spite of this apparent civilisation a witch doctor from this district had been tried recently for killing six people and using their flesh to make medicine. All the medicine which had been distributed was called in.

Certain difficulties of administration are due to the instability of some Africans, who have one foot in the town and the other in the Reserve. Education also creates problems, as for instance the loss of such tribal knowledge as the use of native medicines, the habits of animals, and the methods of making traditional artifacts, which is a pity from every point of view.

Some control has to be exercised over native crops. If it were not they would grow only such cash crops as tobacco or cotton, from which they may make up to £40 per acre and, forgetting about food, might find themselves starving.

I was told that the Matabele had forty different colour names for cattle, every minor variation having been distinguished by a name. There is no word here for "thank you," for the people are without the concept that requires its use. With the African, service to a relative or clansman is expected. Food cannot be refused so there is no need to thank the giver since he too, if he passes another kraal, is entitled to the same hospitality, whereas for the stranger nothing is ever done without payment. We talked about the necessity for creating a middle class from which an aristocracy could rise, and of the importance of catering for the snobbery of the rich — better houses, larger gardens for those who could afford them.

Polygamy is forbidden to Christians. A Christian being defined as a boy who has been educated at a mission school. I said I considered this rather unfair. One could hardly expect a child of seven to decide if he would sooner go to a mission school and be educated and monogamous, or not go and be polygamous.

Everything had been judged before we got to the show but the prize giving remained. The prizes were single-furrow ploughs, trek chains, ox yokes, hoes, forks and other hand tools. To Tiny's astonishment she was asked to present them and, having just seen a newsreel of Her Majesty at a prize giving, she copied her manner and presented ploughs and yokes she could not possibly lift with most gracious smiles and gestures to Africans who understood no single word of what she was saying, but were delighted by the whole affair.

Many of the winners were ladies, among them some old crones who received Master Farmer Certificates — diplomas for good farming practices. They were all dressed in khaki with navy berets, a uniform of their own devising. The chief's youngest wife was one of the winners, a very pretty young woman in her early twenties. The winners received an ovation of shouts, hand clapping and ululations from the women who "*oohed*" into their vibrating palms — a trick that seemed to show some contact with the Arabs. At the end of the show the choirs sang "God Save the Queen" and "Save Africa" in their own language.

I saw some very nice little Mashona cattle in pens which seemed to me to compare very favourably with Afrikanders and red polls. The tests showed them only twenty pounds lighter at the same age. Some were either hornless or had loose horns, and a hornless strain could easily be developed. Their advantage lies in hardiness, and their small bone which makes them dress very high for their live weight. The deciding factor with stock in Africa is their ability to stay alive. Get that, and then improve size and quality by selection within the breed, or by an outcross that is then bred out again — this is the solution of the beef industry's problem in the tropics. This tendency is increasing now in all territories, though when I suggested it thirty years ago no one would have anything to do with the idea, as native breeds are slow maturing.

I was asked if I wanted to meet Sir Godfrey Huggins and declined. He was too busy at that time with the Federation to want to be bothered with a visiting writer.

We were now leaving Southern Rhodesia and starting on our way to the North. The country soon became more heavily bushed and suddenly I saw what I thought was a forest fire. The smoke was visible over the treetops and spread out for quite a distance. Then, as the train slowed down there was a roar in our ears. It was "The smoke that thunders." We had reached the Victoria Falls. The roar increased as we got off the train. As we walked down to the hotel a hundred yards away it grew still louder.

The Victoria Falls Hotel is a magnificent structure, very modern, with an enormous lobby, plenty of public rooms and it must be set on one of the most extraordinary sites in the world. A couple of hundred yards away from it are the Falls. Between it and the cliff is a lawn on which great indigenous trees have been left standing.

After breakfast I tried to call Livingstone but found that elephants had knocked down the line. I then got on to Mr. J. C. Tebbitt, the game warden, who had just returned from chasing elephants away from the rest camp by shouting and firing into the air. He had seen lion spoor on the road quite near by and a month ago had killed a leopard in his cattle kraal. So despite the "Grand Hotel" atmosphere, this was Africa at its wildest and most majestic. A few hundred yards away, a few miles away, things were as they had always been.

The existence of the Falls was known to the Arabs centuries ago, and they told the Portuguese about them. But Livingstone was the first white man to reach the Falls, in November 1855.

The Falls are in the middle of the Zambesi, eight hundred miles from its source and nine hundred from the sea. The width of the river here is nineteen hundred yards. The mean flow in flood season is 120 million gallons per minute, the lowest known flow 6.5 million. The height of the rainbow fall is three hundred and twenty-six feet. The spray, or smoke of the Falls, can be seen over the surrounding bush for ten miles. These are the guidebook figures which can express nothing of the grandeur of the scene.

This was not simply one of the wonders of Africa, but of the wonders of the world.

We hired sou'westers and oilskins and went into the rain forest where the fall of spray never ends and the sun makes endless rainbows in the mist. The trees drip from every leaf, the paths are slippery, the long grass never dries. A specialised exotic flora has established itself in these few acres. The noise from the Falls was too great for us to talk over when we were near them. Some of the trees had buttressed roots which turn into thin, almost flat, knifelike trunks. There was a coarse maiden hair and other ferns. And a feeling of mystery as the dripping forest closed over us. Here in sunshine it was always raining, while two hundred yards away the country was semi-desert bush, the soil merging into soft kalahari sand.

Looking down into the smoking cauldron it was easy to feel the attraction of the Falls but hard to think of anyone deliberately flinging himself into that boiling water. Yet there are so many accidents and suicides that the warden has special gear, including a bosun's chair, for getting out the bodies. Last year a young man was looking down at the water when a pretty girl, who was also staying in the hotel, came up to him and said: "Would you mind holding my handbag for a minute?"

He said: "Of course not." And as soon as it was in his hand she stepped overboard.

Another tragedy took place when a honeymoon couple were photographing each other. To get a better view the young husband moved back a pace and fell into the gorge. I was told there were at least five deaths a year, and soon after we left, a film director went over the Falls through having taken a canoe too close to the edge.

The Falls are almost invisible from the river. It slides on, a great carpet of moving water, and then suddenly there is no bed. Only an emptiness.

Nothing could ever spoil the memory of those few days. Of the river, the great trees; the vegetable ivory palms and the wild dates. The outer covering of the vegetable ivory is sweet and pleasant tasting. Elephants pluck them as they grow like cricket balls fastened to a long fruiting stem and, having digested the core, they pass the nut. Baboons are fond of them and send the young ones up the trees to throw them down. I learned more about elephants from the Ranger. They avoid the rubber hedge, and will run away from wild dogs. An elephant recently killed a four-year-old child in the Reserve here. It was out with some young men who, when they saw an elephant, threw stones at it. It charged and the child was killed. Then the elephant had to be destroyed as another of the treacherous beasts which revenge themselves when wounded or disturbed. In this connection I came across a curious phrase in a newspaper about snakes. A statement to the effect that "forty thousand people were killed by snakes in a year in self-defence." I liked the self-defence.

There is a local legend about the baobab. When God had finished creating the world and everything in it, he asked man if it was to his liking. Everything was fine except the baobab which was useless. Its wood was no good, its fruit no good. Whereupon God pulled it up (it looked like an ordinary tree then) and shoved it back into the ground upside down, which is why it looks so curiously distorted now. This was interesting, because in other parts of Africa we found much use was made of the baobab.

In the hotel garden there was a big clump of most beautiful tall bamboo, its thick, yellow stems tiger-striped vertically with brilliant green. But now it was time to move on. We had seen the Victoria Falls. Today, at this moment, we were among the last of the thousands who, in the last ninety-eight years, had followed in Livingstone's footsteps. His spirit still hung over the place. There was his statue, his great baobab, the place where he'd had his little kitchen garden, the reproduction of his map on the stoep of the Victoria Falls Hotel. How had he made it? Made all those observations, kept it so neat as he trekked about the wilds, half starved and weak with fever? Supported by his belief in God. Driven by his hatred of the slavers. Excited by his curiosity.

How comfortably we trod in his footsteps. We were continuing by rail and air to the great Congo which he had offered to England and which England had refused. That he had delivered from the slavers into the hands of a king who thought only of rubber, and still worse slavery.

5

The Missionary...Northern Rhodesia and the Congo

● WE ARRIVED at N'dola at eight-thirty and asked where to get breakfast. The Rhodes Hotel, we were told. Very much under the influence of the Rhodes myth we went to look for it and found it at last after crossing a dusty square and wandering past a lot of Indian stores. N'dola was not made by God. It was made by the copper mines and without them I imagine it could not exist. It was remarkable for its immense ant heaps, like miniature red cathedrals, that grew out of the red and dusty earth between corrugated iron shacks and modern offices, homes and what appeared to be blocks of flats. There may be more to it than this. But this is all we saw.

Returning to the hotel we got the airport on the phone. "Elizabethville? . . . Oh, we had tickets for Elizabethville . . . Yes that was quite possible . . . There had been planes going to Elizabethville . . . Oh yes . . . But unfortunately they no longer run . . . No, not for some time . . . What had you better do? . . . The train . . . Yes, that was the best thing. The only thing, in fact, unless you have a car . . . "

We went back to the station. Lucky that we had left our luggage. In Africa one looks on the bright side. Lucky to get anything to eat. Lucky to have a roof over one's head. Of course the dust is frightful, but how lucky it was not raining.

More luck — there would be a train for Elizabethville in half an hour. Everyone was most helpful. It was of course a slow train. It took six hours. There was no dining car. Still they thought we could get some sandwiches and beer. The train stewards were Congolese and spoke French of an African kind, but they were friendly, clean and sociable. We bought ham enclosed in leatherlike rolls and beer.

At the frontier we disembarked. There were a lot of bales of cotton on the platform that appeared to have been rescued from a fire. The Belgian flag flew from a white-painted staff. Passports. Forms to fill in in triplicate. Names of father and mother, even if dead. Were parents married? Where had they been married? Where were they

born? On what date? Name of wife even if divorced — almost names
of children if you have not got any yet. A very tight security control
which applied just as much to Belgian students returning from South
Africa to their homes in the Congo as to us.

We now re-embarked. Soon we were hungry again. The charming
black steward "regretted infinitely" that there were no more sandwiches. "Those children" (this was the students) "had had a great
hunger." But there was beer. "Would Monsieur care for more beer?"
We had more beer. The train crawled on. Every few miles it stopped
to pick up wood. It consumed wood, masses of wood, like an animal.
All along the line the forest was eaten off for a hundred yards on
either side of the track. The cutting was planned, controlled, like
everything else in the Congo. The stops must be changed every year
or so to allow the cut over parts to grow again.

The forest was wonderful, a wall of varied green. Some trees had
salmon-pink shoots of young leaves bursting like blossoms from the
ends of the branches. Here and there were isolated trees that looked
like enormous Japanese maples — their foliage a burning scarlet
against the background of solid green. At one place where the train
was creeping up an incline I counted twenty different varieties of
tree in sight at one time.

By now we were hungry again and seeing that our neighbour in the
next carriage was throwing oranges, tangerines and bananas to the
extremely fat black children who clamoured round us at every halt,
Tiny decided to approach him as a fellow American and ask for
something to eat. He turned out to be a Seventh-Day Adventist who
was going round all Africa inspecting the missions of his Church. He
gave us two bananas and two tangerines. We decided he had not
approved our buying so much beer. Tiny felt his behaviour to be
un-American. She had expected more of him — perhaps a kind of
"Dr. Livingstone, I presume" welcome. This let-down plus hunger
produced a condition which, in any other woman, I should have
described as sulky.

The train now stopped in a big way. This was not a wood stop. It
had a sort of negative urgency. People, black and white, poured out
of the train, like the entrails of an enormous caterpillar. Africans
dressed in brilliant coloured cloths arrived out of nowhere, mixed
with the passengers and tried to sell them things. Curious foods to
their compatriots, souvenirs to the white people. An official came
along, and I asked what we had stopped for.

"Be calm, monsieur," he said. "There has been a small drama."

Later I was to become used to dramas great and small.

"What sort of drama," I said.

"An accident," he said.

"To us?" I certainly could see nothing.

"Oh no, monsieur. To the train ahead. It is derailed. By great good fortune we did not run into it."

"And now?"

"A small delay. Four hours, six hours." He raised his hands. "But imagine, monsieur, our good fortune."

So here it was again. African luck. Six hours, plus a six-hour delay meant a twelve-hour trip. And more luck still, I suppose, we had had that breakfast at N'dola. It had only been with the greatest difficulty that I had persuaded Tiny to eat two eggs and some toast. I pointed this out to her. She was in no mood to have things pointed out to her.

She remained silent and glared at the missionary who was distributing more fruit to the Africans on the track. "He knew," she said.

"Knew what?"

"That there was no restaurant car. That's why he brought food."

We lay down and went to sleep. This is the secret of travel in Africa. Carry blankets and, if anything goes wrong, just wait for it to go right again.

Eventually there was a new sort of activity which woke us. A kind of shiver of excitement went through the crowd that stood by the track. It came from the engine end of the train. Perhaps we were going to start. Perhaps the wreck had been cleared off the line. The passengers were implored to re-embark. We would proceed immediately, but immediately.

An hour later we began to move forward at a snail's pace. Showers of sparks, a golden rain of fireworks, illumined the African night. Orange sparks and the silver of the stars pricked the darkness.

Then the train stopped again. The guard came along looking for the missionary. It appeared that he had telephoned from where we had stopped to his brother Seventh-Day Adventists at some mission in the vicinity and they had come to fetch him in a car. We watched him depart in a cloud of dust, like Elijah proceeding heavenwards in his fiery chariot, and then once again we were on our way.

At the station, which consisted of dimly lit platforms and offices closed for the night, we found a taxi which took us through the dead streets out into the country where the Sabena Guest House is situated. It was midnight when we got there.

Food? Oh no, they regretted infinitely but there was no food. The cook was in bed. But we could have coffee. And whisky in the restaurant lounge — a large modern room with a beautiful bar. An orchestra was playing and several couples were dancing amorously. It was very gay.

This is one of the best hotels in Africa. But it would have been nice to have had a hot dog at a Diner. Or fish and chips in a paper bag. But that was a dream, a memory. It was midnight. The plane for Duala left at six. That meant getting up in five hours time and we weren't in bed yet.

Tiny was not at her best. Her mind was still occupied by thoughts of the Seventh-Day Adventist and food. She needs food often. She is an artist. She has not got the temperament of a philosopher. It was no use telling her we had arrived.

She only said: "Arrived? When we leave again in six hours? That isn't arriving."

I said this was a very fine hotel. That Elizabethville was the industrial heart of the Congo. I tried to interest her with some statistics that I had found in a folder on the reception desk. But she was not in the mood. And we were led by a sleepy boy in a white uniform to our pavilion in the garden. A lovely little cottage with a lovely bathroom complete with a bidet. When she saw all this luxury, Tiny burst into tears.

I said, "What's the matter? Isn't it okay — looks fine to me?"

"That's it," she sobbed. "It's lovely and we can't stay and I'm hungry." She brightened up. "But I'll have a bath."

Again we were lucky. There was not only water, there was hot water. There was even a plug in the bath to keep it there. Sometimes, as we were to find later, one or all these factors was missing even in the most luxurious bathrooms. A bathroom is not something to take on faith in Africa. You can't just see it and believe in it.

An airport, even if you are already in it, expects you to be on tap an hour before the plane leaves. The plane left at six. That meant in order to get up, repack and get on to the field of aviation as they called it, we had to get up at five. To get Tiny up at five meant, then, when she was untrained, that I had to start at four. It was now one. Fortunately, I can wake myself at any time I want though I do not sleep so soundly. Anyway a boy was bringing coffee at five. But the period between the initial waking of my wife and the moment when she was dressed and on her feet had to be considerably longer than sixty minutes.

At four I awoke, and put on a bedside light. Fast asleep, with a sort of dormouse reflex, Tiny curled up into a tighter foetuslike ball and pulled the bedclothes over her head. This was always the first or hibernating phase. I added more light. She compressed herself more tightly and retreated, with a sort of rotating motion, to the foot of the bed. I started making a little noise. This she describes as "your banging around." I banged around for a bit. I was now waiting for the next move. This is the result of suffocation. Like many Americans she can live without oxygen for a considerable period, but in the end she has to breathe. As she comes up for air, I say: "Open one eye." She does. Then I say: "Open both eyes. Start waking up." Finally she wakes but it takes time, or did take time. By the end of the trip we were up, packed and out in thirty minutes. But by then I'd taught her not to undress completely. Not to make up in the morning and, above all, not to unpack *that bag. That bag* had all her best things in it. Skin foods, skin tonics, aspirins, hair clips. Things she might need. Things she could not do without. Things one loved but never used. All of which were easy enough to get out but had to be repacked with infinite care or only half of them would go in again. Our bird carved out of ebony, for instance, took up a lot of room. It had come from the Congo originally and now was back again. It was our mascot and necessary to our safety and comfort. It was, in fact, a talisman, exactly like those we criticise the Africans for having.

The plane was a Sabena four-engine job. And both of us were extremely nervous. I had flown only once before, from Miami to Nassau, since the First World War, though then I had been up a couple of times in a fighter and enjoyed it. But I was twenty at that time and courage does not increase with age.

Since that day we have flown all over Africa but that moment, before the take-off, has never ceased to thrill me. The feeling is the one you get on a good horse as you put him at a jump. One of power as it goes into dynamic action. And after that, as far as I am concerned, there is nothing but a feeling of unpleasant boredom. At best, one of a slight hangover, at worst, one of the worst kinds — when one expects to die and swears never to drink again. There is only one advantage to flying. You get there quickly.

We came down at Luluabourg for lunch. Here it was really hot, with a new kind of heat. New even to me, though I thought I was used to Africa. Here the heat was thick, heavy like a blanket. It enveloped one. It was inescapable. The fans only blew it around.

Next stop Léopoldville. Leo as they call it — the Belgians like abbreviations, E'ville, Leo, Stan, Cock.

We saw the Congo, the great mysterious river that I had so often thought about. We touched the tarmac. We had arrived.

We would be here for five days before our plane for Kano left from Brazzaville. Two men came to meet me. They introduced themselves as Monsieur Samuel of the information department and Monsieur André Scohy, journalist and author, of the radio section.

They were enchanted to meet me. I was enchanted to meet them. They were enchanted to meet Madame. Madame was enchanted to meet them and, in a mood of enchantment, they drove us to the Regina Hotel where a room had been engaged for us. They left us with a parting gift, the compliments of Monsieur Rik Cornelis, the Vice-Governor-General, and his invitation to dinner that night. This was the end.

To dinner. When we felt like death. Had had no sleep, were still almost starving and the few clothes we had unpressed.

We had a fine bedroom with a bath. It was full of water. Tiny said: "Fancy that. Fancy people being so lazy that they can't even let the water out when they've had a bath."

The water looked suspiciously clean to me but before I could investigate the matter Tiny had pulled the plug. By the time the water had finally run out I had made some enquiries. There was a water shortage and that was all we would get till tomorrow. By now our supply was down the drain and half way into the Congo.

This was no moment to remonstrate with my wife who was already muttering about "my clothes," about "governors and people like that who had no consideration for other people" — people like her, I assumed. Instead, I thought I would be efficient. These moments come upon me and, fortunately having been born and brought up in France, my French is good.

I called reception. "Madame," I said, "I regret to inform you that a small drama has occurred." I could feel the vibrations over the wire. Every Latin loves the word drama. Had I discovered a dead body in the room? Was some adventuress attempting to seduce me? Had I been robbed? Attacked? Such things are the small dramas that enliven the life of an hotel receptionist.

"Ah!" she said. "Un petit drame." Drama is masculine — I have often wondered why.

"Yes," I said. "Madame has let run the water from her bath."

"Ah," she said again. "A serious matter. There is a shortage of water . . . "

"A bath," I said.

"Impossible," she said. "With infinite regret I assure Monsieur that it is impossible. Absolutely. But absolutely."

"But wait, madame, this is an affair of the greatest urgency. Tonight we dine with the Vice-Governor-General. Can we go dirty? Can we go smelling? Can we go . . ."

She broke in: "It suffices," she said. "My God, the Vice-Governor-General. I will send boys with buckets."

They came in a series, with water, and left with francs. Another boy came to fetch the clothes that needed pressing. When I was in the bath the Vice-Governor-General called up. Very friendly. It turned out that he was a fan of mine and had all my books. He would send his car at seven-thirty.

In the meantime Tiny was muttering about her hair.

"My hair," she kept saying, as if she had just discovered it. "I can't get it done can I?" I said no. Anyway, there was one problem we did not have to solve. There was no question about what she would wear. Her worst evening dress. The only one we had brought.

Then we went down to the open-air café. The band was playing. Everyone was drinking beer and apéritifs. At seven-thirty there was no car. At least no one had heard of it at the desk. At eight I went outside to look around and then I saw a car about a block long with a nickel flagstaff on the radiator. I looked further and found an African driver in uniform sitting on the steps. He was perfectly happy. There is nothing an African likes better than to wait.

"The car of the Vice-Governor-General?" He sprang to his feet, saluted, and said: "Oui, monsieur." I called Tiny and off we went.

The house was on the river. At the gate, Askaris presented arms. A major domo announced us. There was a big party — ten couples. Our hostess advanced. She was a beautiful dark woman, much relieved to find that I spoke French. The Vice-Governor-General came forward and I made my apologies. He understood perfectly. "This is the Congo," he said.

"It is Africa," I said.

I had a cocktail and was introduced all round. The British Consul General, Mr. R. B. B. Tollinton, was there with his wife. So was the Consul General of Holland, Jonkeer van den Brandeler. The other people's names I never got. It was here that I learnt for the first time that most of the perishable foods eaten in the cities of the Congo come from Europe by air.

After dinner Monsieur Cornelis asked me to autograph a copy of *The Turning Wheels* which he had had beautifully bound in brown leather. The conversation was interesting. We discussed polygamy among the Africans and I found that it was being reduced among the urbanised people by the housing situation: A man was allowed only one wife when he got a house. And by giving the other wives no legal rights. Though if he had children by them he had to contribute something to their support. I was much shocked by the view that the Americans practised polygamy — had a plurality of wives, "of course only one at a time, *bien entendu*, but still in principle . . . "

By now I was very sleepy. The pills I had taken against air sickness had begun to operate. They were of the twilight-sleep variety and I sat perfectly happy in a delicious dream. Tiny now took over and asked if anyone was interested in palmistry.

I have yet to meet anyone who does not want his palm read and Tiny was really quite good at it. But she was as tired as I was. The only difference was that she was under neither the influence of alcohol nor twilight sleep. Never, may I say, have I felt more pregnant nor enjoyed a more delightful state of euphoria. Tiny took hand after hand, male or female as they came. If they had rings on they were female. I woke suddenly from my happy daze to hear her say: "Now here's a guy that'll go far." She looked up and saw that she had the Vice-Governor-General's hand in hers, and added "Your Excellency." Her analysis of his character was so good that later Mr. Tollinton told us that he had included it in a despatch to the Foreign Office.

There is no doubt in my mind that Tiny was right. Rik Cornelis will go far. A clever man of great personality, married to a lovely woman, cannot fail. He was one of the first of those men we were to meet who are at the top because they belong there.

Never before in my life had I met so much top brass as I was going to meet in the next few months. From the directors and officials of De Beers at Kimberley, to governors, lieutenant governors, presidents, prime ministers, black kings and emirs. All had in common those qualities which are described as leadership, coupled with immense vitality, and I should say in almost every case wives who were beautiful, understood people, entertaining and, perhaps, even those arts of intrigue which are usually known as tact. Much later Commander Jackson at Accra, who is engaged in promoting the Volta Dam scheme, told me that when selecting people to come to West Africa he took the temperament of their wives into consideration and saw them as a couple rather than as merely qualified men. Africa is not a country where a man can stand alone.

The days now blurred into a kaleidoscope of sightseeing and sensation. Picture and impression merged into a colossal whole that shimmered in the burning sunlight. André Scohy drove us about and showed us everything there was to be seen. The rapids, Stanley Pool, factories which, artistically speaking, were the best I have ever seen. De Tonghe's Circus, with its five ferocious lions, the strongest man in the world, and the charmer of serpents with her terrible rose pythons.

We met a man who said: "Le Congo c'était fait par les célibataires." By the Belgian definition — a bachelor is a man who is not married to a white woman. He said all that was wrong with the place was that the white women had come too soon, and that a bad white man who lived with natives might be better for the country than a good one who ignored them, because the former learnt the language and really got to know the people — a point of view that was to recur later.

We visited the native cities and saw housing schemes where some three to four thousand houses, many of them prefabs from Belgium, Norway and Germany, are being put up each year. They are nice houses and the layout is good. I saw no giving way to expediency. There are plans and they are followed. The ideal price, they say, is about forty thousand francs which is paid off in a period of twenty years.

These Africans are householders. They are city residents of their own city, but not allowed out of it after 9 P.M., nor is any white man allowed in after that hour. Actually there is no colour bar except that enforced by economics and, to some extent, by custom. But today an African can become anything in the Congo, even a functionary — a district officer, if he has the qualities. He cannot vote, nor can the white man. At present the Congo is concerned with progress, not with politics. The troubles and the politics will arrive simultaneously.

We visited two social centres where the women are taught the simplest kind of domestic science. How to clean a room, how to cook good food on the small charcoal stoves they use, how to sew and take care of a baby. Since these women only wear *pagnes* — cloths wrapped about them and artistically draped and tightened to show off their most fetching points — there is no need for them to sew till they marry an evolved man and have to keep house for him and mend his clothes.

We went to a meeting of Africans and white people where the Africans spoke at great length about the things they wanted. These were all evolved, or at least evolving, and what they wanted most were women who were their intellectual equals. Who could take care of them, read and write, and talk French. We visited the art school of

St. Luc and saw the students' work. The teachers are Belgian lay brothers and they try to keep everything African. All they really teach is technique. The results are not primitive. They are powerful, beautiful and with a strange quality of sophistication. This school was started ten years ago with only three pupils. Now it produces work which would be a sensational exhibit in London or New York. There are now sixty-eight hand-picked students and the course lasts four or seven years. These are the artists of the future who will decorate the buildings of their country.

We saw the Red Cross maternity hospital run by Docteur and Madame Lambotte. Nothing could have been better run or more modern.

We met an African writer, Monsieur Antoine Roger Bolamba who had just come back from a conducted tour in Belgium. His questions and ideas were interesting. How do we arrive at the state of the White Man? Why are the women so backward? What do we lack? Why is there not equal pay for equal work? And finally, what actually has the White Man done in Africa? To this I replied: "You yourself are an example of what they have done. You as an African writer. The first of any importance in the Congo is probably their greatest achievement. As to the rest, that is what I am here to find out. In a year's time I may have some of the answers." Before we parted he gave me a most interesting book he had written — Les Problèmes de L'Evolution de la Femme Noire.

Perhaps the most illuminating thing to see in any foreign country is the market. And the enormous native market of Léopoldville is a sight never to be forgotten. To start with, it is almost exclusively female. One is suddenly aware of the immense fecundity and sexuality of Africa. Many of the women were beautiful once you became used to African beauty. One could see why white men took them as housekeepers. They were all woman. They were, in a sense, without souls. I have no doubt that in the eyes of God they had souls, but they did not know it, and the men did not know it. They were bold and without innocence. They said with their dark eyes: We are women. You are a man. We know what you want. Most were pregnant, or carried a child, or led a child, or both. They were dressed in brilliant colours — blues, reds, greens, yellows, beautifully patterned with every conceivable design and combination, their brightness rendered more bright by the sunshine. It was like an immense flower bed that swayed, undulated. There was no smell. These women were clean. There was less smell than in a European crowd. Less than one finds on a bank holiday on Hampstead Heath, or on the Fourth of July at Coney Island.

The wares exposed for sale consisted of everything the African heart could desire. Materials, scented soap, perfume, alarm clocks, beads, hardware, and food in the utmost profusion and variety. Fish from the river and the sea, but even this section was so clean there was no smell. There was dried fish and meat. At one stall an enormous woman was cutting up chunks of smoked elephant flesh with a chopper. At the next, dried caterpillars were exposed for sale. There were piles of manioc that looked like chunks of chalk, and manioc bread wrapped in leaves and tied with raffia. There were medicine stalls where skulls, bits of animal skins, and roots and herbs were offered. There were fruits of every kind, and nuts.

Through all this, past the stalls, handling goods and chattering, went this endless stream of black femaleness swinging its rolling buttocks, suckling its children at breasts the size of jack fruit, content, without a psychosis among the hundreds. Here was the power of Africa.

At last we were on the Congo. The greatest river in the world except for the Amazon. It is wide here, but slowly Brazzaville took shape. This was the French Equatorial African shore, the edge of a vast territory that ran from here to the shores of the Mediterranean.

Near the landing stage is an immense silk-cotton; beyond it the customs house. The examiner was an African. There were no difficulties. I got a taxi and made a price of six hundred francs to be driven round the town before going to the Hotel Relais at the air port.

Brazza bears no resemblance to Leo. It is not highly industrialised. The architecture had a feeling of Indo-China. It is not, I would imagine, efficient, but it has charm of an Old World, colonial kind. The streets are lined with splendid trees. The Governor's Palace is like a white wedding cake magnified a million times. The hotel at the airport is beautiful in the best French modern style. We had some time to wait so we sat in the garden.

Tiny saw an African waiter in wide black trousers, white tunic and black cummerbund chasing a cat with a carving knife and stopped him. I do not feel that he was arrested permanently. We had learnt in Kimberley how fond Africans are of cats. But it was interesting, as an event taking place in this context, in the garden of an ultra-modern streamlined hotel. It was the paradox that is the keynote of the continent. Here the unexpected, the irrelevant is usual. If it does not occur something is wrong.

● *Nigeria*

6

The Camels of Kano...Northern Nigeria

● WE NOW TOOK an Air France plane. Another big one, somewhat dashingly flown. We were given champagne and needed it.

I had more champagne. I was relaxed and thought about what we had seen of the Congo. Nothing of course really, just five days in Leo. But I tried to organise my impressions. Nowhere was the African better treated or better protected from the rapacity of the colonising white. Not that there are many colonists in the Congo, or that colonists are particularly rapacious. Though that is the popular illusion. High wages were paid in the factories, mines and to house servants. There was an educated and an artisan class coming into being. Hundreds of thousands of children were being taught in the mission schools. Becoming, as they say, evolved. But evolved into what? One woman, whose husband was a tailor, had three radios in her house and no electricity. Still, electricity would soon be available. In the meantime it was an attractive example of conspicuous spending. She was dressed in an expensive, dark blue Nigerian handmade cloth, with a black and gold thread design. The upper class was taking its snobbish shape.

We came down at Duala in the French Cameroons. In the native section the cottages and huts were whitewashed, which did nothing to relieve their squalid appearance. Here was dirt in a big way. The palm-leaf roofs sagged on rotten beams. But the people were fat and well dressed.

We had coffee at the Akwa Palace Hotel and then set out to explore the town. There were some fine buildings but they were all stained with damp. New buildings in the process of going up were already patched with black mildew, green with moss. Some concrete building blocks had a vine growing over them, and a young banana had forced its way through the middle of the heap.

The Cameroons have, I think, the highest rainfall in the world — almost four hundred inches in some parts. In the haze of heat and mist we never saw the mountain — either coming or going.

Near the hotel was a fine breadfruit tree and in the gardens I saw, for the first time, the shrub that they call the iceplant in West Africa. It resembles the Australian myrtle but has white blossoms and white spotted shoots that look as if they had been sprayed with paint.

We went to look at a curio shop near the river but it was closed. Once the slave ships must have lain here waiting for their cargoes. The impression was that this was a sad place, a place where men could go mad with the heat and the rain and the manifold exasperations of Africa. The cumulative strangeness which seeks out each man's weakness and then uses it to destroy him. In West Africa the moderate drinker becomes a drunk and dies of it. The passionate man kills someone. The lover of women dies of his loves. Drink, women, gambling — it makes no odds. West Africa will find the weak point and exploit it.

This country wants no strangers, wants no disturbance. Any scene could be set here but one of happiness. Women live in anxiety for their children's health, their husbands' or their own. Their linen is eaten by fish moths, and cockroaches as big as mice. Termites eat the furniture and the boxes in which things are stored, the rain beats its way through roofs whose timbers are destroyed by borer . . . Dreams and memories torture them. But for the bold man, the hard man, there is wealth if he survives. So everything now becomes a question of survival.

I was informed that my best plan was to go to Lagos and on to Kano from there. That is to say, I had to cover two sides of a triangle instead of one.

At five we were in Kano. This was really the beginning of the trip we had arranged. Outside the airport two pink camels were tied to rings in a wall. I assume that they were pale beige but the red dust of the Sahara and the evening light made them appear pink. To me they will always remain the pink camels of Kano. I later found that they had been presented by the Emir to add local colour. The authorities had been delighted to accept them, something they regretted when they found out how much they ate. They did no work, naturally, and were a sulky, bad-tempered pair. I have no doubt they suffered from claustrophobia. Kano must have seemed very built up and suburban after the vast spaces of their desert home.

Mary Potts, a pretty brunette who turned out to be a South African from White River where we had mutual friends, came to meet us at the door of their house in the residential section. It was one of the old ones built in the native style of mud, with immense three-foot walls and arched ceilings and roof. But it had great atmosphere. Our room was like a chapel.

No one understood why Potts had chosen this house. He was a senior official and could have had one of the modern villas that were now being built for civil servants, with plumbing and everything else, had he wanted it. Personally, I agreed with his choice and so did Tiny. We had a nice bathroom. The water had to be carried in but ran out. And a very fine earth closet that was reached by a whitewashed passage that resembled a tunnel. The whole house was whitewashed and hung with native carpets and weapons and had a quite indescribable charm. The garden was beautiful. The birds sang in the trees. There were vases of flowers everywhere. It was a home.

The servants in their white nightshirts, red fezzes and sashes were dignified and good-tempered. It was all very romantic. An outpost of the Empire.

We made the usual apologies about having been foisted on our hosts by our friends Ian and Mickey Gunn in Minna, who had arranged with friends throughout the country to put us up. These apologies were to be continued through the breadth of Africa. The Pottses said they were delighted to have the opportunity, and so forth. After all, what else could they have said? But they were wonderful hosts to whom nothing was too much trouble.

From now on for months, though we did not realise it fully at the time, we were to be handed on from one person to another — rather like parcels travelling by hand. District officers, government agents, private individuals, governors and lieutenant-governors, consuls, all took us in, kept us a few days, and passed us on. This was only the beginning. But what a beginning. From the very tip of Africa, from our farm near Cape Agulhas, we had reached almost the edge of the Sahara.

So this was Kano — the most ancient commercial city of the Sudan, and today a kind of aerial Piccadilly Circus. I went out to look at the signpost. Rio 4248 miles. Jerusalem 2176. Malta 1685. Lima 6006. Nairobi 2150. Cape Town 3244. The Africans paid little attention to the planes that passed overhead. And the passengers who landed here to change planes were in complete ignorance of the old town in which Jesus Christ would have found little to surprise him except perhaps the bicycles. Many of the commodities exposed for sale would be identical, and the cities of the Near East at that time must have resembled Kano. The not-quite-square houses, built of small red mud blocks and plastered with red mud, that leaned inwards from the narrow streets. Houses with rounded roofs or flat roofs whose phallic decorations broke their silhouette against the pale blue sky. Houses with raised designs and painted designs on the walls. And the alleys, so narrow that a loaded donkey sometimes stuck in them. There were no sidewalks, no gardens. At your feet was the sand of the desert. About you the mud walls dug from the borrow pits whose scummy water was the only green thing in sight. The few palms that stand like giant feather dusters in the compounds are not green. Their fronds are white in the sunshine and black in the shadow. They are harsh like a cluster of swords. The Jakara stream running through the centre of the city had magic significance in the early pre-Moslem days. Later it became a cesspit into which all the filth was flung. The heads of criminals executed on its banks were thrown into it, and severed hands of the convicted thieves. But every well was connected with the stream.

In the rainy season many houses collapse but they are rebuilt with the same mud, in the same style, so even the newest houses are as old as the old, as old as the Sahara, as old as God. Twenty thousand people come to the market. A hundred thousand live here in the old town. This is one of the great Moslem cities of the world. When the British occupied Kano it had had sixty kings. A place of multitudinous courtyards, of houses that open into other houses, into little yards, into great circular huts that only prove to be the entrances to further buildings. There are no windows. There are only walls pierced by narrow slits. Thick walls with carved doors that are armoured with nails.

Here, hidden away, is every luxury. Here can be found every vice. There are satin-covered divans, carpets, rich leather work, jewels, pots of silver and vessels of gold. There are rich clothes, caparisons for horses, padded armour, and chain armour that was in use in the days of the Crusades. Here are naked concubines, perfumed boys. But nothing is quite clean. There are no comforts, no lights. No water, save that which is carried in goatskin bags. No sanitation.

When the British came here fifty-two years ago, the mud walls of the city were decorated with heads, prisoners were placed in cells with their legs through the walls, where they were masoned in. Thieves had their palms gashed. The hand was then bound up in green hide which contracted and caused the fingers to grow together in a kind of lump. Or they had limbs amputated and the stump dipped in boiling milk to sear it. Slaves were sent from the great market here across the desert to Arabia, and the North.

And all this is near. Near in time, in memory. Perhaps even near in fact, for who knows what goes on behind those walls? Who is going to bear witness?

The centre of the old town — its pulsing heart — is today, as it has been for centuries, its market. There are miles of stalls packed with merchandise of every kind. Potash from Chad, salt from the North that comes in with camel caravans, sometimes many thousand strong, kohl — antimony in shining heaps. Hand hoes, ju-ju bells — long, narrow bells welded together, one of them being much longer than the other. They have no clapper but are beaten with a little iron rod. Cotton, spun and wound like cocoons on short sticks. Native sugar in brown chunks. There are mirrors, embroidered saddle covers, saddles, fezzes, dates, sweetmeats, cotton-cloth sandals, leather bags, brass and silver ware, jewellery. Long calabashes that the women fill with a solution of henna and wear like gloves on their hands to dye them orange. Beads, stirrup irons, heavy core bits of traditional native manufacture. Medicines — roots, stones, the skins and heads of birds (tick birds, ibis, vultures, crows), the skins of pangolin, hyena and giraffe in small moth-eaten sections, are all exposed for sale in the stalls that cater for the witch doctors.

The fleshers' yard cannot have changed at all. In the passing centuries, time, appalled by the stink, passed it over. Here is the biblical past with its dirt, its vultures and dogs. Its half-naked men scraping the fat off skins, drying them, dressing them, dyeing them. Men had skins wrapped round heavy sticks and were beating them against rocks worn smooth by beating. There were sheep skins, goat skins, crocodile, iguana and snakeskins hanging up. There were goatskins dyed blue, yellow and red, for Kano is where Morocco leather comes from. It is made from the skin of the chestnut Sokoto goat — a breed perfected for this purpose. To tan them the skins are soaked in water and ash till ripe, then when scraped, treated and dyed with vegetable dyes that are the craftsman's secret.

The dye pits cannot have changed either. Here on a platform, some fifty yards by thirty, pits like small wells are sunk. Beside them squat the dyers, dipping their materials into the indigo. Patterns are produced by knotting stones into the cloth. The indigo plant is prepared in the village and brought in blackish lumps to the pits where it is mixed with water, ashes and the ground flour of the locust bean. The longer a cloth is kept in the mixture the darker it becomes. Some of the pits have been handed down from father to son for generations.

The residue of the pits is in great demand as a waterproof plaster for mud roofs and walls. In a hut near the pits, leather workers, naked but for a loin cloth, beat the dyed leather goat skins with heavy mallets, alternating in an endless rhythm on a round log, to polish them by breaking down the fibre.

There are vultures everywhere, and naked children. Small Eastern donkeys, smooth coated, loaded with sacks, are driven along the streets. This is the kind of donkey on which our Lord rode into Jerusalem. A donkey like a sleek grey long-legged, long-eared mouse. A magnificent horseman in flowing riga and turban gallops up the street. At a signal from us he pulls his stallion up into a rear and swings him round on his hind legs. He raises his right hand in greeting — a warrior, a savage desert horseman.

"A photo?"

"Dash?" He holds out his hand.

"A shilling," I say.

For a shilling this magnificent creature poses on his Arab steed. Makes him pirouette and prance. And then departs, again at a gallop, in a cloud of dust.

Had it all been an illusion? Had we bribed a desert king? Or was it just Africa? Was it just civilisation? His father would have cut my throat just for the pleasure of seeing the blood run out on the parched sand. The son had posed for a bob.

7

The Old Emir ... Kano

● To ME the most interesting race in Nigeria are the Fulani. These slim, golden-copper coloured people, almost certainly related to the Masai of Kenya, and possibly to the Swazis of South Africa whom they resemble in many ways, are believed to have come from the Nile basin to the Futa country east of Sierra Leone and to have spread along the desert fringe. The young men dress their hair like the Swazis and have the same love of decoration. Their figures are like those of graceful girls. They even dye their hands with henna and darken their eyes with kohl like the girls. They stand on one leg, resting, as they watch the herds of cattle for which they are ready to die. For again, like the Masai, they are cattle people and their white cattle are among the most beautiful that I have ever seen. Nomadic, they wander homeless with their beasts, often leaving their women alone in semi-permanent camps for months. They pride themselves on their self-control, both mental and physical, and will suffer anything, as we were later to see in Bida, without blinking an eye. They are very race conscious and call Hausas "black skinned." They sometimes live on milk alone, like the Masai, though they generally mix it with fresh blood.

The girls remain faithful to their husbands when left alone — a rarity in Africa, and elsewhere too. Brilliantly dressed in yellow and scarlet cloths, these maidens are most attractive. Seductive, graceful as buck, they stand watchful, knowing themselves to be watched.

I heard of two cases where Fulani herds had been destroyed because they had been exposed to rinderpest infection. The owner went mad in one case, and killed himself in another. There is a cattle tax known as tangali but the animals are so well trained that at a whistle from the herder they will disappear at a gallop into the bush, which naturally makes the counting and taxing, since it is by the head, impossible. A Fulani can call each beast out of the herd by name. They are named for some physical peculiarity — a bent horn, a white udder, or a black spot. In this they resemble the Matabele and the Zulus.

The Fulani is completely identified with his cattle. They are an extension of himself. At one time they were trained for war and would attack at a signal, charging with their masters. I heard of one variety, the Rahaje — the aristocrats of all cattle — large, dark red animals with white horns, which surpass all others in docility and possesses an almost doglike intelligence. This breed comes from the mountains of the Northeast and is, unfortunately, delicate, but the bulls are in great demand for crossing to give their brains and intelligence to the more hardy, more common white animals.

There is another breed — white with black ears and large horns — known as Bunanje, which may be the ancestor of the Royal Zulu cattle.

Both men and women of all ages work and handle the cattle. Butter is made by shaking the milk, which is very rich in fat, in a gourd. The Fulani women are very important, and no sale of stock is made without consulting them. They are a moral, highly strung, sensitive people, who are capable of nursing a grievance for years.

It is essential to grasp the significance of cattle in Africa. They are not just animals, or money or prestige. They are all this and more. They have a mystic significance. The cattle-owning tribes kill them upon occasion, and sell them sometimes, they are often cruel to them because they do not understand cruelty, but the cattle remain almost sacred.

The cattle people run from the south of the Sahara right across Africa till they are checked by the tsetse fly or forests in the West, and down along the east coast through Kenya, Tanganyika, Portuguese East Africa to Zululand and beyond, right down to the Great Fish River.

Being a cattleman I paid some attention to the stock I saw, and outside the city walls I found some Chad cattle — of the Kuri breed with enormous horns. They were of two types. One kind was shortish, two feet six or so long, but gourd-shaped and almost a foot thick in the middle. The second kind was long, very long, and the ox that carried it, a black and white animal that I went up to, must have stood nearly seventeen hands at the shoulder, and was humpless. These animals are supposed to have developed these appendages to help them swim in the lakes of the swampy area that is their home. The horns are honeycombed, very light, and are believed to support them like waterwings. They are capable of swimming ten miles or more and their bones, which are enormous, are equally fibrous in section.

The origin of the Fulani is, like everything else in Africa, in some doubt. They resemble the ancient Egyptians, and one theory is that they are the descendants of the Hyksos shepherd kings, another that they may trace their ancestry back to a migration of Jews into Senegal. At any rate they are Semites, an ancient race, showing blood as the horse shows it. There is no mongrel about them. They breed true and run true to type. But nobody knows much about them, nor does anyone speak their language except, I believe, for one veterinary officer who, because of his job, is forced to follow their migrations.

At any rate in the early nineteenth century the Fulani, who were ardent Moslems, became strong enough to revolt against the tyranny of the Hausa kings and declared a holy war — a jihad — against the seven Hausa states which they considered had fallen into evil ways, and defeated them, the Hausa's ten thousand cavalry, in spite of their chain mail and quilted armour, being no match for the Fulani bowmen. The Fulani replaced their kings as rulers and extended the slave trade, making a big business of what, till then, had been little more than a paying hobby.

Outside Kano the Emir has what might be called a summer palace or farm. This is where in the old days he and his followers rested when they came back from slave raids, their white clothes red with dust and blood. Here fresh horses were brought to meet them, fine clothes, new rich turbans, silken rigas, saddlery. Here the band with its kettle drums and great trumpets assembled, and from here the parade of conquerors, with their chained slaves, entered the city with the full panoply of barbaric victory.

Soon after the Fulani took over, the desert route from Kano to Tripoli was white with human bones. In their raids they killed the men and took the women and children. But they seldom killed outright. They just chopped off an arm or a leg and left their victims to bleed to death. But despite the bones there was always some danger of missing the road. For the dunes drifted and the wind-driven sand covered them. So guides were employed. Blind men who could smell the urine of the camels and the blood and putrescence that marked this terrible road with its perfume.

It was to stop this slaughter that the British came to Nigeria. But the past is very near. Kano fell as recently as 1902. Sokoto surrendered in 1903. Kano has thirteen miles of crumbled walls but the gates remain. The walls were, like everything else in this part of the world, built of mud. They were fifty feet high and eighty feet thick at the base. The old city had fifteen gates. It had been an important place, one of the greatest in the world a thousand years ago. It was still intensely impressive — a city of mud, fast-rooted in the desert sand. Enclosed within the walls were the farmlands that supplied the livestock and people in a siege. There could be no surprising so strong a place for before an assault could be mounted, reserves could be brought into play from the centre of the city. An additional defence was the deep moat beyond the walls that was filled with thorn bushes.

Our next adventure was a visit to the Emir. We went through a great arch into the yard of his palace that was half fort. It covers twenty acres and contains the Emir's private mosque, court of justice, council chamber, reception hall, private apartments, women's quarters, storehouses, stables, garages, barracks, cattle pens and garden, the whole enclosed by a high mud wall. Five hundred people are said to live and eat here at the king's expense.

Above us floated a big indigo standard covered with white Arabic characters. Crossing the yard, we were met by the Emir and his retinue. A tall, dried-up old man, erect as a spear, dressed in a thick-ribbed white silk riga. He greeted us and turned. We followed him through the guardroom where the guards, in loose red and green robes, crouched down in obeisance as he passed. We went through more high, churchlike rooms of immense medieval dignity. They were bare. The walls were mud. The floor was mud. But they had a strange quality. One wondered what intrigues had taken place, what treachery had been planned. Ahead of us the Emir rustled on. He rustled with virility. The heavy silks and satins that he wore rubbed against each other with the noise of steel, like the blades of two knives being rubbed together, as though they were being secretly sharpened. The materials were such as a woman might have worn — rich, lovely — but there was no frou-frou here.

These emirs, and I met several of them, were men, kings who even now, when indirect rule is practised, are still despots in a muted sort of way. I can hardly imagine a man refusing an emir his daughter, or his horse, or anything else he fancied. Or bearing witness against him. Today he would not be dragged out and killed, or mutilated, he would not be tied up for hours or days in a soft tanned-leather sack till he capitulated in agony — he would simply become ill and die. But the end would be the same — he would be dead.

I asked Douglas Potts about this later. I said: "How can you know what goes in in these blind courtyards, behind these faceless walls?"

"We hear," he said. "People come and tell us."

"All?"

"No," he said, "but most. Let's put it this way. Once, for ten men killed we heard of one. Now for ten men killed we hear of nine. A big improvement."

We reached the audience chamber. There was a sofa covered with a shawl on which the Emir sat, sweeping his robes to the side like a woman in a ball dress. We — Tiny, myself and Douglas — sat on European-type wicker chairs. On the floor was a carpet. I was surprised that it was European, and not very good at that. Two of the Emir's advisers sat on chairs opposite to us. The room would have held two hundred people. Would have held a thousand Hausas squatting on the floor almost in each other's laps. The walls and ceiling were painted with mottoes from the Koran in enormous letters and decorated with almost futuristic designs in sepia, buff, black, white and silver.

Potts acted as translator. The Emir asked what I was doing. I said, via Douglas, that I was going across Africa to write a book. He then asked where I came from. South Africa. He said he was glad. Too many people were writing books about Africa who had never been there before. And although I was white I was not a European. It was time a book was written by someone who was not a European. This was a new idea to me.

Compliments passed. He rose. We rose. He went to the door. We followed. In the guardroom the lounging guards prostrated themselves once more. We shook hands all around and crossed the palace yard to the waiting car.

It had been an interesting experience. In the long run these emirs are doomed. Democracy approaches. It is in a way a pity — something of beauty will go with them, of style, of panâche, something original, characteristic, virile. But the male quality is disappearing from the world. Such men cannot be made by machines, by competitive examinations, by business. It is even possible that they cannot be made without horses. There are men today but they are a new design.

I was interested in the ruling class being so dark in colour, as they were Fulanis. The answer was that there were now two kinds of Fulani, the cow Fulani, the golden purebreds — Palominos as it were — and the town Fulanis — Gidan, as they were called — who had mated with their captured African slaves and the defeated Hausas, thus blackening their skins.

In the afternoon we went out of town to visit a Fulani ruga or

village. Stopping the car we walked down a little path through
guinea corn twelve feet high and came to a group of huts where we
were warmly greeted by an old man and his sons. They knew Douglas
well. The place swarmed with children — naked boys and beautiful
little girls, swathed in a single garment of fringed shining Morocco
leather that made no pretence at covering them but served only as a
kind of coquettish invitation, ran about or posed, staring with soft
smiles. A completely naked copper nymph of eleven climbed onto a
donkey and galloped bareback round the huts, guiding it with a little
stick. Other girls picked up naked children nearly as big as themselves, setting them on their hips. The older ones had their eyes
blackened with kohl which made them look more like deer than ever.

There were goats in a little open hut eating grass that had been cut
for them. They stared at us with golden eyes. There were white
Fulani calves tied by collars of hand-woven rope to a cord stretched
between two trees. This was something I wish I had known when I
was ranching. The main rope was slack and the collars made fast di-
rectly to it so that there was no possibility of the animal getting its
leg over its head rope, since there wasn't one, and becoming entangled.

All the animals were tame — cows, calves, donkeys, goats. Chickens
— of the small native type — were pecking round the cook hut. I
have never seen more happy and contented people. From our point
of view they had nothing and knew nothing. But they had a way
of life and knew how to live it. Would they be better off, any happier, if they could read and write? Would those girls be better off in
European clothes? Somehow clothes for black skins seem a kind of
artistic degradation, like hanging a handkerchief on the belly of a
bronze. White people need clothes. They look better in clothes.
One has only to go to a beach to see what they look like without
them.

Clothes mean trade. They also mean disease, and probably the
loss of natural, indigenous chastity. But between them, the businessmen and the missionaries will soon settle the hash of these people,
among the last of the free.

This argument will not appeal to the evolving African in his
lounge suit, and sun glasses, with an array of fountain pens in his
breast pocket. These things, to him, are the outward and visible
signs of his education, his civilisation. But they no more make him
civilised than taking off my clothes and putting on a loincloth would
make me an African able to live on the land, and off it. Able to survive as the African can, survive and still increase. Everything in

Africa seems to me, although here in Northern Nigeria it is at its slowest, to have gone too fast. In grasping at the shadow the bone has been lost. But everywhere the African is complaining that the pace is too slow. He must have more education, better education, higher education. This he is convinced is all that stands between him and the white man. Just education, not history.

There was still more to see in the old town. There was the city of the blind, a section of the old town which we reached after some enquiries and the use of several guides.

We left the car and wandered down alley after alley till finally we came to it. A deserted section. The blind, of whom there are several thousand, were out working. That is to say, begging. At one time a school for the blind — a kind of African St. Dunstans — was established where the pupils got a shilling a day and free meals. After two months it was discontinued. The blind did not want to work, they wanted to beg.

We next went to the smiths' quarter and climbed the iron hill which was the original cause of the city's existence. It was started as an ironsmith settlement at the foot of the slope of Dalla, the smaller of the two hills that stand out above the plain on which the city stands. Near the foot of Dalla runs the Jakara stream that was once fringed with tall trees among which the pagans sacrificed black cattle to the serpents and the sacred tree of Shamus. With Islam the grove disappeared. This was the smiths' quarter and the most ancient part of the town. A settlement predating the Hausa dyers and tanners who are believed to have reached here in A.D. 999.

The smiths themselves were using their traditional tools that I imagine had changed very little, though one of them had a small portable American buffalo forge. But lying beside the huts that were their workshops, mixed with heaps of natural ore, were parts of old motorcars — bolts, nuts and axles — that would, I suppose, later be forged into daggers, spears, hand hoes, bits, spurs and stirrup irons. The men who make these things are the real blacksmiths. Another more modern guild of their craft is that of those who work "white" metals such as silver, brass and alloys.

We went through the market again. I think I could spend weeks there, looking at the articles exposed for sale and making drawings of them. This time I saw some beautiful pink satin pants. They must have been four feet wide across the seat, then they tapered down till they were tight about the ankle. These are the correct wear for gentlemen of high degree. It appears that the Prophet, when he re-appears in a new incarnation, will be born of a man. In consequence trousers must be made large enough to accommodate him when he arrives and tight at the bottom so that he cannot fall through — a pleasing and romantic thought. But I would have liked those pants. In fact, had I lived in the North, I think I would, like some of the early explorers, have adopted the national costume which, apart from being extremely beautiful, is certainly practical for both the heat and the cold. The turban, whose ends come down under the chin, can be pulled up to the eyes like a yashmak in the dust of the harmattan — the desert wind that brings the dust of the Sahara sweeping over Africa in the winter.

(I remember years ago at sea, two hundred miles west of Cape Verde, finding the ship covered with dust as fine as face powder blown out from the Sahara. I never thought then that I would one day be so near the place of its origin.)

Native clothes, native horses and gear all appeal to me. Even the bits, which appear so fantastically cruel, in the hands of a good horse-man are nothing like as bad as they seem. And there is a point that is sometimes forgotten. All the horses here are entires and easily become savage. I talked to a veterinary officer about the effect of gelding them. He had cut eight stallions that were dangerous but it had had a calming effect on only two of them. One of the most interesting things to me was to see how the heavy curb bit and Western saddle was related to those we saw in use here. They had gone north with the Moors to Spain, been adopted by the Spaniards and taken to Mexico, and from there into the United States. Here the same gear has come south over the Sahara suffering some changes but showing its Moorish origin. It was odd to be reminded of Wyoming here, and think of the strange world of horsemen.

Some years ago I had read a fascinating article about a couple who had ridden from Nigeria into the Union, some three-thousand-odd miles without any lameness or mishap, on two local horses. A notable performance. The article was illustrated and one evening as I was driving home with Douglas we passed a horse like one in the pic-ture — an ugly brute. A strawberry roan with splashes of white on him, white stockings, a white face and a wall eye that had a pink rim.

"I say," I said, "what's that horse? I've read about them. They're damn marvellous horses. Who does he belong to?"

He said it was a Bahr el Gazal and belonged to a Mr. Rakar, the Tripolitanian groundnut magnate.

Next day he arranged for us to go and see his racing stud. Mr. Rakar is a charming fat man, whose wife says he is too old to ride now, but he showed us his string of incomparable country breds. Bays with black points, greys, one blue roan which he said had a typical Bahr el Gazal head — the profile was Roman, very like that of an Irish hunter. Each horse had his own syce and when they came near each other they lashed out and screamed with fury. The grooms cursed each other and the horses. It was all very lively.

Rakar has made and lost several fortunes. He told us this as we sat on his stoep on the first floor, the widest I have ever seen — over eighteen feet across — and drank Turkish coffee. At that time there were nearly four hundred thousand tons of groundnuts packed in bags and built up into pyramids of from 750 to 1000 tons each, covered with black tarpaulins waiting to be sent down to the coast. And the new crop, a bumper one, was about to be harvested. This is groundnut country. Thousands of acres are under nuts and probably hundreds of thousands more are available. All that is needed is communications — an extension of the railroad, or motor roads to open up these vast areas. Instead, thirty six million pounds of British money was wasted in East Africa before even a pilot plant had been set up, to see how nuts would grow there. A couple of million would have cured the railway bottleneck between Kano and Lagos. Some new locomotives and loops, with an efficient repair shop, would have done the job and the balance would have been enough to put British agriculture back on its feet and reclaim much of the marginal land in the United Kingdom that is at present useless as its development is uneconomic by private capital.

Perhaps I liked the North because it is still at the animal stage of culture, scarcely mechanised at all. There were horses, cattle, sheep and goats everywhere. Donkeys were hobbled very simply by a rope loop being placed over one fetlock, then twisted up and looped over the other. There were many sheep and all were perfectly tame and you could touch them even in the streets. I saw one newborn lamb, its navel cord not yet dry, trying to nibble at some dry grass growing from a crack in a wall. No wonder they can survive. But this was the period of rams. There were rams by the thousand. Big, beautiful, horned friendly creatures, all waiting to be bought for the Salla, the feast that ends the Ramadan.

We met some interesting people. A doctor about to retire going home with his butterfly collection. Hausa Mallams, learned men, who spoke perfect English and gave me the impression of real wisdom — something we are short of in the West. A man who, some years ago, had seen a white prisoner chained with a gang of blacks in Duala. A very democratic procedure demonstrating equality and fraternity. But we wondered what he had done.

Our stay was now drawing to an end and Tiny needed some shoes — sneakers — so we went out to buy them. The shop was a modern one in the new town. The shop assistants were Africans. With the greatest difficulty we persuaded one of them to show us what we wanted. He was engaged in talking in English to one of his friends who had come in to pass the time of day with him. At last he opened some boxes and handed them to Tiny. He was not going to demean himself by putting shoes on anyone's feet. He was a literate, educated man. He could make out an invoice in duplicate and a man who could do this would certainly not stoop to do up anyone's shoes, least of all a white person's. But it was not that he was simply anti-white. I saw him do the same with African customers. That was the beginning of our disillusion. Most Africans with authority, even that of a clerk, are far from admirable.

So Tiny put on her own shoe, inserted the laces, and we went off with them. Fortunately we opened the box at home. He had muddled the shoes. One had four pairs of eyelet holes and the other only three. Next day we changed them. But the assistant was much annoyed. What did it matter how many holes there were? He was congratulating himself on their being the same size.

When I commented on this I was told all the shop assistants were Southerners, as they are far more advanced. But the Southerner, once he can read or write, is hard to deal with. He at once becomes superior and above any form of manual labour. This presents a serious sociological problem. Because many of them, though they can just read and write and do a little simple arithmetic, are quite incapable of holding down any clerical job. So they billet themselves on their relatives and, filled with hatred for the unjust and jealous white man who refuses to employ them, become political agitators and minor criminals.

8

The Silver Streak...Kaduna and Zaria

● THE FEELING between the North and the South is very violent.
The Northerners regard the Southerners as savages, wildmen, practically monkeys straight from the trees. On the other hand, the
standard of education is far higher in the South, and the Southerner
regards the Northern people as backward, illiterate and feudal. The
Islamic North refused to have missionaries and, for good or ill, it is
the missionaries who have educated Africa. And in the end the
North may turn out to be right, provided they get enough secular
education. After all they have their religion which, in many ways,
is a good one.

Their objection to the missionaries is that they do not enforce
discipline, which is an essential factor of civilisation, though it may
not be of education, and that there are too many kinds of Christianity. Certainly the South is clever. But the North is wise. Discussing
this with an emir, he said the education of the South is like a film
of oil on water. There is nothing underneath it, no tradition, no
history. The South, emulating the Gold Coast, wants the British
out — their "freedom" as they call it — by 1956, though how a few
thousand civil servants, less than five thousand, I believe, can hope
to rule thirty-million-odd people without the use of force is something of a problem. Another thing said to me, as it has been said to
others, was that "if the British leave we shall resume our inter-
rupted march on the South." Actually the horsemen of the North
went as far as they could, and were only halted by the forests and
the tsetse that killed their mounts. There seems, however, to be a
possibility that the Ibos at any rate were defeated by horsemen,
even if they have forgotten about it. This is suggested by the horse-
beating ceremonies.

Hard as it is for us to understand, the African likes blood and
enjoys what we call cruelty. But cruelty is hard to judge and depends

almost entirely, like morals, on public opinion. The same applies to corruption. England, a hundred years ago, was corrupt and cruel. Bull baiting, dog and cock fighting were popular sports. Public hangings were festivals attended by thousands and continued up to 1868. To prevent cruelty, the whole public, not one man alone, must be made to see it as an abomination and this is unlikely to happen in Africa for many years.

It was on this last evening that Douglas told me the story of the recent Kano riots, which were not directed against the British (he and other officials went into the fighting crowds, unarmed, and quelled them) but were against the Southerners of whom there are many thousands living in a separate town outside the walls. This town is known as the Sabon Gari — the city of strangers. It had originally been built hundreds of years ago to accommodate Arab slavers and traders and Tuaregs who came to exchange salt and dates for the black cloth that was specially woven for them here. It was odd that there were so many Chinese place names in Nigeria — Song, Pankshin, Shendam, Hoss, Jos, Bang, Shellen and the like, and sometimes, one came across men with Chinese-looking faces and oblique eyes.

Bushman paintings are known to exist in South Africa showing men in Chinese hats, and it is believed that they may have mined tin in the Rooiberg Mountains of the Transvaal, and certainly they traded in their big seagoing junks to the east coast of Africa thousands of years ago, coming as the Indians, Arabs and Persians did on the wings of the monsoon. In the sixteenth century a giraffe was sent as a gift to the Emperor of China by one of the coastal Arab sultans. Later I found other evidence that made this theory of Chinese penetration of the interior a definite possibility, no more fantastic than many others, and quite worth further investigation.

Our means of transport was the Silver Streak, a 1947 Mercury, which had been treated with a kind of metallic silver paint and which we found had been bought for us by Ian Gunn before we had arrived. Ayo, the African chauffeur supplied by the garage, knew the road and would act as interpreter and guide. He was a big, very black young man of about twenty-five who said he knew all about cars and could effect any running repairs. We carried in the boot everything we could possibly need, except a new engine, which was about the only thing we did need, unless one includes four new tires. The chassis was splendid. The paintwork beautiful. And as long as we stopped every fifty miles to put in water and oil, the Silver Streak lived up to the name we had given her.

Zaria was our next stop; the road was dirt and not too bad. We passed fields of guinea corn, groundnuts nearly ready to harvest and cotton seedlings. There were patches of what we called taro in the West Indies, and is here called koko yam (*Colcasia edulis*) — a kind of arum whose bulbous roots are excellent when mashed, resembling potato. We passed women walking beautifully in lines, with great red water pots, from under which hung the long indigo cloths that protected their necks and backs from the sun. There were herds of beautiful white Fulani cattle pursued by naked boys, tiny donkeys loaded with firewood, a bundle on either side of their backs. We saw some birds — heron, white cattle egrets, coucal, scarlet finches, doves, guinea fowl and, of course, vultures. In the fields men were working by hand. They do not use draft animals here but dig and ridge the soil with short-handled hoes which have very large spade-like heads, out of which sections are cut in various designs, presumably to lighten them or to prevent the soil sticking to them if it is wet. Locust trees were left standing in the lands. The beans are eaten by both man and beast, and their residue — a thick dark brown substance — is used for waterproofing the mud roofs of the dwellings. This indigenous tree is of the greatest economic value and is believed by some people to be the "locust" of the Bible. I do not know if it is being propagated but there seems no reason why it should not be, or why other trees such as the caroe and American locust should not be introduced.

We saw one buckskin donkey on the road and this, with the three chestnut animals we had seen in Kano, were the only ones that differed from the normal, pretty, mouse-grey animal with a black stripe down the shoulder. These donkeys are small, neat and fast, and must be descended from the Nubian wild ass. All the donkeys wore wicker basketlike muzzles and most were hobbled, as were the few loose horses that we saw, for this was the growing season. We passed some horsemen accompanied by servants on foot.

Baobab trees were common but in no way resembled those of Rhodesia or the Transvaal. They were much smaller, less monstrous in their bulging form, and all the branches ended in knots, the result of the leaves being plucked continuously by the Hausas, who use them in soup. This practice may account, too, for their smaller size and shorter life. The baobabs, locusts and shea nut trees all stood in the lands supplying shade for the workers and an annual crop of leaves or fruits. The shea nuts are reduced to a form of butter that is used as fuel, though now they were bare of leaves and covered with the webs of the caterpillars that had eaten them. We saw a few silk-cotton trees, that they call rimi here, standing isolated and buttressed and all along the road rests made of rough poles so that people carrying loads could rest against them.

We stopped in a forest reserve — if there were no reserves there would be no forests — and had lunch by the roadside. There had been some rain and a black lady came and washed herself beside us. She was voluptuous, smiling and quite uninhibited. When she had washed her splendid breasts, that hung like purple eggplants from her chest, she bent over and splashed water on to her back then, kneeling on the bank, she scooped water into her mouth by throwing it up between her open lips with great dexterity. We parted with smiles and gave her the empty gin bottle in which we had been carrying our drinking water. She was delighted and so were we. A very nice lady, I should think.

At Zaria we drove to the Residency section. These areas exist in every town and are official "locations" where the white people are segregated. We found the Residency, a really handsome house in a splendid garden, and our hosts, Mr. and Mrs. Conrad Williams. Helen Williams was a very beautiful blond American. She combined good looks, exquisite taste in her dress and house, a talent for entertaining and a standard of food and service that I have seldom seen equalled. These gifts combined with some private means — dollars, too, in these days of exchange shortages — made her extremely unpopular with some people who were jealous of her looks, charm, capability and position as Resident's wife in the nicest station in Nigeria. But she was equally popular, for the same reasons (but chiefly for her charm and beauty), with other people. There was no halfway about it. You were a Helen fan or you were the other thing. We immediately became fans. There was a certain kindred feeling because we are rather like that ourselves. We have many friends, but when people do not take to us they do it in a big way.

It was here that Tiny had her first bat adventure. Later she got used to them. She had no choice about it. But this evening, leaving me drinking with Conrad, she went upstairs. There was a bat in the passage so she rushed into the lavatory and hid. After a while she peeped out. The bat was still there. She now made a plan. For some obscure reason — perhaps because she thought the mosquitoes and moths that the bat was pursuing kept fairly high up — she decided that bats never flew near the ground and her best way to get to the bedroom safely, about ten yards away, would be on her hands and knees. Just as she got near the door a bug, who did not know of her upper-altitude rule, dived for the ground with the bat after it. With a muffled scream, which was supposed to bring me to the rescue, but which I naturally did not hear — being busy with my whisky and soda — she scuttled through the door of the bedroom and banged it shut, only to find that the bat had come in with her. This was what he had been waiting for — someone to open the door for him. When I went up to change half an hour later I found her fully dressed under the double protection of the bedclothes and the mosquito net which was fortunately down.

I now got rid of the bat by lighting the flashlight and leading it back into the passage.

Tiny is a very remarkable woman, a New Yorker, an ex-fashion artist and, possibly, on the basis of her background and my own, the most unsuitable and most charming wife I could have chosen. When I got her she went lame if she got off the city sidewalk. Since then, and that was eighteen years ago, I have dragged her over half the world, taken her elephant hunting, built her a really lovely home on the farm we had at the Cape and when nicely settled in it, sold it over her head because the wanderlust took me again.

I am a South African of Boer descent and seem to inherit my ancestors' desire to trek, to see what lies over the next hill, to fear comfort and settling down, to mistrust possessions — though I love their beauty — because I have found that in the end they tend to possess you, and you become little more than a caretaker for the stuff you have accumulated.

In all this time we have seldom been more than ten feet apart — and nearer at night — but we continue to interest each other. She remains to me completely exotic, American, and a perpetual wonder. While she appears to consider me a completely inexplicable character. Her personality, since I tend to think in animal terms, combines the courage of the lion (a very small pocket lion) with a dormouse's talent for sleep. Though the lion part does not operate with bats, spiders, scorpions, bees, wasps, hornets and rhinos.

The Residency at Zaria is built on the site of Lord Lugard's first fort. He was Captain Lugard then, and of course, as every schoolboy except me knew, was the founder of Nigeria. A soldier and administrator of the very highest quality, Nigeria was his creation, and I have little doubt that he lies very restlessly in his grave today. Everything that he, and others like him, did to bring order and peace into the wilder and more savage parts of the world, creating an empire on which the sun never set, is being undone today. The Pax Britannica no more than a memory, and the Jack that flew so proudly in so many lands is coming down in most of them for the last time. The critics of Empire have found much to criticise. But is the world today a much better or more peaceful place?

It was here, meeting men like Conrad Williams, who have given their lives and health to what they conceived to be their duty, that one felt this. Good or bad, I do not know. But it was a fine thing, grand in its way.

Owing to the disturbed condition of Nigeria, it is becoming increasingly difficult to obtain cadets — junior officers for the civil service. Their future cannot be guaranteed, and Conrad told me that he was having some trouble advising those of his officers, who had had offers from commercial firms, about their future. A district officer, like a professional soldier, is not much use in civil life if he stays in the service too long.

In the morning we were awakened by birds. From the back window of our room we looked out to the tops of a group of flamboyants that were just going over. In front on the lawn were giant frangipani, and a big baobab which still had a few flowers on it. They hung like large, white, flat five-pointed stars from a stringlike stem. Their centre was a kind of shaving-brush mass of stamens. When fertilised the flower drops off, leaving the pistil at the end of the stem over which the flower had fitted like a tube over a pencil. The fruit swung like goose eggs covered in green plush at the ends of these long strings. The pulp is edible and was once the source of cream of tartar before being superseded, as I imagine it is today, by some synthetic product.

The Williamses had a fine orange cat which Helen believed to be partly wild. The eyes were yellow, set obliquely, and the tail was longer than usual and heavily ringed with dark orange along its whole length. I saw a number of orange cats in Nigeria; they are believed to be descended from the toms the coastal traders had in the old days crossed with the native wild cat.

Our first visit was to the Emir. He was a fine-looking man of medium height about fifty years of age. He was dressed in a white riga with a blue-spotted white muslin turban. With him were various court officials, but he alone wore shoes. He talked in parables and I found that I could do the same, much to his pleasure, with Conrad Williams translating what I said. These people, with their oblique approach, must be interesting to deal with. He talked of the North and South, an endless subject in Nigeria. He talked of his people's old Islamic culture. He complained that they were now growing too much cotton and other cash crops instead of food, which would mean a famine if anything went wrong with supplies from outside in a bad year. Only the loom eats cotton, he said. He expressed the opinion that reading and writing were bad for the memory. He discussed the Moslem virtue of charity to beggars, saying that it reduced crime. No thief has the excuse of actual hunger, which was why, before the British came, theft was treated so severely by amputation or maiming. Thieving, he said, leads to murder.

The Emir returned to the subject of the South. The Southerners have acquired some Western skills, but no culture. Culture, among other things, to these Northerners means manners and dignity. In these qualities they excel.

The Waziri or chancellor sat beside the Emir. He was a small, dark man with very bright eyes and a sharp, foxlike face that radiated intelligence. He was, I was told, a great expert on law. I felt that handling a recalcitrant witness would offer him no problems. When questions failed, the knife and hot iron would produce the answers, or could have in the past. He wore a yellow riga and a magnificent turban that looked as if it were made of carbon paper. This is a material of the highest quality, and can be worn only by men of noble descent, and is most expensive. It is made by beating scraps of mica into an indigo-dyed material with heavy clubs, which gives the material its curious smooth and shiny texture, as the mica is actually incised into the threads thus stiffening them. We had seen it being made near the dye pits of Kano.

After we left, I asked why there were china plates of all kinds built into the walls and ceiling of the palace. Conrad laughed. "For the termites," he said. I still could not see it. He said: "As you know, when they work they must have darkness, so they always leave a thin skin. But a thin skin won't hold a china plate and when it falls it is time to move away from under."

In all the palaces I saw I was struck with the general untidiness of the rooms. Saddlery thrown into corners. Books and papers piled on chairs. Dust and dirt. But it finally occurred to me cleanliness is a new idea and on the whole a woman's idea, and if women live in a harem a house is going to be untidy whatever the colour of the owner.

The sequel to this visit was a dash that consisted of a big wicker basket of small eggs and large cockroaches, packed in rotting straw, plus six live hens delivered at the Residency "for the Resident's guests, with the compliments of the Emir." Before anyone could do anything about it, the eggs and cockroaches were unpacked in the pantry, because the very dignified emissary who had brought the gift wanted his basket back. In the cockroach hunt which followed, the chickens were forgotten — till next morning, when it was found that they had been incarcerated in Helen's Muscovy duck house. These ducks were her pride and joy. So, convinced, and rightly I should think, that the chickens carried all kinds of vermin, she had them removed at once, the ducks dusted individually with insecticide, and their house re-whitewashed and sprayed.

But it was all very splendid and Eastern, this exchanging of gifts. Of course the emissary had to be rewarded in cash. He was given the value of the eggs and chickens at the top current rate for his dash. This would be one of his perquisites in the royal household. Once, I suppose, the present would have been a little slave girl or an Arab stallion. Now it was hens and eggs. Still, one could think about the other things of which they were the symbols.

I was told that some emirs, even today, have several hundred people living in their enormous compounds. Wives and concubines, warriors and guards with their wives and concubines, children by the score, servants, grooms, scullions, butchers and executioners — now a symbolic sinecure — each with a handful of relations and assistants, wives and lights-of-love, and their progeny. There would, of course, also be camels, sheep, mules, donkeys, goats and poultry, ducks and pigeons, the personal horses of the Emir and his cavalry, and a menagerie of pets — dogs, ostriches, monkeys, parrots, warthogs, ground hornbills, cranes, marabou storks, baboons, jackals, tortoises, porcupines, reed buck and duiker.

On our way back we stopped to look at one of the arched gates which was being repaired. I had often wondered how those lovely curved ceilings were produced. Split planks of the giginya palm were used. They were fitted in one behind the other. The effect would be produced in a small way by taking the springs of a car out, fixing the largest one in a wall upside down at the desired angle and then extending the leaves one over the other, masoning them in as one went along, so that each supported the next one that lay upon it. The planks are called azara and only the male palm is used, the female being eaten by termites, which, however, do not touch the male tree. All the building material was carried in head loads — basin-shaped baskets on the heads of women. Though taking it all round, the women here do not have too bad a time because men see no shame in carrying, will in fact carry great cases rather than use a wheelbarrow, and there are plenty of pack donkeys. But once one gets into the tsetse country the women become the donkeys and carry everything.

I was told that each mixing of the building mud — that is to say each time it was completely moved, stirred and turned over — would add a year to the time it lasted.

The palace at Kano had been built in the fifteenth century and rebuilt on the same site in 1800. This palace was newer — at least the part we saw was — it had a villa-ry touch. The hand of the Public Works Department had got into the mud.

Like all the walled cities, those of Zaria are very large, enclosing what seemed at first to be just waste space, or spaces where perhaps there had once been houses which had been abandoned and had collapsed. But this was not the case. The area enclosed had to be big enough to hold the outside population and livestock that came into it in times of war.

It was also explained to me now that one greeted Hausas with the right hand raised in a fist. The Communists must have stolen the gesture from Islam. To raise the left hand or to offer it is an insult, since it is the unclean hand.

At lunch, Helen told us about her scorpion and snake men. Unfortunately, we had just missed the scorpion man who came every three months or so and called the scorpions out of the walls of the house and garden, picking them up in his hands, even putting them in his mouth, and stirring up a boxful of them with his finger. This is something I would have given a lot to see. I had read about it once in a book on Egypt. And later in the day, talking to Colonel Stallard, who runs Gaskiya Printing Corporation, about this phenomenon, he said he had seen examples of it in the war where he had commanded Hausa troops, among whom was a man who always kept a scorpion or two in his haversack to discourage pilfering. The snake man, Helen said, did the same thing, calling out the snakes and catching them without fear. Neither was allowed to kill their catch. They said if they did they would lose their power, so they either dumped them in the bush or left them to starve or devour each other, thus keeping the letter though not the spirit of their contract with their snake and scorpion friends. We discussed the African mentality and his opinion was that they were subject to lapses. The minds of even the best sergeants in the West African Frontier Force would, at times, he said — for a period of a few days — go almost blank and they would remember nothing. It was as if they got tired and had a sort of breakdown.

All the work of the printing presses was done by Africans with reasonable precision, though when binding books, for instance, they would sometimes put in the pages in completely the wrong order, which they did not regard as serious. They were in the book and merely had to be looked for. In the layout they had to be watched or the columns would not be straight or equidistant. This problem of the straight line is one of the keys of the African character. It is, though we seldom realise it, the actual basis of our Western culture and philosophy. Without the concept of the straight line, the shortest distance between two points, there can be no straight thinking, no art that is not primitive, no architecture or planning. In all my experience I have only had one African who could set up a fence in a straight line, and it is only with the greatest difficulty that Africans can be taught to put in plants on one side only of a garden line. The African mind seems to be circular. His kraals are round, his huts are round. His approach to difficulties follows the same pattern.

The paper — its name, *Gaskiya,* means truth, and its motto is "truth is worth more than a penny" — is an attempt to give the people of Nigeria unbiased news, and is the organ of the Northern Peoples Congress, one of whose leaders, Abubakar Imam, is its editor. It is on this party that the British centre their interest, since it is at the same time both moderate and progressive.

I now visited the secondary school, where I was much impressed by both the boys and the teachers. These boys had a serious urgency. They were not smart alecs and had great ability. The subjects were taught in three languages — Hausa, English and Arabic. I listened to an English lesson and the pronunciation was perfect, the smallest error being corrected. These boys would be like some of the Congolese I had met whose French was superb. In the afternoon I spoke to a hundred-odd students at the World Affairs Club. They came from the Nigerian College of Arts, Sciences and Technology and were a very interesting lot of young men, several of them asking many questions about writing which I tried to answer. My idea was that they should develop a literature of their own and not just copy American and British authors.

The Samaru Agricultural Station was the next and last thing on our schedule. Here we saw cotton and groundnut experimental plots, and a dog belonging to one of the directors which looked as if it were part saluki. We lunched with Mr. and Mrs. Emmrich. She was a pretty, dark girl, and he was the engineer in charge of the shops. He spent a considerable time telling me what the drivers and mechanics did to the heavy machinery. What they did not do was nobody's business. The African does not have a feeling for engines, and never ceases to be astonished if, when set impossible tasks, they break down. He regards them as so remarkable that they should be capable of anything.

Mrs. Emmrich had a delightful grey parrot. The house was a nice modern villa, but the Public Works Department had made a slight error in the lavatory. They had put the door in after the pan was in and behind it, so that it would not close. But, as our hostess explained, privacy was easily maintained by the occupant uttering loud cries if approaching footsteps were heard in the passage.

After lunch we visited the cattle. Some experiments for trips (tsetse) were being made. Ndama bulls, which are more or less immune to trips, being crossed with white Fulani cows. The Ndama is also known as the French Guinea. It is a medium-sized humpless animal which, according to one authority is descended from the Hamatic longhorns that were domesticated in pre-Neolithic times. They also had some Muturus, a very small trip resistant breed, found in the forest country.

A milking test was being conducted with white Fulanis which seemed very satisfactory to me. The calving average was sixty-five per cent on a three-hundred-and-five-day lactation period. The cows were mated at four years but were long lived, and fifty per cent of the cows gave over two hundred and fifty gallons of milk with relatively light supplementary rations, and one or two had given up to five hundred. Off grass alone, a few had given one hundred and fifty gallons, some fifteen to twenty pounds a day, testing five to six and a half per cent butterfat when in full milk. The milkers were fed two pounds of seed cotton per day just as it came from the gin, but soaked in water before it was fed, to soften it.

We saw a golden oriole in the garden and watched a group of marabou storks walking about with the stud bulls in a paddock. It was a most enjoyable afternoon — my first close-up of northern cattle, and I was amazed at how tame they were. The calves were far tamer than any European cattle I have ever seen, even when hand raised.

The Zaria visit was over now. We said a sad goodbye — and pointed the Silver Streak south again.

9

Ten Thousand Rams...Bida and Minna

● OUR NEXT HOST was a Mr. Brown, known as Phiz, of the Secretariat. He was tall and distinguished. He drove us round Kaduna, which is an artificial administrative town, with no reason for existence other than its central position. The white population is five hundred, of whom only three are unofficial. There are many beautiful gardens, or compounds as they call them, which are now, with a scarcity of labour and the rise in its cost, too expensive to keep up.

We saw the military hospital — a large gloomy affair of huts surrounded by barbed wire, and the military lines. Two battalions of the Nigeria Regiment are stationed here.

The Acting Lieutenant-General, Mr. Rex Niven, asked us to lunch the next day.

Government House stood in splendid grounds and was approached by a long drive with a guardhouse at the entrance. Lunch was early to enable us to catch our train to Minna, for it was here that the Silver Streak more or less ceased to function. The road south was almost impassable and so it was arranged that we should travel by rail and send the car in a flat.

Mr. Niven, a small, very neat, soldierly looking man, an administrator of the old school, who has written some excellent books on Nigeria and is an authority on its history, took us over the house. He showed us Lord Lugard's desk, which took down into three parts that could be carried as head loads. He showed us the snooker table — the only one in Northern Nigeria — and two very fine lion skins that had been shot in the area. They were very pale skins and almost maneless.

After we had drunk our coffee Mr. Niven ordered his car and we all drove in state — much to Tiny's joy — to the station. At the gate the guard, in khaki with red fezzes and scarlet waistcoats embroidered with yellow, turned out and presented arms as the bugler blew the general salute. Niven waved his hand, Tiny smiled, bowing graciously right and left with her March of Time queenly air. The Union Jack on the hood fluttered bravely, and we swept on.

The station was a scene of much excitement. An African newspaper photographer came and took our pictures with a Rolleiflex, and a very good one it turned out to be, but we, Governor and all, were without significance when compared to the rams which were going south to be sacrificed at the Salla. Truck after truck was being packed with them. I was told that at this time as much as fifty pounds graft, or dash, was required to get a truck, so great was the profit on this trade. The rams were beautiful — big and tame, with eyes like golden agates, roman noses and great twisted horns. The top half of the doors of the trucks were open, and closed with netting made of rope which the rams had eaten through long before we started, out of boredom presumably, because they made no attempt to jump out.

The Lieutenant-Governor and A.D.C. stayed until the train left, which it did at last with a series of shudders, cries from the crowd, and bleats from the rams who, though they did not know it, were setting out on their last journey. This was the Great Salla which is the commemoration of the offering by Abraham of a ram instead of his son Isaac to Allah.

We had stepped into Bible history — into the pictures of the Bible story book I had read on Sundays as a child. Abraham, Isaac, rams, the Salla. My heart was full, but I was sad. They were pretty beasts, so patient, and so near to death.

It was a pilgrim train filled with Africans of every kind going south for the greatest religious festival of the year. They were going to worship, to feast with their families and friends, to trade, or just for the hell of it. There were Africans in business suits, Africans in rigas and turbans, Southerners in loose, pyjamalike outfits, and one half-naked pagan with a tall bow, and arrows in a quiver.

It was not a de luxe train. We had a compartment to ourselves, but it was the dirtiest I have ever been in. Next to us was a rich Moslem who sat with two cocks tied together by their legs at his feet.

We had our chop box — the small crate which we had carried in the car with us and which contained enough food for several days, and plenty to read. But there was too much to look at out of the window to bother about books. At each halt, and they occurred about every half hour, men rushed out to cut grass along the track for the sacrificial rams. Others got out for other purposes. Each Moslem squatting modestly with his kettle of water in his right hand. No Moslem traveller seems complete without an aluminium kettle. Villagers rushed towards the train out of the bush, bringing exotic kinds of food to trade with the passengers — curious flat fried lumps of dough, chunks of meat, dried fish, bananas, green oranges (all oranges are green here), cassava bread wrapped in leaves, chewing gum, cigarettes, tins of condensed milk, kola nuts, groundnuts.

At last, only an hour late, we reached Minna where Mickey and Ian Gunn were on the platform to meet us. We had in fact reached our destination since it was the Gunns we had come to see.

It was dark when we drove past the night market in the native town. One had the feeling of age here, of long custom, of the implacable necessity of trade. Later I learnt more about it and about the mammy traders. Most of the trade is in the hands of the women. It ranges from those who buy in enormous quantities from the wholesalers — the great companies, like the United Africa Company — to the little girls who walk the streets with a single cigarette and four lumps of sugar in a tin plate balanced on their heads.

And the reason for this amazing diffusion? Simply that in most houses there is no storage place safe from ants, beetles, rats and thieves. In addition, there is an enormous floating population of male traders who deal in cattle, leather goods, watches, fountain pens, combs, eyeglasses and the like, and who require food. So these mammy traders are, as it were, the restaurateurs of West Africa, and those in search of a meal go from one to another, buying what they want in tiny immediately consumable amounts.

All this came out at dinner, the main course of which was a wonderful stew of bush fowl served with rice, accompanied by a bottle of good red French wine. The bush fowl is a game bird whose scientific name is the Senegal double-spurred francolin. It has two spurs set one above the other. At later meals Mickey introduced us to palm oil chop: actually a form of stew (though the old Coasters will call this heresy), served with rice and fu-fu. Fu-fu is mashed yams. The consistency should be such that if a small portion is flicked onto the ceiling with a knife tip it stays there. This was the old-time test. I liked fu-fu very much, quite as well as mashed potatoes. The stew was hot with peppers that they call pili-pili, and it was served with a multitude of side dishes such as crushed peanuts, grated coconut, fried bananas, powdered dry fish (known as stink fish in pigeon English). Then over the whole was poured fresh thick orange-coloured palm oil. I enjoyed this dish immensely, but it makes some people sick. It is very rich and it is usually served only at Sunday lunch. The old hands — those who survived — ate it daily, and I am inclined to think that it may have kept them alive, as it is full of vitamins and very laxative. I liked West African food and had only one objection to it — the time it was served. Quite often lunch is not begun till 3 P.M. and dinner till ten. This means too much smoking and too many gins before eating and spoils the meal for me.

As a town Minna has little to recommend it. No buildings of note, no scenery, no history. A new horrible, but hygienic market is being built to replace the ancient and picturesque, but certainly not hygienic conglomeration of mud and rotting mats that used to house it. This is unquestionably progress. But must all progress be concrete?

The Gunns' garden was attractive and the grass was being cut by prisoners with curved swords made out of the iron hoops that go round barrels, sharpened with a file and fitted with a rough handle of rags. This was the first time I had noticed this procedure, but later found it general all over Africa, from west to east, and is the only work I ever saw being done unsupervised, with energy and apparent pleasure. Each blow would have cut a young sapling in half, or severed a head. The drive was bordered with a low henna hedge. It was astonishing to think that so much glamour could be contained in these rather dull, small, green willow-shaped leaves.

On the stoep Mickey grew some lovely roses in tins, and in her kitchen garden she had squash, tomatoes, beans and herbs. She always had lovely flowers in the house and when we arrived had as a centrepiece a vase of what looked like the most beautiful dark red and yellow orchids, whose lilylike leaves ended in corkscrew tendrils like those of a vine.

The view from our room was most un-African — green hills that faded into blue distances. It was an English, almost Constable-like effect. In the garden a group of young Muscovy ducks searched for bugs. They do very well here and seem entirely unaffected by the climate, and are dry-land ducks able to do without water even to mate in.

Unquestionably, from every point of view except that of the artist, concrete and corrugated iron are a great improvement on mud and thatch. But before the trip was over we were to get very tired of them, particularly when handled by the Public Works Department who do not seem to have realised the plasticity of this material when suitably reinforced.

The Belgians, French and Portuguese perform miracles with concrete. The British produce only indestructible atrocities. The new houses built for the civil servants, such as the one we were in, are on the lines of an English suburban villa, relatively functional with bathrooms and plumbing, but totally lacking in grace, architectural charm or dignity. The compounds are generally large and well kept although this depends upon the occupant, and as a rule district officers are moved too often ever to really take much trouble with their flowers and trees. This would appear to be a great defect of the British administration all over Africa, and is much disliked by the Africans because as soon as they get to know one district officer he is replaced by a stranger. This game of official musical chairs is caused by the shortage of political officers. Whenever anyone goes on leave or is sick, a general shuffle round has to take place. The women, too, are affected and some of them never really bother to make a place comfortable since they may be there only a few weeks. Very few people, except the most senior, even spend a whole tour of eighteen months in one place.

Minna was notable for Tiny getting over her fear of bats. They swept through the house at all levels, at all times after dark, and within a couple of hours Tiny resigned herself to them, preferring them to some of the giant moths they pursued.

It was here that I first saw the big agama lizards in great numbers. The males are almost a foot long and have orange heads. The body is indigo that changes to yellow blending into scarlet on the tail. Sometimes there were as many as twelve together on the flat roof outside our bedroom. The females are plain ordinary lizard colour, and slightly smaller. Mickey said they used to steal her parrot's food. I had never thought of lizards being anything but carnivorous before, but it seems that they ate everything including young seedlings in the garden. Inside the house there were delightful geckos — pale yellow, almost transparent house lizards, with suction cups on their feet that enabled them to climb about the walls and ceilings. There were plenty of birds in the garden, among them big dark blue starlings with bright yellow bills, that walked about the lawn and were, I am convinced, the spirits of deceased grass-cutting prisoners, and a flock of large grey and white parrotlike birds which I think were lories.

One night the chief railway engineer, an African, Mr. Egbuna, came to dinner with his wife. She was a tall, very good-looking girl dressed in a long black pleated skirt and a white, almost transparent blouse. Mr. Egbuna had white men working under him and had a reputation for great competence. He talked of the necessity of a new line to the northeast to open up the Chad area, and of new engines to speed up the removal of groundnuts from Kano to the coast. Ian told me that Mr. Egbuna and several other educated Africans had been asked to join the Club but had declined. So segregation at this little social centre was in no way enforced. It was merely the result of two different kinds of people going their own way. At many other clubs there are African members.

We visited a Fulani camp where a family of these nomads was living in association with the local Guari. The Guaris give the Fulani grazing rights and I imagine some of the fruits of the soil, in exchange for milk and the manure of their cattle. Symbiotic relationships of this kind were encouraged by the government, who wanted the Fulani settled. Governments do not like free nomadic people. Perhaps they are too hard to tax. Among the Fulani was a tall, slim, very attractive — and knew it — girl of seventeen or so. She stood high-breasted, with one hip out, leaning on an enormous red water jar in the centre of her compound. Round her, pulled very tight, she wore a dark blue cloth.

We greeted her with raised right fists: "Sanu."

"Sanu," she replied, bold-eyed.

The Guaris are an ugly but industrious people. The women are misformed from their habit of carrying loads on their left shoulders instead of on their heads. The men were working, naked but for a loincloth, in their gardens where they had yams growing in hills, with rice between them under irrigation from furrows that they had taken from a stream some distance away.

The Guari huts were arranged in small groups linked by mud and mat walls. Their granaries were vase-shaped, raised on stones so that smoke could be let into them from underneath. They were thatched, with a ventilation space below the roof. The entrance to these receptacles was a large curved tile set on the side made of clay and straw, held in place by a removable crosspiece of wood.

We saw our first lepers at the Sudan Interior Mission run by Dr. Cummins, an American. He had his wife and two small daughters with him, sweet children who drank Coca-Cola and said we were "welcome, they were sure" in a most homelike manner.

Dr. Cummins was a small, ineffectual-looking little man, dressed in white trousers, sneakers, a blue and white striped shirt worn outside the trousers and a ventilated beige jockey cap with an enormous peak. But I do not think I have ever met a man who impressed me more. In eight months, in the depths of the bush, he had created a hospital, with houses for himself and his assistants, a theatre, wards, compounds and a native village with gardens for his convalescents. In eight months in Africa. In a place where grass was six feet high when he began. When he had to make his own roads.

He said: "Of course it was done with God's help." It must have been. Because to anyone who knows Africa — African conditions and labour — what he has done would have been impossible without it. Usually, when God is mentioned like that, I find it embarrassing. This time I did not. I was listening to the truth.

We talked about gardens and Ian promised him cuttings of aduruku for his compound. These trees are planted six inches apart and form a solid wall of saplings ten feet high, and are much used by the natives in their villages.

I visited the experimental piggery run with great efficiency by Wally Shaw, an ex-sergeant major and captain of the Lancashire Fusiliers. There were over a thousand pigs all told, and the demand for pork, in spite of the big Moslem population who won't eat it, is greater than he can supply. He breeds only large whites and has some magnificent imported stud stock. The piggeries were spotless, the pigs clean and regularly wiped over with palm oil to keep them free of vermin. In spite of the strong sunlight here he told me that he found it paid handsomely to give his pigs cod-liver or fish oil, which seems to show that sunlight does not supply the vitamins necessary in these latitudes. Green feed was another problem in the dry summer season.

In addition to the pigs, he had poultry. He was crossing good Rhode Island cocks with selected native hens for the Africans. It was useless giving them purebred stock, as they will not feed anything. An animal which cannot forage for itself is no good to them. The cockerels from this cross had their mothers' ability to take care of themselves and still transmitted some of the Rhode Island laying qualities to their offspring. The pullets which he kept, he said, laid quite well as long as they were properly fed. The African hens, he continued, had only one virtue — an ability to survive any disaster. His idea was to graft onto this quality some slight improvement in egg-laying capacity and size of egg.

There seemed some relation between Wally's arguments about African hens and the people themselves. Survival is their great quality, and if some extra productive capacity can be grafted onto their present way of life by gradually building it up, a great deal will have been achieved. What seems to be missing in Africa everywhere is the desire to produce a surplus that can be turned into cash and reinvested. As things stand today, an African's best investment is a wife or wives. Women support themselves and bring in revenue. The children are assets in terms of labour when young and, if girls, as negotiable securities soon after they attain the age of puberty. It is useless to talk about monogamy to an uneducated African. And the educated man will question its necessity and produce ample evidence of polygamy from the Bible to justify the practice. Monogamy may not be essential to Christianity but it is to Western culture, and this question is one of the obstacles which stand between the African and his achievement of it.

It was now time to go to the Salla at Bida, where the Gunns had been stationed previously, and whose emir had become their personal friend. Taking the two cars we set off with a picnic lunch which we ate at the Zingaru, which was Lugard's headquarters in his northern campaign. We saw the remains of his fort on a hill. We crossed the bridge over the gorge. It was an impressive spectacle, for here the Kaduna River is compressed to a width of less than a hundred yards between high cliffs. It was not in full flood, yet the tops of the cliffs were almost covered and the water, probably a hundred and fifty feet deep, was running like a millrace, roaring under the bridge and creating little moving whirlpools in its furious urgency. Small trees and bushes swirled down the river, that we had seen flowing so peacefully through the public gardens at Kaduna only a few days before.

The road was bad in places; we were dropping all the time. It became hotter and the trees began to change. There were more palms — some of them kolas, bananas, and a very fine large dark evergreen with a bright orange-coloured fruit called, I believe, the wild apple. Later I examined the fruit. It consisted of several large black beanlike seeds enclosed in the orange pod. Surrounding them was a white edible pulp which had the taste of walnuts, and was most excellent although seldom eaten by white people. It would be very good in a salad mixed with apple, the way they use walnuts in

America. Once again I was struck, as I have been in other parts of the world, at how conservative the white race is when it comes to eating native foods.

At Bida we went to the catering rest house where we had a meal and were allotted adjoining chalets. The word chalet, applied to cottages of this kind, must have come from the Swiss missions which were among the first to be established on the West coast. Before we were settled in, traders arrived with brass basins, silver boxes, ivory carvings and glass beads and bangles. There were big lizards on our stoep, two small geckos in the bedroom, and five large and very friendly toads which hopped about quite unperturbed by our movements as we unpacked. Apart from their not being house-trained, we could have had no nicer companions.

Next day the Salla took place and we went to the crossroads to see the procession. Hundreds of horsemen were already assembled at the place of prayer — we saw them in the distance. Here the Liman was leading the prayers of a white-robed congregation centred about the Emir. All bowed until the benediction was given and the Emir's ram was slaughtered. Then a gun was fired to show that it was over. Till the Benediction no ram's blood might be shed. Now, after the shot, hundreds were dying. Those who were late for the ceremony dismounted from their caparisoned horses and, holding the reins in their hands, prayed by the roadside, bending their heads to the ground and rising with dust on their foreheads. I had a good chance to look at their saddlery. It was most ornate, the bridles being decorated with worked leather ornaments. The reins had triangular pieces of leather attached to them. The brow and nose bands were fringed with tassels and wherever something could be hung it was. The saddles had embroidered silk covers, and the horses' quarters were draped with bright cloths like those of medieval knights at a tourney, a fashion that must have come back with the Crusaders. Beside the horse holders were the sword bearers. Half-naked boys with swords held on cushions before them.

We went to meet the returning procession. The streets were lined with people. In the road cyclists in their best and most flowing robes were doing tricks, racing along, turning, braking with their feet and kicking up clouds of dust. These men are known as "Sons of the Air." The frames of some bicycles were wrapped in yellow dusters; one still had on the brown paper it had been delivered in to prove its virgin newness. Once all this had been done by trick riders on horses. The bicycles were an innovation, part of the world's postwar progress. At last we heard the roar of the crowd and the sound of the Emir's band. He was coming.

First came the clowns and entertainers — jesters, half naked with beards of white cow tail, civet-skin kilts round their loins and big caps of black fur. One carried a club with which he struck his head as if he were trying to knock himself out. There were almost naked men doing belly dances, writhing in ecstasy to the music of the band that came tramping almost on their heels. Drummers with drums of various shapes, trumpeters with copper trumpets six feet long, horn blowers whose instruments were elephant tusks carved and pierced like flutes. There were mounted drummers who beat their drums with little curved sticks. Cavalry in padded armour with six-foot, wide-bladed spears and enormous leather shields. There was one man on a grey horse in chain mail with a lance in his hand. Then came a group of nobles, well mounted and splendidly dressed.

Then came the Emir riding a black stallion. Beside him marched an enormous Negro holding a golden umbrella on a long staff over his head, which he kept twisting as he walked. The noise was unbelievable. There was no tune of any kind. To the European ear it was just noise — the screaming of the trumpets, the beating of the drums. The blowers burst their cheeks to achieve still greater volume, the drummers sweated as they struck.

There was every colour, bright in the sunlight, red, blue, purple, green, yellow and orange blazed. The light caught the scimitars, swords and spears. It caught the gold embroidery of the big umbrella, the silver hilts of the weapons, the brass and copper of the horses' accoutrements. Noise, colour and the smell of sweat, that of men and horses, blended with the dust into a dramatic whole. This came out of the past. It was a triumphal march, duplicating a thousand others which had taken place in Africa by these northern mounted people — Arabs, Moors, Hausas, Tuaregs and their bastards.

The Emir pulled up to talk to Ian whom he was pleased to see. We were to call on him next morning.

We now drove to a kind of thatched saluting base outside the palace. Here we were installed in chairs, on either side of the Emir, with the district officer and some dozen other Europeans. Chiefs and nobles now arrived, galloping up across the open parade-ground-like space and, drawing their horses up into a rear, greeted the Emir with clenched raised fists. They dismounted and, handing the reins to attendants, entered the summerhouse and squatted on the carpet that covered the floor. It was soon full but more and more kept coming and they all managed to fit themselves in. When the last one was settled, the district officer made a speech and presented the Emir with a bag of kola nuts. These nuts will sustain you when exhausted, and are used much as we use cigarettes, but also have a ritual significance as gifts.

The Emir now made a speech, and at the end said: "Mrs. Cloete will now take our photographs," which surprised Tiny, who had had no warning of this till the district officer translated it to her. However, climbing on to her chair, she took some pictures which turned out quite well.

The Emir now put his hand into the bag of nuts which had been opened for him by his chamberlain and began to toss them to the seated chiefs and nobles, picking out individuals and throwing them nuts as if he were feeding grain to poultry.

Between us and the palace were crowds of people — the market women, who are a political power, surrounding the Lelu who was the only mounted woman. She was the queen of market women, prostitutes, dancers and concubines — an official position of some importance, I was informed.

The Emir's palace followed the usual pattern of a big high-walled compound with a guardhouse at the gate. In the audience hall where he received us there was a glass case showing local handicrafts. Borers and termites were busy destroying everything except the glass and metalwork. Below every wooden exhibit was a little heap of white powdered dust. In a corner there were a number of guns and rifles which had been used in the defence of the city in the war with the British.

The Emir remembered the war well. He had, as he put it, just attained the age of puberty. He apparently bore the British no resentment. They won, he said, because they had better rifles. "Just as we won in our older wars because our weapons were better." As far as I could see, nowhere in the North was there any desire for the immediate departure from the British. They all said: "We are not ready yet, you must teach us more." The one thing they would not tolerate was being ruled by Southerners who, if the whole of Nigeria was handed back to the African, would be the only people literate enough to serve in administrative posts, even in the North where the people are, in the sense of education, a long way behind the South. They wanted to rule themselves when they were ready. In the meantime, since they needed help, it must come from white men.

They would have no strange black masters.

I expressed a desire to see the Emir's horses and we were led through various compounds and into a big hut where the black stallion, his favourite, was tethered by a heel rope from a hind leg to a heavy wooden mushroom-shaped peg in the earth floor. When he saw his master he neighed with pleasure, cocking his ears and coming towards him. This tameness of all the animals seemed to me less due to any particular kindness on the part of their owners than to the fact that they lived with them so intimately, walking loose about the compounds or being tied and continually led from place to place. Everything was used to being tethered — sheep, goats, chickens, turkeys. In the compound I saw tame guinea fowl with white wings, such as I had had at home, and white pigeons which I was told were seldom eaten but kept for sacrifice.

There were three reigning families in Bida, each with its own compound, from which the rulers were chosen in rotation. The walls of the town were among the most beautiful I had seen. Parts of them were very well preserved, and in the evening light they were a brilliant Venetian red against which the green of the trees, which grew in profusion, stood out and formed a picture of great beauty. It certainly seemed to me, now that I had seen so much, that Zimbabwe had been built by a people of culture similar to this — some pre-Islamic Arab people. Nor did I really follow the argument that the builders of Zimbabwe did not know how to make an arch, simply because there were no arches. It was a colonial outpost — part fort, part market, part temple. It was built with slave labour and if they had wanted an arch they would have had to build it with their own hands. It may just be that they did not care enough, and so deceived the archaeologists who were to examine their work so many centuries later.

We went to see an irrigation project — a rice-growing scheme which promised very well, and saw cormorants, grey kingfishers, fire finches, and what looked like a scarlet shrike as we followed the canal. We visited a village where there were two lepers — I could recognise them now — but there was no law to force them into hospital. By one of the huts there was a big lizard of a new kind with a head that looked as if it were plastered with emeralds.

In the afternoon we went down to the town and were fortunate enough to run into a Fulani beating ceremony. It has been discouraged by the Government but not stopped. It could only be driven underground. But it remains difficult to see and is now done by small groups whose activities are masked by their friends. It is, like so many African ceremonies, an age-group affair. I first noticed the young people running about in little bunches, the boys pursued by girls. I saw them crouch and dance like fencers and then noticed the sticks they carried and that several were bleeding across the chest and upper belly. We now began to watch carefully. The boys operate in threes, the beater and the two who are to be beaten. The one who is to be struck stands with his friend. Their arms rest on one another's shoulders. The friend is a kind of best man, or a second. Both are stripped to the waist. Their hair is decorated. They wear mid-length Fulani embroidered trousers or loincloths. On their ankles are triangular bangles with bells at the corners. They are curiously beautiful in their young gay arrogance and courage. Like game cocks or bulls or horses. Very male and shiveringly conscious that the moment of dedication and ordeal is upon them.

In his left hand the one who is to be struck carries a short sheathed sword, in his right a mirror fixed on to a little wooden handle. In front of the two, as they sway and dance, a drummer squats. Around them are the crowd, the other young men — some bleeding from having been beaten — some older ones to keep order, some waiting to be beaten, and the girls, brilliant as birds in their plush scarlet or yellow cloths. Eager, excited, their dark agate eyes shining in their golden faces. And about the participants — the drummer, the best man and the bridegroom of pain — circles a young man with a whip. It is a special kind of tree, very supple and as thick as a man's first finger. Crouching, he makes a feint at the dancer, who never flinches but continues to look into his mirror. Another feint and then a blow — a savage crack below the breasts that breaks the skin. The victim shows no sign, only looks at himself in the glass and points to the sky with a moving finger, as if he were watching the flight of a bird. The drummer beats more wildly. The best man points to the blood on his friend's breast. The girls run forward and pour pennies over the head of the victim, who pays no attention to them, leaving the best man to pick them up. The victim now dances, holding the sheathed sword over his head. Shivers run over his body. He is in ecstasy. The drummer drums harder. The victim shouts that he can take more. It begins again. He is struck two or three times. Then he becomes the best man and his friend takes his place. The pennies the girls bring for their special admirer are carried in enamel soap dishes with lids. And the money, after the ceremony, is fastened to leather thongs which the boys then wear, hanging in tails from their waists.

I was surprised to find that I was in no way upset by this performance, brutal though it was. It was without cruelty, there was nothing sadistic in it. It was simply a proof of courage and endurance — a kind of super showing off in front of the girls who, as darkness fell, would no doubt reward such courage. It was a way to get girls — to get the scars of manhood — the proofs of an ordeal. Nor do I think they felt much, autohypnotised as they were by their mirrors, the drumming, and the presence of the excited girls. They were in an almost cataleptic state, a quality which they appear to share with the Masai.

Seeing the ceremony was a remarkable experience and one which not many people have had today. And all the time, through the beating and before it, I had been accompanied by a small African about four years old, who had put his soft pink-palmed hand into mine almost as soon as we got out of the car and never let go. He was a dear little man, solemn as an owl with immense brown eyes. He wore the traditional nightshirt dress and a small dark blue embroidered fez on his head. We parted with mutual regret.

That night we dined with Gordon Rogers, the district officer. A man in his early thirties, who was a personality, a character, with a style of dress and manner of his own who will, I imagine, go far in the service. The dinner was excellent. Boiled paw-paw was one of the vegetables. I had never tasted it before, and very good it was. We drank champagne and after dinner Scottish reels were danced on the grass outside the house. The area was lit by forty little bowls of shea butter, each with a small wick of twisted cotton, set along the wall that divided the drive from the lawn. It was a beautiful sight. They burnt brightly without a flicker.

The music was produced by a gramophone with a loudspeaker attachment that was powered by a motorcar — the whole directed by a very intelligent African clerk who selected and played the records as he thought fit. A tropical African night may perhaps not at first seem an ideal place to dance reels and square dances. But it is cooler at night and even if the dancing is bad, and it was, since only a few of the dancers knew any of the steps, it remained good exercise and another of those paradoxes that are the charm of Africa. Ours is not a normal world functioning in a normal manner. Everything is too big here — the star-pierced sky, the courage of the lonely administrators, the very vices of the vicious.

With his head out of the window of the thatched hut that served him as a stable, Gordon's pony watched the dancing unsurprised. He was an African horse!

10

Lagoon City ... Lagos

● Next day we went to see the native industries. First to the hat weaving. The factory was a largish hut in which four men worked squatting on the floor, their raffia arranged in ordered heaps beside them. They were brothers. Hanging on the walls were the hats. They sold for three shillings and the demand far exceeded the supply. There was nothing to prevent the brothers from employing more labour and building up a quite big business. Ian Gunn, when he had been district officer at Bida, had suggested it. They had agreed with him in every way except one. This was a family business. They were happy working together. They made enough. And why should any man want more than enough? There was no answer to this wisdom. Why should anyone?

We next went to the street of the glassworkers. They worked in huts with several doors and tiny triangular windows. In the centre was the furnace, a pit with raised hearth, built up of clay, like an ant heap. It was about eighteen inches high with a square open top. The forced draught came from two small, drum-shaped bellows that were worked vertically, concertina fashion, by sticks fastened to their leather tops. The fire was fed with a special hot-burning wood, brought to the forge by the women. When the heat was great enough, a broken piece of glass was held in the heart of the fire till it was soft. While this was going on, more pieces of glass were warming on broken pieces of pottery on the edge of the furnace. The molten piece of glass was now applied to one of the warm pieces, which stuck to it at once. It was then put back into the furance till it melted. Then it was twisted off like toffee with a poker by the chief glassmaker, who pushed a second poker into the blob of melted glass, stretched it and then with a poker in each hand worked it into a perfect circular bangle and dropped it into a small heap of sand to cool and harden. It was strange to think that this little glowing affair was the mother of the blast furnace.

At one time it is believed that the people of Bida had the secret of making glass and traded their wares all over the Sudan, but they have lost it. Like so many other arts in other parts of Africa, its secret has been forgotten. Now they use bottles — medicine bottles, beer, any bottles or bits of glass they can buy or steal. In fact, here, in this hut, was the answer to a mystery. Only yesterday the dispenser was complaining to the medical officer about the shortage of bottles in his store. Well, here they were — a heap of blue medicine bottles being smashed into suitable sizes by a naked glassmaker's apprentice.

In Africa medicine bottles are used to make ornaments and telephone wires are cut to make copper bracelets. Railroad spikes are beaten into spears, and pumps broken up for ammunition.

Next we went to see the metalworkers — the brass, silver and tin-smiths who make bowls and cutlery, spoons, measures, bracelets and bangles. The raw material is hard to get now and many discarded motor parts are used. We bought two beautifully cast bracelets which had been produced by melting down the radiator cover of an old car. The forge resembled that of the glassmakers but was not so high. The tools were the simplest — pincers, hammers, files, cold chisels. The anvil was a heavy iron pin driven into the ground — a kind of giant thumb tack.

These arts and industries are believed to have come from Egypt, seeping up the Nile and along the desert fringe with the migrating tribes, but all are in a state of atrophy. European beads are cheaper and brighter, Birmingham brass and metal ware replaces the old handmade stuff, and enamel decorated with bright designs is much preferred to the old handmade articles.

We went back to the rest house for lunch and now a tragedy occurred — a little drama as the Belgians would have put it. Lunch was curry and rice. I heard a crack and looked at Tiny's face. She put up her hand and laid half a tooth on her bread plate. Her teeth were always her weak point and she had bitten a pebble that had been cooked with the rice. After lunch we discussed the situation with the Gunns. It meant a dentist. The nearest one was at Lagos, nearly five hundred miles away. In the afternoon we went to see the medical officer — Dr. Adeniyi Jones — who gave Tiny something for the pain and confirmed our views about going back. We had met him the previous evening and it would be hard to meet a more delightful man. He had qualified in the United Kingdom — Edinburgh, I think — and had worked there in hospitals for more than two years before returning to Nigeria. His father had been a doctor and his grandfather had been well known on the coast in the old days for his leadership and integrity. He had himself married an African girl, who was also a doctor. She was in Lagos, so we did not have the good fortune of meeting her. This is the kind of man, with three generations of education behind him, who completely knocks on the head any idea of African inferiority. He was certainly in every way my equal and, as far as education was concerned, my superior. But because of his outlook he was not liked by some of his fellows. He was giving up the hospital because he could not get on with the staff. The nurses said he was as bad as a white man when he objected to their sleeping on duty, or to their making the patients pay for such attentions as a glass of water or a bedpan.

The main point he proved to me, which was confirmed later on the Gold Coast, was that civilised men must come from civilised homes. Colour is irrelevant. In the end it is the man's mother and what he learns at his "mother's knee," as they used to say, that counts.

There are in Africa thousands of highly educated Africans with university degrees who are not civilised simply because they were brought up by mothers who were all but savages. The citizen of to-morrow must be taught by the mother of today. Here was the answer to the Congolese cry for civilised women, the proof that Africa cannot progress until this is achieved. The colour bar was absurd with such men as this doctor, and many others I have met. Their being black seems to me to be of no greater importance than their being redhaired or bald. You notice it, say: hullo, this chap's bald, or black, and then forget it. It becomes utterly irrelevant. But how many are there like them in the continent?

The decision now made, we decided to return to Minna next day. Knowing we were leaving, the Emir sent his gifts. Half a ram which was put into the guest-house refrigerator, and a turkey which was tethered to a tree outside our room with cord.

We had hardly got up before Dr. Adeniyi Jones drove up to the chalet. He had heard that Tiny was worse. If she was really bad he had made arrangements to give her an anaesthetic and take out the tooth himself. He had had some dental experience and could do it. To make this offer he had got up extra early, and, in spite of all his work, had come to see if he could do anything. Fortunately the report he had received was wrong, but I have seldom felt more grateful to anyone for his help and sympathy.

Once home we sent a series of telegrams to Lagos and found that the road between Minna and the capital was impassable. Two bridges were down. So the Silver Streak continued her journey south by rail. This question of a really good all-weather road from the coast to the interior would, one would imagine, be the most vital necessity in the development of the country. But no one had seen it that way. There were too many authorities all pulling different ways. But perhaps I am being unjust. Maybe they just seemed that way and the Colonial Office really had a plan.

At any rate, the train — it was as nice a train as I have ever been in as far as comfort was concerned, almost as good as those in the United States, and only a year old — was upholstered in green leather with fly-screened windows and a private lavatory. The seat ran the length of the compartment, the other side was occupied half by the toilet and half by an armchair and a fitted table. The food in the restaurant car, run entirely by Africans, was plain but good, the service excellent and everything absolutely clean.

Once in the night I had got up to look out of the window as the train crossed the Niger at Jebba, and saw the sinister black pinnacle of the ju-ju rock sticking up out of the silver water. Human sacrifices used to be made here, and there is a legend that any white man who climbs the rock will be dead within the year. But so many white men who came to the Coast were dead in a year. Some died within a week. When we woke up we were in a new world of heat, palm forests, bananas and paw-paws.

This was the South. The land of ash, chop and ju-ju. Of darkness, of slow rivers, muddy creeks, oil palms; of leopard men, second burials, of blood and slavery. The white man's grave of the past, and a country of swift deterioration still today. The sun is no longer a friend but an enemy. The rain does not resemble rain. There is no refreshment in the terrible downpour that falls with the weight and solidity of lead, and having fallen, rises up again in steaming mist.

It had been arranged that we should stay with the Keelers — the American consul general and his wife. After squalid native slums we went through open country into Ikoyi, the residential quarter. Here beautiful houses stood in beautiful gardens. New buildings — apartment houses — were going up in what was virgin bush. It made one gasp. New modern buildings twenty-five yards from the forest.

We were met by Mrs. Keeler. She was a lovely woman, whose travels with her husband had enhanced her natural charm.

At dinner we talked about some recent robberies in the vicinity. Here the gardens ran down to lagoons and creeks which fed into a veritable maze of waterways that were, in fact, the multiple mouths of the Niger. It seems that the robbers came by canoe, broke into the houses and went off silently with their loot, which was naturally never traced. The police were unreliable and, in some cases, believed to be in cahoots with the burglars. The night watchmen, or "watchnights" as they are called, invariably sleep, and much object to being disturbed. Bill Keeler had been unkind enough, after the burglaries, to make the police call his watchman when they passed the house, which was every two hours. This caused many complaints from the ill-used man, such things being contrary to native law and custom.

Bill told me that one of the more amusing exports from Nigeria to the United States are the gigantic horns of the northern Ankoli-type cattle, which find their way into the bars and saloons of the West as genuine longhorns.

There was a walk along the creek at the bottom of the garden through some bush to a small and very beautiful park. On almost every palm tree, fastened just below the crown, was a bottle or a gourd into which the palm-wine sap was dripping. A refreshing drink when fresh, it soon becomes very potent.

In the park lake there were small black fishes that ran over the surface of the water and along the shore, even climbing onto the roots of the trees. There were land crabs too, which I should think were edible like those in the Caribbean.

The Keelers' house was beautifully decorated, and every window netted. Lights burnt in all the cupboards to keep them aired, but even this was not enough to prevent mould growing, almost overnight, on the shoes stored in them. The master bedroom was fitted with an air-conditioning plant but the water container sent out from America with the machine was far too small, and had to be replaced by a galvanised receptacle, so great was the quantity of moisture sucked out of the room, which was not enormous, in twenty-four hours.

In the morning we went down to the dentist. The waiting room was full of Africans but at last our turn came. I showed him Tiny's X-rays. We never travel without them. He injected Novocain and then got hold of the tooth, which broke off with a loud crack very neatly at the gum, leaving the roots in her jaw. He had not realised how fragile her teeth were. But he assured us that she would have no pain — she did not have much — and that the roots would work out in time. As usual she was very brave. But it took three whiskies to get me back to normal.

Comforted by the drinks and the dentist's promise that the would be no more trouble, we went back and spent three lovely re ful days in real American comfort, which is different from any oth comfort in the world. American cocktails — cold ones — Americ salads, American food, American talk, American books and magazin Americans have the talent of taking their country with them whe ever they go.

From here we were passed on to Government House where spent two days. Mr. E. A. T. Benson, the Chief Secretary, was A ing Governor during Sir John MacPherson's absence. He is a ta very good-looking man, with a brain like a rapier, and is a wonderf host. He had taken over Tony McClellan, Sir John's A.D.C., who h served in the Gurkas before transferring to the Colonial Service. I had been a district officer in the North, and was a most interesti young man.

Government House is on the Marina — the main drag as it were and big ships go past it so closely that we felt we could put out o hands and touch them from our bedroom window. It was odd see them flanked by palm trees at the bottom of the garden.

Mr. Benson had served in Uganda and said that they had h notification of trouble brewing in Kenya even in those days. I talked about Nigeria, about self-government, about the racial hatre jealousies and dislikes which make united Nigeria so difficult achievement. We discussed leopard murders and he said I cou have access to the secret files as long as I did not use all the mater — give names and places and so forth.

These murders are peculiarly West African but part of the patte of ritual murder that is common to the whole continent south of t Sahara, and perhaps north of it as well. There are secret societ everywhere. Leopard men, hyena men, crocodile men and lion me

A few years ago a district officer thought that too many people his area were being killed by leopards. Leopards do kill people ar there were plenty of leopards in this part of the forest, but the deat were rather too numerous. The bodies were seldom discovered t they were in an advanced state of decomposition, which made a c tailed study difficult, but even so, there were odd discrepancies. some the viscera had not been removed as is usual with a leopa The arms were mutilated and in some cases the head was missi But what really clinched the matter was finding a woman's he wrapped in her own loincloth. This emphatically was not the wo of a leopard. Nor were the pad marks satisfactory as they did n correspond with those of a leopard's movements. And now, when at last the wheels of justice began to revolve, there were more than a hundred deaths due for investigation. But the district officer who first brought the matter up was under a cloud for some time.

He had invented it all. Such things did not happen now. In the old days of course, but that was different. But how long ago were the old days in Africa? This is what the home government always forgets. When he was proved right he was promoted but he had taken a risk. He had jeopardised his career. This type of enquiry is not welcomed in any colony. It means that questions are asked. When that happens the Colonial Office comes down on somebody, because Parliament has come down on the Colonial Office. Actually, and this applies everywhere in Africa, not only in British territory, things which do not happen under the nose of an official are assumed not to have happened. Assume, for instance, that a man sees what he thinks is human meat being sold. It is proved to be human flesh. All right. Suppose the girl is picked up. She is a pretty little thing of twelve or so. What was she doing with the meat? Selling it. Where did she get it? A man sold it to her. What sort of man? A big man. And so on and so on. The doctor has proved it to be human but the child knows nothing, or says she doesn't. What happens next. Who investigates what? Perhaps the trail leads up to French territory and then peters out. If it happened in French territory the trail would have led to British territory. The buck is always passed. But nothing has been gained by such enquiries. The district officer gets a bad mark for causing trouble and upsetting everyone, and things settle down again.

In Nigeria the leopard murders were traced to the Idiong Society whose mouthpiece had been, before it was destroyed, the Long Ju-ju of Aro Chuka. When finally, early in the century, this shrine was destroyed and its priests killed by the British, the job was incompletely done and some escaped to carry on the traditions of the cult. Idiong shrines require to be fed with blood and when Africans found that justice could not be obtained in the courts, either through corruption in the native courts or the failure of some technical point being proved in the British, the people reverted to the old Idiong Society and employed them to rectify their wrongs.

The priests did not carry out the sentences. This was done by the Leopard Society, who were their strong arm men. I was to hear more of them in Port Harcourt.

There was an earlier parallel in Sierra Leone where news reached the government that eighty men suspected of leopard murders had been burnt to death. This was done by the Tongo Players, a counter society, who were called in by the villagers when the leopard men killed too many people. After a suitable preparation the Tongo Players would call the people together and the suspected persons were made to submit to the ordeal of plunging their arms into a cauldron of boiling palm oil. If guilty, they were struck down by the chief Tongo Player with a club loosely veiled with leopard skin and set with knives called the "tongora." They were then thrown into a great fire and burnt to death.

The leopard men believed that they would be protected by their fetish, the terrible borofima, the fetish of the Boro Society of which they were all members. This fetish was very strong, containing rice, the white of an egg, the blood of a cock, the blood, fat and other parts of a human body — such as the liver and genitals — a cloth taken from a menstruating woman, and dust from a market place, and was wrapped tightly in the skin taken from the palm of a human hand, the forehead, or the sole of the foot. This was (and perhaps is) the most powerful fetish in Africa, but to retain its strength it had, at intervals, to be anointed with human blood and fat. The fat was obtained by boiling human intestines and skimming the brew. Such fat is believed to be still on sale in various native markets at a very high price. Members of the Leopard Society had marks on the buttocks, hidden by their loincloths, which were made by raising the flesh with an iron needle and then shaving off the raised portion of flesh and skin. The wound was then treated with nikori, a medicine made by grinding up the bark of the wild groundnut.

After the borofima had been strengthened, the body of the victim was generally eaten and, I quote: "some like it raw, some cooked with rice, some roast."

I have written "was," I have put almost everything into the past tense. But borofimas may still exist. And who would recognise one? A little tightly wrapped packet of greasy leather!

The participants in these rituals are not ordinary savages. They are often chiefs and leaders, sometimes educated men. There was a case of a minister of the United Brethren in Christ Mission who had been ordained in 1878 and was accused in 1912 of being a member of the Leopard Society. He was a citizen of the United States and had used his citizenship to escape punishment when previously indicted for cannibal murder. This time, tried by a jury of educated Africans who may also have been implicated, he was acquitted. He returned to the Mission and lectured on their behalf in America. This information comes from *Human Leopards* by Hugh Rees, published in 1915, and is of particular interest as this is part of the African background which continually obtrudes itself. The chiefs of Bechuanaland are educated men. The leaders of the Mau Mau are not savages; they are literate, and more than literate. The rioters of East London who killed and ate a Sister of Mercy, who had spent her life serving them, were educated urban Africans.

All of which makes it difficult to solve the problem of race, colour, education, civilisation and culture. Difficult even to penetrate what lies beneath the veneer of our material civilisation which the educated African often wears with such complete success. One can only believe that it varies from the thinnest veneer of culture to complete civilisation. But since only the surface is exposed, how can we tell the true from the false? The veneer from the mahogany? It would seem that every black man is not only a problem to the white man but to himself as well. That in each there is a great fight between the past he has lost and the future that only a few so far seem destined to attain.

11

The Sacred Slave Chains . . . Lagos . . . Badagri

● THE SILVER STREAK now came to rest at a garage in Lagos — her final target — where she was left to be sold. There were no fond goodbyes. She would now sink to the ultimate automotive degradation. She would become a native taxi.

Ayo, the enormous black chauffeur who had produced so many improbable accounts written in such a lovely clerkly hand, who had never been there when I needed him and who had always turned up at my side when I was seeing an emir or at any other entertainment or place of interest, was now paid off. I shook his big, black, pink-palmed hand with much delight — West Africa is very democratic — and felt myself free of another burden. Not that Ayo was a bad boy. He was just a damn nuisance, always wanting something. Money for food or an advance to buy some splendid piece of apparel that had struck his fancy. I think we parted friends. In a curious way I liked him, but he was very race conscious which made him, at this time when Nigeria can only talk about its freedom, somewhat anti-white. There is no error about the black man being on top here. In any dispute he is always right, even before the law, even if he is wrong. The pendulum has completed its swing, the hour has struck. Black cuckoos are popping out of every clock. Somewhat inaccurately, it is true. Striking three when it is seven, or twelve when it is five. But they are enjoying themselves. They are like schoolboys before the end of term. Discipline is relaxed, the exams are over. They can do almost anything they like. But the masters, those wicked civil servants, are still there to keep the place running. The meals are still on time, the drains are in order, the doctor attends the sick and the mails are delivered.

On the whole the Africans were easy to get on with. It simply was a question of politeness. My politeness. It meant accepting from Africans things I would never have accepted from a white man, such as the friendly arm of a drunken African about my shoulders in a bar. It meant an infinite number of "pleases" and "thank yous" and "do

you minds?" It meant, if it went on long enough, giving oneself
ulcers. A senior Government official once said to me: "Do you know
why we need so much leave here?"

I said: "The climate, I suppose."

"No," he said. "Other climates are as bad. Malaya, for instance.
No, Cloete," he said. "It is the African."

Here I may as well make clear my use of the term "official," or
functionary, in the Congo. I have the names of everyone in my notes
but most of them said things "off the record" so, as we used to say
in the Army: "No names, no pack drill."

We were now in the hands of the P.R.O. — the Public Relations
Office — headed by John Stocker, who sent us in a kit car — a
light truck — to Badagri where we were to spend a few days with the
district officer.

Going out of Lagos we passed through streets of slums and near-
slums, varied by some new balconied houses built of reinforced concrete. The design of the railings in one of them consisted of great
"£'s," the pound symbol, cast in concrete and endlessly repeated. I
saw this symbol in use several times and it interested me as being the
outward and visible sign of West African materialism. The sign of
Mammon, the very opposite of the Cross of God, or even the Cres-
cent of Allah.

We passed a chemist shop called the Golden Gate Pharmacy,
which I would have thought a little too apt. We passed houses where
the hand-lettered shingles informed us that our horoscopes could be
cast, our palms read, or that esoteric literature was for sale. We passed,
and were passed by, native buses — locally known as mammy wagons
— bearing such titles as "Show Me the Way, O Lord," "No Money
is an Abomination," "God is Love," "God Help Us," "God Save Us."
The general idea seemed to be that only by the grace of God would
the vehicle ever reach its destination. In most cases there were no
doors to the driver's seat. This, I was informed, was to enable him to
jump in case of an accident. The percentage of fatalities among
drivers being very low due to this forethought. The driver jumped.
God looked after, or did not look after, the passengers.

We passed a big travellers palm, the first I had ever seen. I recognised it from pictures in books on exploration that I had read. This
magnificent vegetable looks like a cross between a giant banana and a
Victorian lady's fan. The dew falling on the great leaves runs down
the stems and accumulates at their base, and has saved many a man
from dying of thirst, though I must say I do not know where, as I
have never seen a wild one in the bush. But this was the kind of

thing we had come to see. The romantic things I had read about since childhood. That was why we were going to Badagri. It had been one of the great centres of the slave trade, and I was collecting material for a book on the subject.

The drivers of the autos drove like Jehu with their fingers on their horns. There is a special technique for driving through crowds in West Africa. It consists of sounding the horn and accelerating. If you slow down, the people who had leapt off the road at the sound of the hooter, simply relax and return to the middle. It is therefore essential to go while the going is good, and profit from their momentary fright. The standard of African driving is very high as far as speed is concerned. The West Africans are a nation of racing motorists. They only lack a little judgment about pace and timing to be the most perfect drivers in the world. They also suffer from a psychological complaint which might be described as driver's pride. They all want to be first and do not realise that this is impossible. The application of this principle, when two cars meet going in opposite directions over a bridge that is only wide enough for one, tends to create difficulties. This is when the drivers jump.

The upkeep of engines presents no problem. Once a year a living dog is sacrificed to the mechanism, a tribute to the god of iron. Gas is put into the tank when the car stops for lack of it. Water is put in when the radiator cap blows off, and oil sometimes. If there is no regular source of supply at hand, palm oil is obtained from a local housewife. Oil, after all, is oil. Cars do not last very long.

This is naturally a gross exaggeration, but a caricature is sometimes a more faithful picture than a studio portrait.

Leaving the town we drove through the forests that border the creeks running parallel with the sea. The soil was rich, fecund, forest muck which later changed to a sandy swamp land where the character of the vegetation altered completely. Gone were the tall oil palms, lianas and half-wild bananas. It was scrub. There was a very pretty bush with a single roselike mauve flower with a fluffy yellow centre, and a semi-climbing shrub that looked like a white poinsettia except that the coloured leaves were much bigger on the lower side, giving it a cock-eyed, half developed look. Later we saw a scarlet variety of this plant and found that it was known as Ashanti blood, and in the forest the great red bracts do look like drops of blood falling from some hidden sacrifice.

I found our host, Mr. Cecil Iles, in his office. He promised to show me everything: the markets, the slave barracoons and ju-ju houses.

I saw a human skull on a shelf. I enquired about it.

"Oh that," he said. "The A.D.O. found it cooking in an iron pot on the beach. He was walking along the shore and lifted the lid out of curiosity to see what chop was being made and saw it bobbing about in the boiling water."

"What did you do?" I asked.

"Nothing. What was there to do? It's an old skull. We simply brought it here. Interesting, isn't it?"

To me it was intensely interesting. Quite obviously it was not being boiled for fun. Quite obviously, too, there was no nourishment in it. As soup it was purely symbolic, but symbolic soup is good enough for magical purposes. Someone would have drunk it if it had not been taken away. And there is no doubt that they would sooner have had a fresh head if they could have got hold of one. Both the flavour and the magic would have been stronger.

The assistant district officer, Mr. McInnes and his pretty wife, joined us. After lunch we visited the market. An enormous affair spread along the riverbank, or beach as it is called here, for several hundred yards. The goods for sale consisted of the usual articles of native commerce, with a few additions that I had not seen before such as a kind of black plum, red and green vegetables that are called garden eggs and are varieties of eggplant or aubergine, pumpkin seeds in dishes, and little heaps of yellow, purple and green metallic-looking powder.

There were bundles of the eighteen-foot raffia palm-frond ribs that are used for building, shiny leaves from a kind of arum or jack-in-the-pulpit that were sold for use as wrapping paper. There were innumerable pots of every kind from very big, almost circular jars brought over by the Africans from Dahomey, whose canoes, many of them flying the tricolour, were pulled up on the bank, to tiny jars that were used as lamps. Goats and long-snouted, razor-backed pigs wandered about the stall, with the vultures, dogs and children.

The French Africans were decorated with a kind of dappled tattooing that resembled hammered metal, or the markings on the quarters of a young grey horse. There is a tradition of peace in these African markets where tribe must meet tribe to exchange its products. And quarrelling has always been most severely dealt with as a danger to both peace and trade.

Next day when we went back every trace of the market had disappeared. Except for the trampled ground and the pigs rooting for dropped remains, it might all have been a dream. But the ephemeral quality of the market structures was only a little greater than that of the thatched and mud-built huts. It was only a matter of degree. Here things disappear and if, through some cause as war or disaster, they fail to come again, are soon forgotten. Everywhere one feels the forest waiting like a python to swallow man's pitiful efforts to establish himself.

Next day we were taken to a ju-ju house. This necessitated some financial arrangements with the priests, villainous-looking old gentlemen, possibly sullen because their hobbies of murder, sacrifice and skull collecting had been stopped by an administration which had no respect for the ancient gods of Africa. There are five districts in the town, each with its own ju-ju house which corresponds more or less to a church with us. In addition, each family has its private ju-ju altar or chapel. The one we visited was an ordinary oblong, mud-built house, with a corrugated iron roof and a stoep. Its front was decorated with two large, painted clocks whose hands were set respectively at eleven-thirty and four. On each side of the door were painted figures that appeared to represent Portuguese soldiers, and above the windows was a West African concept of the royal arms with the lion and the unicorn clasped in an embrace. The painting was done in brilliant red, yellow, green, black and white. This front hut was empty except for some intricately carved stools thrown into a corner. It was a vestibule to a courtyard in the centre of which was a small thatched hut with a mat hung over the entrance. This contained the regalia and other sacred objects.

Before entering the ju-ju house, the Africans accompanying us took off their shirts, as a mark of respect, as we would take off our hats. In front of the ju-ju house was a large open space scattered with big trees. One looked like a large magnolia. The ground below them was clean and evidently kept swept. Near the big tree was a large clay phallus about three feet in height and one foot in diameter.

Everything, except for the garishly painted front of the ju-ju house, was plain and simple. There was nothing to get hold of except that, in spite of the bright sunshine, the place was sinister. What had taken place on this clean-swept, leaf-dappled yard? What else was there in those huts that we had not seen? Human skulls hidden in the thatch or dangling from strings almost certainly. But how old were they?

There had been some carefully carved wooden figures and against an outside wall, apparently thrown away, was one of a recumbent woman. Who had carved her? Why? What purpose had she served?

Taken in conjunction with the clay phallus and other decorations, the thought behind it all was obvious.

Several times we passed small, open shrines roofed with dry grass, or a bent sheet of iron, containing sacred objects. Some had been sprinkled with blood and white cock's feathers, others had brightly coloured, metallic powder scattered over them.

But there was more to it than this, as I was to find out in a minute when McInnes pointed and said: "This is where Richard Lander was made to go through the ordeal of the poisoned water." He had been accused by nine Portuguese slave traders of being a British anti-slave spy and his trial was ordered by the king. The fetish tree under which he had been examined stood here until a few years ago when it had finally rotted away. In Lander's time it had been festooned with human skulls while the headless bodies were suspended nearby. All had been slaughtered under the fetish tree to please its spirit. And in the midst of all this stink, surrounded by savage warriors, by Portuguese slavers and their assistants armed with guns and whips, Richard Lander was given the poison cup.

The ju-ju priest said: "If you have no evil designs you will come to no harm, but should you have evil in your heart you will die."

Lander took the wooden bowl, drank, and dashed it to the ground. Then he turned and walked back to his quarters. There he took a strong emetic. He did not die.

This man was one of the giants. A gentleman's gentleman who became one of the foremost explorers of West Africa. He first came to Nigeria as the servant of Hugh Clapperton, a naval officer who died at Sokoto. Lander continued his master's work. Africa and exploration had got him. He and his brother John were the first two men to trace the Niger down its course to the mangrove swamps where sea and river meet at its immense delta. The journey took them seventeen months.

Later, in 1832, he returned in a paddle steamer, sent out from England by some Liverpool merchants to explore the possibilities of trade in the interior. It was on this expedition that he met his death. Of the forty-eight white men who left the coast on this trip only nine returned.

So I had been right. There was blood in this ju-ju compound. Over the centuries, hundreds may have died in this spot, sacrificed to these abominable trees.

Badagri was a great slave centre, its barracoons containing at times as many as a thousand captives. Those not required by the slaving captains on account of age, lack of health, wounds or other disabilities, were either pinioned and flung, weighted with stones, into the river that our bedroom overlooked, or were tortured and sacrificed.

It is an interesting reflection that these coastal people, now among the best educated and most vocal of all Africans, who are continually recalling the horrors of the slave trade and the white oppressors' brutality, are not the descendants of the slaves, but of the slavers who captured them. They were the hunters and traders in men, the middle men who took over the raw product and processed it for the middle passage, who sold their own black brothers for rum and guns. Without them there could have been no slave trade. Its continuance depended upon their energy.

In its heyday Badagri had five slave barracoons. We saw one of them. A large courtyard surrounded by a high stone wall, constructed by the Portuguese on the design of a patio. They probably brought the stone from Portugal as ballast. The wall was pierced by a single door. There were lean-tos on all four sides. Open sheds, some with rings masoned into the walls, to which slaves could be tied like animals, and small rooms, prisons for recalcitrant or special slaves, rooms for overseers, guards and stores. In the centre of the yard was a wooden or iron post. Here the slaves were examined down to the smallest anatomical detail. Here they were branded.

In another compound we saw a heap of slave chains and one small war-canoe cannon. They are now all ju-ju, and at times have libations of palm oil and gin poured over them by the fetish priest. The iron neck shackles were jointed so that they opened, but ended in loops through which a very heavy chain was passed. There were also handcuffs, some for small children like tiny bracelets through which a fixed bar was passed. Once on they could only be removed by a smith.

I asked about the poison ordeal and McInnes, who is a student of native custom, told me that it was made from the bark of the Erythropleum and is known as the red-water ordeal. The material produced has the properties of raising the blood pressure while slowing the pulse and decreasing the powers of respiration.

Another ordeal in use on the Cross and Calabar rivers is the esere bean. This is the seed of a creeper which contains several poisonous alkaloids. Here it is believed that if the accused is innocent he will vomit up the concoction and suffer no harm, but if guilty will die in agony.

An ordeal in use in the north was that of the red-hot iron. Here the accused had to lick the iron with his tongue. If guiltless, he suffered no harm. And here there is, as in so many of the witch doctor's tricks, an element of scientific truth, for the guilty man, conscious of his guilt, has no saliva in his mouth.

African witchcraft is a mixture of primitive medicine, sound psychology, absolute mumbo-jumbo and some inexplicable factor which no one, who has lived on the continent for long, is prepared utterly to discount. It has always seemed to me that the medical and esoteric knowledge of the witch doctor is un-African. That it corresponds to nothing else in the culture of the native. This idea appears to be confirmed by a new theory which is now being considered — that Africa was once much more civilised and is now in a state of decadence. In which case the knowledge of the witch doctors is something left over from a higher culture that once existed. Like the great rocks from which the soil of Africa has been eroded.

Iles told me of a previous district officer who had to be transferred because he offended a sorceress who put a snake ju-ju n him. Snakes are rare here, months go by without one being seen. But suddenly they became common in the district officer's house and compound. He would see one lying on the path in the garden, find one in his car, another curled up in his chair. I heard of another similar case when I was on the Gold Coast and I believe it to be possible. In Tanganyika something of the same sort is done with lions. When a man is cursed by a lion-man they suddenly appear from all directions. The rational explanation is that some substance is used that attracts them, as catmint attracts cats. This may also apply to snakes. But most witchcraft consists of either causing death by suggestion — and the African is very susceptible to suggestion — or by direct poisoning.

Here are some of the methods by which a witch doctor will discover a thief. The suspects are each given a twig of the same length. They are told that when they bring them back in the morning, that the one held by the thief will have grown by the width of a hand. Naturally, next morning, the thief's twig is one hand shorter than the others. He wasn't going to be caught that way, so he shortened it.

In another test, a goat, covered with mealie meal, is put into a dark hut. The suspects are sent in one at a time and told to rub the goat's back with both hands, and only the hands of the guilty man would be marked. Of course the guilty man goes in, does not touch the goat and comes out clean handed. The others, who knew themselves innocent, are covered with flour.

Of course, as far as trial by ordeal is concerned, there is a great deal of corruption. The guilty man, who is prepared to share his spoil with the doctor, will either get a very weak dose of poison or be given an antidote that will save him.

Only the slave path remained now. This tragic track across the sand was the last the slaves would tread in Africa. Captured up country in some savage raid, they had been marched down to the waterways where they were bound and flung into the bottom of the great war canoes that would transport them to the barracoons of Badagri. Here they had suffered every indignity, every cruelty. Children had been torn from their mothers and had their brains dashed out against the walls, young girls had been taken by guards, chiefs and slaving captains. Many had been killed as useless, drowned in the creek or sacrificed. The picked stock which remained was now chained and marched, wailing, from the barracoon to the beach (river bank), re-embarked once more to cross the narrow channel and forced out on to the sandy shore of the opposite side. Here they were driven along the track that led upwards in a gentle slope. There was a new sound that stopped them, that made them cry out with fear. A dull roar, something they had never heard before. The ground still sloped up and then suddenly they saw the sea below them. None of them had ever seen the sea before. The thunder of the surf grew louder, the wind lashed them in their cold nakedness. The great palms rustled, bowing before it. Out beyond the bar, the slaver lay. The ground fell steeply now. The coarse, harsh grass grew sparsely, the sand was thicker, clinging to their ankles. They hesitated. The slavers' whips cracked. On the steep, shelving beach the big canoes waited, the foam of the savage surf licking their sterns. Hundreds of little red fiddler crabs dashed into the tiny holes that pocked the silver beach. Other crabs, almost transparent, with eyes set out of their heads on sticks, ran like spiders in and out of the foam. They were like the ghosts of dead crabs, or dead men. The fiddlers stood at bay waving one big red and purple claw, and then dived like rabbits into their burrows.

The canoe boys laughed as they watched the surf. They launched their canoes, standing naked, wet, glistening, half in the water beside them, holding them down as they rose to the incoming waves. The slavers now loaded up their cargo, forcing the slaves into the water and over the sides of the heaving canoes. The paddle captain watched the rollers pounding in as if he knew them. Now, now. This was the moment. With a wild cry the paddlers launched the canoe and sprang in, paddling furiously. The timing was right. The bows rose to the sea and the paddles struck the water with renewed fury. A wild yell of triumph drowned the desperate cries of the slaves. They were over the bar.

Never have I been on a more terrible or more desolate beach. There were no gulls. There was no life except for the crabs. There was only the sighing palms and the pounding, death-dealing sea. Over there was America. Behind me was Africa. Between the two lay the middle passage where millions had died.

12

● WHEN WE GOT BACK to Lagos we stayed with the chief secretary, Mr. Leslie Gobels, his wife Mickey, and Ferdinand. Ferdinand, a brown dachshund, was as much our host as his owners — a splendid animal of immense personality, who certainly could have spoken had he wanted to take the trouble.

Ferdinand had a small bed of his own in the Gobelses' bedroom. He had his own blankets, pillow and mosquito net, but one night nothing would make him get into it. As fast as he was put in he got out again. At last the Chief Secretary parted the mosquito curtains and found a solitary mosquito inside. Ferdinand knew about malaria. Once it had been killed he went to bed quite happily.

Leslie Gobels had some twenty-five years service in Nigeria and his wife had been with him most of the time. She was one of the earliest women to come to the colony. Things were not easy then. All treks were done on foot or horseback. There were still lions in the northern parts and the natives were far from pacified. She told us of one adventure, crossing a flooded river that could not be forded. When her husband had swum over she was put in a large tin bath and ferried across by two Africans, one swimming on either side.

Mickey is a small, white-haired, highly strung and extremely charming woman. Leslie is tall, good looking and, I would imagine, a most able and experienced administrator. He is always remarkably well groomed and cuts his own hair, which would seem to be the ultimate sign of efficiency. These are things that are not generally appreciated — hair cutting, managing in a hot climate without a refrigerator or ice, taking care of your goods and stores in a land where the ants can destroy a saddle in a night.

Once even in South Africa, where things are not nearly so bad, I remember dropping my shirt on the ground beside my bed. In the morning there was no shirt; only the buttons remained. Then there are snakes, scorpions, centipedes, ordinary ants in variety and driver or safari ants that put even lions to flight. These are everyday problems in the bush, apart from malaria, guinea worm, tombo fly — which lays its eggs on the skin and hatches out a maggot in your flesh — and water, every drop of which must be boiled. These are subjects of ordinary conversation like the price of food, or servants, or children at home.

As to the water I heard one amusing story. A hostess said to one of her guests: "My dear, do you know what I found? The boy was putting the water for the ice cubes into the container after he had washed it under the faucet. So I said (she went on): 'What's the good of boiling the water if you do that?' "

The boy said he did not know. In fact he did not see why the water should be boiled at all.

"Make him dead," he said, meaning boiled water was flat. "No agree for boil water."

To him it was just another piece of white man's madness.

The guest went home and discussed the matter with her chief steward. On enquiry it turned out that the water for her ice cubes was not even boiled. It was taken straight out of the tap.

"No drink. Ice like stone, so why?" was the answer that she got.

The servants in Nigeria are graded. Chief steward, he's the one you tip and he keeps most of it. A second steward, a third steward if the establishment is fairly large, and a Small Boy everywhere, who ranges in age from twelve to fifty. Small Boy does all the hard work. Number three does the floors and makes the beds, number two cleans silver, lays the table and waits. The chief steward's function is one of decorative responsibility. He waits, pours out wine and arranges the flowers. He does the table napkins. This is not just a matter of doing them like a sort of hat as one finds them in hotels. Oh no. A good steward knows thirty or forty ways of doing napkins. They are never the same. Each night he waits with modest, down-cast eyes for praise at the new design. The one we liked best was the duck pattern. Here the napkins seemed to be swimming round the table. A favourite for a big party is a bridgelike twist, a sort of continuous arch that goes in a series of loops from one glass to the next and is ornamented with flowers.

It is the chief steward who says "Welcome" when a guest arrives, answers the telephone and knows all the private affairs of the family. Some boys remain with their masters for their whole service of twenty-five or more years, and apart from their wages and perquisites, receive, when their masters retire, a lump sum, often amounting to ten pounds for every year they have been with them. A very genuine relationship of friendship and loyalty often exists between them.

The Gobelses, for instance, decided to give their chief steward, Moussa, a bicycle for a present. He was sent out to choose it. He came back.

"No bicycle, master."

"What?" Mrs. Gobels said, "no bicycles in Lagos? Why, the shops are full of them."

"No bicycle, madam," Moussa repeated. "No Hercules bicycle."

"Won't another kind do?"

"No, madam, not for us, not in our position. What would people say if they saw the chief steward of the Chief Secretary on an ordinary bicycle?"

The Hercules is the Rolls-Royce of bicycles on the West Coast, and Moussa waited till a new consignment came in. The African can be very loyal to a brand of goods, or to a master, if they are good ones.

We set off for Abeokuta in the same kit car. Here we stayed with Colonel MaCrae, the Resident, who had a house on a hilltop with a lovely terraced garden.

At lunch we discussed native languages and the Colonel named seventeen main languages of which three — Hausa, Yoruba and Ibo — were the most important. He quoted an area — Kukuruku, four square miles in extent, under one chief — where there are four languages and whose people cannot understand each other without an interpreter. The total number of languages and dialects in Nigeria is believed to be four hundred. And this is the kind of thing which, it appears to me, makes a really united Nigeria more a dream than a possibility for a long time to come. The same naturally applies to the continent as a whole where there must be at least two thousand language groups, each with cultural differences that make them dislike all strangers.

After lunch I went to visit the agricultural officer, Mr. J. N. W. Nicholls, who came from Barbados and had some excellent ideas about tropical agriculture. The first of which was to destroy all office files. This is a general feeling in all departments everywhere. Too many returns that are pigeonholed and never looked at once they have been sent in. He believed in the native system of working the land and letting it go back to bush and he was, as far as the African here was concerned, against clean cultivation. He said the trees and bush should not be grubbed out but cut back so that after the harvest they could ratoon and grow again so that the sun could not burn up all the humus in the soil when it was left uncovered by a crop.

They were practising an interesting form of strip contour farming in the forest land, which struck me as very practical, the two alternating strips of forest and garden being approximately a hundred yards in width. This was particularly good for both cocoa and oil palms whose root systems must be kept cool, the ground cover making a difference of up to six degrees in the soil temperature.

When we had finished with the lands we went to the cattle byres and I saw more of the Muturu cattle. They are very small, cobby, with fine bones and almost invisible udders. Many of them can scarcely feed their own calves. They are forest cattle and, like the goats in similar conditions, appear to have been reduced in height by some form of natural selection. The goats are certainly the shortest legged I have ever seen; in fact, if heavily in kid, their bellies hardly clear the ground.

We next went to see the mental hospital a few miles outside the town. It was being run by two very high-salaried white doctors, mental experts, who had lovely houses with the best gardens I have seen for a long time. In fact, gardening seemed to be their main preoccupation since the hospital was empty while a departmental argument went on about it. The Government wanted to put lunatics into the institution but the doctors only wanted people they thought they could cure and rehabilitate. Meanwhile nothing happened except that the correspondence about the matter must have been mountain-high.

But this was a most beautiful asylum, the last word, *le dernier cri* in asylums, suitable for the very highest grade of lunatic with every provision for their comfort and security. It could probably be equalled, but not surpassed, in Europe or America.

Meanwhile, because there do not appear to be enough high-class lunatics in Nigeria, it stands empty and the insane, apart from those in the two existing asylums, are kept in jails without treatment, or chained in their villages by their relatives who fear to let them loose, being held responsible for their actions by the community.

In this splendid institution the patent locks are bronze, the patent toilets white china. There is not a knob or a projection anywhere — nothing that can be torn loose or come adrift. The only complaint one of the doctors had of the construction was that the polished mahogany handrail of the stair case had not been correctly bevelled and did not follow, with complete exactitude, the curve of the stair. This, he felt, might cause some further psychosis, or even trauma, in the minds of the nonexistent African patients who have never seen a staircase and have no conception of a line, either straight or curved.

Nothing is easier than to condemn or criticise but there seem to be times when it becomes inevitable, when mistakes seem to cease being mistakes and become acts of madness. The money spent on this institution could have been spread over ten less complex structures, where the insane could at least have lived in some comfort, in charge of men who, if they were not skilled psychiatrists or alienists, understood the handling of the mentally diseased.

This was one of those examples of complete misunderstanding, both of Africa and the African. At this stage what is needed is something (anything is better than nothing) that will just work. At the moment what is needed is quantity, not quality. Get the mad under cover, feed them, treat them with humanity and then go on from there. Nor do I believe that psychiatry in the American or European sense will work with the African until some first-class men have devoted themselves to understanding the African psyche. First of all, they would have to know the language, for how can an analysis ever be conducted through an interpreter? In addition, they would have to be anthropologists who knew native law and custom backwards, and understood every stress and strain to which the black child is subjected in his kraal or compound. Only then could the cure begin. The Oedipus and other myths, the Freudian fantasies, may apply to the African but if they do the context is absolutely different to our own.

Such work has been begun by Dr. J. C. Carrothers, M.B., D.P.M., who has written a book on the subject — *The African Mind in Health and Disease* — in which he sets up the groundwork for further investigation. He has also made a study of the Mau Mau for the Colonial Office (*The Psychology of Mau Mau*).

That night Colonel "Crocus" and Mrs. "Tony" Andrews dined with us. She was a very pretty blond woman with laughter wrinkles round her eyes. We arranged to go up to the lines on the following day to see some of the regimental trophies.

Next morning we went to see the Alarki, or King, of Abeokuta. When we reached the gate of the palace a native trumpet sounded. The Alarki came to the doorway of the palace with his umbrella bearer behind him, and advanced into the yard. The large crowd of men and women, waiting for audience, prostrated themselves on the ground shouting his praises.

He greeted us and we followed him into the palace — a largish villa — and up the stairs into a long narrow audience chamber. He was a dignified, middle-aged man dressed in white with a round white cap on his head. There were numerous thrones in the room. One had carved figures supporting the seat, another was completely covered with varicoloured bead work. The one he sat on at the end of the room was more ordinary — an everyday throne as it were. Behind it was a kind of glass-fronted bookcase filled with theatrical-looking, heavily jewelled crowns, some were gilt (or perhaps gold), others were beaded to match the throne.

He told us about the umbrella which his father had captured in his victorious war against the King of Dahomey, defeating his forces, including the famous Amazons, decisively. On the wall there was the biggest, most heavily carved cuckoo clock I have ever seen — the face was more than a foot across — and when the hour struck a cuckoo the size of a Bantam popped out of its hutch. On a sideboard were twin silver cups presented to him by John Holt and the United Africa Company, respectively. These rival companies have watched each other like hawks for a hundred years.

A very pretty young African girl came in, curtsied, and put down a tray with glasses of beer and cigarettes. The Alarki's son was educated in England and is now a judge. One of the few with a first-class reputation for incorruptibility. There was a picture of him in his robes. The Alarki, too, had been to England and must have had quite a time there judging from the enormous book of press cuttings he showed us.

In the afternoon we called on the Andrewses. The Colonel showed us the regimental silver which included a model palm tree — the regimental badge — and a silver model of the carved ivory tusk captured in the attack on Benin, which replaced the original that had been presented to a museum.

Next day we drove on to Ibadan where the new University College — the Oxford and Cambridge of Nigeria — is coming into being. We were met by Colonel Thorn with whom we had lunch. He was an artist and he showed us some very attractive pictures he had painted when crossing the Sahara. He was also a naturalist and had made many sketches of birds, which interested us as so many here were unfamiliar, although we did see some old friends from the south now and then.

Ibadan is the largest African town in the continent, with a population of half a million. It is of natural growth and does not owe its origin to the white man. It is a Yoruba town — a blue town. I say blue because this is the only colour the Yoruba women wear. Blue of the sky, of the sea. Deep indigo blue that is almost black. The town is filthy and unplanned, the roads unpaved; the houses are mud, their unpainted rusting corrugated iron roofs ornamented with the usual frieze of resting vultures. Between the houses run narrow alleys that serve as paths and drains.

Straggling out from the old city are the houses of the rich, the educated and the evolved. Gardenless, they stand like blocks of tenement flats — apartments. For each must accommodate a family, almost a tribe. Through this custom the rich members support not only the poor, but the idle, and here is one of the basic causes of corruption. As soon as a man gets a reasonable job his family descends on him with its demands. What is more, this is accepted and regarded as normal. It seems right to the African that ten pounds of petty cash should be taken from the company's cashbox to buy medicine for Auntie who is ill, or to help a cousin to buy a bicycle. After all what is a company? What is the government? They have no hearts. They do not need medicine or bicycles, or gin for a second burial.

The University College is one of the wonders of Africa. Of course Maxwell Fry and Jane Drew have not created anything that can compare with the Big Hole of Kimberley in terms of historic significance, but they have built some very odd and very big buildings in the heart of the African bush. These resemble a series of enormous square wedding cakes which have been attacked by termites possessed of a sense of design. The ants have bitten out squares and crosses and flower-petal-shaped openings. Everything is brilliantly coloured with great washes of pale blue, pink and white.

Inside the sun strikes through the pierced walls making fantastic shadows and dapples the parquet floor so that it looks like a wood on a sunny day.

The planning and decoration have a Brazilian feeling, which is interesting as even today there is a very close relationship between certain families descended from slaves in that country and their relatives on the West Coast.

But one wonders how such buildings will age and weather.

The British taxpayer has spent £1,500,000 on the University. It has seventy thousand books already in its library, and room for a million. But what, after all, is a university but an educational oven? The real value of the University will be seen when the cakes that it bakes are consumed by Nigeria.

We met Dr. Kenneth Mellanby who created the University College in less than five years out of bare bush — a wonderful achievement — and some of his staff, all of whom were very pleased with everything as indeed they had reason to be, superficially at any rate.

In the agricultural section I was told that the members of the faculty considerably exceed the numbers of the students, and I believe only one is going in for veterinary science.

There is no doubt that this university will produce excellent scholars, that diplomas will flourish like mushrooms in a cellar. But how many students will take such subjects as agriculture, forestry, mining, geology, zoology, engineering, surveying or architecture? And what use will they make of their knowledge once it is acquired? And there is a danger that the knowledge acquired is often not put into practice, or even correlated with reality. An examination is one thing. Actual, practical work is another.

Our next visit was to Ife where we saw the Oni, who had been on the throne for twenty-three years. He had been to England for the coronation and had enjoyed the ceremony very much. His English was perfect. He was a man of great personality, and a political power in Nigeria, being the spiritual head of the Yoruba nation.

He was dressed in a grey nightshirt-like garment with green trousers and a white brocade cap. We sat for our interview in his reception chamber. The carpet was plum coloured, the chairs of the brown leather club variety with yellow velvet cushions.

An attendant brought in a golden, wheeled table with a bottle of champagne — Mumm — and a new box of fifty Players cigarettes. The conversation followed the usual unproductive line of compliment and platitude. Such subjects as racialism and the future of Nigeria were skirted. We drank one another's health. The Oni hoped we would have a good trip. I hoped he would reign for another twenty-three years. We had come on an opportune day — the anniversary of his coronation.

Racialism is the new religion of Africa. At the moment it is anti-white, rather the way our new religion is anti-Communist. Only their feelings are stronger. And the white man by his colour is so easily distinguishable. If only Communists had red skins how much easier everything would be. But once they have dealt with the white menace — and they are well on the way to accomplishing this in West Africa — they will seek new enemies. Each race and tribe is going to demand living room, to feel itself surrounded and proceed with the usual measures that such feelings induce — alliances and defensive wars. Each nation wants the senior position, the greatest powers and the majority of privileges to which, in its own opinion, its glorious history entitles it.

Leaving the Oni we went to the museum, a beautiful modern building where the exhibits are exposed in glass cases. There were terra cotta heads and torsos, finally the famous bronze heads that Leo Frobenius first brought to light. Some had been thrown away in old compounds, or buried; others had been found in ju-ju houses. The terra cotta is lined with a glass-like ceramic a quarter of an inch thick, and just uncrated were some flat, twisted tapelike bangles of metal. And there was still a whole room full of boxes that had not yet been opened and catalogued.

Nothing comparable to these works has been found in Africa before. The features are not negroid, and the workmanship is comparable to that of the Romans, although to me they seemed to have an Oriental touch in the form of the headdresses and the oblique setting of the eyes. There are other treasures still in the forest — small, stone figures over whom white cocks are sacrificed at yearly ceremonies.

The bronzes were not believed to be very ancient, possibly not more than five or six hundred years old, until recently. Now, most experts believe the bronzes to predate the Portuguese influence by centuries, although after their coming Portuguese motifs became incorporated in their traditional designs. But why is the art now lost? Why are there no traditions, no fables? Nothing is left but the art of casting bronze by the ancient *cire perdue* method, though this, too, has degenerated and few are capable of doing skilled work. And why were the bronzes buried and the terra cottas smashed and thrown away?

The last thing we saw at Ife was the Episcopal Church whose steeple, mounted in the top of a square tower, was two feet off centre. We met the incumbent who was dressed in a flowing robe or surplice, whose design consisted of "First Anglican Church" and pairs of open scissors, infinitely repeated in dark grey. We saw the old mission — one of the earliest in West Africa — and the usual graves. Tragic reminders of the swift death that overtook the Europeans who first came to the coast. After that we visited the Bishop, an old gentleman of eighty who lamented the past and said that the young educated men of today were ashamed to work in the gardens and went to live by themselves in the cities instead of staying in their family compounds. He did not come out for polygamy but I had a feeling that he thought the church would have more converts if it were allowed. Which seems a reasonable supposition.

And so back to Lagos. This time to the Olympic Hotel where we had booked a room before leaving.

13

The City of Blood...Lagos...Benin

● THE OLYMPIC HOTEL was run by two Greek brothers. It is a modern building with a large pillared lounge on the ground floor. The chairs are stainless steel with slip covers of blue and white stripes and have low, glass-topped tables between them. The floor is tiled in red and black, varied by an inlay of white marble chips. Outside on the pavement Hausa traders have their goods laid out — leather bags of all kinds, python skins, carved ivories and ebony heads.

On the first floor is a wide gallery-dining room, the reception desk and the kitchens. Over that are the bedrooms. Our room was large and comfortable and for a while this was our base. We looked out on to a small hospital. The street was shaded by enormous wild almond trees whose big leaves were turning scarlet. This is an interesting and common tree in West Africa, growing in natural canopies. The branches spring out horizontally from the trunk in a series of layers and if the tree is topped they can be pruned into one enormous summer house.

At night the fruit bats called to each other with a plaintive squeak which had a kind of rhythm like a metronome.

We had time to explore the city. Lagos, so named by the Portuguese, means lakes and is an island surrounded by swamps. It was an important slaving centre and at one time was attached to Benin. Later the coast was overrun and five hundred thousand people in this area were believed to have been killed or sold. With this surfeit the price of slaves fell from fifty dollars to a roll of tobacco worth fifteen dollars, or a keg of powder worth eight. In 1852 the Obi and his chiefs signed a treaty with Britain by which slavery and human sacrifice were abolished and all slaves expelled. But the slave trade continued to prosper and only about ten per cent of the slavers were captured. Finally, in 1861, Lagos was ceded to the British.

An immense amount of reclamation work has been done by blowing in sand from the sea to increase the inhabitable area, but basically

Lagos, like Manhattan, must grow upwards. The problem, however, of building even miniature skyscrapers on a foundation of semi-liquid mud is one that the engineers have not yet completely solved.

We found the ju-ju stall in a market. Here was the stuff to cure syphilis or yaws, which are believed to be identical, or gonorrhea that is called a "cold in the head." Stuff to cure belly aches, or to give them. Here were simples and poisons, if you knew how to get them, and charms to make a lover faithful or a maiden desirous. Here was the mixture that epitomised Africa.

We drove out to Victoria Beach. It is lined with cocoanut palms and casuarinas, dotted with sunbathers and swimmers who are warned not to go out beyond the surf of the bar. This is the only beach where I have seen a notice board, painted in red, stating: "This Beach Is Very Dangerous."

Oddly, it does not look it. The sand is golden, the sea is blue. The waves look like other waves. But like so many other things in Africa, they are deceptive. They do not just come in on the beach, they dig it away in every charge, turning themselves over and over in their fury, pounding their frothing heads on the sand with a revolving somersault movement, so that anyone caught in them is not swept shorewards, but beaten down to the bottom and ground there into the sand by the angry water, beaten and rolled, and then beaten again.

While we were there a dead African was pulled out of the sea. He had been missing for a couple of hours — all this time being rolled and pounded. Two white men had only just been able to get him out when, for an instant, his body drifted into some slack water beyond the bar. They carried him in by his legs and arms, his head sagging. A mixed black and white crowd collected round the body. No one was perturbed. It was the run of the mill. Young mothers lay playing with their babies a few yards away. Later, he was carried off into the shade of the trees and laid on the rough sea grass. I assumed that sometime someone would pick up the body (though he was still there when we left to go home). The bathers continued to bathe. The mothers and children to play. A dog chased a long-nosed pig away from its master's towel and clothes. The surf continued to pound. I have an idea the Africans who were bathing were pleased. The gods of the sea had had their victim for the day. Perhaps they would be satisfied.

At lunch a day or so later we saw our first mixed couple, an African with a white wife and a mulatto child of six. The woman spoke with a Scottish accent and was probably a landlady's daughter. They often marry their African lodgers who have told them that they are princes at home. The man left the table first and sat down in the lounge for coffee. When his wife joined him he did not get up. This was presumably to show his superiority. This sense of superiority was continually on display in the lounge. Africans sitting sprawled in their chairs, with one leg over the arm. Some in Western clothes, some in their own pyjamalike suits with little round caps on their heads. When they want more beer they shout: "Boy!" It all makes a fine show of independence. And of course that is what they come for. To prove something to themselves. To prove their democratic equality to the white man and their superiority to the uneducated mob. Here, in principle, every man not only can be President but ought to be.

The best type of African never acts like this. His manners are impeccable, his clothes perfect, his voice cultured and restrained. There is only one thing wrong about the really educated African. There are too few of him.

A neat little household racket was described to me by the woman involved. Eggs in Nigeria are like gold. Native eggs, about the size of pigeons' eggs, cost sixpence each and European eggs, as they are called, eightpence. Native eggs are seldom fresh since the hens lay in the bush and they have generally been sat on by the time they are collected. So when she was offered eggs, this lady put them in a bucket of water and bought only those which sank. She told the trader to come again and she would buy all that were fresh according to her test. A week later he came back with four dozen in a basket. They all sank and she bought every one. But when she came to use them not one was fresh. They had been hard-boiled which drove the gas out of them. All this is very clever, very neat, but a country cannot prosper on a basis of a hundred per cent dishonesty. And that is the problem that the African on his own is going to have to face.

In a recent scandal, an expert on embezzlement was brought out from England and is believed to have said that he learnt more on the subject in Lagos, in six months, than in the whole of his previous experience.

The African does not look upon dishonesty as we do. Corruption is normal to him. What after all is a bribe? And everything is run on this basis, even the elections in which the seats are bought and sold, sometimes to both sides, and here, sometimes to ensure honest corruption, a fetish is brought in and unbreakable oaths are sworn. And of course, behind everything, behind every act, there is always the threat of accident, of poison, of being cursed or bewitched.

I asked about the native buses and was told they are bought on the instalment plan. Only by running the truck day and night without servicing can the payments and the driver's wages be met. At the end of a year the purchaser has paid expenses, got a few pounds in hand to pay the deposit on a new truck and still has the old one which he can sell for fifty pounds or so to some enterprising African garage, which will take it to pieces and sell it piecemeal — the bolts, nuts and engine parts to other garages, and finally, the wornout tires to a shoemaker for sandals. Nothing is wasted in West Africa. Not an empty aspirin bottle, not an old condensed milk can — these are made into lamps by fitting a little tin nozzle and equipping them with wicks of twisted cotton.

Another experience was a visit to the local night clubs. Leaving Tiny at home, I went with Tony McClellan and an African subaltern in the Nigeria Regiment, who had been to Sandhurst. He was a very good-looking and pleasant young man, a member of a noble Kanuri family. We dined at Government House and left about midnight in Tony's car.

The first place we went to was the "Corporal's" — it was run by an ex-corporal of police. It consisted of a walled compound inside of which was a kind of beer garden. There were tables and chairs, all somewhat rickety, and a few fairy lights strung from the branches of the trees. On one side was a green wooden shack rather shakily lettered with the words: DRINKING ROOM. A loudspeaker blared. The corporal kept putting records on the victrola and asking how we liked them. On a seat that ran along the wall of the drinking room, two Africans were fondling a pretty boy dressed in green plush cloth. Beyond a small dying palm was another notice which said: LATRINE, also in large, white letters. In the drinking room, which was also a dance floor, a young white girl of sixteen was dancing with an almost bare-chested African. Her father, who I was told had been a member of the British Council, was sitting, somewhat befuddled, in a cane armchair.

The British Council is supposed to introduce British culture — good music, pictures, books and other cultural factors — to the African. But no one has been able to explain to me its effect, if any, beyond providing jobs for a number of artistic young people. I fail to see how explaining a Constable water colour to an African is going to achieve greater collaboration or lead us towards a multi-racial society in which the white lion and the black lamb lie down together to listen to Gilbert and Sullivan Operas. In England the British Council may be of more use explaining English customs to African students and, a harder task I should think, the African habits of emigrant labour to the people among whom they have come to settle.

One of the Africans now began to sing, accompanying himself on a guitar by striking the strings with a Gillette blade. His friends supported him by tapping empty bottles on their sides with table knives. It was an effective performance. It was all very natural, all very relaxed. This was an African club. We white men were like the other guests, neither honoured nor particularly disliked. I have no doubt we could have had pretty, velvet-wrapped boys, or girls if we had wanted them. Certainly the girls. The place had a particular atmosphere. It was not evil, not criminal. After all it was run by a police corporal. It did not have the feeling of a West Side dive. It was infinitely safer. One was not afraid of a knife in one's back, or a stick-up. One just wondered if the glass the beer was in had been properly washed. Then one hoped that the previous drinker had not got syphilis too badly.

We moved on to the Universal. This is an important club.

We went into the house through several drinking parlours, passed a bar and into a yard. The first sight that met my eyes was the sign, very large in shaky red: URINARY MEN, followed by an arrow. On the opposite wall was a similar sign for ladies. The place was dirty. Everything was rickety, nothing stood level. I was told it was much used by the top politicians. Next to us a political celebration was going on. Beer mugs were being banged on the table and every second word was *Freedom* . . . "When we get our Freedom." The *dom* part loud and vocally underlined.

The most excited gentleman was well known in political circles. He was dressed in a Cambridge-blue pyjama suit with a design, in paler blue, of enormous Prince of Wales feathers — the final ignominy of the proud crest of the poor blind King of Bohemia. Out of the Cambridge-blue back rose a black bull neck and a bullet head. "When we get our *freedom* there must be an Opposition," he shouted. I assume he saw himself as its leader. The leader of the Opposition in a West African democracy is in a very strong financial position. The more he opposes the greater the amount required to buy him off. Some of his friends were rich men in plush nightshirts, with embroidered collars.

We were now disturbed by two women fighting over a man who

sat smugly watching them. One called the other a dirty Calabari bitch whereupon the insulted lady slapped her face and she sat down with a bang on the bench from which she had risen. These regional quarrels appear to be carried right into the nuptial couch. While they were fighting the man slipped away and hid in the Urinary Men, where the winning lady, undeterred by the notice, pursued him.

Our politicians rose and, seeing a fight was going on in the men's department, went to the Urinary Ladies. Loud screams followed, as it appeared to be occupied.

We got our beer. It was served by a very pretty African girl in a smart, well-cut black frock with a clean white apron.

The political party continued to talk in loud voices, using the longest words they knew. The longer the polysyllable the better the argument.

We finished our beer and went to the Yaba Rex club. The last thing we heard was the Calabari lady shouting.

The Yaba Rex club was the biggest place we had been to. There was a regular band. To reach it we went through a house, passed a couple of pugilist chuckers-out and down some steps into a big compound where trees grew out of the concrete. There was a regular floor and there must have been a couple of hundred people drinking, eating supper and dancing.

We ordered fried eggs, chips and beer. I had hardly taken my seat before a black girl, coming from behind me, slipped a velvety arm round my neck, rubbing it caressingly with her forearm, and took the cigarette out of my mouth. More girls surrounded us, pouring themselves like warm, black water over our shoulders, taking our hands, asking for cigarettes with their mouths and other things with their eyes. They were all young; some were really pretty with beautiful figures. They were brilliantly dressed and talked with soft, pretty voices. They stroked with soft pink-lined hands. It was like being mobbed by a flight of butterflies.

Here was disease, vice and corruption of the body and the spirit offered in its most tempting, orchid form. There can hardly exist a man who has had no dream of the strange woman. Well here she was, in one of her most exotic and lascivious manifestations. We gave them cigarettes and bought them beer. They perched about us, showing breasts that glistened like black fruits. Showing black and golden thighs — inviting, asking, teasing, promising. They represented one of the greatest dangers of the coast, for the women, as much as the gin and fever, have killed off the white men who have paused here.

Now and then one of the girls would find a client and go out with him. In a few minutes she would be back, having lain with him in the deserted streets.

Some white sailors came. They looked like engineers from a freighter. They were not fine specimens. In a second they were overwhelmed by our black, perfumed butterflies.

We had our fried eggs and chips, drank our beer and went home, driving down the Marina whose grassy bank was littered with recumbent couples. It had been an interesting evening.

A strange, dark land in which the whores carry themselves like queens.

Our next trip was to Benin. Here we stayed with Kenneth and Anne Munro. From the air the town was very tidy, laid out in neat squares. Nothing from this angle could have been less sinister, but slowly the picture changed. I cannot explain how, but it was a matter of feeling. Ghosts walked here, there was still fear. I was told the people's name for Benin is "The Country of Hatred."

Our host's servants, who were Ibos, would not go out at night. Why not? No reason except that they were afraid. Why were they afraid? No reason except that they had reasons. Ken, without adequate evidence, considered their reasons valid. Or to put it another way, he said: "If I were an Ibo I think I would stay at home."

It's the same old story. Like witchcraft, no white man believes in it, but . . . There is always a but or an if.

Our first visit was to the Oba in his palace. He came to greet us. He was a tall young man in glasses, wearing a long white robe closed to the neckline like a cardinal's, and a white biretta-like cap. He was in council and led us into the chamber, placing us on his right. It was a long, narrow room. Down each side sat his nobles, chiefs and captains. They were wrapped in white sheetlike garments. Their chests were bare, and draped with necklaces of coral, darkened and polished by age and sweat, a sign of their nobility. In the past, if they lost their beads even in battle, they were condemned to death.

To me they looked cruel. They were not negroid. Their features were sharp, pointed as daggers, their eyes like agates.

The discussion was apparently about the ancient glories of Benin. Of how once it had stretched north as far as Sierra Leone and how, if things went on this way, it was time to secede from the west and re-establish their ancient glories. The time for a come-back was approaching. The time to prove that the Beni were a superior and warlike people and that no one could put anything over on them.

The Oba spoke to us of the old days, the good old days, when slaves were currency. After them in value came cows and then ivory. He spoke against divorce. He felt that women once acquired should be retained. In the old days, the good old days, there was no divorce. If a woman became intolerable she was poisoned or sacrificed or sold. Life was much simpler then.

We were given beer and cigarettes. I thought of the Benin throne that I had seen in the Nigeria Regiment's Mess and looked at the armchair on which the Oba sat. Behind it against the wall were other chairs of Portuguese or Spanish origin, like some my parents had when I was a child in Paris. On them were masses of stacked newspapers, some of them yellow with age.

When we had drunk our beer and exchanged the usual compliments, the Oba passed us on to a chief to whom he gave the necessary keys and told him to show us round. Along one of the narrower ends there was an altar that ran the whole length of the wall — a shelf of clay which, in the centre, bulged out into a semicircular altar. Here there were cast bronze heads reminiscent of those of Ife, with carved elephant tusks inserted into the holes in their skulls. There were long, carved clubs, and figures of gods and men in brass and bronze. Near the bells were some Neolithic stone axe heads which they call "thunderbolts" and are considered very sacred. It was all very innocuous and innocent, and yet this grass-covered yard was redolent of blood. These altars that we were looking at had once been so caked with human blood that it came off in flakes when it was touched. This compound so full of dead that British soldiers had thrown up at the stench when they entered it. We were in the very centre, the sacred pulsing heart of Benin, the city of blood.

Here is the story written by Commander Bacon of the Royal Navy who accompanied the expedition against Benin in 1897, the year of my birth.

This was the palaver house, the ju-ju compound. Long sheds ending in raised altars on which were bronze heads with carved tusks stuck into them and carved clubs all smeared with blood. The whole compound smelt of death and corruption. In the centre was an erection of iron with hooks for hanging portions of the victims' bodies and near it a well into which the bodies were flung. The streets of the town were filled with the bodies of sacrificed slaves, in front of every house whose owner could afford it was the body of a human being. In front of the others was the

body of an animal, a goat, or a dog, all rotting in the heat of the
sun. There were avenues lined with skulls. On the crucifixion tree,
shaped like a great bed with a sloping back, two men were lashed
together in the form of a double cross, the right wrist and ankles of
one tied to the left wrist and ankles of the other Below them the
ground was strewn with the skulls and bones of previous victims.

In another description, Captain Alan Boisdragon wrote:

When the column approached the city they found live women,
gagged and pegged out on their backs, their abdominal wall being
cut in the form of a cross with the uninjured gut hanging out. Men
slaves, their hands lashed behind their backs and their feet tied,
were also lying about. As we neared the city, human beings were
lying in all the paths and bush, even in the king's compound — my
God, the sight and stench of them was awful . . . The bush, too,
was filled with dead bodies, their hands being tied to their ankles
so as to keep them in a sitting posture. All along the road decapi-
tated bodies were found, blown out by the heat of the sun.

A fire broke out shortly after the town was captured and that was
the end of old Benin. The king gave himself up and died in exile
in 1914 in Calabar. His son became Oba and twice was accused of
sacrificing a wife but was acquitted each time through lack of evidence. One does not get evidence in West Africa against kings. The
present Oba succeeded him in 1933.

Men who are sixty were small children at the time and must remember some of it. Men who are seventy, and were adolescent then,
must remember a lot. Like all old men they must talk of their memories — of the wars and battles, the sacrifices they have seen — to the
children who group themselves about their feet. And we like to
imagine that we have here the material from which to manufacture
a democracy on the Western model.

For this is the picture all over Africa, where the savage and cannibal
past impinges on the living present.

Among the relics found in the old city was a brass image of Our
Lord and some small metal crucifixes. And this, the crucifixion of
human beings, was the only residue of their Christianity, all that had
been acceptable — a new and more decorative form of torture. This
was all that remained of the earliest Christian missions in the country, which began in 1456 when the King of Benin, then a great king-

dom, had sent his ambassadors to Portugal. They returned with the Christian priests, who started the first mission here. For a while Christianity rivalled the religion of the fetish cults but fever, no doubt assisted by the ju-ju doctors' poison, slowly decimated the missionaries. Black deacons took over and they slowly succumbed, sinking back into the more exciting religion of their ancestors — to human sacrifice and torture, with the added refinement of death upon the cross.

It had been said that the African takes what he wants of an alien culture. What does he want of ours? Bicycles perhaps, and deck chairs.

We visited the museum. It had a mass of most interesting material but it was too crowded and insufficiently labelled. There were bronze bulls' heads reminiscent of Assyrian art, and horses that looked Chinese. A carved bronze stool made of a large snake, rolled into a figure of eight, the head appearing between the folds at the bottom. A big war drum four feet across and four feet high which, I was told, could be heard seven miles away. And smaller drums all constructed in the same way of hollowed logs with a skin stretched across the head that was tightened by pegs driven diagonally into the body to act as wedges. There was a large carved chest on feet, all cut from a single log, like the one at Government House. There were models of Portuguese soldiers in bronze. Two eastern looking execution swords of very heavy iron which curved upwards and became much wider and thicker at the end of the blade. The office of executioner was hereditary. The head had to be removed at one blow — should he fail to do this the executioner himself was executed by his apprentice who was his son. This produced a titillating situation and added pepper to the salt of the event. There were an ivory leopard, carved ram's horns containing a thunderbolt (neolithic flint), and bronze birds that reminded me of the soapstone birds of Zimbabwe.

More and more I was feeling the impact of other cultures in Africa, seeing things that reminded me of other things. Richard Burton writing of Benin in 1863 said: "We find in every house a perfect Tuscan ATRIUM with a gangway running round the rectangles IMPLUVIUM." Why not? Why should there have been no influence from Rome? What about the cloths worn on the Gold Coast that are draped like togas? Among the looted treasures of old Benin were such things as a carved ivory SISTRUM whose origin is Egyptian, a staffhead with a leopard motif common in Assyria, carvings ornamented with snakes, lizards and faces reminiscent of Phoenicia.

Benin is very old. A thousand years ago it was a kingdom. No one can date its dynasties or tell its origins, but many strange influences have touched it. Strange fingers from over the seas, from across the deserts and down the rivers have poked into its cultural pie and left their mark.

A private ju-ju house was the next thing. We were taken to a compound through a heavy door of adzed planks that were fastened together vertically, like clapboards, by clinched iron pins. Inside was a darkened, empty room, beyond it a covered compound in the usual design, with lean-to sheds all round it.

The centre received little sun and was green with slippery moss. We went down a passage whose walls had been polished with bees-wax and which were ornamented with a design of formalised female organs arranged in a patterned border. Then we came to the shrine itself. Here life-size red clay figures, painted in black and white, wearing necklaces of beads and coral, flanked an altar which was covered with a collection of curious objects. Swords, spears and arrows were embedded in it, point upwards. There were slave chains and manacles, clay and bronze figures, old car parts — all sacred to the iron god — and, in a kind of trough in front of the altar, offerings of fluted phalli and vulvas, carved in some soft white chalky stone. There were white feathers scattered about and the altar was coated with dried blood. In the yard there were more drums, some of them painted white — these were women's drums — and a life-size nude woman's figure, kneeling facing the wall with her breasts upon the ground. What happened in these dark, moss-grown courts?

We took some pictures of the altar and got very strange results when they were developed. The whole background is flecked with light although no sun penetrated here. Nor was the film defective because the exposure which preceded and followed the fetish pictures on the same roll were perfect.

Among other sacred articles that we saw was a chest filled with Toby jugs, some very old and some new. There was even one of Sir Winston Churchill, complete with his cigar. And with them was a gourd filled with leopard fangs. Mr. Law, the assistant district officer, told me that not far off there was a village where pythons are still sacred and take chickens with impunity. They are allowed in the huts and on more than one occasion, according to the stories, have swallowed small children that they found sleeping.

We dined with Mr. Butcher, the Resident, and had manillas that he had had silvered for napkin rings. He gave Tiny a bronze one and told us how they had been reclaimed. They had been used for centuries as currency, but with the coming of real money their employment became too complex as the rate of exchange was arbitrary and could not be controlled. A manilla is an open ring of copper alloy, two inches across, whose ends are flattened into heart-shaped ellipses. The weight is about five ounces and its value fluctuated between twopence and sixpence — £3 worth, as much as a strong man could carry, weighed fifty-six pounds. They were bought up at fivepence each and the transaction cost the Government £350,000. Some were sold as scrap at £120 per ton in London, the rest were dumped into the sea. The collection centres were visited by trucks which conveyed them to the railhead where they were taken to the coast. Of Portuguese origin, this curious coinage is now illegal and has almost disappeared from Nigeria, though an odd one still turns up now and then.

Next day we went to visit another ju-ju house some distance away. We passed the remains of the city walls and defences. One was a great ditch filled with green scummy water covered with what looked like lotus leaves. There were once three defensive walls, the most distant being fifty miles away from the town. It was here we saw our first rubber trees and native cured rubber, hanging out in matlike squares that looked like tripe, on bamboo rails.

All the house roofs were blackened with smoke which was said to preserve them by coating the rafters and palm thatch with its deposit and killing ants and borers.

It was raining lightly and we passed people carrying single banana leaves as umbrellas. The older women were naked to the waist. Breasts are an important factor with Africans. A woman's age is measured by her breasts, which are described as buds for young girls, cups for adolescents and gourds for adults.

All along the road there were small ju-ju shrines, thatched or covered with a bit of tin, in which sacred objects hung from strings or lay on the ground. Again, all along the road we saw the big-leaved, small-flowered, semi-wild red canna. There were small forest goats, black, smooth, shiny-coated sheep that were very attractive, and groups of tiny Mutura cattle — black or black and white in colour. All the animals were fat.

We came to the village we were looking for and the priests were found by the court messenger. This was a big ju-ju house that looked, from the outside, rather like a stable or a barn. There was a figure of a naked woman made of clay on the left of the door and near by was a big ju-ju sasswood tree.

Inside we got a shock. On the right, on the raised walk that was protected by a lean-to roof of corrugated iron, was a life-size figure, beautifully modelled and coloured black, of a decapitated slave. It was most realistic. The hands were made fast behind the back with tie-tie, the head was separated from the body by a few inches. It was, to me, the very height of realistic symbolism. It was what they used to do. It was what they would do again if they could. It was here, in this sacred spot, as a reminder, a fragrant memory of the great free past.

The main altar was a kind of Madame Tussaud's affair of grouped, life-size figures of clay, the central piece being a representation of the Oba, his bracelet-weighted arms outstretched, supported by slaves. The altar was conventional, like the other we had seen. The walls were decorated with designs of snakes and tortoises, the male and female emblems of fertility. There were drums in variety. The drum must have come to us from Africa. In a separate yard was an enormous phallus covered with dried blood and white cock's feathers which Tiny was not allowed to approach or photograph. This was not for women. The priests were content with their seven-shilling dash, or seemed to be, though no doubt they would sooner have sacrificed us to some dark forest god. The white man is irrelevant here, something that passes over the forests, like a wind and then goes back again. He can never be everywhere at once, and one wonders what happens in his absence.

Here, for instance, after a bad harvest a number of people, chiefly children, were accidentally drowned in wells. These are holes about twenty feet deep and almost every family has one in its compound. But everyone is used to them and in normal years there are no accidents. Again, in a recent census, in the seven- to fifteen-year group, the boys vastly outnumbered the girls in a most unaccountable manner. Had they been sacrificed? Nothing could be explained.

There were recently two cases of thieves being found with a six-inch nail driven into their heads, but the courts did not convict, through lack of evidence. There is never evidence. This is the jungle still, with only the faintest overlay of justice and order.

We now called on the local Oba. His house was a new one. The door panels were asymmetrically painted in green, white and red. Up-stairs on the reception room table there was a magnificent white plush cloth with a design of two Bengal tigers in colour. The royal bedroom had an enormous brass number with knobs on it. We were shown clocks. The Oba liked clocks. One of them, under a big glass dome, showed all its intricate innards, much to his delight. There was another clock with a picture of Little Red Riding Hood on the face, which played a tune — "The Big Bad Wolf" — when it was wound up. The only clock that worked was a kitchen clock. There was a large safe but the key was lost or the combination forgotten. The Oba asked the district officer what he should do about it. And the fridge was not working.

While we were entertained with warm beer I looked round the room. The windows had coloured glass in them. The curtains, mounted on sagging strings, were tied in knots. Children swarmed. One of them, a little boy, had quite red hair and was, I suppose, a near albino, though his skin was dark. The men present, some of the councillors and advisers, said very little, but listened to the Oba with respect. Munro asked if we could hear some stories but we were told that stories were taboo till after dark. The Oba was dressed in a white robe patterned with grey which had an ecclesiastical-looking cape that fell halfway down the arms.

He took us into the assembly hall of his compound. Here the walls were covered with curious paintings and designs, both inside and out. There was a thirty-foot snake, a crocodile, a cock and hen surrounded by eggs in a very surrealist design, and a coronation seat of mud whose three steps were greasy with blood. All the walls, which were white-washed, were spotted with dabs of Reckitt's Blue between the decorations. He took us to his private ju-ju house where there was a ju-ju which sang when a chief was about to die. He had heard it before his father's death. The centre piece of this chapel was a large clay phallus, ornamented with knobs.

Then we went to the dining room on the ground floor. He told us that his father had four hundred and fourteen children, and that after his father's death he had taken over twelve of his eighteen remaining wives, as is the custom. I wondered what had happened to the other six, the ugly ones.

Then he pointed to the floor below the table. There, outlined in cowrie shells in the beaten clay, was a human figure.

"My father," he said.

This, too, is the custom. Men are buried in the floors of their houses. And here we were, drinking our last bottle of beer with our feet resting on the body of a recently departed king, the late Oba of Abayo.

God save the king.

14

● THE LAST THINGS we saw at Benin were the brass foundry and the wood carvers' shop. The smiths had suffered great deterioration. Their art, once supported by the king and nobles, is in decline and their only outlet today is the tourist trade in Lagos, which is in no way a tourist centre. Men can make more on the cocoa farms than they can by producing brass masks and figures, and the work that is done now in no way compares with that of the past. The process — the *cire perdue* method — has almost certainly come from Ife. In fact it is believed that men from Benin were sent there to learn their trade. The lost wax process consists of modelling, somewhat roughly, the object in fine clay and covering it with layers of wax which is carefully worked in great detail. A thick layer of fireproof clay is now put over the model and it is baked. The wax is melted out and replaced by molten brass or bronze. The making of a mask or plaque is relatively simple, but how the complex figures of horsemen with lances, chiefs and kings complete with their ornate crowns, jewellery, umbrellas and weapons, were ever cast by this process in these primitive conditions is much harder to understand and represents a very high standard both of art and technical skill. Most of the objects they made were connected with ancestor worship, religion, and joined the carved tusks and other ornaments on the family altars of the rich. Bells, and plaques depicting historical scenes were also made and worn on the breasts of notables. (The ancient Egyptians are depicted wearing similar decorations.) In fact history was recorded in bronze, writing being unknown. Here at least was something that the termites could not destroy.

The Ife heads were pierced by small holes, possibly for fixing real hair or skin. Heads so decorated have been found at Ikom. One wonders what skin was used.

Leaving the brass foundry, we visited the house of the senior smith, who showed us some really old things. One was a magnificent bronze leopard head, in which the black spots were represented by small raised whorls. The expression of the face was perfect in its savagery.

Right through Africa one finds this leopard theme. Leopard ornaments, leopard stools, the use of leopard skins and tails by chiefs, necklaces of leopard fangs and finally, the terrible secret society of the Human Leopard Men with their murderous insignia. The leopard is a giant forest cat — a man killer and a perpetual menace, and fear may have been blended with respect through the sacred cat legend coming from Egypt in some vestigial form.

The wood carvers were much less degenerate than the brass workers. They followed the old tradition, copying ancient works and producing heads, torsos and panels, representing allegorical scenes, with the greatest skill. Their work is more salable than that of the brass workers, cheaper to produce and more suitable to the décor of modern apartments where African sculpture seems to fit in without difficulty. It has export possibilities.

Tiny, to whom one of the men appeared to have taken a fancy, was given two small ebony fish for which payment was refused.

At the airport, not only was our baggage weighed, but we were weighed as well. And then began a curious procession of Africans carrying rocks from a heap outside the waiting room to the scales, where they were solemnly weighed as if they were groceries. A big one was taken off and replaced by two smaller ones and eventually, when the pilot was satisfied — he was a big man, redhaired, with a splendid fiery beard — they were carried off and put into the tiny vest pocket plane that sat looking very lonely on the airfield. They — the rocks and our luggage and ourselves — were now equalised in some way and the plane properly balanced and ready for flight.

We followed the rocks and took off.

At Port Harcourt we were met by Mr. Charles Crowsdale, the district officer, in a fancy blue convertible Jansen. We found that he was full of information, having passed twenty-five years in the country. He told us of how when crossing the desert he had found the bones of two camels that had died of thirst beside a small well. They must have been lost and returned to the water that they knew. But there was no one there to draw it for them. An African drama. I saw them watching — waiting for the men who never came.

He told us that the desert salt, on sale in the native markets, is twenty times as expensive as the European because "it gives strength to men, women and camels, enabling them to have children." This seems more than possible as it would contain minerals and trace elements that are removed from our salt in the process of purification.

Nor are chemicals added to it to prevent it caking in the damp. We pay a high price for purity which seems to be confused with whiteness. The idea of white salt, sugar and bread is somehow mixed up with white lilies, white satin and virgins in our conditioned minds. This was, in fact, the device used to drive brown sugar off the market. Brown was dirty, white was pure. I was once told that fourteen minerals are removed in the process of refining sugar.

Crowsdale told us about a diamond-smuggling affair in which a policeman, who had been to South Africa on leave, was asked as a great favour to bring back a wedding cake on his ship for the daughter of a Syrian trader. Too many wedding cakes had been coming into the country, so this one was opened and several stolen stones were found. The policeman was quite innocent and had only done it to oblige.

I was told of another Benin custom — the slaves to be sacrificed had their lips pierced and padlocked to prevent them eating before the ceremony.

Our host had an amusing custom of whistling for his boys. He had a different whistle for each of them, and they replied by whistle, like courting birds. Tiny picked up the trick and began calling them in this manner, which amused them but did not please our host. She said, very rightly, that if the boys liked being whistled at, it seemed rude to call: "Boy!" This whistling is apparently an Ibo custom — one of the pleasanter ones.

We met two Swedes, Lars Ottoson and Bengt Lindstrom, who were touring Africa — "Cape North to Cape Town" was their slogan — by Volkswagen. They gave a lecture to a number of Africans at the invitation of the British Council, which we attended. At the end the African representatives asked if they would like to see some Ibo dances. When the performance was over they were told that they would have to dash the dancers seventeen guineas. Which I believe they eventually did, though why they did not reply that their fee for a lecture was twenty guineas and ask for the two pounds three shillings balance owing to them, I do not know.

That evening we were with the Swedes when an African newspaper man came to interview them. He was a West African intellectual of the worst kind. Brash, insolent, lolling in his chair and spilling the ash from his cigarette on the floor. When he started to write, he found his pen had no ink in it. So ink was fetched. It was very African. He had brought everything except the one essential necessary for an interview.

He asked the Swedes what countries they had come through.

They said: "Sweden, Denmark, France . . ."

"No, no," said the journalist. "I mean what countries in Africa? That is all that interests us."

This took me back to the University College of Ibadan where there was quite a large bookshop. I asked what books were sold? What novels? What biographies? And I was told nothing was sold that was not about Africa. They wanted only to read about themselves.

When our journalist had this information — the Swedes had come through Morocco, Algeria and French West Africa, as he must have known — he gave us a lecture. Nigeria must be industrialised at once. It would then be free of the British. What was to be industrialised or by whom, or where the money was to come from, he did not say. Then he said why had the British, who had been here for hundreds of years, done nothing about the naked pagans on the plateau? It was a disgrace. They should be forced to wear clothes. This would certainly be part of the programme when Nigeria got her freedom. What must foreigners and tourists think? They always took pictures of them. It was disgusting.

I suggested that if he was interested in the impression Nigeria gave to the outer world, it might be better to stop African gentlemen from urinating opposite the Kingsway Stores (the Saks Fifth Avenue of Lagos) on the Marina while they looked in at the windows.

But educated Africans are very touchy about the nakedness of their fellows. They do not like pictures to be taken of naked tribesmen. They do not even like Europeans taking off their shirts and playing tennis or working in their gardens stripped to the waist. They think it is done out of contempt for the African.

It is difficult for most people to understand that this line of thought, in which pride, envy and contempt are blended, is of the greatest importance in the African mental approach. Gold Coasters and West Indian Negroes have a contempt for the less educated Nigerians. The coastal Nigerians despise those of the interior. The Moslems of the interior despise the coastal boys. Every grade and category and race appears to be infected with notions of superiority towards someone, and hatred, due to inferiority, towards someone else. The best thing is to be educated. The next best thing is to appear to be educated.

We now met Tessa Conroy and her husband. She ran the Catering Rest House and Captain Conroy was in charge of the prison. He told me about one of his warders who had had to be transferred because he was known to be a slave. Of course there is technically no slavery in Nigeria now. But if a man knows he is a slave, that is to say comes of a slave family, and if everyone else knows it, it is no good telling him he is not a slave. As a slave, the warder had no authority, so he had to be moved to a place where he was not known.

Prison is no disgrace here. Quite the contrary in fact, since a prisoner is better off as a rule than he would be as a free man. He has better food, better quarters, plenty of congenial companionship and the chance to learn a trade. The best tailor in Jos, I was told, had a notice over his shop: "Trained in His Majesty's Prison, Port Harcourt." And for a political career, a prison sentence is almost essential, as a proof of good faith and genuine patriotic anti-British feeling.

The prison was beautifully kept and had the finest and biggest cannas I have ever seen. They were of all colours, over six feet high, with blooms the size of my open hand. I mentioned this and found that they had been planted on top of a three-foot layer of night soil. Some gardeners have all the luck.

The prisoners were occupied in various ways. First offenders worked in the carpenter's shop. Well-behaved long-termers worked in the shoemaker's and tailor's shops. These were the aristocrats of crime. It was here in the tailor's shop that I came across Nafor Orizu again. The case had been tried while we were in Nigeria, which was a curious coincidence, as the last time I had seen this gentleman was at a cocktail party on Park Avenue, where he was being fêted as a Nigerian prince. I had met him several times. He even gave me a copy of a book he had written about the West Coast. His thesis was that his people were too happy and contented to achieve much. He was a little upset when I said: "Then why not leave them alone?"

That was ten years ago and he and his kind have succeeded in stirring up a lot of trouble since then. I told his social sponsors that I questioned his royal lineage, and I learnt from the Chief Secretary at Lagos that in the end pictures of his palace had been sent to Washington, which had made enquiries about him. It was, of course, the usual small swish (mud) hut with a corrugated iron roof.

His crime was, to me, one of the most despicable and yet one of the commonest among educated Africans — the exploitation of their own people's desire for education.

The newspaper said:

Dr. Abyssinia Akweke Nafor Orizu was a well known American trained politician and educator, one of the right hand men of Dr. N'Mande Azikiwe — the founder of the National Council for

Nigeria (the Ibo party) and president and founder of the American Council on African Education. He was found guilty of conspiracy to defraud, and of stealing on five counts . . .

The judge, Mr. Stephen Thomas, said that no less than £32,000 was collected from the public. He went on to say: "This has been a terrible trial. Here is a man in whom we had great hopes, one who is known to all the world."

Orizu's method was to promise to obtain scholarships for African students in the United States on the receipt of fees from the boys' parents. The fees were large and, when nothing happened, the complainants were staved off by one means or another until finally the matter was brought to light by the Owa Improvement Union for education in America, who wanted to know what had become of the £400 they had deposited for the training of their representative.

Of all the money collected, only £1000 was shown on the books as petty cash used for stamps and cables, which seemed excessive since there were no tangible results. This is a typical example of the kind of crime perpetrated by the educated African, this time on a grand scale, where the educated use their prestige and knowledge to prey on their simple minded fellows.

Working with Orizu, in the tailor's shop, were the members of the Human Leopard Society who had had their death sentences remitted after the famous trials of this society a few years ago.

Between 1945 and 1948, one hundred and ninety-six men, women and children were known to be murdered by the Leopard Men in a single area. Probably, the actual figure is much greater than this. They occurred in forest country where there were good roads, missions, schools, churches and native courts. There were numbers of leopards in the district. The people were poor but did not suffer from shortages of food. The villages consisted of separate compounds, two or three hundred yards apart. There were no chiefs. The government was by elders and headmen. (This forest country, the government by elders and the scattered dwellings, resembles the Kikuyu way of life and has a psychological bearing on these types of crime and secret societies.)

The primary cause of these murders was the corruption of the Native Authority courts and presents a preview of what will almost certainly occur when the British withdraw from the country. Failing to get justice, the Africans revert to their ancient methods of murder, employing professional assassins through the agency of witch doctors and diviners, who profit from the deaths.

The Idiong Society, whose original function had been to mete out arbitrary justice to evildoers — having them executed or sold into slavery — was revived, if indeed it had ever died completely, with its subsociety — the Ekpe Leopards — who carried out its orders.

When the British took over, seven hundred and fifty Idiong shrines with their regalia and apparatus were destroyed. They included the famous doll ju-ju, on which mass oaths could be taken, which would bring death if it were broken. It was held against the back, head and chest during the ceremony and those were the parts that were affected.

The Leopard Men killed to obtain charms for subsequent murders, and for parts of the human body that they could sell to priests of various ju-ju cults. They simulated a leopard by their dress and the mutilation of their victim's body to give colour to the popular belief in lycanthropy.

Any man wanting to commit a murder was initiated into the society and inoculated with the leopard charm, which would enable him to turn into a leopard whenever he wished. He then went to a diviner who told him who was responsible for his troubles. Next came the local ju-ju man who told him that in order to make the medicine he needed, he must have, as an ingredient, the skull of someone of whom he was very fond. To obtain these materials, one prisoner confessed to having killed his sister. For this medicament he paid the doctor a hundred manillas, a cock and a bottle of gin and, in addition "a dog to be sacrificed to your god before you can do this thing." He now went back to the diviner who told him where and when to perform the murder, and whose payment, among other things, was certain parts of the victim's body, which would increase his ju-ju's power of attracting people to his oracle.

The would-be assassin was now quite fearless as he was immune, even in front of witnesses. He was told what weapons to take. A matchet, a small knife, a club and an iron spike of the kind often employed as a roasting spit, were used to inflict the injuries. The possession of these articles was in no way incriminating since all were normal household utensils. And finally he was instructed to wear a headdress of ferns about his head when he did the killing.

The witnesses — there were witnesses on some occasions — said they had never seen a man. They had seen a leopard, or a *thing on two legs* and then they had run away to call for help. Even if they knew the murderer they would not say so, not merely because of their fear of reprisals, but because, to the African, a man becomes the thing he says he is, even if he isn't, by an act of faith. They can, for instance, know a sorcerer quite well, but as soon as he puts on his regalia — his mask, his raffia suit or his feather headdress — he becomes, by this act, something else — the terrible spirit of the forest, or the river or, as in these cases, a genuine man-killing leopard.

The assassin has a very good idea of the path his victim will take — having been told by the diviner who has informed himself as to his habits. He blows medicine into the air, calling the name of the person he wants to attract. He has with him a padlock and key to lock up his voice so that he cannot cry out, and an edible leaf, a koko yam, some fruit and manillas — which he puts on the path. These are the bait which will attract the victim. And when he comes he falls upon him.

These killers are really as much the victims of the ju-ju men as are the murdered people. The whole business has been built up for profit. (The victims are not selected at random. The societies and doctors are always on the lookout for people who have a grudge against each other, and offer them every assistance on the understanding that sacrifice will be made, and parts of the body given to them. They even have agents who report all quarrels to them.)

The regalia of the true Leopard Men consists of a crown of plaited fibres, a raffia mask and a complete leopard skin so fashioned that the mask comes over the head. Iron claws are sometimes made of a poker-like rod — a sort of trident whose prongs are bent into sharp hooks — or sharp steel spikes easily concealed in a hollow cane are used. Artificial leopard pads carved out of wood are worn on the feet. A modern innovation is the use of cloth (now quite fashionable in America) printed with a spotted leopard-skin design. One uniform, complete with trousers made of this material, was found when the last leopard shrines were destroyed. But the men who wear the full regalia are charter members of the society — professional killers, and not simply men who want justice or revenge.

The mutilations of the examined bodies were peculiar. Here are some medical details that were typical:

1. Removal of tongue and neck tissues, cervical vertebrae and tissues of face and skull (eyeballs intact).

2. Severing of both arms, complete or partial stripping of arm tissues.

3. Arm removed with large portion of throat and thorax so as to expose internal organs of chest.

4. Removal of heart and lungs.

5. A few punctured wounds in chest and back.

There was, in many cases, only a symbolic attempt to develop the leopard motif. But with Africans the symbol was enough. Bodies, for instance, were discovered in which the leopard had removed singlets and shorts without tearing them, or had wrapped the head of the victim in her loincloth, and extracted manillas from raffia bags. Human footprints were left near the body. Leopard hairs were found in one case which proved, under microscopic examination, to be completely dry and to have come from an old skin. The scratch wounds were symmetrical and did not come together as those of a leopard do at the end of the stroke, nor were the bodies eviscerated as is usual when the killing is done by a wild beast.

It was later found that pieces of flesh — the left arm, heart, intestines, facial skin and skin of the skull — had been sold for medicine in a nearby town for eighty manillas. The left hand fetched twenty manillas, the skin of the face and skull fifteen manillas, the heart twenty manillas.

The motives for some of these murders were as follows: Revenge, 19. Jealousy, 17. Dowry dispute, 16. Land dispute, 9. Debt, 6. Dispute over succession of property and ownership of children, 6. Refusal to allow sexual intimacy, 4. Dispute over property, 4. Society dispute, 2. To conceal another murder, 1. Various unknown causes.

These crimes were of particular interest to me because of the Mau Mau atrocities in Kenya which had some procedures in common with them, such as the strong binding oath, the intimidation of witnesses, and the use of parts of the body for medicine. They also fitted into the ritual murder pattern of the Basutoland Protectorate in the south, which are, in fact, less ritual than medicine killings, the victims being bled and dismembered alive to obtain protective medicines required by the witch doctors for their ceremonies. The object is not the death of the victim (which is incidental) but possession of his organs whose extraction causes the death.

In South Africa similar murders occur in Swaziland and Zululand. So the continuity is complete from West Africa through the Congo to East Africa, and down the coast to within a few hundred miles of Capetown.

It must be remembered that among Africans there is a very strong belief in the medicines which the witch doctors prepare from all kinds of materia medica — animal, vegetable and mineral — ingredients whose effects are as much psychological as physiological. Modern psychosomatic medicine takes a similar line of approach and the miraculous cures of faith healers all point in the same direction — to the power of the mind, of faith, over matter.

The basis of all these cures, and for that matter, deaths (by suggestion) in the case of the African who has been bewitched, is faith. It is immaterial, philosophically speaking, whether the patient believes in a sacred relic or an empty gin bottle which he has been told contains a strong but invisible ju-ju, so long as he believes it utterly. It remains faith, and it is this fact which the European, unacquainted with Africa, finds so hard to grasp. The African distinguishes clearly between good white and bad black, medicine and magic. That is to say between those means which are employed to harm specific persons, and those medicines or formulas which benefit society or an individual.

Since the African still tends to think tribally, he is quite prepared to have a member of the tribe sacrificed to make a good strong medicine. What does one life matter if it is a question of the failure of the yam crop, or if the fish expected in a certain month have not arrived? Such a disaster threatens the existence of the tribe. Nor can he understand the European feeling about murder, particularly that of a stranger. Many tribes take theft much more seriously. All that is necessary in a case of murder is to compensate the family in cattle, goats, hoes or spears for their loss.

Blood in all its form has great mystic importance to the African. A drop of woman's menstrual blood is sufficient to bring death to cattle in a kraal among some peoples, and is an ingredient in special medicines among others, such as the Kikuyu who employ it in the Mau Mau oath-taking ceremonies. The blood of sacrifice, that of cocks, goats, rams, horses and bulls, is universally demanded by the gods and it is only logical to assume that the flesh and blood of man, the highest animal, must be even more powerful and effective.

In the old days there were plenty of dead enemies from whom medicine could be made, and prisoners or slaves who could be sacrificed. But today, since this no longer is the case, some member of the tribe or a passing stranger is seized and killed.

Now for the reason that these murders are not reported. First, there is the solidarity of the tribe whose members all believe that it was necessary for the fertilisation of the crops, or to bring rain, or victory or peace. (In Kenya the Mau Mau attribute the forced evacuation by the Government of several farms to be due to their ritual burying alive of Mr. Leakey.) Secondly, comes the fear of retaliation of some kind, even the possibility that they will be sacrificed themselves by the murderers, which is a great deterrent. Thirdly, that there exists among all Africans two points of view about any act. The official and the private. An incident may have happened. People may have seen it happen. But if the official version is that it did not happen, then it did not happen.

And fourthly, the witnesses may have been given medicines designed to remove all memory of the deed they have witnessed. Medicine which enables them to work themselves into a state where they genuinely believe that they know nothing of the matter — a combination of a drug, hypnosis and faith functioning again. And finally there remains a general lack of interest in the whole matter. The danger of drought, of crop failure has now passed. A victim has been sacrificed. The witch doctor has his medicine. It is obviously good that one's own witch doctor should have a store of such a powerful remedy, and bad that he should ever run out of it. The feeling would be the same with us if our doctor had run out of penicillin.

In principle, the good and bad elements of witchcraft are always at war with each other. A comparison might be the churches' attack on the witches of Europe in the Middle Ages. The churches' magic was white. The witches' black. The good witch doctor, by a process of divination, seeks to destroy the evil ones, the sorcerers who cast spells and do harm, bringing sickness to men, death to cattle or barrenness to women by means of the evil eye. This accounts for the great smelling-out ceremonies of such tribes as the Zulus.

The good witch doctor, festooned with entrails, dripping with snakeskins, skulls, tortoise shells and ostrich eggs — all the tools of his trade — was easily recognisable, like our local parson or doctor. But the wicked sorcerer or witch was much harder to find. He worked under cover. He might be anyone. That is why the good witch doctors were so important. Only they could smell them out.

There is no doubt that these doctors can sometimes effect cures that are inexplicable to Europeans and have herbal knowledge that is unknown to us. But the white administration everywhere has attacked the whole witch doctor system and the good have been eliminated, that is to say driven underground, with the bad. Of course the good, who practised openly, were much easier to destroy.

A great deal has been lost by this ill-considered action. Fear of the ju-ju man kept the criminals indoors after dark. Kept the women faithful, protected the crops and disciplined the children.

Ju-ju, voodoo and obeah seem to be an essential part of the African's psyche, though naturally there are hundreds of thousands of true Christians who have broken away from all such things. Yet I believe that few would defy a ju-ju priest, and still fewer have no friends or relations who do not belong to one cult or another.

Brutal and inhuman as it seems to us, there was in Africa a certain necessity for these wise men. They were not only the doctors and the policemen, they were also the explainers of phenomena. And to the African, everything that is not normal is due to magic and requires explanation. A man can only die of old age, be killed in war, or by smallpox or starvation. Any other form of death is due to witchcraft. If a hunter is killed by a bush cow or a woman taken by a crocodile as she draws water, someone has sent them to do this evil deed. If a woman is barren, a child sick, someone is to blame. And only the witch doctor can say who it is. If things are stolen the witch doctor will discover the thief. If illness or an epidemic comes upon them, he will cure them by placating the gods whom he alone understands. But behind all this there is some curious knowledge, of which Pierre Ryckmans, an ex-Governor of the Congo, in his book *Dominer pour Servir*, gives a wonderful example. He tells of a dance during which seventeen people were killed by order of the witch doctor. There had been a number of deaths in the village. What we would call an epidemic had struck a forest community. Someone was guilty. The witch doctor must discover the culprit.

He organises a dance. Great fires are lit. Much pombé (banana wine) is brewed. The witch doctor puts on his regalia, paints his body with white zebra stripes and put on his mask. The dancers are told to bring clubs.

The dance begins. Sweat rolls off the performers. One begins to falter. The witch doctor points a finger. He is clubbed to death. The dance continues. More weaken and are killed, irrespective of their sex. At last the dawn breaks. It is over. Seventeen lie dead, murdered according to our views. But actually there is the possibility that those who were killed were already infected by the disease, that they would have infected others and that their deaths arrested its progress. The dance was a prophylactic measure, the excessive drinking and the exertion eliminating the weakest, the carriers of disease, and sweating it out of the others.

The witch doctor was hanged on the scene of the crime. Justice

was done but it is doubtful if the Africans saw it quite that way since no more people died.

The African has no knowledge of cause and effect. He knows a poison will kill him but he does not know how or why. Kill him whether it is sprinkled on the floor of his hut, concealed in the shell of a forest snail in his thatch or drunk in his beer. He sees no reason for swallowing medicine. It will work just as well if he rubs his body with it. It is good medicine and its application in any way is therefore good, just as a bad medicine is bad in every way.

In the prison the recidivists made bricks or wove cocoanut matting and doormats. The husks were rotted in tanks, then the fibre was stripped from them and twisted into long strings that were wound into balls. I got a glimpse of half a dozen men condemned to death. They were a savage-looking lot, dressed in blue and wearing heavy leg shackles. The shortage of warders made this a necessary precaution. I did not see the women's section of the prison as they are much harder to control. Among them were two child murderesses. Both had killed out of jealousy the children of another of their husband's wives. A favourite method of murder, I was told, is the "Ihalla murder" that was once peculiar to the Owerri but is now relatively common, where the victim is killed by a big nail being driven into the forehead between the eyes.

As well as a thousand prisoners there were twenty lepers and three hundred lunatics, who were not criminals, in Port Harcourt jail. But Captain Conroy, by kind treatment and giving them tobacco and teaching them handicrafts, had got all but the worst cases leading relatively happy lives. They all clapped their hands and leapt and shouted when they saw him.

There were two hundred and fifty literates in prison, of whom fifty were well educated. They included one senior station master, two members of the House of Representatives, one B.S.C. Ceramics Oxon., one doctor of literature, Columbia (my friend Orizu), and five rich businessmen. There were two white men in the prison — one for embezzlement and one for forging gun powder certificates.

I picked up some other oddments of information. There were six thousand known prostitutes in Port Harcourt for a population of fifty-eight thousand. Albinos were not liked and the men were generally pimps meeting the ships and leading the sailors to the brothels in the slums. Their colour simplified their approach and they had no difficulty in dealing with seamen who might have shied away from a Negro.

One sees no old albinos and it is my belief that until recently, say thirty or so years ago, they were killed at birth, though this was denied.

A curious thing about albinos is that no matter where one sees them in Africa, whether in South Africa, Nigeria, the Gold Coast or the Congo, they all resemble each other very closely. Tribal differences seem to be ironed out.

I was told that prostitution increased enormously round Christmastime when the women wanted to buy themselves new clothes.

Sex, particularly where they have been circumcised, means very little to many African women, since the instrument of sexual pleasure has been removed by the operation. Some anthropologists believe that this is the cause of the operation — an effort to restrain their lubricity.

It would certainly appear that the women are very demanding. I saw an essay by a young man on the subject of "Family Life." He described it as a "load on his head with women, insatiable creatures, giving him much work in the night."

But there is the possibility that the male African is neither highly sexed nor quickly aroused. And that erotic dances by the women are required to excite him. Crawley, in his *Studies of Savages and Sex*, says the sexuality of their festivals "indicates rather the contrary, and demonstrates the need of artificial excitement." Richard Burton the explorer, who had considerable medical knowledge, writing about the sex life in damp jungles says the "sexual requirements of the passive sex exceed those of the active."

I discussed prison reforms with Captain Conroy who was most interested in rehabilitation. He thought that criminals should be given the choice of prison, or labour camps where they would receive pay and could do useful work. We agreed that quite obviously prison was no place for lunatics and he said he had the feeling that a slave was often substituted for a real murderer, if he was important. He would accept his fate in silence. What choice had he? He would be killed anyway. And no one else would talk.

He said all hangings should be carried out reasonably quickly and that someone from the village should witness it. The Africans still have an impression that the condemned prisoners are sold as slaves by the British.

We talked of other things. The Hausa guards and warders had to be paid in silver shillings. They would not accept paper money. To pay out fifteen hundred pounds in this way took a long time. He told me how many Africans dye their hair with a mixture of steeped cocoanut fibre and shoe black. Age is respected, but on the other hand white hair would indicate lack of virility. Time has no value to the African.

Age is dealt with very approximately. Few men know when they were born. They say: "The year of the yam failure, or the year the soldiers went to war." Historical time here seems to begin with the big queen — Victoria.

In spite of their cry for freedom, most natives do not trust one another and do not want to see the white man go. They want him to go in principle, as it were. But most want to keep just one white man — the local district officer, or someone else who takes care of them, and with whom they can leave money if they go on a journey. This cuts both ways right through Africa. Even white men who do not like natives make exceptions. Most of them like one black man. Perhaps race relations may eventually be established by means of these exceptions.

Not once, but several times, I heard from Africans that if the white man went it would not be long before the blacks were "chopping" each other. And this was certainly confirmed by a very senior official who said: "If we go, there will be civil war at once — not one civil war but ten or a dozen." And here again is a pattern that I think is common to the continent.

15

The Palm Oil Ruffians...Port Harcourt...Calabar

● MR. R. H. AMBLER took us over the tropical testing station at Port Harcourt. First we saw the laboratories in the town, where he had a complex sea of apparatus, very efficiently but economically housed in buildings that were no more than big sheds. Here every sort of material, from pieces of felt to a complete camera, is being artificially deteriorated under various combinations of controlled heat and moisture. The place was a mass of intricate gauges — thermometers, barometers, furnace and refrigeration units, and so on, which improved on God's job of climate creation. Machinery was being taken apart to see what the climate had done to it after specified tests. I was told there were other controls: one on the beach at Lagos — this is supposed to be the ultimate nadir of the deterioration curve — and another in the desert North of Kano to test the effect of wind-driven sand and dust erosion, combined with that of the burning heat in those parts. This is an outfit dedicated to constructive destruction.

Then we drove about twenty miles in the drizzle to their outdoor plant in the jungle. This was fascinating — a series of barbed-wire-fenced and Askari-guarded compounds in the thick dripping forest where the subjects of the tests were exposed to the worst that the tropical jungle had to offer. It appears that the climate of Malaya or the East Indies cannot exceed the local forests' power of destruction.

Wearing macks and borrowed gumboots we wandered along little paths that ran with water through tunnels of strange moss-covered tree trunks — some were blotched and patterned like python skin, others were caught in the twisted coils of lianas that throttled them like snakes, none were normal, sensible trees. It was an arboreal nightmare. Big arum-shaped leaves, apparently made of thick green patent leather, brushed our legs, sometimes even reaching to my waist and Tiny's shoulders. Mr. Ambler said that if it had been the rainy season we would have been covered with leeches. An intriguing thought.

Here were the test stands — frames on which tissues and materials were exposed to the wicked elements. There were sheets of metal being tested for corrosion, a whole series of wooden plaques covered with various kinds of paint to see which stood up best. One type of material was the kind of hard, thin felt that is used in making bowler hats. I did not see why the London hatters should want to know how long a bowler hat would stand up to West African conditions without shelter. Perhaps it was only idle curiosity. There were aero engines, ammunition dumps, containers for gasoline, half sunk in the humus, almost buried like corpses in the newly fallen leaves. Every month or so they were examined.

There were some beautiful moulds growing in the laboratory. Some were grey, shading into various tones of rose and shell-pink. I was told that they were all mutations of the same variety. Like white man and black, I thought. The same but different. And that's about what we really were — moulds on the living green surface of the earth. Actually, I supposed, in volume these moulds were very much larger as individuals on the surface of the moist cloth that was their home than we were on the surface of the earth. Such thoughts always comfort me when I begin to worry about my importance as a person, or that of the human race as a species. We are only important to ourselves and while we live.

We left in the rain the next morning and were met at Calabar by Mr. David Smith, the senior district officer and acting resident, who put us up. This is one of the embarrassments of travelling in countries where there are no hotels. It is all very well to say that people are only too glad to have you because they see so few strangers, especially people who are not official, but on the other hand their salaries are not enormous and the cost is at least a pound a day per person and probably, with even moderate drinkers like ourselves, comes to nearer two pounds. There is some truth in their liking to see people. I felt like that when I was ranching. But the visitors I had were either friends or had been recommended by friends — passed on as is the English custom — whereas we were strangers whom the Information Service or Public Relations officers foisted onto people.

Among the other officials we met was Mr. James, whose house had a ghost — that of Sir Roger Casement, an early British consul. The children had seen it several times. Casement was a remarkable Irishman who, in 1903, was commissioned by the British Government to investigate and expose the horrors of the Belgian rubber traffic in the Congo, and in 1916 was hanged for planning an insurrection against

Britain with German invaders during the First World War.

Calabar was another highlight in my life — one of those places whose names had always fascinated me — Calabar, Zanzibar, Manila, Malacca, Havana, Nassau, Timbuctoo, Martinique, Sarawak, Zimbabwe. Why are certain names so attractive, and so charged with romance or horror? Certainly there was no disappointment here. The Residency was a beautiful Victorian house which had been brought out in sections a hundred years ago, long before the term "pre-fab" existed. It was a museum piece inside and out and had been the residence of governors of Southern Nigeria, before the North was conquered. The dining room had the biggest punkah in Africa — an immense affair of white canvas which had been painted so many times that it had the consistency of steel. The walls were painted brown for three feet, and then cream. The ceiling was white matchboard decorated with a border of rosettes. The doors and stair rail were mahogany. There were the skins of big dark forest leopards, with leather braided edges, on some of the chairs, and magnificently carved native stools. One was supported by naked figures, male and female alternately. Another had a border of sexual organs, both male and female, in deep relief and another had the usual leopard motif. All the polished fittings were solid brass, the carpets were of muted colours worn by many feet. Our room was enormous with a colossal bath in the dressing room that communicated with it. The pictures were in keeping — a cavalry charge with a "Floreat Etona" caption.

Below us was the compound with its lawn of swamp grass, flowering shrubs and trees, and beyond that the Cross River and Duke Town. This was one of the great slaving centres of West Africa. Hundreds of thousands of captives must have been shipped down this wide, sullen water. The Bonny River, the Cross, Old Calabar, Opobo — the names from all the books I had read came back to me. The slave ships had lain out there waiting for their human cargoes, having brought gin and guns, powder balls and brandy. In 1833 human skulls were used for steps to the houses in Calabar, or lay about in the streets with other rubbish. White men found human joints being smoked in huts, the fat as it dropped into the fire causing little spurts of flame. They found old men grinding skulls to powder and licking their fingers as if it were sugar.

The Calabari had some interesting tortures — ear cutting, crucifixion round a large cask, the extraction of teeth, chili peppers pounded up and forced into the nostrils, eyes, ears and anus. For a change they sometimes tied men to posts at low tide for the sharks and crocodiles, or chained them to stakes without shade or covering and so little food that their shackles fell off, or impaled them slowly on iron rods continuing till the point came out through the skull.

They honoured their dead chiefs by interring their wives and slaves alive with them, first breaking their arms and legs with hammers. When the Hope Waddell Mission, which still exists though on a new site, was first established on the hill overlooking the river, that we could see out of our window, they found it the haunt of leopards and full of bodies in all stages of decomposition. As they worked at building, more bodies slung on poles, carried by two bearers, kept being brought and dumped in the bushes beside them. Only gentlemen, house slaves, or those who would be required by their masters in the next world were buried, but these had to be specially killed for the purpose.

Apart from slaves the ships came to the Bight of Benin for gold dust and nuggets, elephants' teeth, parrots, monkeys, beeswax, dry and green hides from the North, gum arabic, ostrich feathers, ambergris, cods of musk, tiger teeth, teeth of seahorses, santalum wood, crystal, long peppers, manequette pepper, rice, cotton cloth, blue stones and jasper, Benin cloth, mahogany and palm oil.

In exchange the Africans wanted iron bars, red, blue and scarlet cloth, silver and brass rings, Dutch pointed knives, steels to strike fire, calicoes, cowrie shells, red worsted caps, Dutch cutlasses straight or bowed, beads, musket balls, looking glasses, cloves and cinnamon, thread, Dutch mugs, round padlocks, shirts with bone lace at the neck and sleeves, brass trumpets, shoes, brass kettles, white sugar, red cords, tallow, empty chests and Leyden rugs.

The rate of exchange was worked out in a complex manner. A slave was worth from twelve to twenty bars, and a bar plus a cutlass was worth eight hides.

It is of a certain interest that nothing really useful was ever asked for by the natives. No carpenters' tools, no wheelbarrows or agricultural implements or building tools. What they wanted were weapons to capture more slaves, decorations for themselves and their women, and condiments and liquor for their feasts.

The coast was deserted between December and March when the "smokes" or mists smothered the river, the traders believing them to be unhealthy. This was the dry season, when the harmattan blew from the deserts of the North, and rivers and marshes gave up their water to the sun.

The ships, once they reached the rivers, unstepped their masts, rigged up roofs of native mats, mounted swivel guns to repel attacks, and converted their holds for slaves while they did their trading. It had been found, by trial and error, that living in this way right out on the water there was less malaria, although they did not know then that it was carried by mosquitoes, since there were many less away from the heavy foliage of the shore. Later, when slavery was abolished, the palm oil traders known as "palm oil ruffians" (many of whom were ex-slavers) developed this custom into the permanently anchored and roofed houseboats called hulks which, slowly, as things became more orderly, came nearer and nearer to the shore, finally tying up on the beach. The cables were replaced by gangways which were superseded by wood and iron sheds that linked the ground with the water, and some of these half-ship-half-shed edifices, named after the hulks that once lay in midstream, such as *Matilda House*, still exist in their original berths. Ashore they had had their factories, so called because they were looked after by a factor, and if there were slaves there were the slave sheds or barracoons in which they were kept. Now the whole concern was merged into one large trading store.

The traders who lived the longest were those who ate native food such as palm oil and groundnut chop, with rice and peppers. These foods are said to contain protective vitamins but even so, few men survived long on the coast when the effects of malaria, black water and yellow jack were offset by square-face gin and black girls.

The Residency section was on a hill — Calabar is built on a series of hills — overlooking the river and town, with the beach and trading section along the bank. Big ships with a draft of up to twenty feet can tie up, deliver cargo and load bulk oil, for which the holds must be heated so that it does not solidify when it reaches the colder latitudes of European waters.

This is a change from the old hulks that used to lie waiting to imbibe the rancid orange palm oil delivered in puncheons by canoe. But the picture remains in one's mind. Looking out over the river one can imagine the ceremonial visit of a black king, his being rowed out in his six-oared gig with his official striped umbrella held over his head, wearing a silk cloth that reached to his feet and a white beaver hat. With him would be two attendants carrying his pistols, sword and gold snuffbox. On either side of the gig come two war canoes, each with twenty-eight armed paddlers. King Eyamba called himself "the king of all the black men." He had an iron palace which is still standing, a two-storey affair built on a wooden frame and sent out in sections from Liverpool. Its outhouses and sheds were filled with trade goods of every kind; courtyards were piled with things — mahogany chests of drawers, bales of Manchester cloth, hogsheads of tobacco. The main room contained a live peacock that screamed and strutted in from the yard where Muscovy ducks, bare-necked Portuguese chickens and vultures picked about in the offal. Large mirrors with gilt frames lined the walls. Under a velvet canopy there was a brass throne. Guns leaned against the walls. Half naked warriors stood on guard, and, wearing little more than their bangles, slave girls drifted in and out. At a feast specially fattened girls brought in great dishes of palm oil chop on their heads. Brandy and gin was drunk in unbelievable quantities.

Palm thatched huts were built along irregular streets that were all but impassable owing to the mud, heaps of rubbish and rottenness in which the vultures scavenged. Drunkards, black and white, rolled in the gutters dug by the torrential rains. Naked children, fat and sleek as seals, played on the doorsteps made of human skulls. Everything was dark — the people, the rich soil, the sepia and dull red mud plastered walls, the ancient thatch lit only by the livid green of the banana leaves, the flowers of the tropical trees that grew in the compounds, and the brilliant cloths — scarlet, purple, blue, magenta, yellow and orange — worn by the richer men. Over everything was the miasma of the river. The stink, almost palpable, of putrescence that covered everything with a blanket of the mixed odours — rotting vegetables, fruits, fish, putrid meat, excrement, urine, wood smoke, sweat and the dirt of a hundred years trodden into the bloodstained mud. It all rose into the hot humid air and hung there.

The king had a four-wheeled carriage which was borne on the shoulders of slaves when he went abroad and which, for some reason, possibly because a horse was called a white man's cow, was known as "the white man's cow house."

This was a terrible world, the more so because it was not entirely indigenous, but a bastard civilisation which combined the barbarities of Africa with all the worst of the European slums.

To give some idea of the figures, between October 1820 and July 1821 no less than 163 cargoes of slaves are known to have left Old Calabar. Never was a place more redolent of an abominable history. Even today, as in Benin and other parts of Nigeria, strangers still disappear. We were shown some of the thirty slave children who had been picked up in a war canoe down the river in a raid by the police a few months before. They had been stolen from their villages or sold by their parents. In these parts, when the people go to their gardens to work, some young men are always left as guards to protect the children. The missionary, who was explaining the whole affair, was saying how thin they were when taken, and put out his hand and touched the arm of the boy about whom we were talking. The boy trembled. To him the gesture meant only one thing — we were going to buy him to eat.

One incident in the history of Calabar illustrates the whole of it. In 1856 the missionaries complained to the consul — he was then at Fernando Po — that Duke Ephraim, the chief, had caused "Egpo to be blown" on their houses because they had refused to surrender three fugitives who had taken refuge with them from an ordeal by esere bean. The ban was lifted at the Consul's insistence but there are still deaths from the ordeal, and Egpo is still blown, though secretly today. And this, to an African, is a death sentence. He must die as surely as a bee excluded from the hive. No one dares deal with him, dares speak to him, give him food or shelter. The Egpo Society has many grades and each step has to be paid for in money and sacrifice.

We visited the King of the Qua's — Ntoe Ika Ika Oqua II — an attractive middle-aged man with grown-up sons, one of whom was in the police. He wore a crown of crocheted white string decorated with red parrot feathers, leopards' teeth and claws. The king's palace was a modern concrete villa. In the window a protective ju-ju of dried birds' wings hung on strings. The king showed us his robe made of beaten-out bark, and the royal talking drum which lay on its side in a shed in the backyard. It was a long hollowed-out log, at one end of which there was a carved and painted human head. It was played by being struck on the side with a short stick.

Next day Mr. Smith had to go on tour in the launch and we accompanied him part of the way. He took his car with him on a float that was tied to the launch's side. We were now going down the river towards the open sea — down one of the most famous (or infamous) waterways of the world. On each side of us the forest crept down to the water, encroaching upon it with great hands of leaning mangroves. Their branches thrust fingers into the water which developed roots as soon as they touched it. The roots sought the muddy bottom and then sprang upwards with new growths. One had the

The Big Hole,
Kimberley

Digger shaking out
first wash (note
coarse mesh of sieve)

Ruins of Zimbabwe

Desert horseman
(Hausa)

Kuri ox
from Lake Chad

Kano shop

Kano house

Fulani girls,
near Kano

Mounted Bida spearman in chainmail believed to date from Crusades

Emir of Bida

Emir's trumpeters

Medicine stall,
Lagos market

Ju-ju house,
Badagri

Altar at Benin. These ju-ju objects were all thickly coated with human blood when the city was taken.

impression of the fingers dipping themselves into the stream and great gnarled hands reaching upwards out of it.

Naked fishermen, who hardly looked up at us, had built fragile huts on platforms on the roots above the water.

We passed a clearing where the mangrove had been stumped out and rice was being grown — satisfactorily, I was told. This seemed a valuable experiment.

Then we passed the Isle of Parrots, from which hundreds fly out at each dawn and return to roost at night. These are the grey West African talking parrots that the natives call "Pollys."

At Oron the car was landed. We went to look at the museum. It was a temporary mud and thatch shelter in which were assembled some five hundred of the famous Egpo carvings made in the image of men who had died. They were all male, very much so, and most had beards and wore top hats. They belonged to two hundred and forty-three families and some were believed to be several hundred years old. No more are made today (we saw one modern attempt and it was almost unbelievably crude) and the families to whom they belonged come and borrow them for their sacrificial festivities. A few held a child in their arms, and drinking horns in their hands. The figures are intricately carved of camwood and are about three feet high. Their function is to mediate with their god upon demand and when refreshed with libations of gin and blood.

It was here we met Mr. Allen, who had a timber concession — who told us about the twins whose lives he had saved in the last twenty-six years — over a hundred. The custom was apparently to kill the mothers and boil the babies in a large pot.

That evening we went to the Calabar Club which had once, when Calabar was in its glory, been the headquarters of the 3rd Nigerian Regiment. We saw the old mess, the anteroom and regimental offices. It was a sinister two-storey building that seemed to have come right out of a Somerset Maugham story. There were no walls to the mess, just great matted shutters held open by sticks. The matchboard interior wall and ceiling were a kind of livid yellowish grey. The bar was the original bar of the mess and the stools had been carved to fit the buttocks of various notable officers. I had no idea that bottoms could leave so varied a spoor. The mechanics, too, interested me. Presumably the initiate sat himself down in a basin of plaster of Paris to make the mould. The matrix was then cast and the wood carver worked till he fitted his artifact into the hollows so romantically produced. The stools were all named and it appeared from this data that the more senior the officer was the finer bottom he had. It is an idea that might be tried in Hollywood where the footprints of the great are such an interesting exhibit.

I was fortunate enough to find a comfortable seat but Tiny was too small to fit into the spoor of any officer mature enough to merit such an honour.

On the way up, between the Residency and the mess, we crossed a line of soldier or safari ants, the first I had had a good look at. The workers marched down an avenue lined with soldiers, with enormous mandibles, that stood two deep, vertically, one on top of each other like a wall. There must have been millions of them. They were marching when we came. They were still marching when we left two days later. They marched day and night. I went out with a flashlight to verify this. Nothing will face these insects. Lions, elephants, leopards, men — all run from them. They will eat babies if they find them, and have eaten prisoners in their cells. The only thing that will stop them is fire or fresh ash that smells of fire. When they bite they cannot be detached and in pulling them off the body comes away leaving the head. The natives use them sometimes for holding wounds together, first closing them and then applying the living ants whose heads act as stitches.

This part of the world has something special, steeped in ju-ju, its present perhaps potentially as evil as its past.

This was Aro country, its centre the grove of Chuku, their terrible god. It was a dark ravine, dense with bush. The sides were seventy yards deep, it was sixty yards long, and fifty wide. Down its centre ran a slow stream with a small island on which there were two altars, one made of trade guns planted butt upwards in the soil, and the other composed of human skulls. Beyond the altars was a rock screened with mats and cloths and roofed with skulls. Here the priest and his assistants lurked in a cave. Tame sluggish fish with yellow eyes and long feelers swam with slowly moving tails in the pond, which lay below the sacrificial altar, waiting for their share of the offering. The Aro had agents in every village. The fees were enormous and the customers came in never ending streams to consult this famous oracle. They came in groups, blindfolded, led backwards by guides through secret paths. Of all who went, only a few returned. The sacrifices offered had to be all white. White cocks, white sheep, white goats. The watchers saw blood in the waters but it was animals' blood. The men who had consulted the oracle were clubbed unconscious and sold as slaves. But sometimes the word went out that the Chuku wanted a human sacrifice and on these special occasions there was a cannibal feast. All towns gave their quota. Hundreds were killed and the flesh sent to kinsmen and to chiefs. The victims were regarded as sacred and those who ate them partook of the god's power. When in 1901 the shrine was attacked by the British and destroyed, hundreds of skeletons were found hanging from the trees and enormous heaps of skulls were discovered in the bush nearby.

This picture of ju-ju and gri-gri seems consistent in West Africa between the deserts north of Dakar to the deserts south of Angola. It is a product of the mystery of the great trees which, since time began, have held man in their thrall by their unchanging immensity. What are these priests but black Druids?

Nothing is new here, and nothing so far as I could see completely ended.

16

The Naked Pagans...Enugu...Jos...Five Mines and Natives

● WE NOW FLEW to Enugu where we stayed with Mr. Cuthbert Mayne, the acting Lieutenant Governor — a tall, slight man with a cavalry stoop and immense charm of manner. He was one of the old school of administrators who had made Nigeria, and who were now attending what might well be the funeral rites of the child they had brought into the world.

It was here that I heard some more stories of the old days which were not so far away. Mr. Mayne told me of a vendetta in Calabar in which three men were kidnaped. One escaped and while hidden saw the other two skinned alive, and watched the mother of the victim — the one whose death was the cause of their capture — dancing with their heads, one in each hand. When the case was investigated some fragments of human flesh were found and some skin pegged to a ju-ju tree, but no bodies.

In another case a mad woman was sold like a cow, for £2 10s. to a neighbouring village. When she had been butchered there was a profit of 7s. 6d. on the meat.

Mr. Mayne told us of a wonderful racket: a Jamaican came to Nigeria and taught the people to make stills for £25. He could not be stopped because he maintained he was teaching them to purify their water. If they put palm wine or a banana mash into it it was not his fault. The whole country was full of illicit stills which could not be controlled, so much so that a motion had been put forward in the House of Assembly to make illicit stills licit!

Mr. Mayne had a splendid dog, part spaniel and part schnauzer. He also had two cats — a grey Persian and a fluffy pale yellow one. On the lawn there were a dozen light Sussex hens and two tame sheep, all of which, including the hens, became our friends.

Tiny enjoyed dressing for dinner in her one evening dress and drinking "the Queen" at dinner every night. I did too, and thought of how that health was being drunk all over the world each night in regimental messes, by Englishmen at parties or alone. What is this feeling? One of sentimentality, of loyalty, of continuity, of history, or a compound of them all?

We met Colonel and Mrs. Davies of the 2nd Battalion Nigeria Regiment that was stationed here. We arranged to go over their lines the following day and saw some very nice close-order drill, signalling, radio communication, and musketry work. Colonel Davies told me that they had a lot of trouble with their fatigue hats. The men persisted in carrying things on their heads and their wiry hair wore holes through the material. There had been endless correspondence on this subject with the War Office in England, who could not understand why these hats wore out in West Africa and nowhere else.

At the airport of Jos we were met by the district officer, Mr. Counsell, who drove us to the Hill Station. Jos is the health resort of Nigeria and is much patronised by people in need of a holiday or a change. It was completely modern and beautifully furnished with a large and very beautiful garden in which there was an aviary and a compound for a very large desert tortoise said to be three hundred years old. There were also two West African parrots, one of which had laid an egg. After an excellent lunch we were driven to see a pagan village. The road was very rough and stony, even for Africa, and went through low hills covered with a straggly kind of bamboo. When we came to the village we found every compound hedged with high euphorbia. Narrow lanes twisted and turned in all directions till we were almost lost in the dark spiky maze. These people were never conquered by the horsemen of the North, as mounted men were helpless in these dark alleys which, in some places, closed over one's head into impenetrable tunnels from which there was no escape. Nor could the euphorbia be cut down with axes as the white milky juice is poisonous and blinding if it splashes into the eyes.

The men were away working on their lands but an old crone showed us her compound, a series of small huts welded into the rocks. This ancient Eve was naked but for some scraps of wilted spinach thrust before and behind into the string she wore about her waist. In her hut there were a smouldering fire, a couple of clay pots and a log cut lengthwise for a seat. There were no blankets, mats or other utensils that I could see. She lived as Stone Age man must have lived, and yet these people mined tin and melted it into straws which they used as articles of commerce. It was through following these straws to their source that the tin deposits were originally discovered.

We dined with the Counsells and the Director of Medical Services.

He told me that in that part of the country, if there was an accident, one should never stop but go on to the nearest police post and return with a constable, as there was liable to be trouble. In fact, African truck drivers who had injured someone had been dragged into the bush by the infuriated villagers and chopped. He said there were still supposed to be head hunters within a hundred miles of Enugu. In some parts of the plateau, it appears that the natives eat both hyenas and leopards. Human meat is believed to come down, hidden in the trucks, from French territory near Lake Chad. And a retired district officer who had been stationed at Maiduguri told us that during the war he had been requested by the postmaster to be present while he opened a sealed can about which he was suspicious. Parts of a dismembered girl were found in it. She was being sent down to the coast for the Christmas festivities, rather as we would send a turkey. I also heard another story about a member of the Eastern House of Assembly who was making an address on "freedom" when, having glanced at a note that had been passed to him, he fainted. It appears that his father had been killed and eaten. True or false?

Perhaps the most extraordinary, and certainly the most publicised thing in Jos are the "naked pagans" for which the place is famous as far as tourists are concerned. They walk about the streets with nothing on but their spinachlike leaves or, among the more coquettish young women, little twigs that seem to grow out of them like tails. A few carried dirty army blankets — this was a missionary innovation and, I should think, less sanitary than nakedness and not likely to improve their morals which, I was told, like those of most naked people, were extremely good.

We went over to look at an old man working in a field. His only garment was a penis sheath made of beautifully plaited fibre and he carried a thin, loose scrap of leather the size of a lady's handkerchief tied round the waist that supported a small pouch in which he kept a primitive pipe and a flint and steel.

Some of the pagans cultivate terraced fields which, combined with their ability to process tin, points to some forgotten culture having once existed here — possibly Egyptian or — following an earlier and more exciting train of thought — Chinese.

In the museum there is a terra cotta pagoda-shaped pot which is so described, and further evidence to support this possibly quite untenable theory are the pagan ponies. They are Mongolian in type and resemble no other horse in Africa, which are all Arabs or Barbs with unmistakable signs of such blood in their big prominent eyes, wide nostrils, dish faces and general appearance and temperament.

On the way back we had a look at a tin mine. These are open cast dragline affairs worked by enormous cranes. The red tin-bearing soil is caught up in gigantic scoops and processed by being washed through a series of small, shuttered dams in which the tin, being heavier, is caught at the bottom while the mud is swept away with the water. The tin miners are very prosperous, but are resented by the natives though they could not live at all without the wages they receive from the mines in this agriculturally poor country. Their interests are well guarded by the authorities and large sums in rent are paid to the various clans which inhabit the tin bearing land.

The next thing on the programme was a visit to the Agricultural Station at Vom a few miles outside Jos where there is a veterinary school, and the West African Institute of trips or trypanosomiasis research known as "Waitr" under Colonel Marshall. He showed me round and introduced me to his assistants — a very remarkable bunch of young scientists who put the problem of trips into a series of nutshells to explain it to me:

1. The study of the fly. Its love life and habits.

2. The control of the fly, that is to say methods of attacking its love life.

3. The production of cattle that are immune to fly.

4. The production of a serum which will immunise stock from the effects of the tsetse bite — one had been produced which lasts for three months, thus enabling them to cross the fly belts.

The experimental flies were kept in jars and incubators in a room at the end of a long passage. To reach them we had to pass through several locked doors, metal screened — like a prison — for the male and female flies were criminals and must not be allowed to escape. The females flies were in glass jars and lived in old refrigerators where the temperature and humidity was most scientifically controlled. The young man who took me round got out one of his favourites to feed her. Her jar was covered with mosquito netting. An African assistant brought in a live sheep — her host. The African reversed the sheep. The scientist reversed the bottle onto a part that had been shaved clean of hair and wool. His little pet immediately flung herself onto her victim and began to suck up her meal of blood with a delicate proboscis. I thought it all wonderful. At that time I had not been in tsetse country.

I saw the crêches where the larvae were kept in separate labelled bottles, so that their pedigree would be in no doubt. The tsetse gives birth not to an egg, but to a maggot which turns almost at once into a cylindrical black pupa with two breathing holes. It soon hatches out and starts breeding on its own. A fly gives birth once every week or ten days for its life of from four to six months.

There are seven or eight kinds of tsetse or Glossina, and these tame Nigerian flies did not compare in size or savagery with the varieties we struck in Tanganyika later.

Then I had to see the experimental animals. They had hundreds of rabbits running in looseboxes in lots of fifty to a hundred. The secret of raising such large numbers, I was told, was the removal of does to hutches as soon as they were pregnant, and the separation of the young into groups as soon as they were old enough to be sexed. There were also large numbers of extremely prettily marked guinea pigs, a few red monkeys and nine thousand rats which had been bred up from a foundation stock of four. The smell in their house was unbelievable, and the rats in such quantities utterly revolting, as they crawled like white pink-footed lice over the cage fronts along the alleys down which we walked. There were just bellies and pink feet and scaly, scurfy tails. No heads were visible, at least no eyes from the underside. I am fond of white rats and have kept them as pets for years, but I suddenly imagined what it would be like to be locked in here with all of them loose and hungry.

The cattle that were being experimented with were the N'dama from French Guinea. Pale yellowish animals whose points darkened to sepia and near black. In spite of the fact that they received no supplementary food they were pig-fat, especially the bull, and though the aim seemed to be to kill them by injecting as many trips as possible into their blood stream, only one of them did not look well.

This trips control is the only concern I have seen anywhere where there appears to be a full international exchange of data and information. Nothing like it exists in the various agricultural departments of the world or even, supposing some experiments are secret, between those of the various dominions and colonial services.

I am convinced that many West Indian fruits and crops would do well here, but none so far as I could find out have been tried. Nor is there any explanation of why the leaves of the baobab are eaten only by the Hausas, or that only in the Congo are the leaves of the manioc or cassava used for greens. There should surely be the greatest possible exchange of information on foodstuffs, their culture and methods of cooking between tropical countries.

At the Veterinary School where assistant veterinary officers are trained, there were very few students — only about twenty as far as I can remember. It is extremely difficult to get young Africans to become anything but doctors or lawyers, these two professions being the only real money earners. Nor does the problem end there. The northern people, who are born stockmen, are, as a rule, not well educated enough to learn the theory, while the Southerners who qualify academically are generally useless with stock.

After lunch I visited Mr. Marshall, the Director of Veterinary Services. He had a very nice cocker spaniel bitch, and told me these dogs did better here than any other breed. The Marshalls had a lovely garden — everything grew wonderfully in the volcanic soil — and after tea I saw the files about the Ibo horse-killing ceremonies, and very shocking they were.

The horses, which are aged, wornout animals, are brought down in the dry season from the North by Fulani and Hausa traders. On the trek from Kano, Sokoto and Katsina, more than a thousand miles, the best horses, that is to say, those that do not stagger as they walk and still have a few months work in them, are exchanged for animals that are in even worse condition. More horses are added as they go, and this unhappy snowball grows as it reels across the burning plains, till at last the horses reach the southern markets where they are bought by the retailers who will finally distribute them.

Their cost price in the North, as wornout animals, is about £3 per head, and now they are sold for up to £60. So it is easy to understand that the copers engaged in this lucrative traffic are loath to have it stopped.

The buyers are rich men. They must be — lawyers, storekeepers and traders, and merchants — since no one else could afford to pay such prices. Many of them are well educated.

The buyers are of two classes — those who want to sacrifice horses in the second burial festivities and those who wish to kill them to obtain "horse-killing titles." This is perhaps one of the most curious of the world's customs, and is performed by men who call themselves Otigbu Aninya (the man who has killed horses by beating), and whose emblem is a horse's tail. The more they kill the higher the title they obtain. A man who has killed one horse is known as Amusi, more than one horse, Ogbu Zulu (killed and satisfied), over ten, Osi Milli or Ori Mili. Osi means sea or river and is meant to give a picture of vastness. There are still other titles, all expressing further grades in this society.

A horse may be killed in honour of the parents of a favourite wife, in connection with the yam festival, to the sun, to the players of the egele drum, to the erection of a tin-roofed house, even to a tree. In all cases it is a form of conspicuous spending, a means of showing wealth. A poor man sacrifices a chicken worth 2s. 6d., the rich man a horse worth £50.

The other form of sacrifice is connected with the second burial rites, and here the whole clan, all the relations including clerks and people working at a distance from home, have to subscribe if they ever hope to return. Not to subscribe might even cause their death by poisoning.

The tail is always cut off before death, and the methods of killing are horrible. Sometimes the miserable beast is dragged to the ju-ju house where its throat is cut to bleed over the altar. Then it is pulled into the open and beaten to death with clubs. Sometimes it is hauled up by a rope round its neck to the limb of a tree, or its legs are broken and it is burnt alive in the yard of the homestead to the glory of the purchaser and the honour of his ancestors.

An official, who was taken to see a horse killed by his steward, states that the animal first had its tail cut off, then its throat was slowly cut with a blunt knife — a piece of metal nine and a half inches long by one and a half inches wide — after it had been cast. The crowd then jumped up and down on its barrel and chest to drive out the blood. After death the horse is eaten and its skull placed on a wayside shrine. One district officer stated that his steward attended a horse killing and then went to Mass and when questioned, said he saw no relation between the two functions.

There have been numbers of questions from England about this matter — the R.S.P.C.A. and U.F.A.W. have taken it up. There have been letters to the *Times*, and the only thing that has come out is that some £600 has been raised by private subscription for the purchase of humane killers at £26 a time, but there is no reason to suppose they are always used even when they are supplied. The authorities are afraid to stop the practice, particularly where the second burial rites are concerned, in case human sacrifice is substituted for it, and now with the power moving from white hands into black there is very little chance of anything being done to end this practice, particularly as the traffic is so profitable and that those who go in for this hobby are rich and influential men. It is in such things as these that the difference between education and civilisation begins to become apparent. I suggested the use of a leather mask with a fixed spike which is driven into the brain, such as I saw used at the abattoirs in Switzerland many years ago, as being both humane and cheap. But why should humane methods have any appeal? The charm of the ceremony lies in the horse's screams, kicks, struggles, and the spurting blood.

Thousands of dogs are also brought down from the North each year, coupled in packs for sacrifice, so are mules and donkeys. All these animals are eaten.

There are no explanations for the horse-killing ceremony, although among the Ibos there might be a psychological reason such as a great hatred of horses through once having been defeated by mounted men. It might be a kind of long-distance revenge whose cause is forgotten, lost in the pre-history of the nation. And what is the answer? Education? It is not education, if reading and writing and an ability to make a living is considered to be education. It is not religion, not Christianity, since the African is so often both Christian and pagan at the same time and seems able to weld his diverse religions into a single comprehensive cult that combines all his beliefs.

I now met Mr. R. G. D. Horsley, the general manager of the U.A.C. at Jos, whose knowledge of the West Coast was most extensive. Through him I met in the U.A.C. an African, Waziri Ibrahim, almost their only successful native executive. He had risen from manual labour to the head of the Transport and Packing department. He was a good-looking Kanuri of about thirty. And his ideas were interesting. He said there would be civil war if the British left. I found no one, black or white, who really believed the contrary. He was against the feudalism of the emirs. He had tried to help some of his friends by getting them into the business with him. They had not lasted. They wanted short cuts. He said the African was interested only in academic qualifications, which meant, of course, that they learnt a lot of things which were quite irrelevant and useless to an African in Africa. I was much impressed by this young man, as I have been with all the really intelligent Africans I have met all over the continent. There are no problems about a multi-racial society with men like this. But a country cannot be administered or ruled by "short cuts" and corruption. Mr. Horsley told me of one of his clerks whom they were going to transfer to his home town and who they thought would naturally be pleased. The opposite, however, was true. He begged to stay on at Jos. He said if they sent him home his relatives would batten on him and he would be finished.

The flight to Lagos was uneventful. We visited the office that

Francis Morrisey had just rented. It was a new concrete building with an apartment over the top floor. From the kitchen one looked down on the church compound next door, and into the bucket lavatories of the mission school attached to it. As I looked out an African woman settled down next to the latrines and, unperturbed by the surroundings, made a little fire and began to cook her chop. From one of the other rooms there was a good bird's-eye view of an unutterably squalid rusty corrugated iron house in which twenty or so Africans seemed to live. There were women doing each others' hair, women suckling children, women cooking and women preparing food. Children swarmed. This was Lagos, where the new blocks are surrounded by old tin shacks and crumbling houses of masonry and clay. Some idea of the conditions of the city can be gathered from the government report on the Municipal Administration. The investigator, Mr. Bernard Storey, O.B.E., an experienced English town clerk who had been asked to go into the matter, stated:

> In arriving at my conclusion I in no way overlook the fact that the present Lagos Town Council only came into existence in October 1950. . . . Neither do I overlook the fact — and I say this in no derogatory sense — that it was an all-African Council. . . . But although the Lagos Town Council has to cope with special factors which do not exist in the United Kingdom, it proudly and vehemently proclaims its right to local self-government, its fitness to undertake it and its unwillingness to surrender it. All this was made clear to me both at the public Inquiry and in private. If it is correct in the first two of these proclamations and justified in the third, it must be assumed that it accepts certain standards of conduct and efficiency. . . . Running like a brightly coloured thread through the tangled skein of a Council's administration has been the subject of honesty or the lack of it — of corruption. I could not get away from it at the public Inquiry; it was mentioned in connection with almost every matter which was brought before me. . . .

It was usual when such a charge was made for the person making it to swear solemnly and in the most circumstantial detail to the occurrence, and for the person who was alleged to have received the "kola" to take the witness stand shortly afterwards and to swear solemnly and in the most circumstantial detail that "nothing of the kind ever occurred."

We now come to the matter of latrines in the capital city.

On the ninth of December, 1950, Mr. H. O. Davies, a solicitor, wrote to the acting town clerk regarding the latrine in Balogun Square on behalf of his client, the manager of the Savoy Hotel. Balogun Square, Mr. Davies pointed out, was an important trading and residential area and much frequented by visitors. The public latrine did not serve the surrounding buildings, which had adequate conveniences, but the "floating visitors" who would not mind if it was removed to a more satisfactory place.

> As it is now [wrote Mr. Davies] the enormous stench emanating from this latrine every night is a serious discomfort to the occupiers of the residential buildings around. In particular it renders useless all the front rooms of the Savoy Hotel facing the Square because no guests who stay in them ever liked to continue to do so. The result is that the front rooms, which ought to be the most popular parts of the hotel are abandoned and my client has been losing income for over a period of time.

On the twenty-third of February, 1951, the manager of the Livingstone Academy had written to the acting town clerk protesting against the proposal to remove the latrine near his premises on the grounds that the "usage of this very latrine has been since the school was established, approved and granted to the children of the school . . . and the demolition will certainly deprive the school children of this important amenity." Before there was time for him to receive a reply, however, he was overtaken by the swift march of events, and on the eighth of March, 1951, he is writing "reference the above letter on the latrine demolished, the surroundings are now an eyesore; parcels of faeces are deposited overnight in another man's premises especially the school compound . . . forcing the children to choose between putting up with the filth or becoming night-soil boys and girls." The manager suggested, as a measure of relief, a temporary erection on the east side of Thomas Street, facing Ibandan Street. The Council's object having been achieved, the pace slackens, and it is on the seventh of August, 1951, that a recommendation of the Public Health Committee is accepted "that the above suggestion of the manager of the Livingstone Academy be not entertained." There the whole matter appears to rest.

These extracts give some idea of the difficulties experienced in West Africa of administration. The pattern is consistent on almost every level. All the forms and titles of a democratic executive body exist but few of the duties are performed.

We now visited the government dairy farm at Agege where milk was being produced at great expense for hospitals and children in Lagos. They had a very fine Friesland bull in a big fly-netted stable where hand-picked white Fulani cows were served in an attempt to increase their milk potential while retaining the hardiness of the original native stock. There was also a small herd of Montbelliard cattle from the French Cameroons where, after about thirty years, immense herds of this breed have been built up. They look like grade Herefords, being red with white faces and, like Herefords, are susceptible to eye trouble. It is a curious fact, as I found myself, ranching, that white-faced cattle have this weakness, but I believe a new strain now exists which has brown rims to its eyes and is relatively immune to ophthalmia.

I was entertained by the manager. He was a keen horseman and had some very good books on Arabs, my particular interest.

We talked about milk production and how extraordinary it was that milk was now being flown over from England in cartons at 2s. 6d. (I think it was) a quart, more cheaply than it could be produced here. Outside the cow stable in a basin of half-dry manure were some large white grubs about the size of my little finger. They were the larvae of a beetle which the natives are very fond of eating. This time I was beat. I will eat anything — snake, iguana, locust, ant, elephant, lynx — but I don't think I could have faced those grubs even if they were disguised with a nice white parsley sauce.

The papers were now carrying headlines about a murder case which I found interesting. A Moslem preacher, Alfa Bisiriyu Apalara had been killed by the members of the Awo Opa Cult for saying that "God alone could cause childbirth." And he condemned the Ifa Oracle, saying that the palm kernels which were sacred to the Ifa Oracle could not carry such powers as to "give children." When he had stated this heresy a riot ensued which ended with eighteen men in the dock being charged with murder, the preacher's body having been found much mutilated in a creek.

Before leaving Nigeria we called on the Governor, Sir John Mac-Pherson, who had just returned from leave. And at about our last dinner party in Lagos met a lady who ran a children's school, who told us that in the last two years four bodies had been washed up from the creek at the bottom of her garden. One of them had been headless. This was in Ikoyi, the residential section of Lagos. She said that now the first thing the children did in the morning, as soon as they arrived, was to run and look for bodies.

Another guest, the district officer of the area which included the airport, said he had had an interesting case lately. According to custom, after the death of the chief his successor had eaten certain parts of his body, a necessary ritual. It then turned out that another man had a better claim to the chieftainship but the parts he should have eaten, which would ensure his legitimacy, had been consumed. The consumer now went in fear of his life because the only way to carry on the tradition would be for parts of his body — since he had eaten those parts of the late chief — to be eaten by the rightful claimant. It was in fact a problem of gastronomic succession. An example of African logic. Here was real continuity.

I was told of a chief's burial to which a number of white officials had been invited. They had come a little early, only to find the coffin unscrewed and the African guests engaged in eating the corpse. Very tactfully they withdrew. I was told about a native dispenser who had been found guilty of cannibalism. He had, it appeared, been asked to dissect a body into joints, as he had the necessary skill. When he came out of prison the Native Authority re-employed him since they had paid for his training and did not want to waste it. Another district officer, also at the party, who had served in the North said in his opinion slaves were still exported via Chad and probably reached Abyssinia or even Arabia.

This depressing conversation was enlivened by a story about a local locust officer who sent the following telegram to his chief: HAVE FOUND LOCUSTS COPULATING. The reply came: STOP COPULATING KILL LOCUSTS.

I had not sought horrors. They had been thrust upon me. All I had done was to lift the veil of progress and education and sophistication, and see what lay beneath it. Granting the possibility of tall stories, even lies and exaggerations told to a stranger, a substratum remained, the pegs on which the tales were hung. Actually, I think most were true or nearly true. The people I talked to were all responsible men, all wanting to get something off their chests, to tell someone what they knew.

We were now going to the Gold Coast. Things might be better there. The Gold Coasters were said to be the most advanced people in Africa. They had been the longest in contact with the Europeans. But so far the picture had been very dark. Under a superficial veneer of education and culture, under a government which had every appearance of democracy, with local Native Authorities, school boards and almost complete self-government on municipal levels, I had found nothing but corruption, cruelty and a people living in perpetual terror of their fetishes.

Little of this showed on the surface where everything was on the up and up. Outwardly there is much progress. There are fine buildings — houses of assembly, schools, universities, and the rest. But they are the result of British initiative and are supported by the white civil servants who still remain though they are now in the unenviable position of having responsibility without authority. As things become Africanised they seem to go downhill. And since government may be defined as the use of the national revenue to the best advantage of the population, how will self-government succeed with a people who admire honesty in the British but cannot see how it applies to themselves?

● *The Gold Coast*

17

Castles of the Coast... Gold Coast... Accra...
Tembe... Elmina

● THEN THE ACCRA PLAIN was below us. Bare, golden, khaki
spotted so symmetrically with patches of olive bush that they looked
as if they had been planted. We were met at the airport and driven
to the Information Service Offices where James Moxon, a fat fair man
of immense ability and understanding of the country — our cicerone
to be — was waiting for us.

We lunched at his house with Monsieur and Madame Cartier,
French journalists who lived in New York and were touring Africa
getting material for a series of articles. They had just come from
Kenya and the Congo. She was a pretty, plump, dark-haired, blue-
eyed woman, and he a thick-set, balding intellectual, who missed very
little of what went on.

After lunch we went to Tembe where a modern harbour is to be
built, and saw a model of the project. At the moment it was still a
fishing village of palm and thatched mud houses, with canoes drawn
up on the sandy beach round which everyone who was not fishing
appeared to spend his time.

From here the sailing canoes go twenty and thirty miles out to sea
for their catch. We watched some come in. When fairly near they
drop their sails and lie parallel to the surf, just behind the breakers,
till they feel the time to come in has arrived — the right wave. Then
they turn the canoe and come, riding the wave like a surfboard. As
it breaks they paddle furiously to keep ahead of the swirling waters
which would swamp them. Their trident paddles, painted green, red
and white, flash like weapons as they drive them into the water. Before they touch the paddlers jump out and run the canoe up onto
the beach, defeating the pounding waves that leap at them.

We saw some of the fish they brought in. Among them was a tuna
of ninety or a hundred pounds, beautifully green and blue, like a
giant thick-set mackerel. There are tarpon, sailfish and marlin here,
too. West Africa holds some records.

But we were seeing the last of the old Tembe. By now it has gone. By now the wild beach has become the foreshore. Once more beauty has been sacrificed to efficiency and another piece of Africa has died. For what is new cannot be Africa, and I sometimes wonder if it will survive or go the way of the other things that were once new here too. Once, in the distant past.

We were staying at the Gold Coast government hostel that was run by the wife of an official — Mrs. Sparkes — a very capable and charming woman. Another guest was the new Indian Commissioner, Rajah Rameshwar Rao, an attractive young man who had abandoned his princedom — it is now incorporated into Hyderabad — and gone into the service of his government. He was, as can be understood, very anti-colonial, and I think he disliked the English but seemed nonetheless to get on with them.

Rameshwar and I discussed black and white relations. He thought there must, at some time, be mixed education and that the Africans must participate in the government of their country. He was, of course, right. The difficulty was to produce conditions where this could happen without the deterioration of either government or education.

We dined with Moxon and met Sean Graham who was in charge of the Gold Coast Film Unit. A very exceptional man, a real artist. And Mr. Raymond, a bearded young man who did the publicity for the Volta Dam scheme.

After Lagos, Accra was very clean and tidy. On every street there were children standing in basins washing themselves, or being washed, from their woolly heads to the soles of their pink feet. The big ones were washing themselves, the babies being washed by someone a few inches taller than themselves, and all stared up with big dark eyes through the soapsuds as we passed. Some little girls wore a tu-tu, a most attractive sexy little garment consisting of a strip of red cotton cloth passing between their legs and dangling in a tail over their shiny buttocks. It was held in place by a string that went round their waists. The Folies Bergères could learn something here. Even the smallest girls wore something, but the boys seemed to go naked up to puberty.

We went down to the harbour and watched the surf boats come in. The big ships lie out beyond the bar and everything is brought in by these lighters. Everything, that is, which does not fall overboard. I was told there were quite a few cars on the sea bottom of the anchorage.

I picked up some odd bits of information. A thousand years ago the University of Timbuctoo was in touch with both Spain and Egypt, and had a thousand students. There were empires then in Africa and kingdoms like those of Ghana and Songhai, where the standard of civilisation was probably higher than that of Europe at that time.

We forget the debt we owe to the Near and Far East. Astronomy, algebra, navigation originated there and luxuries such as silks, spices and perfumes all came from there. According to Rameshwar, the Indians had the zero before the Arabs, and geometry before Euclid. He told me, too, that his grandfather had had a regiment of cavalry composed entirely of African slaves, and that he had seen old books, written in India five thousand years ago, in which the horoscopes of men alive today, including the date of birth and names of parents were sometimes to be found. He had seen this happen to a friend of his. This is a "believe it or not, Ripley" story, but I have reached the stage where, even if I do not believe something, I am still not ready to deny the possibility of its existence.

We dined with Sean Graham — and had one of the best evenings I have had in Africa. The guests were an English school principal, Mr. Coleman Porter, an African surgeon, Dr. Charlie Odamatten-Easmon and his wife. She was a very pretty and gay young woman of Sierra Leonean descent. He was acting senior surgical specialist on the Gold Coast and was a fine musician and sculptor. The other African girl at the party was a Miss Gloria Addae, who was a research fellow in economics at the local university — also charming and most intelligent. Both girls were beautifully dressed and had lovely speaking voices. This was something that struck me several times. The voices of educated African women — soft, yet full and wonderfully modulated.

The conversation could not have been more interesting. No one had a chip on his shoulder. Colour prejudice, on either side, did not exist and even seemed hard to believe in. We discussed some of the mysteries of native African medicine and Dr. Easmon told us of some of his experiences. One was a case of a woman dying of septicaemia on whom penicillin had no effect. Her parents wanted to take her home. The authorities said they thought she should die in hospital because it would be easier for her. The parents insisted and she left the hospital. Three months later she walked in cured. There was not even any scar tissue. Another man refused to have an anaesthetic for a serious operation, and it was done under autohypnosis. Another said they could not cut him and the sharpest scalpel in hospital could not even break his skin.

I was told of a girl who had had her heart cut out while she was still alive, as a sacrifice to ensure the winning of a football match.

Next day we drove with Moxon to Aburi where the king — Nana Osae Djan II, Ohene of Aburi and Abur Adontenhene of the Akwapim State — was celebrating his silver jubilee. We drove up into the mountains to the village where the festivities were to take place. It was filled with hundreds of people, all in their best clothes. Some were wearing kente cloths from Ashanti, made of ribbed silk with beautiful designs, that may cost as much as £80. Many of the women wore long strings of ancient beads, the largest being almost the size of a golf ball.

There was a procession of chiefs preceded by dancing ladies who, I later found, were the local Methodists — my mother-in-law's co-religionists — and who, despite their mature figures, leapt high into the air brandishing twelve-bore hammerless shotguns. The way for them was cleared by running footmen carrying elephant tails that had been flattened into fan-shaped whips, and a guard of men armed with dane guns and brass-bound blunderbusses. Then came the executioners with their swords, who were followed by officials splendidly dressed with their rods of office, and the linguists with their sticks whose heads, carved into the shape of birds and beasts illustrating the principal figures of various fables, were heavily plastered with plates of beaten gold.

Next came the drummers. Men with small drums that they carried under their arms or wore slung round their necks with leather bands, and the big drum — a long affair, carried on a man's head and held there with raised hands and played by the man who followed him who beat it with a short elbow-shaped stick. Accompanying the drums were the trumpeters whose instruments were made of carved and ornamented tusks. Among them, distributed through the procession, were the stool bearers. These stools, or carved seats, are symbols of royalty and have a sacred significance of their own, divorced from that of the holder of the title to which they are attached. They can, for instance, be insulted like people. The chiefs, gorgeously dressed, reclined in palanquins while over their heads attendants twirled great multi-coloured umbrellas. Each was a little entity, with his stool, his linguists and his band which strove to prove his importance with bursting lungs and madly beating drums.

And then finally there came the hero, the king, the Adontenhene. He came lying in a litter carried on the shoulders of four immense black men. Before him on his litter stood a small, almost naked boy of eight or so — his soul. The child's face was whitened, he wore a golden headdress and ornaments that rivalled those of his master, who was dressed in the most brilliant garments with a golden helmet and heavy golden chains about his neck.

The chiefs and notables sat on the covered dais that had been prepared for them, and the dancing began in the hollow square that was left open before them.

First came the Methodist ladies, dancing alone and in groups, holding their shotguns over their heads, twirling them, waving them. They moved with the happy ponderous grace of suitably lubricated maturity. Then came the male dancers with enormous feather headdresses, who leapt and capered.

The rain, which had threatened, now began to come down and we retreated to the chief's house. It was floored with cement that was red with the blood of recent sacrifice, which the pelting rain gradually paled and washed into the gutter at our feet. The blood of a goat I was told. But once, and not so long ago, it would have been that of a man, and the decorated child on the palanquin would have been sacrificed at the death of the king.

We had been near to the heart of Africa in its most sophisticated form. The cloths, the beads, the hand-wrought golden jewellery, the gold-plated linguists' sticks, the palanquins, the umbrellas, the magnificent ribbed and patterned clothes had all been here before the white man came, even before the Portuguese. What was new here was negligible. The shirts, the white singlets, the khaki trousers, the store clothes of some of the women — they did nothing to alter the ceremony, and seemed to me to represent the slightness of our impact on the continent.

Shirts, pants, Coca-Cola, some reading, writing, hymn tunes, bicycles, sewing machines — and you've about had it. I do not discount my African friends of the other night but there are not enough of them, and their influence is more than offset by the pretentious young intellectuals who abound.

We now went to stay at Christiansborg Castle with the Governor and his wife — Sir Charles and Lady Arden-Clarke. We were taken to our suite, an enormous bedroom, bathroom and balcony that overlooked the sea. Going to the parapet I found a battery of old muzzle-loading guns pointing at the roadstead where so many slavers must once have ridden at anchor. Below us, their muzzles sticking out of the wall, were three more big guns with two crown birds, already perched for the night. I had never associated crested cranes with the sea but there they were in what was apparently their usual roosting place.

Sir Charles was a remarkable man, an administrator to whom the Gold Coast owes a great deal. Lady Arden-Clarke resembles a freckled Watteau shepherdess, very young looking, with her almost white naturally wavy hair piled above her lovely face. Sir Charles was the first governor of Sarawak, and his successor was murdered by an assassin who did not know he had been transferred. He was a lucky man. There seems little doubt that luck is a kind of faculty, a talent.

One of Sir Charles's pet ideas was a multi-racial colonial service in which men of every race and colour would serve all over the British Commonwealth. If this could be done it might solve a lot of problems.

Christiansborg was my first West Coast castle, and it was really to see them that I had come to the Gold Coast. Castles were being built in Africa when they had become outdated in Europe. They run all along the coast from Dahomey to Cape Verde in Senegal.

Of all the castles, Christiansborg is probably the finest. Magnificently restored, it had not been turned into the most beautiful Government House in Africa. Every modern comfort and convenience has been blended into an historic whole without ruining its character.

From our room we looked due west into the sunset over the sea. We walked along the battlements wondering how many others had done the same in the centuries of the castle's existence. How many governors and officers of the watch had searched that same horizon, looking for the topsails of a craft from overseas. Friend or foe? How many had stared, pining for home? How many had died here of fever, of dissipation, of wounds? How many Africans had been flogged, raped, branded, tortured? The very cobbles of the yard, with its magnificent trees growing out of the cobblestones, stank of history. We saw the kennels of the great mastiffs that guarded it at night. We visited the slave quarters under the walls, and the well, like a sump, through which the slaves were lowered one at a time onto the tiny beach where canoes would pick them up and convey them to the slaver, that lay with furled sails in the anchorage.

The castle was once taken and held by the Africans for more than a year. They came to buy guns and asked if they could try them with blank charges. But they had brought bullets with them and once the guns were loaded they had the garrison, weakened by fever, at their mercy. Then apparently becoming tired of living such a restricted life they were, after twelve months of dressing up in the governor's clothes and exercising his prerogatives, quite ready to sell the castle back again.

In the evening we went to see *Where No Vultures Fly*, produced by our friend Harry Watt. It was interesting to see the timing required for even so simple a thing as going to see a film. Watches had to be synchronised so that the escort should be ready, the buglers standing by at the entrance to the bioscope, the police cordon prepared to keep back the crowds, the red carpet down and the manager prepared with his best smile and bow. It gave us an idea of how the Queen must live — all her life in a kind of split-second publicity, illuminated by the almost continuous flash of exploding magnesium bulbs. We enjoyed the film, the animal photography particularly, and then went back and had a nightcap on the castle terrace which was floodlit like a film set. Nothing could have been more romantic or more beautiful — the light, the shadows of the palms and guns and grillwork on the white walls. Above us the star-pierced sky of Africa, and the slow, endless beating of the surf upon the sand below us. We were for that instant poignantly a part of history. Included in it without relevance, but very much aware of both past and present. Very alive, sensitized as it were by emotions which had once existed here.

Barbara Ward, Mrs. Jackson, also a guest, was that almost unique combination of a beautiful woman with a hundred-horsepower brains. She was on the board of the B.B.C. and a regular contributor to the *Economist*, but had retained her charm to such an extent that one in no way resented her being more intelligent than oneself. In addition, she was a cat lover and promised to show us her two Siamese kittens as soon as her husband returned from England the following week.

Our next trip was to the university college of Achimota where the medical officer, Dr. J. M. Wilson, took us round. There is a lovely dining hall and the buildings are splendid, more or less a Spanish mission style, reminiscent of California, which I preferred to the more modern Ibadan effect, as I thought they would age much better. The students I met seemed intelligent and their rooms neat and tidy, each had its own small balcony. I heard the usual story — learning by rote, a desire to be lawyers and doctors rather than anything else; but there is plenty of scholarship and the pupils are keen to learn.

The next afternoon we went to see a football match between Nigeria and the Gold Coast. The players were without shoes but their feet were taped. They played well and fast and used their heads more than is customary, and with great effect. At half time one side, I forget which, poured a libation of gin on the ground to ensure victory. The crowd was enthusiastic and dressed in its best — in European clothes that varied from well-cut lounge suits to singlets and drawers — and in native cloths of all kinds and qualities. Many chiefs were there with their intricately carved and decorated sticks of office.

This was our last day in this beautiful place. Tomorrow we were off again. Off to see more castles. Leaving Accra we drove through a rich forest belt and then into open rolling country, a kind of downland, that followed the seashore. We passed cemeteries bright with red and yellow crotons and alcalifa which in West Africa replace the funereal cypress of other lands. Orange is the mourning colour.

When we got to Cape Coast, another famous slaving centre, we went to see Mr. John Matson with whom we were to stay. He had some interesting curios — small brass boxes in which the Ashanti kept their gold dust and old Ashanti gold weights. They represent animals and tools of various kinds. One was a trumpet decorated with human lower jaws. The lower jaw is very strong ju-ju and always kept separate from the skull which is more of a trophy or decoration. It is the lower jaw that talks and this is what makes it so significant. According to Richard Burton they were used as ornaments for umbrellas and sword handles, and were taken with horrible cruelty, the muscles severed with a knife and the jaw torn out with the left hand from the yet living victim.

Mr. Hughes, an African in the Information Service, took us round. We visited a girls' school in the Ibadan style. The girls are good at dressmaking and, like most girls, more interested in marriage than education, but they realise that the best educated will get the best husbands. Mr. Hughes told us about African medicines, of an ointment made of palm oil and banana skins for skin disease, about plantains for cancer, and of a dressing made from a concoction of herbs which cured rheumatism. He gave us a wad of stuff that looked like wood wool and is called chewing sponge. It is very astringent and produces a strong flow of saliva. Something might be extracted from this for use in the desert, I should imagine. I chewed it several times when thirsty, with excellent effect.

We went to see a retired judge whose wife was a dressmaker and she showed us her jewels and her cloths which she put on and modelled for us.

Ashanti gold is very pure, guinea gold in fact, which was worth 21s. — because it was better than the ordinary sovereign. On a black skin it looks magnificent, but on a white, or if held in the hand it looks brassy and unreal, partly perhaps because it is not polished and finished the way our jewellery is. But the work is very fine — filigree with knobs and traceries.

Then we went to see another man, an old lawyer, who had been a well-known politician and was full of complaints. One of these was that there was no gold now for the goldsmiths to work since it was so tightly controlled by the government. It was controlled because so much was being stolen. And gold was no longer found in the streets after rain — another complaint — because they had been paved.

Cape Coast Castle was used as municipal offices and for stores, but was in good repair. Part of it was a prison and I saw some of the warders' wives putting their laundry out to dry on the battlements, weighting it down with old iron cannon balls. On the stairway there was a charming putty-nose monkey that was most affectionate, and once it had my hand hated to let it go. These are among the nicest monkeys for pets, as they seldom turn nasty.

We now called on the local chief. He lived in a two-storey stone house, built in 1728 when the slave trade was at its height. Its design was the classic one with the central courtyard or compound that was only reached through a twisty passage that ran through the lower floor. These secret yards always filled me with horror. It was surrounded by a balcony. There were drums standing in the corners and the palanquin that looked like a kind of large cradle, in which the chief was carried on official occasions, hung on the wall. Outside the house was an ancient fetish tree — a very large wild fig. At its foot was a collection of sacred objects, including a broken stool, beautifully carved, that lay on its side, and the differential of a truck.

A little way off there were a series of concrete monuments belonging to one of the Asafo companies. These are warrior associations that correspond to the circumcision groups of other parts of Africa — bands of brothers linked by their age and their ordeals. The monuments were large and consisted, among other things, of a big lion and a whale, both realistically painted. Between the lion's feet a puppy, about six months old — safe there, I imagine, from interference — was dying of distemper.

We drove on to see another chief, past fields of sugar cane, whose flowers looked rather like pampas grass. The chief was a charming old man, wearing a red cloth and a folded white napkin flat on his head.

It kept falling off as he talked and finally he held it in his hand. His councillor, who accompanied him, was dressed in a torn white vest, khaki shorts and a golf cap, which he wore all the time. In his hand he carried his gold-topped stick of office. Children ran in and out like puppies, the boys naked and the girls in scarlet tu-tus. The houses here were flat roofed and Moorish looking, possibly a result of early Portuguese influence.

I was struck by the curious dignity of these West African chiefs. I do not suppose they are admirable old men, but they are men, and their power is being shorn from them — less by the British than by the young men who now govern the country. Only the chiefs stand between them and absolute power.

In the afternoon we went to visit a leprosarium that was about to be officially opened, although a number of patients were already there. Among them was a dear little girl of seven or eight. She had been so covered with sores when she came in that, in order to keep the flies off the pus that covered her, a small meat-safe-like affair had been built for her to live in. It stood on legs like a big hutch in the middle of a ward. She was nearly well but would not give up her house, and popped in and out of it like a tame rabbit. Leprosy is beaten now. It is only a matter of getting the lepers to come in for treatment.

We now went on to Elmina, the real show place, hardly altered in any way since it was in use. This was one of the greatest of the strongpoints that dot the beaches of this terrible coast. It is now a police training depot and commanded by Captain Barry Lane, a very fine type of executive officer. The castle was built in 1482 by the Portuguese, who brought out all the stone, marked and cut, from home, so that it was in a sense prefabricated. Don Diego de Azambuja founded the settlement and Bartholomew Diaz was one of his captains. Christopher Columbus is supposed to have come here. It was considered impregnable. The Dutch, however, took it in 1637 by getting guns up in the darkness to a hill behind the castle where the Portuguese had built a church. This is now also a fort and inhabited by Mr. Peters, who is in charge of all castle restorations. We had a drink with him and played with his grey parrot, which liked climbing over me and biting my ear. The view was magnificent and it was easy to see how guns had enfiladed the defences of the castle from here. Outside the castle there is an enormous compass set made of round pebbles of two colours, fixed into mortar, by which mariners were said to check their instruments.

Inside the main courtyard was the slave market, a surprisingly modern looking building with a kind of sentry box that had a side entrance and slits through which the chief could watch the sale of his slaves and people without being seen by them. There were immense slave dungeons under the walls, and the yard for the female prisoners was surmounted by a balcony that led from the officers' quarters so that they could pick their fancy from the girls and women who were paraded naked below them.

All the iron work in the castle was original and some had a typical Dutch design of tulips, the result of their occupation. Everything was in perfect condition, but Barry told me that it all had to be continually painted, which was why the place had such a smart appearance. The iron work and the old guns, battery after battery, which pointed out to sea, each with their little heaped pyramid of cannon balls, were all painted black, and all the walls a dazzling white. It was moonlight, and after dinner we went round the ramparts to stare at the phosphorescent sea. Then we came in and talked. We talked about the famous Kibi ritual murder. This occurred when Sir Oforin Atta died in 1944. He was the Omanhene or chief of the state of Akim Abuakwa, and normally, that is if the British had not been there, several hundred slaves would have been sacrificed at his death. This was now impossible but one man, a subchief, did disappear, and his relations very unpatriotically complained. His bones were found. Some witnesses sang and told how he had been killed in the traditional manner, bled to death with a knife thrust through both cheeks and tongue, and a basin beneath his face to catch the blood which was needed to wash the royal stool. Later he was beheaded. Eight men were found guilty of murder by a jury of eight Africans and one European. In the end, by a series of legal manoeuvres, in which the African advocates excel, the case was dragged on for nearly three years — and finally only three were executed though no one doubted the guilt of any of them. It should be remembered that the burial was that of a distinguished chief who had been knighted by the king and that the defence was conducted by Dr. J. B. Danquah, the leader of the United Gold Coast Convention, a barrister who was related to both the deceased king and several of the murderers. He was defending a custom which he considered normal, with every device open to a trained legal mind. These are the anomalies of Africa — the place where ancient murderous customs and modern education meet in brotherly love. Although very few of these cases come to light, they are known to everyone with colonial experience.

We spent a very happy night in a big bare whitewashed bedroom overlooking the sea. It was entirely unimproved and it was interesting to think of the previous occupants. Nothing has been altered in the castle, lavatories and bathrooms being the only additions.

We were awakened by bugles tearing the pale silken dawn and getting up we watched the sailing canoes skimming over the sea like swallows. Perhaps they had done it two thousand years ago. These projections from the past through into the present are very moving. They give one a sense of continuity and reality.

Captain Lane told us about the ghost which his two little boys had seen several times but were quite unworried about. He was, they said, a nice white bearded old man who came to visit them occasionally when they were in bed.

Next day we drove past Takoradi, the big port, and went on towards Tarkwa. The castles of the Gold Coast had now been visited, but the grim picture will never be forgotten. The monuments to the first collaboration of the white man and the black in an abominable trade.

18

Ashanti Gold... Tarkwa... Kumasi... King and Customs...
Baden-Powell

● WE REACHED Tarkwa in time for tea with Mr. Arnold Jones and his wife Helen, with whom we were to stay. Our bedroom had a view down over a valley and on to the spearlike shoots of some giant royal palms that were growing a hundred feet below our window. On the ledges under the roof hundreds of little finches were nesting, and when the windows were open they flew across the room diagonally, using it as a short cut. On a big tree we saw our old friends, a pair of West African fish eagles, looking magnificent as the sun caught their white heads and mantles.

The local bank manager came in to dinner. He told us that in spite of the wealth from the cocoa crop and the diamond fields near by, no more money appeared to be banked than usual. No one knew where it went. I asked why the term government agent had replaced district officer and found that it was more acceptable to the Africans, just as they prefer "expatriate" to British or European when referring to white men.

African officials are beginning to replace the white in the process of Africanisation, and I was told of one two-bedroom house from which sixteen beds were taken when the occupant was transferred. Here one is up against the old problems of uneducated African women, who have no idea of how to run a European-style house, and the custom by which a whole family move in on their more successful relations. The answer is time but there is no time.

We passed a small pineapple plantation. The house was built of bamboo slats with palm mat, but was very isolated and in some disrepair. It would have been a wonderful background for a murder or suicide story, with the forest closing in on the garden on three sides and the melancholy rubber trees on the fourth. There it was rotting away in the middle of a sinister little green oasis.

We were taken to see a forestry concession where they were installing new and very expensive machinery. On the road we met

enormous logs off on their way to the outer world. At the mills men
were trimming by hand — great mahogany curls — these are the
heads of the trees where the branches begin and are used for the
best veneers, having a bird's-eye grain. The logs go about three to
four tons and are a full load for a truck. The most ever got from one
giant mahogany tree was forty-eight tons of salable timber. The
forest is selectively cut — only trees nine feet in circumference above
the bowl may be felled.

We saw the house of a white man, a gold miner who had turned
Moslem and lived there with his four African wives. He had brass
crescents fastened to his door and a curious arrangement of what
looked like armour decoratively arranged in his front yard.

It was a most interesting day, particularly as we were accompanied
by Peter, a woolly collie-like dog with very soft eyes and a beautiful
nature, who participated in everything.

Next day we went to see some gold dredging operations. This
was the ultimate paradox. Here in the depths of the high forest
on the shallow arm of one of the rivers that drained it, was an
enormous dredge creeping over the muddy water, its great buckets
scooping out the bottom.

We went out in a punt, edging our way past dead floating trees,
roots and rubbish. The moving staircase of the scoops, each as big
as a bath, their edges polished and sharp from the friction of the
bottom, revolved on their endless belt, repetitively scooping, carrying up and emptying their contents of forest muck, sand and ore-
bearing gravel. Water was pumped over the locked screens and the
gold caught by gravity as it was washed over the tables that were
arranged in steps — nuggets at the top and the finest dust at the
bottom.

In the pre-British days the nuggets belonged to the chief and the
miners got the dust. There is a story of one chief who had a nugget
so big that he used to tether his horse to it. This area must have
been worked by the Ashanti, because one of the men on the dredge
had found Ashanti gold weights among the stones of the discarded
sludge.

There was a definite cause for African resentment in this development. The natives had always mined gold here. It was alluvial and
there were no great complications. These operations in no way resembled those of the Rand. Nor do the highly sophisticated Ashanti
resemble the Zulus or Matabele who roamed the South African high
veld.

Some idea of the magnitude of the operation may be gathered from the cost of the dredge — £300,000. This one was shortly to be dismantled and moved. The cost of doing this, including repairs and replacements, would be about £180,000. The dredges work for approximately twenty years in one place and the four dredges belonging to this company process a million tons of gravel a month, with a target of three thousand ounces of gold.

We lunched with the director of the mine in a very comfortable bungalow centrally situated to all four dredges, and saw the electrical installations necessary to their functioning. Power lines and roads ran out to each ship, for that is what they were, and the organisation and capital entailed were enormous.

We went off next morning to see the site of the proposed Volta Dam. On the way we passed the area where General Baden-Powell got the idea for his scouting movement during the Ashanti war. It was difficult to relate the little wolf cubs and scouts I knew to this wild country. I was also shown the mountain where once surplus girls were flung over a cliff. It appears that they were selected at puberty and those whose initiation exams had not been up to par were thrown over. One can imagine no greater incentive to good school work. The aim, of course, was to control the population and prevent overcrowding.

This dam, a £150,000,000 project, will supply the power needed to work the enormous bauxite deposits of the Gold Coast. It will take twenty years to complete and the capital is to come from England, Canada and the Gold Coast government. The big snag appears to be self-government, that is to say the possibility of an unstable government. Another snag is the god of the river. A very large area will be submerged, forming a lake two hundred miles long, and the local witch doctor, quite properly in his opinion, demands a sacrifice of a hundred human lives. The present plan is to offer a substitute of goats, though I do not feel that the god need be worried. In a scheme of this kind more than a hundred lives will be lost before it is completed. But things like this must look very odd on the financial reports, though I have no doubt they will be dressed up acceptably and the hundred goats listed as compensation to local authority.

The dam across the river will be two hundred and sixty feet high and the impounded water will form the biggest man-made lake in the world.

We were accompanied as far as the Volta by a very beautiful

blonde, the wife of one of the officials, attired in what seemed like a shirt only, but it turned out that she did have shorts on under it. They were almost the shortest shorts I have ever seen but I expect they were cool and she had lovely legs.

We dined with the African district officer, Mr. B. C. B. Nutsugah, a charming man of fifty-five or so, and his assistant Mr. Crepi who was considerably older and remembered the Germans being here — we were in Togoland now. I asked him how he liked the Germans. He said in many ways they were preferable to the British. They were hard but just, and, above all, they were swift. At dinner, Mr. Nutsugah and his friend, who were beautifully dressed in lovely cloths draped like togas, had gone to great trouble to produce a European meal. I wish they had given us some local dishes.

Next day our host piloted us to Palime in French Togoland. The cloths the women wear here are the most beautiful we have seen, being in designs of squares that are brilliantly marbled and patterned and look as if numbers of differently patterned materials have been sewn together. Cloths vary from section to section and the manufacturers are continually wondering if such and such a design will be popular. It is almost impossible to guess, and the women will follow any fashion they fancy, just like European or American women. The country was tidier than usual and the houses better built. There were old mango trees planted in avenues, a relic of the previous German occupation. What they taught seems to have had some lasting effect. There is evidence of this in the Cameroons and in Tanganyika. The Africans liked the Germans and that is all there is to it. If they did not, why did their Askaris fight so well and so few desert from their forces in the First World War? My idea is that they liked the discipline, even the brutality which amuses those who are not being brutalised. They enjoyed the pomp and ceremony of the administrators who were all army officers. At least with the Germans they knew where they were. They beat them, they took their women, but they acted like masters and chiefs. It would sometimes seem that they mistrust our friendly attitude. In our position as masters, which we were until recently, they would not have been friendly. Among themselves they are not friendly except to their own tribe and they are very hard on those below them in station or power.

To get to French territory we went through a forest that was a kind of no man's land. Mr. Nutsugah told me that they had quite a bit of trouble with smugglers bringing spirits and perfume over the border. They were armed and there had been fights with the police.

The people in French Togoland seemed somewhat depressed. I assume they wanted self-government with its manifold, but at present invisible benefits. One thing I noticed was that the cocoa here seemed more healthy than on the Gold Coast, perhaps because more of the natural forest had been left and that, apart from the greater shade the big trees gave it, their rotting leaves supplied some trace elements brought up from the lower levels by the roots. We went into one plantation and it was most beautiful. The trees, whose young shoots were a golden bronze, grew under a canopy of forest giants. The fruit was just ripening at this time and clung to the trunk and older branches like golden elliptical, slightly flattened lemons. I opened one and found the beans to be fastened to a central core rather like mealies to a cob. They were white and soft, and surrounded by a white pulpy mass.

Coming out of French Togoland we went through the customs again. Had we bought anything? Any tobacco, perfume, or alcohol? Oh no, we said. We had not. But when we got home we found our driver had bought a litre of scent which his wife would decant into little bottles and hawk on the streets.

We now climbed a high mountain to the unused rest house of Jasikan. Here there was an immense view. All Togoland was spread like a carpet of forest, field and villages below us.

Our next stop was Ho where we stayed with Mr. and Mrs. Allan. They were charming and amusing. They complained about how much the sheep they were "dashed" by the chiefs and notables cost them. A dash of course carries with it the implications of a dash in return of slightly higher value. At the moment they had a dozen sheep picketed on the lawn — when they did not get loose and run about the compound. They had to have an extra boy to look after them and though they did eat some of them, they became so attached to others that they could not kill them. They had a lovely pink cassia in full flower, the first I had seen, and one of the few trees which in actuality equalled the illustrations in books on gardening.

Other guests were Mr. and Mrs. Canham. He was a remarkable man to have made a trip to West Africa, being almost crippled by arthritis. They were interested in African students visiting England and found them accommodation, and friends. They had now come to visit their protégés in their West African homes. He, I think, was somewhat disappointed to find some of the university graduates he had entertained living in primitive squalor. But she pretended such things did not exist and took a dislike to me at once. Perhaps she did not like my appearance, or perhaps because I was a South African — a race notorious for its ill treatment of the aborigines. Though one South African problem is the presence of the thousands of "foreign" natives who come there to work — something they would hardly do if conditions were so intolerable. At any rate, no deep friendship was formed here. Tiny and I have a great talent for making friends, which is balanced by an equal knack of being disliked with the utmost cordiality.

Next day we drove back to Accra where I called on the Minister of Commerce and Industries, a most highly educated man. I also saw the Prime Minister, Dr. Kwame Nkrumah. Looking for his office, I asked a very beautiful golden coloured African girl the way. She surprised me by answering in one of the prettiest American voices I have ever heard, as soft and caressing as satin.

"Why," I said, "you're an American girl."

"No," she said, "I'm Liberian."

I wondered how many more there were like her at home.

The Prime Minister was a personality. One felt it at once. About forty-five years of age, sleek and beautifully dressed in a dark blue suit. He is a man of destiny, and knows it. We talked about South Africa and he seemed pleasurably surprised to find that I was not anti-Negro. I said I had no feeling one way or the other. I had coloured friends in America, I thought I had made some in West Africa, but I neither disliked a man because he was black nor liked him because he was white. The Prime Minister could not have been more charming. He talked about the Gold Coast, about his desire for it to attain dominion status. I said I saw no reason why the experiment here should not succeed. Nor do I, if corruption can be controlled. Its short-term progress depends on the kind of white men they get to help them when the officials go home. And long term, on the education of their women.

To replace the officials they will have to get out men on contract. These will cost more than civil servants and be without their ideals of service. They will be there for what they can get out of it, and many of them, though they will have the necessary qualifications, will be lacking in character. No one goes to West Africa for fun. Service to one's country, and what was the Empire, is one thing, and a contract is another. Then, seeing the general corruption here, there will be a tendency to do in Rome as the Romans do.

As to the women there the problem goes even deeper, being tied up with the land, with fertility, the gods, with money and above all with taxation. At the moment the women traders are not taxed and some of them make enormous sums, several having monthly credits, with the United Africa Company and other companies, of a thousand or more pounds per month, and one at least has a turn-over of more than £100,000 per annum. Once the Gold Coast is free and the United Kingdom ceases to pour millions into the country, this source will have to be tapped and the abounding law-yers will come into their own, particularly as no books are kept and many of the women traders are completely illiterate and carry all their manifold transactions in their heads.

In the afternoon I went to see the government experimental farm and had a very pleasant time among the livestock. I met one of the biggest Hausa cattle dealers who, I was told, had been discussing aphrodisiacs. He must have been about seventy, a magnificent figure in his riga, tall, slim, and still as straight as a spear. He had tried them all, he said, including some from India but there was only one which always worked.

"What is that?" the veterinary officer asked.

"A new young wife," he said complacently.

This is probably one of the world's great truths.

The Nungua Experimental Farm is about eighteen miles from Accra across the plain and their great difficulty is water. This has been got over by making a big concrete catchment for the rain, and it is run into a concrete storage dam. There is no fly here so it is healthy enough for stock. They had a big herd of white Fulani cattle, some Adamawa working oxen that were among the biggest and finest animals I have ever seen, and a herd of dwarf Gold Coast shorthorns — the Muturu — which were nearly double the size of those in their natural state in the forests, through being properly fed from birth. The bull was remarkably savage and charged at sight. I was also shown one Anglo-Nubian goat — the £600 goat they called him, as he was the only surviving descendant of a group which had been imported at the insistence of the Minister of Agriculture at that time. Only by the grace of God had he been stopped from bringing in Shire and Clydesdale horses, which had impressed him in England but which were utterly unsuitable in West Africa. The next importation was to be some breeding stock of the Adamawas from the Cameroons which seemed a wonderful idea. They are splendid beasts.

In the last few days I had picked up some interesting bits of information. That cattle trekked down from the North lose one third of their weight on the way. That rinderpest inoculation is no longer compulsory since the Gold Coast is self-governing and should there be an outbreak it would be uncontrollable. The cutting out of cocoa for swollen shoot had also been abolished when the government passed into African hands, but had been reintroduced as the disease was getting out of hand. Freedom naturally had meant freedom from such controls as these.

I was told that in the Sudan where wells had been sunk the cattle had increased enormously. There had, of course, been no corresponding increase in grass, in fact quite obviously it was grazed harder than ever and was more tramped out, so that the last state of the stock would be worse than the first. We discussed the checks and balances of nature and the danger of interference with them. At one time they had given away improved Fulani bulls to stock owners but they were either allowed to die or were sold for slaughter. They were then sold to villagers at a nominal price, but still they disappeared. Now they were sold for £30, double their market value of £15, and were well taken care of.

No one takes much care of things he gets free and this is particularly true of the African who would often sooner buy medicine than get it free from a dispensary. The dispensers often cash in on this and sell it to him. There is a great call for injections. They like them, and say they make them strong. Dispensers have been found giving injections of distilled water and charging £3 for them. But one really dangerous practice here is the sale of small amounts of penicillin and sulpha drugs which is done by pharmacists. People are rendered immune to the effects of these drugs by the use of small doses and then when they are necessary they are useless. Worse still is the fact that strains of bacteria are bred in their bodies which, when picked up by other people, are resistant to these drugs.

Our next safari was to the north to Kumasi, the Ashanti capital.

The road was first class, much of it through thick primary forest. We saw a few monkeys and more red Ashanti blood. There is a legend that when it fades the Ashanti will lose their country.

In one particularly dark patch of forest the sun struck a brand-new canoe as it lay there — a long, hollow cylinder of golden wood on the edge of the gloom, waiting for a truck to pick it up. Wa-wa wood is used for canoes and they are always made in the forest since the log would be too heavy to carry.

We stopped to have our sandwiches in a little clearing where, as always in a forest, butterflies abounded, and there were some beauties — yellow, red, white. Blue swallowtails, and some that might have been cut out of black velvet. Looking at them fluttering it is hard to believe that their favourite resting place is excrement or putrid meat.

We drove to the Information Service Office in Kumasi and met Mr. Arkhurst, a young, very personable and intelligent African who was more than helpful in arranging and explaining everything to us.

We were to stay with Mr. W. H. Beeton at the Residency. This was a lovely house with a very large and beautifully kept compound. The old trees had been left and in the middle of one of the big lawns there was an enormous silk-cotton surrounded by a bed of white scented spider lilies.

That night we dined with Miss McInnes at the new School of Technology, which is to train the engineers and technicians of the Gold Coast. Among the guests was a Mrs. Wilkinson who showed us the gold ornaments which had been taken at the capture of Kumasi by General Baden-Powell, and which his widow, Lady Baden-Powell, had given to her to return to the Asantehene. The collection consisted of rings, gold necklaces, gold weights and a small portable balance with two thin metal dishes suspended by strings to a central bar. General Baden-Powell had given them to his wife as a wedding present — they must have been his finest trophies, fitted into green leather velvet-lined cases. Granted that it was creditable to return them to their rightful owners — the Royal House of the Ashanti Nation — Tiny was nonetheless much upset at the lack of sentiment involved.

At dinner one amusing incident was repeated. A student had said he thought it was shameful that a man could not be a Minister until he was twenty-five years of age. He was twenty-two and when he was asked if he would be prepared to take over a ministry he replied of course — any of them. This African self-confidence is admirable. Beautiful as a bubble, but just as fragile when exposed to reality. It was their self-confidence that most impressed the Canadians when they talked to the African Commission which went to Canada to discuss the Volta Dam project.

That night we heard tree bears for the first time. They are tree hyraxes and make a peculiar and rather frightening cry. They scream "Woman . . . woman . . . woman . . ." Each time it is louder. Then they stop. A moment later they start again. The story is they do this when they are coming down a tree head first, getting more and more hysterical as they lose control.

In the morning we had an appointment with the Asantehene. We drove up to the palace past two Assyrian-looking whitewashed lions made of concrete with heavy brown painted beards. There were guards on duty. The house was clean and shiny, floored with patterned Italian tiles. The sofa and chairs had loose covers of crimson velvet and on a big sideboard were dozens of signed photos of royalty, governors and officials, the centre piece being one of the Queen.

The Asantehene came in. He was dressed in a splendid kente cloth of blue with a golden border. His left shoulder was bare. He was a handsome, clever-looking man of late middle age. He told us that in the old days the silk to make these cloths had to be unravelled from materials that came presumably from the East, and that to make one for him took nearly a year. He said he was very fussy and if there was a single mistake he refused to accept it. He spoke very good English and was addressed as Nana. As usual nothing was achieved except for us to say that we were glad we had met him. I could not ask him leading questions. He could not have answered them if I had. I did gather that he was, like all the chiefs and kings, against self-government, which was shearing them of all their rights and turning them into decorative puppets. He was an aristocrat and had no use for these jumped-up young men without breeding or background.

There was a certain interest and a certain tragedy in meeting this, the last of the Ashanti kings who was being slowly shorn of power and reduced to impotence. He was probably alive, though only an infant, when the British took Kumasi in 1896, then in its full glory of gold, blood and sexuality.

The king then had had thirty-three hundred and thirty-three wives, as was the law. He had three execution grounds and a staff of a hundred executioners. A grove filled with hundreds of skulls and bones was found, and a brass bowl five feet across that was used to collect the victims' blood — a bath for the golden stool. Human sacrifice reached its height in Ashanti, as elsewhere in West Africa, on the death of the king. Literally hundreds of slaves were now sacrificed, their heads retained and their bodies thrown into the bush. Hundreds of the king's wives, dressed in their best and blind-drunk, were strangled so that the king, when he went into the next world, would be suitably served at board and bed.

When Sai Quamina died in 1799 two hundred slaves were killed each week for three months, and at another king's mother's death three thousand victims were sacrificed from the royal compounds alone. Subject chiefs each contributed hundreds, and no village sent less than two. Then, according to custom, every other family that was also mourning one of their loved ones, performed a sympathetic sacrifice as a gesture of goodwill, in which more thousands must have died.

The Ashanti of that day were not uncivilised, if by civilisation we mean having a complex culture, laws, taxes and order, any more than the people of Benin were. Blood does not destroy the artistic instinct. Their protocol and laws were far more complex than those of the modern democratic procedures which, at the instigation of Whitehall, have been grafted on to this strange and bloody stock. What odd fruit will it bear? Apples where once there were human skulls swinging on strings from the sacred fetish tree?

Only a few years ago the Asantehene was taken ill at a dinner party in Accra from eating some fish which had gone bad. He got better but had he died there might have been war. Another time he was ill at home and as soon as the news got out hundreds of strangers left the city. They left on foot, on bicycles, they hired trucks. But they left. Why? Because if the king died, Kumasi was no place for a stranger who wished to keep his head. That was yesterday. In the present. How odd that people think they can play with time in Africa, muzzle a savage with a hymn, or smother a fertility cult with a pair of pants and a mother hubbard. How odd that those who devise these tricks have never thought of the boredom they induce, or wondered how long such boredom could be endured.

This is the new sickness of the African. Boredom of the most intolerable kind. Playing at politics is one outlet, but how long will it suffice? And to what will it lead? Certainly not to what we think and hope. It may not be good, but it will be something different. It is extremely doubtful if the psychosis of transition can be dealt with by a political formula. This is a problem that Dr. Nkrumah and his friends will have to solve. When the white man has gone, who will be the new scapegoat? Who will be blamed when the new present does not equal the glorious past?

19

The White Elephant of Kumasi ... Accra

● WE VISITED the fort built by the British after the occupation of Kumasi. The building was a classic Victorian fortification with the guns mounted in what looked like a cross between a bandstand and a summerhouse. To change the direction of their fire their trails must have been moved by hand.

We next visited the sacred Lake of Busumtwi which is situated at the bottom of a volcano, filling the whole crater. The legend is that it was made by a giant thunderbolt. It is exceedingly beautiful and so sacred that no boat or paddle is allowed on it. All fishing must be done from floating logs propelled by either the hands or feet. The lake god, who is very powerful, has strong prejudices about such things. Way down by the water, little villages were clustered. The whole area was protected by a wire fence and the guardian had to unlock the gate for us. There is a rest house here which is most romantic with its view over the water far below. This was once the home of a powerful fetish which consisted of two life-size models of a woman's breasts in clay, with a knife between them and a wooden idol above. It grew so strong that the government had to suppress it.

From here we went to see the new hospital that is in the process of construction. It is to have five hundred beds and to be a training centre for three hundred nurses. Though not yet finished, it is a remarkable building which would be an ornament to New York or London. It has everything. A magnificent mortuary for six cadavers, all on ice, with metal trays on rollers to move them in and out of the great metal cabinet container looks like a fixture in a giant office. A splendid dissecting room, very large, with two enormous china man-shaped sinks in which post-mortems can be performed. It has an automatic laundry, air-conditioning plant, its own generator for electricity. The concrete floors are covered with beautiful smooth tiles, the wards have extra insulation under the thick rubber floor. The windows have a special kind of yellowish glass which lets in the light but keeps out the heat of the sun. The walls are painted in pastel shades of pink, pale green, blue and grey. Nothing could be more restful — or harder to keep clean. It was the most magnificent white elephant I have ever seen in my life. A joy to behold and an expense forever. So far it has cost three million pounds of, I presume, British taxpayers' money, and it is not done yet. There are no beds, linen, silver, theatre equipment or crockery. There are, in addition, no doctors to staff it and no technicians to run all the very modern and fancy equipment, no nurses, and not even anyone who knows how to keep such a place clean unless they get houseboys that European women — the wives of officials and business people — have trained in their homes.

With a population of five million there are only eighty-five doctors in the civil service and thirty-three in private practice on the Gold Coast. Yet a place like this would probably need a staff of at least a dozen. The answer might be to hand it over to the United Nations for use as a research station for tropical medicines.

And now, having built such a hospital here, there is a clamour for a similar one to be built in Accra. Hospitals appear to be a form of competitive civic expenditure. I have talked to many doctors about the matter and most agree that the army cottage-type huts are perfectly satisfactory, much cheaper to build, easier to staff and simpler to take care of, particularly in a hot climate. Patients are less afraid of entering such an institution. It looks more like the kind of house they have seen before. Their friends can visit them more simply. It is even probable that in Africa there should be cottages where the families could live while one of their members is undergoing treatment and possibly even cook their food under some kind of supervision. And a hundred such hospitals could have been built for less than what this super structure will have cost. It would also seem that doctors should come before hospitals and that very good work can be done in very poor buildings as long as they are clean and weatherproof. One of the reasons for the shortage of doctors is that many of the best young Africans who go to England to be trained remain there. While I was on the Gold Coast, the Prime Minister appealed to them to return. The ones who do come back, with some most notable exceptions, are those who, having qualified, never even work in a hospital to gain experience. They read no medical literature and begin to practise a curious mixture of what they remember of modern medicine and native ju-ju. I have, for instance, recently received a letter from a friend in Nigeria who writes as follows:

I do not know if you met X, the Minister of X. He died sud-denly and it went round that he had been poisoned. He actually collapsed under the accelerated mental strain of his present life and became insane. He did not respond to treatment so they handed him over to African doctors who tied him to a bed and beat him unconscious, and suddenly he died.

There is no reason to assume that this is not true.

One interesting thing about the Kumasi hospital is that it is being built near the famous fetish tree upon which the sacred golden stool of Ashanti descended and was received by Oka Okonfo Anokye, the high priest who climbed up to meet it. Near it is the sacred sword and iron shield that came down from above at the same time. The sword is embedded in the ground and no man is believed to be strong enough to pull it out. The buckler lies beside it. Both are en-closed by a strong barbed-wire fence put up by the contractor who is building the hospital. If anything happened to them, all work would cease and it is doubtful if a single patient would ever come into the place, even if it were fully staffed and equipped.

I had a tooth loose and Mr. Beeton arranged for me to have it out. I went to the old hospital, a very ramshackle affair that will soon be scrapped. It was quite painlessly removed by an African dentist who did a very nice Novocain injection job but was, I felt, anti-white and not friendly. The conditions certainly left a lot to be desired. While I was waiting we saw a typical African scene. A proud young husband had come to fetch his wife who had had a baby. He was dressed in a very nice grey lounge suit, a grey felt hat and brown shoes. She followed him carrying her new rather pale coloured baby in her arms and her suitcase balanced on her head. He naturally carried nothing.

We now went to Mapong, a beautiful drive through mountains and forests. We stayed in the rest house and the district officer, Mr. Grieve, an ex-Ghurka, fed us. He took us to see the mission and the Teachers Training College. This was another Maxwell Fry building, of the perforated wedding cake style. The future young lady teachers were making a most incredible noise, screaming like parrots at each other, but apparently enjoying themselves.

In Kumasi there were masses of cars, mammy wagons and bicycles. We saw one small hand hearse — like a glass case mounted on a coster's barrow. And I made a note of some more mottoes that were painted on some of the vehicles. "Pretty woman never stay long with one man. Why?" "Hate me to the end," "Who knows his end?"

"God Save Al Taxi," "No sweat no sweets," "Charity begins at home," "Seniority is always hated," "People will talk anyway," "Perseverance overcomes difficulties," "Not yet, O Lord," "All days are not equal," "Please be kind," and then a banal boy series — "Strong boy," "Happy boy," "Easy boy," and "Still boy."

The market remained to be seen. This was very large with a somewhat uninteresting and sophisticated selection of objects for sale, and we walked through the crowd rather bored by it all till, passing a Hausa stall, I saw spread out on the ground among a lot of modern trash some really lovely beads, some blue like those dug up in Chaka's kraal in Zululand, and some others that looked even more ancient. I bought two strings and some odd ones — of crystal, and one old twisted glass bead that I thought was Venetian. In the afternoon I went back to buy more but found them gone. The trader had only just unpacked them and from what I could gather through an interpreter he had got them from someone who said they came from some tomb in the desert. When Tiny wore them later in Accra, I found her surrounded by women who certainly knew their value, and when I showed them to Professor Leakey at the museum in Nairobi he told me that some of them dated from about 850 B.C.

Next day we had lunch at the Hotel de Kingsway, the best hotel in Kumasi, before catching our plane back to Accra. Some of the upstairs rooms had open umbrellas over the beds to keep off the rain, and in the ballroom and bar a big palm tree came through the floor in a most decorative manner. One whole wall was open for coolness and we drank beer and watched the vultures on the neighbouring roofs.

Our first day back we were taken to Odumase to see the N'mayem or millet festival by James Moxon who had once been district officer there. This was a very remarkable and historic, although obviously emasculated function. We sat in a grandstand on one side of the show ground. The chiefs in all their glory were seated under their state umbrellas opposite to us, but before they sat down they paraded round the field.

First came the Konor, or local king. He was preceded by two dancing girls and two women in pink evening dresses with straw hats. One carried a wooden paddle and the other had a recently severed goat's leg, fastened to a string round her neck, which she worried in her teeth like a dog right through the proceedings. Other chiefs followed in their palanquins and with their entourage of elephant-tusk horn blowers, drummers, executioners, guards, running footmen and stool bearers. Over each was a twirling, brilliantly coloured state umbrella, held by a slave. One chief came in riding piggy-back on one of his subject's shoulders. Each stool was reverently carried by an attendant, one was shaped like an elephant. The king's stool was particularly grand and carried by two men; the first had it on his head while the second held two long reins of leopard skin to which bells were attached, that he jangled violently. Some of the drums were square in shape, something we had never seen before. Among the retinues were men armed with whips made of iguana tails with teeth set in them at three-inch intervals. The king's drum, a long two-man instrument, was ornamented with human skulls wrapped in white cloths, presumably to disguise them, but if one looked carefully the eye sockets were quite apparent.

We greeted each chief, and the ceremony began. Two ju-ju priests dressed in white sheetlike garments blessed the seed millet, poured a libation — probably gin — on the ground, and then went round throwing handfuls of the blessed seed at the chiefs, ourselves — the assembled white people, and the gaily coloured crowd.

We now drove back to the chief's house where we had very nicely served sandwiches and lemon squash. We met some of his lady relations. Very pretty girls, beautifully dressed in white frilly blouses with magnificent kente cloths draped round their hips. On the whole, most African women are too heavy behind to look well in European frocks or skirts, though there are exceptions and I saw some girls with most beautiful figures. In the afternoon we went to call on the Liberian consul, Mr. Lloyd Whisnant, who was most helpful about my visit to Liberia, where we had been invited by the President, thanks to Dr. Nkrumah's good offices on my behalf.

The next day, being Sunday, we went on a picnic with the Sparkeses to a ruined fort at Senya Beraku. What a beautiful place for a weekend; nothing could have been more glamorous. Ruins, sands, the pounding surf.

I found that in some places the fish eagles are called palm-nut eagles because they have taken to eating them. They also dig up groundnuts and hunt the lawn for worms, like chickens. Mr. Beeton told me to watch for them in the morning when we got up. This struck me as most ignoble and uneagle-like behaviour.

Mrs. Sparkes told us how, if one gives a big party, the boys borrow the household silver from one another and one is quite likely to go out and recognise some of one's own stuff on the table. Nothing, however, is ever lost or stolen. We discussed swollen shoot, the cocoa disease, and I found that there was another variety of cocoa which is immune to it and produces ten times as many beans, but there were two objections. The chocolate making machinery might not be able to handle the beans as they were of a different size and, of still greater importance, no one seemed to know what the flavour of the finished product would be like. Cocoa butter is the basis for that most frightful of liqueurs, Crème de Cacao. I had always wondered what it was made of. Oddly enough, the beans, before they are fermented, have no taste of chocolate but are said to be very nourishing although indigestible.

I learnt about a special class of African girls called bungalow girls who consort only with Europeans, and of a woman who proudly said her family had supplied mistresses to the governors of the Gold Coast for generations.

We met the partner of a big firm of accountants who had come to audit some books which had proved to be too big a headache for the local boys, a charming man and his wife who was investigating the possibility of starting a building society on the Gold Coast, the chief difficulty being complete insecurity of title. With the exception of a few very small areas, the land was distributed by the chiefs who held it under God. Since the land was God's it could not be sold, which presented certain difficulties under European law. And now there was a French African who had brought down an exhibit of native sculpture from Dakar — a very nice fat little man, who was delighted to find someone who spoke French. But he was much disliked by the chief steward who addressed him as "African," nothing else, and who had the greatest objection to waiting on anyone of his own colour. He was a good boy but a real blue-white-ten-carat snob, who had worked for one master for twenty-one years, until, in fact, he died, and did not think much of the continual boardinghouse-like coming and going of the hostel.

Another reason we liked the place was because we had tamed the big lizards that lived on the stoep to come for scraps when we called "Liz . . . Liz . . ." They liked bread, bacon, fruit, fried fish and, had we stayed long enough, would have eaten out of our hands. There was one big male with a red head and chest and indigo tail, that changed to orange at the tip, who did nonstop press-ups. There were about half a dozen less decorative females. When we finally left, I wrote out instructions for the feeding of lizards for future guests on the notice board in the dining room.

We now went to a most interesting entertainment — a High-Life dance — with Sean Graham at the Rogers Club. Our party consisted of ourselves, Sean, Gloria, Joyce Gidden, the Prime Minister's secretary, a handsome West Indian woman with greying hair, most intelligent, sophisticated, and cagey, as far as the Prime Minister was concerned, and another couple whose name I have forgotten. He was an African barrister married to a white wife.

We watched the dancing which was in the open air and then a beauty parade of the girls who were beautifully dressed in European evening clothes. The three judges sat in front of us. As far as I was concerned, the choice was restricted to two most lovely tall young women, as graceful as deer. But neither of them got the prize. It went to a girl whom I would not even have placed, but on enquiry I found that one of the judges was her auntie and another one of her mother's friends. Some of the girls carried themselves beautifully, like slim arrows balanced and swaying on their high heeled shoes, others walked no better than white women. These were the sophisticated young ladies who had been raised in town and who had never carried a pot on their heads. It always amused me to think of our schools where girls used to be made to walk with a book on their heads. A good walk is not just a balancing trick. The secret is the thrust upwards from the loins against a real weight. Most African women carry weights that are too heavy for them to lift alone, and quite small girls will swing along with a paraffin tin of water on their heads that weighs forty pounds. The secret is the thrust, the stillness of the torso, and the swinging action of the pelvis. This pelvis swing of the African woman is very interesting. In some it seemed to move fully four inches either way as they walked.

The dancing — "high life" as it was called — was of a very high order and most graceful. The men, in evening dress, were beautiful performers and everyone most well behaved. There were no quarrels, no drunks, which is more than would have been the case in a European assembly of a similar size in comparable conditions.

A few nights later I dined as a guest at the Accra Dining Club which is a mixed stag affair at the Avenida Hotel. It was most enjoyable and I sat between two African barristers, both good company. We discussed mixed marriages, which they were against. The brother of one of them had a white wife, which he said made things very difficult. He even went so far as to say a man should not marry out of his own tribe since the difference in custom and upbringing varied so greatly between one people and another.

It is not surprising that Africans in Europe go with white girls, since there are very few of their own race there. No more surprising than white men in Africa, before the advent of white women — a postwar innovation — taking black mistresses.

I made discreet enquiries on this subject, asking some very senior officers what the official attitude was about it. Did it ruin a man's career? They said it did not as long as the association was not flaunted and there was no open scandal.

But there were dramas and crimes of passion. No greater or more numerous than they would be in any other society, but pointed up by the colour of the protagonists. One man, who had kept an African girl for years, came back with a wife, was seduced into sleeping with his mistress again, and she killed him in her bed. In a non-British colony a white district officer's wife gave birth to black twins. She was shipped back to Europe at once but his career would be ruined. A cuckold might be considered amusing, but this was beyond humour. In another colony I met a man with a charming young wife who had gone back to his black mistress, and was living with them both. Perhaps by now the wife has found out. Even then, as is usual in such cases, everyone else on the station knew of the liaison.

All these are normal tragedies, to be found in any newspaper on almost any day, in any country of the world. The drama here is one of colour, of miscegenation, of a background of tropical palms and tom-toms, of sweat and prickly heat, of palm wine and gin, and dashes and fetish. This raises the emotional and artistic temperature from the purely sordid into the dramatic. It is the *mise en scène*. The barbaric beauty, the pulsing beat of the surf. The python draped over the branch, the leopard coughing in the night. The maddening reiteration of the fruit bat's cry. The nostalgic madness of the white man seeking an escape — any escape — from loneliness.

I got an interesting story from my friend Dr. Stewart Simpson, the Director of Veterinary Services, about an incident that occurred in the northern territories when he was staying with a district officer. One day when he was out he met a lot of women carrying a guinea fowl trussed up in grass. They were singing very happily and it was obviously a triumphal march of some kind. They said: "We have got the killer." The killer? The killer of what? He told the district officer and neither of them could make head or tail of it. Two days later some men came in with a litter. They said they had killed the thing. What thing?

The thing.

The guinea fowl?

No, not the guinea fowl.

They had put it on the fire to burn it alive, but it was very strong, and had escaped to join the wild ones.

"Then what is this?" the district officer asked.

This is really *it*. *It* had attacked the women in the fields. They had screamed and as the men came *it* ran into the bush. They had shot *it* with arrows and speared *it*. And here *it* was. They had brought *it* in.

The two white men went out to see what they were carrying. It was a man who had been speared to death.

"This is serious," the district officer said. "It is murder."

The men said: "But we have a woman, too. The one the *thing* attacked. She is torn open from scalp to belly. We have taken her to the dispensary." And they had.

Once again, believe it or not. And how does one deal with such an event? How is it reported? Is it any wonder that many odd things never appear on the official files. What would Whitehall say? What would happen if questions were asked in Parliament? Africa is the country of the whitewash brush and the great hush-up.

Another case is that of a man-eating hyena which was supposed to be a woman. Not believing a word of it, the district officer set a spring gun up where it was supposed to pass. Next day it was reported that the gun had gone off and an old woman was found in the village who had bled to death from a gunshot wound in the thigh. A coincidence, of course, but try to persuade the villagers that she was not the hyena.

Some more curiosities. On a road near Accra there is a ju-ju stone which had not been known about when it was surveyed. Result? The Public Works Department had to split the road on each side of it.

As to slavery, the *Instructions to Political Officers*, published in London in 1919, have the following headings: British Policy on Slavery. General Emancipation. Reasons For and Against Slavery. Relations of Women Slaves to Their Masters. Methods of Slave Dealings. Holding Persons in Pawn. Disposal of Freed Slave Children. That is not so long ago. And there is no doubt that even today a form of slavery exists on the Gold Coast which I heard about and which was subsequently fully reported by Eric Downton in the *Times*. He says he saw at Bolon Bolgatanga, in the Northern territories on the French Ivory Coast, the notorious traffic in migratory labour being conducted by African collectors and middlemen. These labourers are rounded up and sold between middlemen till they reach the cocoa farmer where they are shamelessly exploited.

In Abyssinia there are still slaves. They still raid into British territory and export slaves to Arabian harems as concubines or eunuchs.

Some of them are made full eunuchs — an operation necessitating the removal of all external organs which only thirty per cent of the victims are said to survive. As to cannibalism, there is plenty of evidence of that too. And why not in a land where protein is short and people think of meat the way we think of chocolates?

I quote an extract from Hansard (Legislative Assembly Debates of 27th February 1953, page 40):

> *Mr. Ayinibisa. Re shortage of meat on the Gold Coast. The Government is contemplating getting meat from the French colonies. I do not think it will be correct as in the French colonies they have certain meats . . . intelligent and non-intelligent. In most of the French colonies they still eat the flesh of man even as far as the Congo. If you import meat excuse me to say you are not going to get the heads, feet, hands or anything else to show and prove the fact, therefore it is dangerous to contemplate the Government bringing in meat from the French territories, particularly intelligent meat. We want animal meat. Animal meat is termed non-intelligent in those territories . . .*

Evidently the legislature believes in the existence of cannibalism in the adjoining territories, where no doubt they accuse British territories of similar habits.

Two more amusing questions were asked in the House of Assembly. Mr. Kusi asked Mr. Casely Hayford, the Minister of Agriculture and Natural Resources, what was the estimated population of the tsetse fly. To which the Minister replied: "There is no record of the tsetse fly population."

Another question was about the humidity of Accra "which induces pulmonary complaints."

The chief medical officer was asked what he was doing about the humidity.

This is the lighter side of such debates. There is always a light side in Africa, just as there is always a dark and tragic one. Like its own sunlight and shade, Africa is a continent of extremes, of tropic downpours and bitter droughts, of laughter and murder, of burning heat and icy cold, of contrast, violence and paradox.

We were now all set for Liberia. Only one thing remained, and that was rounding up the traveller's cheques and letters of credit. When I went for them they had disappeared to the tune of £1237. They had been locked in a briefcase and I had had no reason to look at it for some time. In addition to the money, the yellow fever and vaccination certificates had gone and so had the plane tickets to Zanzibar.

I went to see the police — a European colonel of the C.I.D. who sent two African plainclothes men down to the hostel. They filled in forms most meticulously in a fine round schoolboy hand. They asked where I was a native of?

I said: "South Africa, but I thought you boys didn't like the word 'native'? I was told that I must not call Africans 'natives' and yet you call me a native."

There was no answer to that. They just went on writing in their fine round hands and asked our fellow guests if they had seen anyone with my briefcase. They questioned the staff, who were remarkable for their honesty, and finally they asked me what I thought had happened. I said I knew. The luggage had been left in charge of the government chauffeur, who had driven us up from Accra, for a period of three hours while he had some minor repairs done in Kumasi. That was when it had happened. Why had I not noticed it before? Because he had relocked the case and I had had no occasion to go to it.

Of course the two parts of both letters of credit, which should never be kept together, were together. The traveller's cheques being on the American Express were guaranteed but the whole thing meant that, even if we got the money back, it would be the best part of a year before it was all cleared up.

I got a letter from the health people saying that I had had my certificates or I could not have got into the country. I wrote to Sir Charles Arden-Clarke, asking him to give me a letter saying that my papers were in order when I came to the Gold Coast and asked him to put his most official seal on it, which he did. A splendid red sealing wax affair, about two inches across.

I found that there was quite a racket of this kind. Everyone was most kind and sympathetic, which did not make me feel less of a fool. But I was much touched by two offers to lend me money if I was short. The police, with their usual efficiency, of course traced nothing. Not even the government car which had been lent us by the Ministry of Transport.

After a few hours' sleep, we walked over to the airport — probably the ugliest in Africa. The cocoanut matting of the waiting room is filthy. The Morris chairs are black with sweat. The naked light bulbs blaze down from the flyspecked ceiling. It would be difficult to imagine a more unattractive point of arrival to the capital of a rich country. This objection was partially made up for by the African personnel who were always most helpful and obliging.

● *Republic of Liberia*

20

The Love of Liberty ... Monrovia

● LIBERIA is the most interesting country in Africa. The only Negro republic in the continent. A colony seized by a handful of liberated slaves who, in a series of colonial wars against the indigenous inhabitants, have now conquered forty-three thousand square miles of rich mountain and forest land. The masters are some twenty-thousand-odd Americo-Liberians who came with the motto "The Love of Liberty Brought Us Here" and, with this slogan in one hand and American arms in the other, took possession of the interior in the traditional manner. The only difference between them and the white colonists was that they did not settle in the interior and did not develop the country. They merely exploited it, raised taxes and even, at one time, indulged in the slave trade, selling natives to the Portuguese islands of San Tome and Principé and the Spanish island of Fernando Po, at so much a head.

The peculiar interest of the country lies in this colonial exploitation by black men of black men, and the necessity for pointing it up is due to the continued attacks by Africans and their friends upon all white-administered territories, from the Cape to the Mediterranean.

Liberia was the first experiment of this kind. The Gold Coast is the second. Abyssinia is an African land ruled by Africans but apart from the short Italian occupation has never till today been much exposed to Western civilisation, and both slavery and slave raiding still go on.

Let us look at the beginnings of Liberia. Nothing could have been more auspicious than the arrival in 1816 of a band of freed slaves sent to Africa to establish themselves in their ancestral homeland by the American Colonisation Society. The United States Government furnished appropriations. Arms and ammunition were bought. (It is interesting to reflect on why they were bought in such quantities.) Ships were chartered to carry the settlers to Africa where they were to found new colonies — the hateful word. America was glad to get rid of her freed slaves who were clamouring for the emancipation of their brethren — so it was not all good will and charity. To the five thousand freed slaves sent from the U.S.A. fifteen thousand others, captured from slavers on the high seas, were landed as they were taken.

The first expedition sailed on the *Elizabeth* in 1820 and settled on the little island of Sherbro on what is now the northern boundary of Liberia. Disaster struck them — disease and hardship were too much for them and they were taken to the nearby British colony of Sierra Leone. A year later the *Nautilus* arrived with more settlers and picking up the survivors sailed South to a pleasant fertile tract which had been bought from the natives and in January 1822 landed on what is now known as Providence Island in the estuary of the Mesurado River. From this base they moved to the mainland where they met every sort of difficulty, including attacks by the natives who now regretted selling their land and who, but for the arrival of Captain Spence and the *Cyane*, who came to protect the settlers, would have finished them off.

This is the story of most colonies. Natives being tricked into selling land, then finding the settlement is becoming permanent, regretting it and attacking the settlers. They never understood the transaction in the first instance, which is contrary to all native law and custom, since among them land cannot be alienated.

The settlers defended themselves bravely. Colonials always do this. Against Red Indians, Zulus and other savages, fighting to protect their homes and lands. And again, as usual, guns and cannon overcame the spears and arrows of the natives and peace was made. More settlers arrived, and the town of Monrovia, named after President James Monroe who had at one time headed the American Colonisation Society, was founded, and a war, which has never really ended, was begun with the natives.

Here is a list of actions fought by the Frontier Force with American help, the troops often being led by American Negro officers, against the savages of the interior, in 1852, 1856, 1875, 1884, 1893, 1910, 1913 and 1916. The Kroo war of 1916 was settled only by the arrival of the United States Cruiser *Birmingham*. But for this American intervention, the Liberians would probably have been massacred. During the Second World War it is almost certain that the natives would have revolted but for the presence of strong American Negro forces.

Writing of Liberia in 1906, Sir Harry Johnstone said that there were no means of transport, no roads, no bridges, no telegraph, no medical or educational facilities, and that only the possession of arms enabled the few thousand coastal Negroes, who controlled the country, to exist. He described Americo-Liberians as not industrious. They grew no fruit or vegetables and even had to import their rice. Few of them had been or dared to go thirty miles from their capital, and they were without any feelings of sympathy for the natives whom they described as bush niggers, enslaved, and never regarded as citizens.

Henry Fr. Reeve, writing in 1923, describes the Liberians as fond of litigation, whether they win their case or not. They like to be lawyers or parsons and do not want to work. He said there were no roads, even in Monrovia, no hospitals or professional nurses, no drains and sometimes no doctors. Slaves were shipped to Fernando Po at fifteen dollars per head, which was paid by the Spanish Government. Fetish men, devil men, leopard and other societies exist and among the members are to be found educated men.

Delafosse, for a time French Consul in Liberia, says the people are dirty, eat bad food and produce weakly children. Superficially, many Liberians are civilised, reading books and living in good houses and regarding themselves as superior to the natives, when actually they are inferior, both from a moral point of view and one of well-being. The interior is still unexplored.

This is the picture from a research point of view. A story of colonial exploitation of the worst kind, something far worse than anything done by any white race in Africa. Exploitation of black men by black men, by freed slaves who reinstituted slavery, both on a domestic and export basis. An example of black rule in which the masters made no effort to assist the subject races.

That this has occurred in a country which, though not a colony (this word being anathema to the American people), is still one in which the United States takes a "particular interest," is a grave reflection on those who have kept the truth from the general public. In the outer world Liberia is regarded as an American possession in which "indirect rule" has been given its head and only profit has been considered.

Now for my personal experiences as the guest of President William V. S. Tubman, who has recently been elected for his second term. His administration cuts the history of Liberia in two with the knife of his personality. There is before Tubman and after him. Things are not good yet, but they are certainly much better. Liberia which was once no more than a tragic joke is taking shape of a kind. The President is an outstanding man, but my impression is that he is alone, that nothing would be done without him and that he carries the state upon his shoulders. Nkrumah does much the same. In Africa it is men, not systems, that count — individuals on whom everything depends and without whom everything would slide back.

When we landed at Roberts Field, the big airport built by the Americans during the war, we were met by the Honourable Ajassiz Knuckles, a very pleasant young Liberian from the State Department.

His car was a new dark red Pontiac. The first few miles of road were first class — this was while we were on the Firestone property. Once we passed their barrier, the road went to pieces. Many of the women and children were powdered with white chalk as a form of medicinal ju-ju protection against devils. Most of the women's breasts were bare. They did not seem a very cheerful bunch, much less happy than the Gold Coast people.

The huts and houses increased in number and suddenly we found ourselves in Monrovia. The houses vary from ultramodern structures to Victorian homes and tumbledown corrugated swish and iron buildings.

Ducor Hall, the government hostel, was one of the Victorian numbers, solidly built of stone and furnished with an interesting mixture of the new and the old. In the sitting room there was a large-painted cupid fountain standing in a waterless zinc bath five feet across. There were two plaster bronze-painted Arab heads on stands, and several vases with artificial carnations. By contrast, the draperies and curtains were new and of a very attractive bold floral design.

The bedroom was most comfortable, with a bedside lamp and a three-speed floor fan. The maids — Miss Brown and Miss Brooks — who expected to be called "Miss," were cheerful and fat and wore Topsy hairdos of tight hedgehog twists.

We were driven around town by the Honourable James Morgan, Chief of Protocol of the State Department, a very handsome powerful man with a deep Paul Robeson voice. We crossed the St. Paul River by the new Tubman Bridge and followed a splendid coastal road for ten miles or so till it petered out.

We saw the island where the first settlers landed and the site of one of their battles with the natives. Then we drove back along the bluff where the best houses are — those of the richest Liberians, high officials and the foreign consulates — and saw the enormous quarry from which was obtained the stone for the harbour. One of the finest in West Africa, it is semicircular with a wide entrance into the open sea. And so home to Ducor Hall.

There were other guests — three Americans, including a botanist, from Akron, investigating a possible concession for a rubber company. It was their first visit to Africa and they were somewhat shaken by the experience.

This was the residential area where white people other than government officials lived, but it was a kind of uncongested slum. I saw from our window chamber pots being emptied out over second-floor verandas into the tangle of grass and heaps of empty cans piled up against the house. The side roads were unpaved and big rocks had just been roughly levelled off. And all this was what one saw easily in passing by, as it were.

In the morning we called on the Secretary of State, the Honourable Gabriel L. Dennis, another big, very handsome man in his late fifties. He was dressed in a pale cream suit with a gold brocade tie in which there was a large diamond stickpin — clothes which no white man could have carried off, but which on him looked splendid. He is a much travelled man and has, since his childhood, covered more than a million miles. We were then taken to visit the President by the Honourable George Padmore, the Assistant Secretary of State. The long waiting room of the white executive mansion was crowded with people waiting for an audience. I was told the President often started work at five in the morning and sometimes went on till late at night. There were sentries standing about in rather sloppy battle dress, paratrooper boots and rifles with short fixed bayonets.

After some waiting we were ushered in. President Tubman is a small thick-set man of great charm of manner. His room was obviously modelled on the study of President Roosevelt. His desk was covered with souvenirs of various kinds, and a crucifix. There was a Liberian flag behind him, with its six red and five white stripes, representing the eleven signers of the Declaration of Independence. The blue field in the corner represents Africa and the white star Liberia, its only republic. The President was smoking a cigar and was sorry we were staying so short a time. I was sorry too, but our plans had been upset by the loss of our money, and we still had a long way to go — right across Africa at its widest part. No one could have been kinder than this President, who has really put Liberia on its feet.

In the afternoon we went to see the Le Tourneau houses. These are cast in a single solid piece of concrete and can be built in a day if nothing goes wrong. But they had proved too expensive to be practicable. Later we saw the machinery — immense things — for making these houses on the dock on its way back to the U.S.A.

The next day we went to see the iron mine at the Bomi Hills. It took us two hours by rail. The ore is fed from the trucks to the holds of the ships by long conveyor belt. The toy train takes up supplies and brings back ore, which is said to be the richest in the world and tests at sixty-nine per cent pure iron. We rode with the engine driver, who was an Englishman, sitting on chairs beside him.

We were met by Mr. Davey, the manager of the Liberian Mining Company (an eighty-year concession), a big, extremely able American engineer whose hobby was town planning and architecture. The layout of the mine showed it too. It was a beautiful job, like a small garden city. We had an excellent American lunch and then went to look at the machine shops where, as far as I could see, they were able to do everything except build a complete bulldozer. Then up to the mine. It is a solid hill of ore which dips like a saucer and reappears further on, so that it will be many years before it is completely exploited. Africans do all the driving of tractors, trucks and bulldozers, and there is the usual difficulty of getting them to attend to maintenance or not overload their machinery. This was the same story that I had heard everywhere and it knocks on the head the idea that African labour is cheap. It is not economical to have a cheap man handling an expensive machine. Yet, paying him more will not increase his ability.

There were diamonds three days' walk away in an alluvial deposit in the forest. Mr. Davey said he had had them offered to him. I asked if he had been to see the area. He said no one had — it was unexplored. There were no roads, only tracts, and it was probably not even very safe.

He had designed and built a very fine one hundred thousand dollar hospital with twenty-five beds, and all the staff houses had every modern convenience. It was, in fact, a little piece of America and could have been removed intact from the United States or returned there and no one would have been surprised to see it. This was an example of the Americans' great gift of organisation.

The native houses we saw along the line were built of swish or tar paper on wooden frames with very high-pitched untidy thatch roofs that made them look like haystacks. Many of them had open sides with pillars for supporting the roof beams.

When we returned we visited Dr. John W. Davis, the head of the foreign operations administration in Liberia — the Point-Four Programme. The office buildings and equipment seemed first class. An assistant then gave me a half-hour lecture on the aims of the programme, which amounted to no more than the most ordinary plans for the improvement of crops and such rural amenities as wells for water and the establishment of latrines. My impression is one of too much paper, too much planning, too much talk, too many reports and too little done. It reminded me of what a golf pro once said of my style — "all swing and no hit."

In the evening we went to a party given by our friend Mr. Padmore, where we met the elite of Monrovia. The house was delightful, the food excellent, the drinks first class. It was an evening no different from a thousand others, except that we were the only white people present. I was asked to say a few words, something I had not expected, and so spoke about my feelings on colour, which are very well defined. They are those of Cecil Rhodes — equal rights for all civilised men. Where this falls down is in the definition of civilised. I said what I had said to the Prime Minister at Accra: "I do not like a man because he is white or dislike him because he is black. I remain a snob, as most people are, even if they will not acknowledge it. I prefer educated people with adequate incomes to the poor and uneducated, whatever their colour. This, whatever anybody may say, is the usual approach. We all choose our associates from our own income and educational strata and by and large the colour problem is mostly a question of economics."

It is remarkable how prejudice disappears in the presence of gold. Indian rajahs have never been considered dark in colour. The West Indian heiresses in the eighteenth century were soon snapped up by impoverished noblemen, however frizzy their hair or dark their complexions.

It was a black tie — and evening dress for the ladies — party. And among them was a perfect beauty — a sort of chocolate-coloured Dresden china figurine. Very gay and charming, with immense black eyes in her heart-shaped face. She was going with her husband to the Liberian Legation in Paris the following week, where I have no doubt she is a great success and will do more to put Liberia on the Paris map than a dozen diplomats. But I should not like to have to pay her dress bill. The Liberians are very clothes conscious and very well dressed. Also very formally dressed. They all wear collars and ties and do not take off their jackets however hot the weather.

Next day we drove to the experimental farm at Suakoko. There was very little livestock to be seen.

Quite a few African gentlemen were taking their rest in hammocks — the first I had seen on the coast. They seemed to replace deck chairs here. We were not greeted with any enthusiasm. Not even the children waved as we passed. I had the feeling that this was not just an anti-white demonstration — it was an anti-car and all the Americo-Liberian authority and oppression that the car represented. This was the first country in which I had seen hungry men; that is men with so little to eat that their ribs stood out. We stopped at an inn called the Cuckoo's Nest, and passed an eating house called the Big Belly Restaurant.

Some of the village houses were decorated with drawings of human hands, some with spots and one had a big scorpion with a human head. The wild almond was common in the villages as a shade and council tree, but I was surprised here as elsewhere to see so few fruit trees such as avocado pear, citrus or paw-paw, which grow so easily in this climate. There were of course, bananas.

We passed two soldiers of the frontier force carrying their rifles. I was told they patrolled the area to keep order. A dangerous business, as native soldiers alone are inclined to abuse the populace they are supposed to protect. Later I found this to be true, and I also heard that there had been some cases of suicide among the troops, several having shot themselves. A phenomenon of transition.

This station is difficult to describe. There was everything there with which to experiment, but although it was started in 1947 there was very little to show for the time and money that had gone into the place. A new laboratory building, very fine indeed, with a lot of nearly empty rooms and only two scientists that I could see. Two big Brahma bulls imported from the United States running with about twenty grade N'dama cows. I asked which cow was the mother of a half-grown young first-cross bull and no one knew. I asked about "trips" and no one knew whether there were tsetse fly here or not. Obviously not, or the bulls would have been dead. But where were the fly belts? In the poultry section — a nice building — too many birds had been bred and owing to insufficient perch room they slept on the floor. Most of the pigs had been killed, I was told, but they might have died judging from the condition of the few that remained. They were covered in lice and flies, without bedding, and crippled with rheumatics. Their food — a mixture of bran — was fermenting in the sun. The runs had not been cleaned for days. There were experimental fish ponds but the man who knew about them was away. The man who looked after the tree nursery was away too, otherwise I would have liked to ask him why the cocoa seedlings, that were planted far too close together in the open ground, were entirely without shade. I was told they were trying six varieties of bananas and

saw a rice mill that was being erected. It was hoped that the natives
— or tribesmen as they are sometimes called — would bring in their
rice to be hulled. There seemed to be some question about whether
they would or not, owing, I imagine, to their doubt about how much
of their produce would stick to the fingers of those who handled it.
The administration is by district officers, supported by frontier force
troops, who deal with the local puppet chiefs.

It is easy to understand the African's dislike of the white man but
he still prefers to do business with him. This is one of his problems.
To hate the man he trusts and mistrust the man he is told to love
because he is the same colour. The African does not have an easy
time, and must face and solve tremendous psychological problems in
the near future.

But we met some very nice people here. The director — an American Negro — a graduate of Tuskegee, was extremely friendly. Miss
Simpson, the poultry expert, who gave us a very good dinner, could
not have been nicer. Nor could a young Jamaican doctor who had just
arrived, or his very pretty American wife — a Rutgers girl who seemed
rather lonely, and pleased to talk to us about the States although she
had been there much more recently than we had.

The station had, I was told, fifty thousand dollars' worth of equipment. Most of it seemed to be in need of repair, or was actually being
repaired. I was glad to have seen Suakoko but astonished that I had
been shown it. I can only think that it was believed to be on the up
and up by the Department of Agriculture and Commerce. It certainly was an experimental station even if no experiments of value
were carried out there.

Next morning we set off for Firestone. We were held up for a
couple of hours while a bridge was mended. This is the only road to
French Guinea. The bridge consisted of two big logs as bearers set
about a foot above the stream, and the usual sapling crosspieces. They
had been at the repair work some hours before we arrived and there
was a long line of cars and trucks on both sides of the stream. We
were the only white people but everyone was friendly enough. We
were offered a very nice monkey for a quarter. Only American money
is used here. There is no local currency, though a quarter is often
called a shilling. The work was watched by a mixed crowd that included a number of young ladies in clean white sweat shirts with the
words "Seventh-Day Adventist Mission" printed across their chests.
The job would have gone faster if there had been more than one
hammer and if each nail had not had to be straightened.

We reached the Firestone experimental station at last and had about an hour there which was most interesting. In fact, here they were doing, and had been doing for years, with the greatest efficiency, all those experiments which the Liberians were about to begin at Suakoko. Was some curious form of African pride involved? The information was here. The experts were here. The best thing the government station could have done would have been to carry out field experiments among the villagers under the supervision of the company and in conjunction with them, and so avoided all duplication.

The work I saw in those few minutes impressed me very much — as has everything American that I have seen in Africa. Varieties of rice were being tested and many kinds of fruit tried out.

At the club we settled down in real American comfort to drink real American martinis. I have never needed them more. We had some lunch and then started on our tour. There was a lot to see before our plane left that night.

We drove miles and still more miles along perfect roads with the tires singing in the fine gravel. All Firestone — every block numbered, every tree a pedigree, and we only touched the fringe of it. Ninety thousand acres of rubber — the biggest plantation in the world. A million acres the total concession. This accounts for some of the "bad blood," as the French say, against the white man. This once was farm land. The tribal owners were dispossessed, and their sacred soil rented to Firestone at six cents per acre. What an outcry there would have been if the French or British had done it. But these were Africans who were renting the land to which they had no right, so it was all right.

Leaving Tiny to rest, I went over the factory. It had the smell of a tannery which I was told was due to a bacterial action, similar to that which attacks hides. I had never thought of rubber like this or realised that if it was not smoked or treated it would go bad. It was hard to think of it as white tree blood. Just as it is hard to think of water as molten ice, or ice as a rock which melts at low temperatures. But there it was, and it stank.

The procedure of getting the rubber is more or less as follows: the boys tap the trees by cutting off the bark in strips, and fasten on at the base plastic basins to collect the latex. When full they empty the latex into big milk buckets of shining stainless steel — it even looks like milk — and carry them on either end of a long bamboo shoulder pole to the collecting centre where it is transferred to the tanker trucks which either transfer their load to the tanker boats waiting on the river at the factory dock, or put it through machines which look and operate like giant cream separators and process it on the spot. It is then rolled, dried and smoked in sheets that look like skins or tripe, and finally compressed into bales. When transferring latex from the trucks, compressed air is used. It cannot be pumped because the bubbles could not be got out, and in order to prevent coagulation a solution of ammonia is added to it in the tanks of the ships.

By selection and experimentation the yield of rubber has been pushed up from five hundred to twelve hundred pounds per acre, and the new trees, or clones, although they produce more, are smaller, which saves time, the tapper having a much smaller cut to make since the tree has a smaller circumference.

There are approximately six hundred African-owned plantations, belonging naturally to the ruling caste of Americo-Liberians. The company supplies them with grafted trees, cups, advice and buys back all their produce. It is quite obvious that none of these plantation owners, who are members of the government, are likely to vote for any measure which would be against their own or Firestone's interest. The company pays standard wages of twenty-five cents a day. They want to raise the pay but the government would not allow it because that meant they would have to pay their own labour more. However, the company issues rations, sells extra food at cost or below it, and supplies two ounces of Mulipurpon, a concentrated food which is equal, in terms of calories, to half a full working ration.

Firestone employs about thirty thousand men with a basic wage of twenty-five cents that goes up to one hundred and fifty dollars a month for a few skilled men. David Soper, who deals with the labour, told me what I had heard everywhere else and experienced myself. That it was very difficult to raise an African's pay. If he works well and you pay him more he feels either that he has done too much and relaxes, or that he is indispensable and becomes impossible to handle. Or where, as so often happens, the labour is simply "target labour" the target becomes more easily achieved and the man leaves earlier than he would have done if his pay had not been increased.

The term "target" is used when describing a man who comes to work who need not do so. He has all he wants at home, but feels he would like a bicycle or a phonograph or a sewing machine or a new wife — his "target." So he gets a job and works till he has the necessary money. Then he quits.

The Lotz' house and place was delightful. American designed, American built and American furnished. Firestone is a piece of America. Roberts Field is on the concession so there is direct communication with America — New York is only nineteen hours away.

There is every sort of modern convenience for the white Firestone staff who number about one hundred and fifty — hospitals, club, sports grounds of all kinds.

There were things I wanted to ask but did not. Rubber is not a thing one asks about. Not in the Congo, not in Brazil. The Firestone Company is a good master but it is a master — actually the master of Liberia, because Liberia is Firestone and Firestone and America are synonymous. Liberia is actually an appendage of the great Republic, a colony which America does not administer but nevertheless controls.

I wondered what had happened to the natives who had lived on this land. Who got the money Firestone paid out? Of course I knew the answers. They may not like it but the Liberians know that they depend on the United States for financial help, for advice, for military assistance — though how long they will get it when the country wakes up to the way it has been used, remains to be seen.

Of the total exports in Liberia 1950/51, forty-five million out of the fifty-one million came from the Firestone Company. Now there is Bomi Hills iron mine, taken over by the Liberian Mining Company which will help to produce income for the country. There is African Fruit Company, the first of a projected series of proposed German concessions, some of them very large. Then there is the Le Tourneau Company of Liberia which is going into the country in a big way, and the new shipping arrangements whereby it becomes advantageous for ships to fly the Liberian flag. These are all money making devices which keep the state functioning. But they are all foreign, none are native, none are worked or directed by Americo-Liberians and very little of the money that comes in from them is spent on the aborigines whose taxes form the rest of the national revenue. And with each land concession someone is displaced.

The flight back was the worst I had ever made — a tornado with thunder and lightning the whole way, and our big four-engined job fluttering like an illuminated leaf in the wind. I felt like death and did not feel much better when we landed at Accra at four in the morning, and here at this curious time of night, while going through all the passport and other formalities, I met Count Roussy de Sales of the U.N. Information Centre who had just arrived on the Gold Coast and whom I had not seen since 1937 in New York. He was on his way back to America so, except for shaking hands and wishing him bon voyage, a better one than I had had anyway, I saw nothing of him.

What we wanted now was a nice cup of tea but all we could get was warm beer. Really warm, off the shelf, with a temperature of eighty degrees. Having swallowed it we staggered off.

What was my impression of Liberia? It could be no more in the inside of a week. It was chiefly one of disappointment, a cumulative one. I had hoped for more than this of the African. In Liberia I felt there was a great deal hidden, that it was a whitewashed sepulchre, that, like the road along the sea front, it was pretentious and led nowhere. Everyone I met belonged to a government that did not govern, that lived on the exploitation of the tribes of the hinterland, and the taxes mulcted from the great white companies who really ran the country. Protocol, black tie, white tie, no one took their coats off and did any work.

I found that in 1933 President Barclay passed a sedition law which punished any criticism of the government, or the giving of any information on domestic affairs to a foreign government with imprisonment and confiscation of property. No wonder I had been moved through the country in an atmosphere of cotton wool. Cushioned in political silence. This accounted for the fear that I had felt about me — a silence on the top and a seething resentment underneath. I found that Eslanda Goode Robeson, Paul Robeson's wife, who certainly could not be accused of bias against anything African, called the ruling class a shameful picture . . . a disgrace to the Republic and the U.S.A. which sponsors it. And that when President Barclay and President-Elect Tubman visited America, the *Afro-American* and *Chicago Defender* were critical of them as representatives of the Negro race and commented on the fact that the President received a salary of thirty thousand dollars a year while the workers received a wage of twenty-five cents a day. But which was the real Tubman? The one I had met or the one I had read about? Probably both were the real man. For almost every educated African is a Dr. Jekyll and a Mr. Hyde.

I found that in May 1943 a dressed-up monkey was taken to the polls and that a small precinct of a dozen houses polled 5100 votes for the Whigs and 7 for the Opposition. That natives were held in pawn (slavery) up to twenty years for debt and were often framed. That the frontier force soldiers demand "dashes" from the natives — anything from a Kola nut to sleeping with their wives. That rice was imported because it was not worth growing if the Commissioner took the crop. I found that the Vai, one of the Liberian tribes, were the only people in Africa to have invented an alphabet, and that the grain coast derives its name from the red pepper which made it famous.

Liberia is well documented. There is plenty to read about it and very little of it is good. But the yoke of the African lies heavy on the African's neck here.

There were now only a few goodbye days left in Accra. One of them was spent with Sean Graham who drove us out to see his friend Dr. Oku Ampofo, the sculptor, who had a very lovely modern house at Mampong. This was a notable afternoon in more ways than one, as Sean drove in the Jaguar at a hundred miles an hour though we slowed down to seventy for the corners.

It was nice to see Gloria Addae again, who was staying with the Ampofos, and at tea we were given a fruit that I had never seen or tasted before, which they called passion fruit but which does not resemble the grenadilla at all, being a largish green gourd about the size of a paw-paw.

Dr. Ampofo was one of those Africans I had come to find — a black man equal to any white man and superior to most, both in education and devotion to his people. He has independent means from his cocoa farms and would sooner work at his sculpture, which would create a sensation in New York, than be a doctor, but feels it his duty to continue in medicine.

Unfortunately, his type exists only in hundreds, if that, instead of in thousands and most of them, like most decent people everywhere, are unpolitical. This type of man is the high point in any civilisation, any culture, black or white, and the proof that colour, as such, is quite unimportant.

When I came back I went to see Rameshwar again to say goodbye and while I was with him a young African student came in to talk about philosophy. He felt that Rameshwar, being an Indian, might have the answers. He asked how he could get "freedom from himself." He had tried religion and it had failed him. It seems that religion here is very strict and members of the congregation — he was Methodist — must question nothing. Freedom from self. Surely that was what we all wanted in some way, but it presents a special problem for the African who, till this generation, has had no self, being a unit of the family, or tribe, without the necessity of personal decisions, or even possibility of individual choice. What worried him was his self-consciousness, what, I suppose we would call his ego. This conversation was most interesting, as it pointed up something I had been thinking about for some time — the psychological problems which the African was going to have to face in the transition period.

The last day came. We packed up and went to dine with the Jacksons, who lived next door.

Standing on the veranda with Mrs. Jackson (Barbara Ward), Commander Jackson, the old American Quaker couple who were staying with them, and Tiny, I watched the sun go down in a sky of grey and orange taffeta and sink into the sea. The two Siamese kittens played at our feet, chasing each other, hiding, boxing with soft sepia gloves. There were drinks on the table and small chop in little dishes.

I was very content. Happy, in an interesting place, one that I had always longed to see, with interesting people. We were off to the Congo in a few hours — the Great Congo, the Zaire of the slavers. Forests, the greatest in Africa, palm oil, pygmies, okapi, crocodiles, cannibals, Mississippi steamboats, gorillas, Watussi and big horned cattle were in my mind. This, the setting and the company for a short story's end or beginning. And then I saw one of the wonders of my life. On the pillar beside me a big moon flower began to move. It was rolled up like a paper spill. It began to unroll, slowly, counter-clockwise. And then suddenly it snapped open like a big white con-volvulus, letting loose its scent, shooting it out, bursting like a bomb of perfume — onto the astonished dusk. More flowers burst open. The pillar was white with blooms, the early purple of the night heavy with the scent that was already bringing the great moths that would fertilise the flowers that had called them. I do not know why this moment meant so much to me. It joined other wonderful moments when, in some way, I had felt near to God. Once in the lilac of a Transvaal evening, I had watched a native girl coming back over the veld from water with a pot on her head. She was singing. When she stopped for a moment a hunting jackal called. Again, near Cape Agulhas, I watched from some high dunes two hundred porpoises playing in the great Antarctic rollers that smashed against the shelving beach. The waves were between me and the sun. I could see through them, and the porpoises were caught as they played in the water like black, toy fish in the bright blue-green aspic of the sea. Once in the Bahamas a great school of little fish almost flew out of the water and landed in a shimmering sheet on the rocks by the shore. They were being pursued by bigger fish and behind the bigger fish were still bigger ones, and behind them a company of monsters. In Florida, a screaming, diving swirl of gulls feasting on something in the sea. A solitary pelican flying low, its wing tips touching the water. A hum-ming bird hovering as it drinks nectar from a red hibiscus flower. Something seen for an instant in the eyes of a beautiful woman. The circling eagle in the sky. The thunder of a galloping horse. What are these magic moments? Memories burnt into the heart.

21

The Leopard of the West

● THERE ARE three great apocryphal figures in Africa today —
Mr. Nkrumah, the black leopard of the West; the imprisoned hyena,
Jomo Kenyatta, in the East, and Strydom, the Afrikander bull hold-
ing his ground in the South.

In the West, Nkrumah dominates the scene. Highly strung, un-
tamed, untamable, bitterly resentful of any bars that stand between
him and the forest of complete freedom. He purrs round the legs
of the masters whom he wishes to destroy, while he roars defiance
into the ears of his lesser fellows. He is a man who radiates mag-
netism and danger, a black political leader, king-sized, packaged in
dynamite. With him it is dominion status, Ghana, freedom or bust.
He is believed to have said that anything, even the slave days, was
better than the present situation.

The election when Convention Peoples' Party swept the polls, of
February 1951 placed Nkrumah in power as Leader of Government
Business, a title which has since been changed to that of Prime
Minister.

He was born in 1906 and is the son of a goldsmith and a market
woman. He received his education at a mission school and Achimota
College. At the age of twenty-six he came to London for a short
period. Then he went to America and obtained a degree of Bachelor
of Arts at the Negro university, Lincoln, in Pennsylvania, and is a
Doctor of Theology. In 1945 he returned to London where he
studied at the London School of Economics, and became secretary
of the Pan-African Federation of which Jomo Kenyatta was president. He maintains that he is the friend of Britain, and desires for
the Gold Coast dominion status within the Empire. He has said:
"I am not even thinking of a Republic. I am a Marxian Socialist
and an undenominational Christian."

Already he has made history. He is the first African prime minister
of an almost self-governing territory, rich in population resources
and potentials. He is not a big man but he is powerful. He moves

quickly, neatly and is unlikely to change his spots. He fits into the West African leopard mythology — omnipresent, dangerous and beautiful. He is not married; he does not drink, except champagne in private; he has no resources except his personality — his brains and political talents which are unequalled in Africa. His enemies accuse him of being the Show Boy Premier, of taking bribes, of strong-arm methods in suppressing all the opponents to his party. To his own people he is a god. They believe Jesus will not return to the world because Kwame Nkrumah is the second Christ . . . He is also "the Star of Africa . . . symbol of the common peoples' aspirations . . . defender of the faith of the common man . . . and the torch of Ghana's emancipation." In this he resembles Jomo Kenyatta in East Africa, whom the Kikuyu regard and worship as a god. Africa is not a place where parties have any meaning. Democracy is only a word. It is the men who count. And the great men who can fill the minds of the people become gods, near gods, from whom all blessings will flow once the white man has been flung out. There is a tendency to regard the Opposition as an enemy to be destroyed. It was reported in the *Ashanti Pioneer* that Mr. Nkrumah had said that anyone who joined the Opposition party was a traitor to his country. This may or may not be true. West African reporting tends to be more interesting than accurate, but it shows the direction of thought.

The same religious and fanatical spirit is shown by the press in Nigeria. Dealing with political opponents, a recent leader began: "The monster is here and there camouflaging the track with confusing scenes in order to divert the seeker's attention. Satan did the same, yet Jesus conquered the devil. Prove as wise as Jesus taught and as witty as Mohammed demonstrated by voting for the N.C.N.C." Politics and religion are inextricably bound together in Africa.

Nkrumah himself is a student of theology. The Dinis of East Africa are religious political revivalist movements. The Watch Towers of the Congo and Rhodesia have a religious background. The ancient gods of Africa are those of the soil, the rivers and the trees, so politics which concern their ownership are bound to have a religious tinge.

Nkrumah lives in his mother's house, a modest villa painted red, the bricks being picked out with white. He lives simply as a man of the people — the political hermit whose only wish is to liberate his land.

But he has his dreams. First — independence. Next — dominion status. Then — a West African Federation which would eventually include Nigeria, Togoland, Liberia, Gambia, Sierra Leone and presumably the French Territories that separate these lands. But he goes further. His interest is in all the African dominions, colonies and protectorates. He has unofficial representatives in South Africa. News of the Gold Coast experiment reaches the Congo from Matadi and passes up the river. All news from Kenya is carefully watched and reported in the Gold Coast press and printed in heavy type, or in a box. This news is always so many Mau Mau executed or the story of some crime committed by a British soldier or a settler. No mention is ever made of the African atrocities, of how the Mau Mau have killed and tortured between one and two thousand of their own fellow Africans.

In his political moves, Nkrumah has been most astute in using what he learnt of the political machine in the United States — organisation, advertising, ballyhoo — and combining it with the Russian techniques of cells and strong-arm methods of intimidation, and perhaps worse, that he learned during his flirtation with communism. I have been told he was once a Communist and have even seen his party number quoted somewhere, but this is probably untrue. But it is not untrue to assert that he had many friends and contacts among them. Turkson Oran, the secretary of the Gold Coast Trades Union Congress, who organised the anti-British strikes that helped him into power, and who was recently suspended by Nkrumah for communist activities "because being associated with the party might jeopardise the Gold Coast's demand for Dominion status," was once his friend.

There are at least two Nkrumahs. To succeed it was absolutely necessary for him to placate the British while inflaming the mob with anti-British sentiment. The only chance for an African politician is to create a wave of hatred and then to ride to eminence and affluence upon its foaming crest. At the same time it is necessary to tell the British not to pay too much attention to what he says to the people, as it does not mean anything. And then to inform the people that his association with the hated white man is only a matter of expediency — just a means to an end. Nkrumah has been much more intelligent than Jomo Kenyatta. He had better material to work with, was younger and more energetic. But it was probably his success which caused the outbreak in Kenya. Not his fault. No one could imagine his having had a hand in it. He had too many fish of his own to fry. But had there been no Gold Coast experiment, there might have been no cooking up of attempts at premature self-government elsewhere.

So here is the picture. This very remarkable man comes out of prison, where he has been incarcerated for inciting violence, and becomes Prime Minister and the idol of the populace at home, and the Great Black Hope of every African on the continent south of the Sahara. Self-government, he says, "is only a step away . . . we are ready to claim the right to our independence."

In the meantime European officials do the work, shield the idle and incapable, and take the blame for anything that goes wrong. In my opinion, the Gold Coast is now at the happiest stage of its history. It has freedom without responsibility, wealth without taxation, services without payment and a glorious feeling of achievement, of being heroic and in the news. At the moment they are under the rainbow, their hand is stretched out for the pot of gold at its end. Will the future disillusion them? Will the responsibility overwhelm them? Will they succeed when they are no longer fed with Western skills, Western capital and Western subsidies?

The naïve British hope of a democracy on Western lines — with an incorruptible judiciary, civil service, and smooth functioning utilities — is unlikely to be fulfilled. But the experiment may still succeed. There are other formulas. The African tradition is of chiefs and kings. It is authoritarian and it is unlikely that Nkrumah, having entrenched himself at the head of an invincible machine like the C.P.P., will allow a strong opposition to grow up that will endanger him.

The question is: How well will these "chauffeur driven" countries drive the car of state on their own? First they were passengers with no say at all in the route. Now they say where they want to go and are taken somewhat too slowly for them in that direction. But the day is coming when they will be free to go where they will at any speed they want. Even today there is some deterioration. Thousands of pounds worth of diamonds have been lost in the registered mail between the mines and Accra. The Prime Minister himself has been accused, and acquitted, of corruption, but no one doubts that there has been corruption somewhere, in a big way, along the line.

This enquiry began with the resignation of Mr. Braimah who was Minister of Works. He admitted receiving £2000 from a Syrian contractor and then said that his conscience forced him to resign, and demand an enquiry into other similar irregularities. He alleged that the same contractor had paid nearly £2000 for a car for the

Prime Minister, Kwame Nkrumah, and that another contractor had paid Nkrumah £40,000 for another contract. Nkrumah denies these allegations and says that the money to pay for the car was borrowed from a Dr. Djin, the acting managing director of the government-controlled cocoa-purchasing company. Dr. Djin is said to be a cousin of a Mr. Djan, Ministerial Secretary to the Ministry of Finance, who has been committed for trial on a charge of accepting a £150 bribe from another contractor!

So far the only references to a certain firm have been in connection with a contract for a thirty-seven-mile road near Accra. It seems that two local firms quoted £15,000 a mile.

In March 1952 Nkrumah wrote to the Minister of Communications and Works saying that this firm was prepared to send a mission to the Gold Coast provided they would get pilot work on a cost-plus basis. It seems that the firm's original tender was unacceptable and Nkrumah advised them that the maximum figure acceptable was £12,000 a mile. Braimah says that this message was sent without his knowledge or consent and conflicted with his policy. Finally in October 1952 Government decided to award them the contract on the basis of a fixed fee plus off-site costs. It has been stated that the cost of the work will be £20,000 a mile.

A great deal of attention was paid to the report by Mr. Braimah that the cost of the new Winneba-Weija Road, constructed by the Astaldi Company, had risen from £12,000 per mile to £22,000 per mile. It appeared that the increase had had Cabinet sanction and that the contract carried a "rise and fall" clause. Much time was spent on the elucidation of this affair.

The *West African Daily Graphic* of October 12, 1953, stated that the auditors' report on the Gold Coast for the financial year ending March 31, 1952, "shows a series of extraordinary errors, arrears of income tax amounting to nearly half a million pounds, and cash frauds of seven thousand pounds."

Meanwhile the country must be developed and Professor W. A. Lewis, a West Indian who holds the chair of economics at Manchester University, was asked to investigate the matter for the government.

He said that the Gold Coast must have foreign capital, which meant that foreigners, or expatriates as they are now called, must come in to deal with their interests. He told them that management was an art that could be learnt only by management and not out of books, so that until they are trained by working with Europeans, there could be no Africans capable of dealing with large concerns. He concluded by saying that whatever they might think of the foreigner they needed him much more than he needed them. This news was not particularly palatable but it appears to have been accepted. The next thing is to persuade foreigners to invest capital in a country whose government is far from stable and notably corrupt. Corruption remains the greatest weakness of the educated African and the greatest impediment to his progress.

There is no doubt that England, until comparatively recent times, was corrupt. It continued to be so till long after the Napoleonic Wars. There is much corruption in Europe and in the United States. But limited corruption can be balanced by natural resources and human efficiency. Where a country is neither rich nor efficient, corruption can prove an insurmountable obstacle to success. The mind of a corrupt man deteriorates. Where profits are calculated to the last penny, where the price is cut by quantity buying and mechanising, leaks all along the line must end in disaster. It is unfortunately true that many Africans regard their education as a tool dedicated, not to their employers or the interests of their country, but to their own personal gain. Many Africans who have studied law in England or America use this knowledge to cheat their fellows legally. They have learnt the law but have no idea what it means, or its tremendous tradition. They have merely extracted from it those elements which will enable them to swindle their neighbours without being found guilty in a court.

The African has been conditioned by centuries of savage competitive life to seize what he desires wherever he can find it. He could be restrained from doing this only by fear of the atrocious punishment meted out for such crimes within the tribe. Once detribalised he had no restraining sanctions.

A favourite method of swindling is to get in touch with Chambers of Commerce in various parts of the world, from whom the trader obtains the names of important exporting houses. He uses good paper with a fancy engraved letterhead. He then makes an order with a bank credit against the goods, or gives a thirty per cent deposit. Legally, the consignee must check the items on the invoice before the consignor can receive his money. So the recipient now lodges complaints with the authorities that he has been cheated and refuses to take delivery of the goods, which are still housed in the customs warehouse with demurrage being charged to the exporter. The consignor has paid freight and insurance which are debited to the consignee's account but which will be paid by him only when delivery is made. The purchaser, who has refused the goods, now suggests a compromise — that he find another buyer, as the goods are not up to sample, or in some way do not comply with his specification. This is agreed to. It is cheaper than paying the return freight and insurance. The goods are now sold at auction for a fraction of their value and bought in by a collaborator of the original purchaser for next to nothing.

The other possibility is that the consignor complains of fraud and cables to have the credit attached, only to find that the business is closed. And the bank has never heard of the transaction and the letter of credit has been forged by a clerk who cannot be found. No one knows anything about the matter. The businessman has disappeared — having packed his fine lounge suit in a tin trunk, he is digging peacefully in a forest clearing dressed in a loincloth and completely indistinguishable from the other millions similarly attired that surround him.

He is now a big man in his village with many wives, goats, land and honour. Having no conscience there is no remorse. He may even have cleared enough to start a transport business with a truck or two. Education has paid off handsomely.

There is no gratitude to his teachers. None to those who enabled him to achieve his doctorate, the missionaries who taught him his ABC or the Europeans who helped him on his way. All this is forgotten. A thousand kindnesses are lost with one insult — real or imagined. He has had his revenge and it is sweet.

But these methods will not make the wheels of industry turn or produce justice in the courts.

I have heard corruption explained like this. Five pounds is a gift, fifty pounds is greedy, five hundred is a bribe. I have also been asked if I give a present when someone has done something for me.

"Of course I do," I reply.

"Very well," comes the answer, "all we do is to give it before we get the favour."

Bribery is a factor in a jury trial — to which must be added intimidation, tribal rivalry, blackmail, witchcraft and, in a political case, chicanery on a large scale, with so many men in high positions involved and all the books concerned in such a state of disorder, or even nonexistent, that nothing can be pinned on anyone, though it is probable that some of the smaller fry will take the rap and be suitably recompensed when they come out.

We can now begin to define some of the necessities of good government — incorruptible magistrates, an efficient postal, medical and transport service, a trustworthy police force and government departments in charge of ministers who are beyond reproach. How many of these exist even at this stage? Still, the West Africans are filled with confidence and hope.

But two psychological factors must be taken into consideration, which appear to be typically African. The first is the fatigue period which seems almost universal among Negroes when suddenly, for no apparent reason, interest is lost. The second is pointed out by Dr. J. C. Carrothers, one of the few experts in African psychology, when he says the African shoots up from a sense of impotence to one of omnipotence and suddenly feels he has nothing more to learn. Then if this bubble is pricked, omnipotence collapses and gives way to the opposite in which he seems himself as an impotent victim of a cruel world.

They still talk of the slave trade but the debt to the slaves who died on the middle passage has long since been paid. Very few American Negroes are willing to return to the country of their origin to help develop these lands, though they are very ready to criticise the white men who are doing this work. It was the white man who stopped the slave trade which the black man, not the white, began, and which, where it is possible, they will still carry on.

Yet the Anglo-Saxon people seem to suffer from a guilt complex whereas the Africans, ignoring their own part in the traffic, blame the white man for all its horrors. The white man even seems to be ignorant of his own history and forgets the thousands of political prisoners, felons, prostitutes and honest indentured servants who were sold, or sold themselves, into slavery before Africans became a current article of commerce — a practice which continued long after it, so that white and black were sold, and worked, side by side for centuries.

The idea of a West African Federation, of a great Pan-African Republic developing like the United States of America is a wonderful concept, and might be a possibility if there were no linguistic or tribal differences. But there are perhaps two thousand languages in Africa and there are almost certainly no two tribes who see eye to eye on anything except getting rid of the white man. There are great Moslem races who hate and fear the Negroes of the coast.

There cannot be for a long time technicians enough of any kind to develop or run the country, and no means of obtaining capital or capital goods except from the despised white man. The problem of the African is not how to get rid of the white men but how to do without them.

At the moment the African gives lip service to democracy. This is to please British and American public opinion. It will enable the politicians of today to destroy the chiefs, and having done so, they will almost certainly revert to some authoritarian form of government, which is likely to be unstable enough to make the development of their countries by European capital a difficult and uncertain business.

There are no answers. There is only trial and error, and patience. But two great truths emerge. There can be no real civilisation till African women are civilised; no efficiency till the African accepts the Western concept of time. Nor can the average African be accepted as an equal till he proves his equality, till his conscience makes him conscientious, till he develops what the Belgians call a "conscience professionelle."

No one can civilise the African. He must do it for himself. The question remains. Does he want to? Will he pay the price? There are riches in West Africa — gold, diamonds, tin, iron, manganese, coal, cocoa and coffee, palm oil, palm kernel, groundnuts, copra. Riches in the forests and mountains beyond all dreams, but they will not be wrested from the rocks and soil by evolved intellectuals, or the near literates who refuse to pick up any instrument heavier than a pencil. Industry must precede culture, hard work must come before politics, and a social system be built up from the bottom, not suspended on the string of a subsidy from the top.

We were now on our way back. The furthest point had been reached and though the rest would be new, it was still on the way home — the long way round. We had seen West Africa, and I tried to build up a sort of composite picture of the coast in my mind.

What were the salient points? Superficially, the greatest thing was a passion for education, for politics, for progress. Both the material and social progress seemed to me to have in common a kind of hysterical haste, both magnificent, but both built upon an insufficient foundation.

It seemed to me that self-government should take twenty years to achieve, with young Africans acting as reliefs in every administrative post, going up in the scale over the years so that the best would reach the top at the age of forty.

Nigeria was more of a political dream than a country, with the three main sections — North, West and East — divided against each other, and with even greater tribal animosities within their borders than outside them, which might at any time break out into a series of civil wars.

The Gold Coast was a one-crop and one-man country. Everything seemed to depend on cocoa and on Nkrumah. The same applied to Liberia — there, Tubman carried his little republic on his shoulders and was carried by the Firestone, which in turn was supported by the giant might of the United States. What then is the future? Good, one must hope. A slow movement forward to a series of orderly African states where justice reigns, even if the form does not correspond exactly to that of our concept of parliamentary democracy.

And the alternative? The political machine coming slowly to a standstill, halting, poised like a ball on a jet of water in a shooting gallery and then gradually accelerated disintegration. One has hopes and fears for Africa. Can she overcome her history? Will people work who can live without working?

An answer? Of course there is an answer. A basic Christianity, that of Christ divorced from all dogma or creed. A Christianity of the golden rule that might even accept polygamy. In which all men are brothers. Thinking over what I had seen I kept going back to the substratum of death and cruelty that lay beneath the apparently prosperous surface.

Can the young, emancipated university-trained Africans overcome these forces of superstition? Are they themselves immune? Would they feel no fear if, on coming out of their doors, they found a dab of blood on the lintel and some white cocks' feathers on the threshold?

It is difficult to write as I have and still assert, as I do, that I am the friend of the African, but our relationship — black and white — cannot be built up on a tissue of lies and misrepresentation. I think many Africans will agree with much that I have written. Many do not believe in freedom now, many are afraid of it, knowing where it may lead. For them to say so might mean their death.

But there is a danger that, with freedom, "may the beloved country cry," indeed.

22

The Long-Tailed Cat

● The FLIGHT from Accra to Léopoldville was uneventful — part
of it in darkness. We saw the sunrise over the forests that were
black below us. We saw the Congo — a wide silver ribbon — we
rocked in the air pockets above the rapids and came down. We were
met by Monsieur Jean Labrique of the Information Service who
took us through the customs and to the Health Department where
new temporary yellow fever and vaccination certificates were waiting
for us. A government car was put at our disposal. Our room at Le
Regina had been reserved. We were once again in an efficient
country where, to use their own words, things functioned with some
degree of accuracy. It was still Africa, where the unforeseen factor
is always high, but the machine turned over without continual break-
downs. It was fastened with wire and not with string.

Here there were no politics for white or black, though this was
resented by the white settlers and probably would be resented, in
the near future, by the Africans. But for the moment everything
was for the Congo, for the development of the country and the
people in it, particularly the black people. The political situation
was hard to evaluate, the future hard to foresee, because progress
obscured it. Buildings were going up everywhere, roads being built,
an immense airport under construction, the whole structure of the
colony was humming like a top, kept vertical by its own momen-
tums under the whip of success.

After a drink and a bath we went to see the enormous sports
stadium which included a physical training school where the in-
structors, who would later go into the Bush, were being taught under
European teachers. We saw the dormitories and gymnasiums of
the students. There was nothing shoddy or cheap about any of it.
It was fully up to any European standard and the buildings were
artistically built of dressed stone.

Then we visited the TB hospital where five hundred people are examined daily. The native cities are divided into sections which are dealt with, one at a time. Every African has a personal book which gives all his particulars — name, age, race, place of origin, married status and his full medical history. Every doctor who examines him makes an entry. This would be a good idea in any country, enabling the doctor to see the whole picture when a patient came to him.

Next we went to see a technical school and were shown complete machines which had been made by the pupils, and ended up with a visit to an African carpenter who employed thirty workmen. An African middle class of this type is the Belgian aim. They want to foster people with a real stake in the country, who are interested in its progress. A university is under construction and an African elite is coming into being. But the authorities are against sending Africans to centres of learning outside the Congo, where students are exposed to political ideas which they are not sufficiently advanced to criticise. The Belgians say they have profited by the mistakes of other nations, and certainly every revolutionary in French or British territories has been trained in European or American universities. The Belgians are very logical and believe it an error to teach their African nationals to run before they can walk. But there are no obstacles placed in the way of their advancement within the framework of the country. They can become functionaries — district officers — and the sky is the limit if they are prepared to reach for the stars. All the laws are to their benefit and for their protection. Striking an African is a serious offense with a fine of five hundred francs. Even calling one a *macaque* or monkey is punishable, and every white man coming into the country has to deposit fifty thousand francs with the government as a guarantee of good behaviour. Provided this is done, anyone can come and work here — there seems to be no bar on account of nationality.

There was a flower that was new to me in the garden, a most beautiful big pink waxy bloom, like a heavy water lily, called the Sceptre of Solomon. The leaves, which grew like those of the ginger plant, were eight feet high and the thick, pokerlike flower stems about three feet long. It lasts well in water and should travel, so that it would be worth growing in Florida for sale in the North, since it would go well with the décor of a modern apartment.

While eating, and drinking a nice bottle of French wine, we heard a cat and finally found it. A very thin, black and white female, which at once ate what we brought her from our plates. She was, I think, one of the ugliest and nicest cats we have ever seen, with an extra-long and extra-thin, almost ratlike tail. I saw several like this in the Congo and imagine them to be a local variety with some long-tailed wildcat blood in them.

Next day we went to the bank and while waiting we saw some very pretty and well-dressed women. It occurred to me then that this was where one did see such women who, by virtue of their appearance, belonged to men with sizable bank accounts. A sad and cynical reflection with world-wide application. Most of the clerks were African and they were just trying African tellers for the first time. Some earn as much as eight thousand francs a month, or approximately one hundred and eighty dollars, after taxes are paid. This is more than many working men earn in Belgium.

In the afternoon we went to see the new airport that was under construction. This was going to be one of the biggest in the world and so designed that a jet plane could land and go on again without having to turn on the 5460-yard runway.

Then we went to one of the satellite native cities, all of which have light, water and sewerage laid on. I was told that there was very little crime or trouble because the people had high wages, legal protection, good food and plenty of amusements — playing fields and cinemas — as well as social and medical centres, where they could get any help or advice they required. In fact my feeling was that everything was planned for, that here one had progress, discipline, humanity and sentiment. And a young African of any talent or character had a better chance of leading a full and happy life than most young white men in Europe.

I now called on the Vice-Governor-General, Monsieur Rik Cornelis, to tell him about our West African experiences. He said the aim of the Congo differed from that of the British territories, whose plan had been to create a politically minded elite. Here they were trying to build from the bottom upwards because, in his opinion, when you started at the top things could go back so easily. This was my own impression.

He said one of the most noticeable things was the difference in the children of parents who were literate and could speak French. He commented on the value of instructional documentary films, and said the aim was to create a strong bourgeoisie and not a handful of intellectuals.

We talked about insect control. It was surprising how few mosquitoes or flies there were — many less, in fact, than in parts of

South Africa, Europe or America — and how curious it was that yellow electric light bulbs did not attract night-flying insects.

He stressed the *foyer* or home life, and the education of women — a point I had already grasped as basic in the evolution of the African. Once again I was struck with his ability.

There is little colour prejudice in the Congo because there is no competition. The colour problem in South Africa is actually an economic question — a projection of the Western class war into that continent, where it has become confused in the boiling emotional cauldron of pigmentation. The higher the income and educational status of the white man, the less, on the whole, will be the prejudice, owing to the absence of fear. The doctor, barrister, writer, veterinarian, surveyor, architect, engineer, accountant or other professional man is not worried about African competition. The Africans who can compete with him are few and far between. The journalists, for instance, in Rhodesia have just admitted an African into their society as a colleague and meet him as an equal.

But the moment we descend the economic ladder and come to the artisan, the skilled and the semi-skilled man, the picture changes. Here men of colour whose competence equals that of the white man come into direct economic competition with him and, owing to a lower scale of living, are able to undercut him.

The mean whites, or poor whites of South Africa, America and the West Indies, are the real nigger-haters, since their whiteness is the straw to which they must cling to keep themselves afloat. Having nothing but their lack of pigmentation, they base their superiority upon it.

More and more I was coming to see this problem as the African version of Marxist orthodoxy. Industrialisation is the only means by which the African millions will escape from their struggle on the very margin of existence. But industrialisation is dependent on the white man. On white capital and know-how. At the moment, many black races who have little else in common are united by colour prejudice. This partly accounts for the Indian interest in Africa, which is perhaps why Indians are not encouraged in the Congo. But here an interesting point comes to the surface. The caste system of India, which still exists, owes its origin to the race consciousness of the early Aryan invaders towards the dark-skinned Dravidian natives of India — even the word for caste, *varna*, means colour. But the future of Africa and the African is dependent on the solution of this problem. There seem to be three main trends — assimilation and miscegenation, which the Portuguese seem to favour, and which the French and Belgians accept, in the sense that the mulatto has a definite place in society which is equal, in principle, to that of the white man; the absolute separation envisaged, but probably impossible to achieve, by the Nationalist South African Government; and a multi-racial society where all men live together in symbiotic association which is the aim of the British Labour Party. Where this may fall down is that the African leaders, once they get into power, may not enter fully into the parliamentary system but create an opposition based on colour alone. If they do this they will find the European resisting any further advance. A typical example of this approach is the sentence recently passed by an African judge in Lagos against an Englishman who ordered his dog to attack a native trader. He was fined £120 and three strokes of the cane. This sentence was subsequently reduced on appeal by another African judge to a £20 fine.

Justice had obviously not entered into the original judgment — the maximum penalty of the law had been used to implement a racial hatred. Things like this do the African much harm. They are the legitimate, legally permissible form of the same feeling which animates the Mau Mau terrorists of East Africa. The Congo, though there is little trouble there now, is not immune to pressure from the outside. News of the Gold Coast experiment comes down the coast to Matadi and creeps up the Congo and its tributaries. French Equatorial Africa has Communists whose propaganda gets into the country. The Sudan and Uganda are on her borders in the North and East. Northern Rhodesia with its labour troubles adjoins her own industrial areas.

Dr. T. B. Davie, the Principal of the Capetown University, said when he came back from America that some of the older members of the faculty of a Negro university he had visited said "they were no longer afraid the white man would not accord justice to the Negro but that the young men, in their hurry to get everything done at once, would antagonise even their white friends and then, finding resistance, become unhappy and even embittered."

I was asked at one dinner party not to mention the Mau Mau. They said they never talked about it. I found confidence everywhere but it was limited to so many years. No one really expected that there would never be any difficulties in the Congo. And yet the African could not, so far as I could see, have it any better. Here he was really babied. The point however seems to be: does he really want it? Would he sooner be left alone? He has forgotten, or never

THE LONG-TAILED CAT · 245

been told, what Africa was before the white man came. But perhaps, with all its horrors, there were compensations in the accompanying excitements.

We now went to the Unilever works — the H.C.B., Huileries du Congo Belge — central office and factory, and we saw soap being made in great white blocks four feet by three feet by two feet. It was then cut into slabs like paving stones, into strips and then pieces that were finally compressed, stamped LUX and packaged. How odd it was to see it being made. When one uses something one seldom thinks of its origin or the hands and lands it has passed through.

Next day we visited the Bata Shoe Factory. Everything they used was produced in the Congo — the skins for leather, the canvas for uppers and the rubber for soles. They did their own tanning. The wages, government-controlled, ran from five hundred francs to two thousand per month, plus allowances of various kinds. They had very little loss due to absence, and only two to three per cent through illness.

The production figures were interesting. Tennis shoes, sneaker type, were made here at a rate of twenty-five pairs per man. In South Africa the rate was twenty-nine pairs per man, and in England, where they had the most modern machinery, fifty-five pairs. I was astonished at the speed of the work and it was hard to believe that people could work faster, but presumably African labour was, at present, incapable of handling more complex machinery.

The *allocation familiale* — family allowance — is an interesting factor in the Congo. Here a man's pay varies with the number of his children; that is, there is a basic wage plus a family allowance. This seems to work well enough except where the salary is low and the worker highly phyloprogenitive. I was told of a night watchman — a job which the manager described as "purely symbolic," since he slept most of the night — whose salary was far less than the allowance which had to be paid for his wife and five children. The result being that they had to let him go and replace him by a bachelor.

Ten per cent of the salaries went into a savings account which enabled the bachelors to amass a bride price, which ran from 1500 to 5000 francs according to the tribe and the lady — an interesting feature of African factory management. In spite of the family allowance the company favoured married men because they were more stable and their children were being brought in to work at the age of fifteen. Families were thus being built up whose interests were identified with those of the company.

At Le Regina there was a very pleasant outdoor café where we had our tea and apéritifs. There was music in the evening and a gay Continental atmosphere. Parents came with their children, who ran about and played or slept in their mothers' arms.

While sitting here one afternoon an African policeman came round with a printed notice which people signed. When it came to my turn I saw that it was a "notice of death." Someone had died and this was a method of notifying the public. The news then got around quickly — more quickly than if it was published in the newspaper — which it was, of course, on the following day. But people have to be buried quickly in this climate. It was curious to be sitting listening to the music in the café with a drink in one's hand, and to be suddenly reminded that it still was Africa . . . .

Everything had now been arranged for our tour and we left Leo by air for Kikwit, the nearest landing ground to Liverville, the original H.C.B. factory and plantation. We were met by Monsieur A. G. Lorent, acting director of the station, a delightful man.

The previous week an elephant had been shot here by the troops, since it insisted on spending a great deal of its time on the airport and the authorities were afraid of its causing an accident to a landing plane. Once again the paradox of Africa, a meeting of the primeval jungle and the modern machine.

We drove through the forest. There were thousands of white, brown and yellow butterflies on the road. Lorent told me that sometimes they are a plague here and fatally infect all the poultry, which eat them avidly, since they appear to carry a virus of some kind which has not yet been isolated. A plague of butterflies was an interesting phenomenon. As the country opened up we saw palms covered with finches' nests. They wove them from the palm fronds and killed the trees by stripping them of all foliage. They call them "republicans" because of their social habits.

There are three kinds of time here — official Government, Mission and Company — so that if you make an appointment you have to ask what time you are to use. With plantation time six o'clock is always sunrise — when it is light enough to read the workers' roll call.

We passed through some native lands which had been burnt off. Lorent told me they do this to obtain snakes and forest rats, of which they are very fond in spite of the fact that in burning the land they often kill the palms on which their principal source of food and revenue depends; a family can make a living from thirty trees. He told me that carotin is extracted from palm oil, that sleeping sickness is now under control — this had been a bad area for it, but inoculations every six months had eliminated it, and that once the people are immunised the disease cannot be communicated and dies out.

Lorent was an efficiency expert and he told me that through changes he had made there had been gains of from twenty-five to thirty per cent. He described his job as dealing with the relationship of time and space and he was looking forward to getting back to it once he was relieved of the direction of the plantation. He said they were paying boys to go to school, and promised them good jobs when they completed their studies, but still found it hard to get pupils. Another trouble was that educated boys, once they could read and write, refused to climb another palm tree. This was going to be a big problem.

To meet one phase of it the company was trying to produce a dwarf oil palm which did not require climbing. There had been a few in the East Indies from which they had hoped to get seed but they had been destroyed by the Japanese when they had occupied the islands. I was told that eighty-five per cent of the oil the company processed was from wild palms belonging to the natives. That TB was common in this hot, moist climate. That red soldier ants had eaten eight of his tame rabbits, of a quarrel caused by a native lady squirting some of her own milk at another girl in the course of an argument.

This was the kind of conversation that I enjoyed. An exchange of ideas, of comments, of observations, of fact and fantasy, tragedy and humour.

Then we saw Liverville lying across the Kwilu River below us, a pretty toy town dominated by a toy factory, its miniature chimney smoking like a cigarette stuck vertically into some moss. We went down a steep hill and pulled up at the bac, the pontoon that was to take us across.

We went over, up the steep hill of the opposite bank, and pulled up at Lorent's house — a bower of flowering trees and shrubs — where his wife came out to meet us.

Susanne Lorent was a tall, very beautiful girl in her late twenties, who used no aids to beauty except lipstick. Like almost everyone in the Congo she talked excellent English though she was, I think, relieved not to have to do so. Tiny had now picked up enough French to follow a conversation, to which she replied in English, so there were no language difficulties.

Lunch included a new delicacy — a salad of walnuts and the white bases of the pineapple leaves. These were pulled off the central core like the leaves of a globe artichoke, and the short white portion at the base cut off. It had a most delicate flavour.

It was strange to think that this station had been begun only in 1911 by an Englishman, that this had been the pilot plant of an immense industry and that then, when I was a boy at school, this had been the heart of darkest Africa inhabited by savage cannibals, and parts of it depopulated by sleeping sickness.

I would have liked to be here as a young man then — when Africa was still Africa. Not that it is completely tame today. It is rather like a circus lion — apparently tractable. It responds to the economic whip, it is caught up in the modern technical circus and unable to escape. Now and then it revolts, turning on its masters, on its fellows, with a kind of desperate nostalgia for the past that it remembers faintly.

This was what we talked about at the Jesuit Mission. The good fathers were without much confidence in the results of their work. On the whole I found the Catholics more realistic than the Protestant missionaries. They did what they could with unbelievable devotion; most of them went home on leave only after ten years' service, and then never returned to Europe again, but the general feeling was that only a thin veneer had been achieved, a superficial civilisation which it would take a hundred years to perfect.

The Africans, the fathers told me, had no idea of service or of a *quid pro quo*. But the work that was being done was excellent. I saw a class learning to touch-type. I saw carpenters' shops, blacksmiths' shops, machine shops, shoemakers' shops. The boys who were going to be engineers began by making all their own tools, including gauges and calipers, which became their own property. In the engineering section they had completely rebuilt an ancient truck, making by hand many of the missing parts, after having taken it down completely and removing every nut and bolt.

I was told the ideal plan would be to set up shops in the villages on the European model where these young artisans could ply their trade, but this was impossible because the chief would demand furniture to be made for which he would not pay the carpenters. The shoemaker's uncle would demand shoes from the shoemaker, and so on. The result was many trained boys with no place to practice their craft.

We went to the technical school where really advanced engineering was taught, including mechanical drawing and designing. Of fifty-four qualified pupils only four had turned out to be no good. These young men were hand picked and destined to be in charge, under a white man, of the company's factories and machine shops.

We visited a mission where girls were being trained as teachers, a happy crowd of young African women, who were being taught by black lay sisters wearing the same coif and dress as the nuns.

We visited the social centre where women were taught house-keeping, and the school for the workers' children. We drank orange wine made by the sisters and ate biscuits in the cool shade of their veranda. I felt myself in the presence of something very good here, of a godliness that was combined with a certain liberalism and under-standing, but the difficulties are unbelievable. I was told, for instance, of one African priest who had been ordained for twenty-five years and then suddenly decided to give it all up, get married and return to the Bush and the ways of his fathers. And all black priests had to be visited at very regular intervals to see that they did not revert under the pressure of the forest.

While having our siesta we heard a curious noise and traced it to the wire mesh which covered the ventilator in the ceiling. There we saw twenty little white stomachs palpitating above us. They were tiny bats who resented having their peace disturbed. Our veranda was covered with pink Honolulu creeper which Susanne said was called *Sourire de Corail* in French. The smile of the coral. How beautiful! Like calling moths "night butterflies." And there were plenty of them — many more than Tiny liked. I had thought to comfort her with the name. I said you can't be afraid of butterflies, of night butterflies. But she said she could, and she was. Small flying things continued to upset her. And she was still worried about her long-tailed cat at Le Regina in Leo.

23

The Land of Masks ... Liverville ... Kikongo ...
Gungu ... Kwango

● WE DROVE OUT to a nursery where pedigreed seedlings were being grown in boxes, and I now began to learn something about oil palms.

When they showed four leaves they were transplanted to branch covered nurseries, where the shade was slowly reduced. After a period of three months none was left. At the end of a year the young trees were planted out in their permanent positions, approximately nine yards apart both ways. They began to bear four years later and continued to do so for another twenty-two. By this time they were giving less fruit, were very tall and dangerous to climb, all the frond stubs which cling to the trunk in its earlier life — giving a toe-hold to the climber — having fallen off. The palms are climbed by means of a kamba, a climbing ring made of creepers which passes round the climber's back and the tree trunk, enclosing both within its loop. The climber engages his toes in the branch stubs and holding the kamba in both hands jerks it upwards. There are some dangers. The kamba may break, sometimes there are snakes among the leaves at the palm's clustered top, and the great fronds which have to be kept cut so that the fruit heads are visible may cause an accident as they fall. But on the whole the work is not arduous and, being on contract, it is not hurriedly performed.

The workers contract to produce a given number of "regimes" — or bunches — and as they and their families are well housed and fed they take their time about it. The food is of good quality — manioc, pepper, palm oil — all their usual diet — with additions of protein in the form of dried fish from the Canary Islands and dried caterpillars.

Remarkable improvements have been made in the oil palm by selective breeding. A wild bunch in the forest weighs about five kilos while the selected average is twenty-five (the record being fifty kilos) in the plantations. The plantations are divided into blocks. Small feeder paths from the roads run along each line of palms, and there is a small cleared circle round each tree so that fruit which becomes detached from the bunch as it falls can be picked up. At the end of the feeder paths there is a tablelike stand made of branches on which the bunches are placed for collection by the trucks.

The aim of the breeders is to obtain not merely a dwarf palm but one with either no kernel, or a kernel with a paper-thin shell. Should they succeed, the problem will be seed which will have to be bred — like mules — from the two parent palms. The undergrowth of the plantations has to be cleared completely at least every nine months. I saw one area — they were just coming back to it — where there were bushes ten feet high with stems as thick as my wrist. The power of the forest here is shocking, something palpable and menacing. The palms grow best in low-lying ground and do not grow at all in savanna. Driving through the plantation was an extraordinary sensation. It was like driving through an enormous, endless steam-heated conservatory. The palms almost met over our heads, the narrow road was bordered with big, thick leaved plants — where the plantation had not been recently cleared — every seed in that fecund soil was springing upwards towards the light, creepers were clinging to palm stems which were green with ferns and moss. The heat and silence were a blanket over us when we got out of the car. A big black butterfly alighted on a piece of decaying wood beside us. There was a wild cry from an unseen bird and everything was silent again.

There is little rain except in the valleys where there are trees. The natives have cleared all the upland country and not a tree is to be seen except in the actual villages where a few have been kept for shade or some sacred purpose, but such trees are old and prove that all this country — even the hills — was once heavily forested. In fact I saw the attack of the forest going on in one place. First was an abandoned wornout land without so much as a scrappy bush on it. Then was the burnt-over forest where the dead giants stood up, extending their black tortured arms to the brassy sky. Below them the natives had planted forest manioc and maize. Beyond the devastation was the black, green wall of the primary forest — great trees rigged like masts with creepers — that too was doomed.

The villagers refuse to eat the savanna manioc but insist on the forest variety, which necessitates still further destruction and a lessened rainfall, unless they are forced to plant it by the government. In fact many of the women now even refuse to process the manioc carrots — the long, white carrotlike roots — and buy the prepared flour in the stores.

We now set off for Gungu with Monsieur Fosseprez, a tall good-looking young man who was responsible for the company's legal work at Liverville, and with whom we had dined the previous night on palm oil chop that they call Moambe here, with excellent local rice almost as good as that grown in Liberia which was the best we have ever tasted. Madame Fosseprez was a very young, pretty, fair girl — she was, I think, under twenty — and had a new baby. He was very worried about her because she was so slight and still kept losing weight. This is Congo phenomenon. Nobody stays the same weight in this climate — they seem to become either emaciated or fat.

We drove through a vast and empty downland country, which had once been forest, and reached the Kikongo plantation in time for tea. Here Fosseprez left us with our new hosts, Monsieur and Madame Roger de Gaulle. He was a tall young man, exactly like his uncle, Charles, with whom he served during the war. He has the same great height, profile and prominent ears. She was a lovely, gay, blond Parisienne, whose worry at the moment — they were about due for leave — was her pets, two putty-nose monkeys and a grey parrot. Their home was delightfully decorated with her sculpture, African trophies, curious weapons, drums and pottery and masks on the wall. Many people try to pretend that they are not in Africa and to duplicate a home atmosphere — this we had seen everywhere in our travels — instead of profiting by the exotic and creating a blend, a home in the colonies, where the savage and sophisticated meet in decorative marriage. Africa can only be supportable to those who are interested in the native, his arts, crafts and cultures.

The house was on a hilltop and looked out over the rolling, palm-clad hills. The mist rose from the valleys in streaks like the smoke of a thousand fires and settled, as the evening fell, into white lakes out of which the hilltops rose like islands.

After tea we went down to the factory which, like them all, was on the bank of a river so that the transport of oil could be by tanker. This was still the Kwilu, which was a tributary of the Kasai, which joined the great Congo. This was one of the veins that ran into the greatest artery of a continent, linking this little factory with Léopoldville, with Matadi on the Atlantic, with the ocean, Antwerp and the North Sea.

The factory was one of the newest plants in the Congo and was run by one white man. Everyone else, even the chemists who did the oil analysis, was African. We now knew a little more about the process of oil production and could appreciate it better. The fruit heads were first sterilised by steam which killed the bacteria and loosened the fruit. They were then fed into bins where two rollers, armed with spikes, scraped off the fruits and discarded the great husks. They looked rather like the fenders carried by small boats, and once stripped were used to heat the furnaces, or for compost in the plantation. The fruits were now crushed and the oil separated from the water content by centrifugal machines, which resemble giant cream separators, after which it flows by gravity into the waiting tankers. The kernels are now cracked, the shells separated and squeezed to extract their oil in gigantic presses, and the residue made into cattle cake.

We saw small grey hat-shaped toadstools growing on the discarded fruit husks outside and were told that they were excellent eating. I tried one raw and it had a pleasant mushroomy taste.

De Gaulle told me an amusing story of a man who had just been sent home on leave. He said he heard bells. He kept hearing them at night, and ringing up the doctor to tell him about it. After a week or two of this he was evacuated — it was more than the doctor could stand.

We visited a mission where women who wanted instruction came to learn sewing and housekeeping. One woman came every day and walked five miles each way. When we got back we were greeted by the parrot shouting: "Vive De Gaulle!" Madame had taught it.

In the morning we said goodbye to our distinguished host and his most decorative wife. The parrot's shouts of "Vive De Gaulle!" were our final memory of Kikongo.

We were now on our way to Gungu via the Chutte Rutten where we were to be met by Monsieur Renders. He took us to see the falls, which were impressive, hurtling their dark, almost blood-coloured water over a precipice that was brilliantly green with moss and grass. The falls smoked like those of the Zambesi in miniature. We set off again for the river, whose banks were clothed with giant bamboos. We waited for the pontoon that would take us across. Among others also waiting were some African beauties with red-painted naked breasts, filed teeth and glass ampoules, obtained from the local dispensary, in their ears. I was told that they file their teeth because they do not wish to look like horses. They consider white peoples' teeth horselike, and a white skin like that of a dead man. Some call a white man a peeled man, because he is white like a peeled wand. The ladies were much intrigued by Tiny's lipstick and painted fingernails.

At Gungu, a largish place, we stayed with Monsieur Renders. His job was the recruiting of native labour for the plantations in this area so he knew a great deal about the Africans and their customs and laid on some dances for us. One of the most impressive sights we saw in Africa was a dance by some thirty witch doctors' assistants in the circumcision rites. They were clothed from head to foot in tights of raffia, woven to resemble chain armour. They had wide ruffs of raffia round their ankles, wrists and necks, with short stiff balletlike skirts of the same material. Their masks were circular, with tubes six inches long over their eyes. These tubes projected like the eyes of snails and ended in white painted circles three inches in diameter. Their leader had the same round mask but it was ornamented with an immense circle of feathers so that it looked like a sunflower. Each man carried a twig with palm leaves on it in one hand and a wand in the other with which they used to beat any women and children found in the streets at night when they ran through them — a custom comparable to that of the Poro dancers of West Africa.

The suits were striped with black or leopard-spotted; some of the men wore bells at their waists and the dancing was of the highest order, very fast, varied by rapid running — chasing imaginary victims. The leader had a routine of his own — running, stopping suddenly to raise himself on his toes, throwing up his arms in a diving position and bowing like a courting pigeon. Then he would bend forward and point with one hand, finger extended, throwing back the opposite leg, then repeat this movement of accusation with the other hand and leg. It was not difficult to imagine the effect of this performance in the moonlit street of a silent village. Even in the sun of midday it was sinister and frightening.

I was shown the circumcision knife — a small, sharp blade attached to a flat wooden handle pierced with filigree carvings. It was polished with age and friction, the blade worn down and scalpel sharp. In modern terms of castration complex, it was almost impossible to exaggerate the fear that this little implement, wrapped in a dried corn leaf, must have inspired in hundreds, perhaps thousands, of adolescent boys.

These raffia-mesh-clad men were those who collected the initiates and conducted them to the sacred groves where they would be circumcised and go through the various initiations, and the training required to fit them for full manhood in the tribe. The groves are the universities of the Bush. Secrecy, no contact with women, the painting of the initiates with kaolin, or chalk, which is the custom throughout Africa. The music for the dance consisted of drums alone which were warmed over a fire of palm fronds to tighten the heads. One man carried a bell in his hand. The bell in religion seems to be universal. We have our own church bells which must have been taken over from our barbarian past, and even our curse of bell, book and candle.

After an excellent lunch we went to another village and saw women preparing red cam-wood dye by rubbing blocks of it on a wet stone mortar. This was used before the coming of the white man, with his manufactured materials, to dye the woven raffia cloths before waterproofing them with palm oil. Then we saw bows that were cut from a big tree and which in section looked like palm fronds, having raised edges on the inner or string side. The arrows were interesting too. One ended in a lump of beeswax through which was passed a double cross of thin twigs that projected about an inch from the shaft. It was used for small birds and gave a bigger striking surface than a point would have done. Another type was a two-inch wedge-shaped arrowhead with an edge like a razor; the third type had a Y-shaped head, also razor sharp, whose tail fitted into the shaft.

Then we were taken to see a big drum. It had been completely hollowed out through a slit no more than an inch wide along the top. This was one of the famous talking drums.

I asked to see their hunting dogs and two were brought — a yellow and white one and a brindle; prick-eared animals, rather like a heavy whippet, and obviously related to the dogs I had seen on the desert fringe in Nigeria. When hunting they wear wooden bells tied round their loins so that they can be followed, since they cannot bark. They do not lift their legs to urinate. When hunting big game, I was told their masters prime them with palm wine, but even without it they are most courageous and will attack gorilla or even elephant and lion or bush cow.

I was surprised to find no white man interested in them as a breed, calling them native or kaffir dogs, though I believe some have now been taken to America where they are called Basenjis, which simply means bush dogs, the same term being used to describe unsophisticated natives from the interior.

After lunch we went to see some more dancing. An immense crowd had collected to watch the performance, and we met several chiefs who wore horned ceremonial hats covered with bead embroidery like Indian wampum. The dancing was really miming, archetypes being represented by costumed and masked figures. The Chief stepping daintily accompanied by an attendant. The Dwarf. The Young Woman, simpering, with enormous artificial breasts which the Dwarf ran out and pulled. The Young Lover who courted her and drove off the Wicked Dwarf. The Doddering Old Man. I had the feeling that the show was suitably emasculated for white consumption and that after we left it became more interesting.

We saw the men with arrows through their cheeks. Actually fakes. There are certainly holes through their faces but the arrows are cut in half and join inside the mouth with a long tongue on one and a groove on the other which fit into each other like the sword into its sheath. Neither the big barb nor the feathers that fletch the arrow go through the cheeks, only the central shaft.

The women wore masses of different-sized brass bracelets on their arms, that looked like tightly fitting sleeves of shining gold.

Renders was very comfortably housed, with an excellent boy, who had been with him for some years, called Innocent. It was amusing to hear him shout "Innocent! Innocent!" when he wanted something. He did himself well, like all the Belgians. He had rabbits and pigeons that he bred for the table. We drank excellent French and Portuguese wines. White men are well paid here — a minimum of thirty thousand francs a month — but they spend a lot on food, for they realise that in this climate it is essential to live well, which is more than most British officials do, who tend to keep up their morale with spirits and do not make themselves as comfortable as either the French or Belgians.

Renders had a fine collection of small carved ivory pendant heads, which are worn only by chiefs. He gave Tiny a beauty, which she mounted as the central piece to a string of Gold Coast fertility beads and wears quite often. There are many of these heads now on the market for tourists, but the real ones are quite different in size, feeling and craftsmanship. They are made, astonishingly enough, with a small axe, and finished off with a knife and file. I sometimes wonder what that Bapende head of Tiny's has seen. What deaths? What tortures? What lovemaking? Between how many black breasts has that carved face lain?

Many of the Bapende men wear headdresses and hairdos of sculptured mud and wax, into which they insert brass-headed nails, like studs. The tribe came originally from Angola in Portuguese territory and still exists on both sides of the frontier, which to them is a completely artificial barrier. They obtained **guns** from the slave traders and pushed their way into the interior, now the southwestern part of the Congo.

Part of Renders' job was to buy dry caterpillars for the company's labour. They come from the forest of Kahemba which is peopled by the Batschok, who export one hundred and fifty tons of dry caterpillars a year. They looked very appetising to me though not so to Tiny, and I wanted to try them. Although dehydrated they were very pretty — black with yellow and green stripes running round and round their bodies. Unfortunately Innocent did not, or said he did not, know how to cook them.

Renders had been in the Belgian resistance and had been taken by the Gestapo. While being examined by them, he saw a girl hanging by her hands, her back completely stripped of flesh. One is surprised and shocked at ritual murder and cannibalism among Africans, and one forgets the horrors of the concentration camps of Europe — of the Gestapo, the Russian secret police, even the chain gangs of Florida and the lynchings of the South. Yet the African killings of the fetishists and doctors are, to them, a form of preventive medicine, of worship and religion, which gives them some justification.

The irritant, as far as I was concerned, was the educated Africans' assumption that these things did not exist, and the lack of knowledge about them in Europe and America, where sophisticated Africans are accepted as having the same principles as educated white men and being equally capable of parliamentary democracy. The new African political parties are likely to act as the tribes did in the past, and the elections to turn into party wars as happened at Oyo, in Nigeria, when six people were killed and twenty-six injured when the N.C.N.C. clashed with another party.

This whitewashing of such things as Liberian slavery a few years ago, of Nigerian leopard murders and horse- and dog-killing ceremonies, of sacrifices of live chickens tied by one leg in the ju-ju houses and left to die and rot, of the human sacrifices at the death of chiefs and notables, should be considered in any African evaluation. They are part and parcel of Africa but are unknown outside it, seldom reported in the press, and often not understood in the Colonial Office, where the actual files are scarcely read. The higher officials get digests, or documents so annotated and with so many comments attached to them that what the man on the spot had to say is lost or too much interpreted. These deaths are as much a part of Africa as deaths from car accidents are a part of Europe or America — our sacrifice to the god of speed. Eventually, perhaps both will be reduced but neither can be ignored.

In the evening we went to see Monsieur Caps, the administrator of the territory, and had a drink with him and his wife.

Monsieur Caps told us that the Africans were now becoming ashamed of their own costumes and music and were dancing to the phonograph in European clothes. And of girls who committed suicide by inserting wild lilac into the vagina, which produced an agonising death. He talked of the many springs of Lukwila, a tributary of the Kasai River, which he had explored. They are a curious phenomenon, having eaten away the ground in a series of cups and canyons, some four hundred or more feet deep.

We went to see them on our way to the ranch at Kwango.

At one village we were given wine made from the raffia palm. It was sweetish, refreshing and alcoholic. I could have done with more of it. Wine is apparently made from a number of palms. It can also be made, I was told, by tapping the sap from the big bamboos and, naturally, from plantains, bananas and sugar cane.

The comfort in which an African in the tropics can live is possibly the greatest check on his cultural advance. It is difficult for me to see why he should want any change. In his position, I am not sure that I should want to. He has everything he needs — cassava, yams, palm oil, pepper, home-brewed alcohol, women for his pleasure and to work for him. In fact, his life is that of a playboy, scaled down to its basic essentials of drink, food, women, sport and conversation. To this has now been added a just administration, free medical attention and the possibility of earning extra money for any luxury he wants, such as a phonograph or a bicycle, by going to work for a white man for a few weeks or months. Six months' work will provide him with six months' leisure. Of course this does not apply to the detribalised native or to those living in poor farming areas, but it does include millions in West, Central and East Africa whose lot, in terms of comfort and leisure, is far more to be envied than that of most Europeans or even Americans. In the Bush the native of today seems static, held fixed by the magnet of money pulling one way and the drag of his past the other.

The source of the Lukwila River, when we got there, was well worth seeing. This was erosion on the grand and colourful scale. Acres of ground had collapsed over the centuries and been carried away as silt in the water. One came on them suddenly on the flat, and pulled up the car on the edge of a multi-coloured precipice. The bare soil of the cliffs was red, ochre, brown and almost blue. At the bottom the watercourses could be seen — silver threads that dis-appeared into a jungle of green trees which, from above, looked like a watercress bed but which, I was told, was full of baboons, monkeys and other game.

Some villagers appeared and a boy ran down the path, disappear-ing like a buck over the edge, into the void, to show us how it was done. And it was from down there that every drop of water was brought up by the women.

Beyond the springs there were mountains in which a white hermit had once lived. He had thought the natives would flock to him, but they never came, and he was finally killed in his mountain eyrie by lightning, which the Africans took as a sign that they had been right in not following his teaching.

We packed up and set off again for the ranch at Kwango. We were met by Monsieur Delbeke who was much relieved to find that I had been a cattleman, and we spent three most interesting days with him.

I now learnt a lot about cattle which would have been of the greatest value to me thirty years ago, though of course some of the medicines and techniques were not known then. Besides being a wonderful host, Monsieur Delbeke was one of the best stockmen I have met in my life, either in Africa or in America. He had thirteen hundred head of stock running in an area which had been declared unsuitable for cattle raising, and where two previous managers had failed, and I have never seen finer cattle. Not one blind, not one lame, not one had a tick on it, all very level in each class with coats as glossy as race horses. They were running on forty thousand acres with no loss except four per cent among calves due to lions and leopards. The foundation stock was Afrikander, which had been trekked up some five hundred miles across rivers and through forests, crossed with our old friends N'dama bulls from French Guinea. The chief difficulty had been to train herders, since the natives here are not accustomed to cattle. But Delbeke had done a wonderful job with them. No whips or sticks were allowed. No noise or shouting. The cattle were all tame and did not move off till one was six feet from them, and then only drifted a yard or two before settling down to feed again. There were four herders for each two hundred head, two of whom remain in the kraal and two, accountable for a hundred head each, who accompany the cattle. Their business was to see that the animals grazed the grass closely and did not leave it half eaten. Monsieur Delbeke believes that in time five hectares (approximately ten acres) will be enough grazing per head. It may even be much less when he has his pastures sufficiently improved. This was his key to cattle and grass management. Each night the cattle were kraaled in a wired enclosure, two hectares in extent, which was changed every seven days by the two boys who did not go out with the stock, but spent their time putting up the new fences. In this way, as the kraals were moved along, the grass was progressively improved by close feeding, tramping and manuring with the dung and urine. The change in the areas that had been treated in this manner was remarkable — the gaps between the tussocks, so usual in Africa, had disappeared and creeping finger grasses were covering the ground. At this rate a herd of one thousand improves the land at a rate of well over a thousand acres per year, turning it from rough grass into real pasture. The fence poles were set about nine feet apart and the distance between the three wires starting from ground level was twelve, fourteen, and fourteen inches.

The bulls do not run with the breeding stock all the year round, but are removed when the first calf is born. The calving lasts two months and when the last calf has been dropped the bulls are returned, the ratio being one bull to twenty-five females. The calves are weaned at seven months and the bulls cut at three months. They are branded on the quarter with the year of their birth and earmarked for the month. All cattle are dipped every seven days in an arsenical dip to which Gamatox, to keep off flies, is added every three months. I did not see any flies on any of the animals. Every two months the cattle receive a dose of phenoteazine, a vermifuge. The dip, and therefore the swim, was the longest I had ever seen — sixteen and one half yards. The water for it was collected from its roof into tanks.

Every beast had the long hairs shaved off its tail to prevent ticks harbouring in their roots and all stock was dehorned with a heavy barrel-shaped Texas iron, about five inches long and two inches wide, with a concave centre. There were mineral licks in the kraals that were made up on the ranch of a mixture of salt, calcium, phosphorous and trace elements of copper, cobalt, iodine and iron sulphate. This mixture, dampened with water, was left to set in wooden moulds.

When the herd was taken over by Monsieur Delbeke it was in very poor condition and he treated each beast with a twenty-cc. injection of soludagenon to clean up its blood. Three South African riding horses were used and they were injected against trips every six months. This was the routine of ranch management in a nutshell.

I recorded it in some detail because the results were so extraordinary and could only have been achieved by a man who thought and dreamt of cattle, and who had been brought up with them since childhood, like Monsieur Delbeke, who was the son of a big farmer and stockbreeder in Belgium.

As usual we lived very well, with excellent food and wine. Actually, the food was better than usual as our host had a wonderful kitchen garden.

He told us the best way to disinfect salad in the tropics was to soak it for thirty minutes in a fifty per cent mixture of water and vinegar — a useful tip and according to him much better than the permanganate that is generally used.

The house was very comfortable, with a big raffia mat on the floor of the living room of a kind which the natives can no longer make. On the first evening there was a very large, almost foot-long centipede above Tiny's chair. It disappeared into the ceiling before we could kill it. I told Tiny if it landed on her to brush it off the way it was going and it would not sting her. I had been told this and hoped it was true, but she moved her chair.

We talked of the Africans and Monsieur Delbeke told me they no longer fished in the big lake where fish weighing up to twenty kilos have been taken, but bought smoked fish instead; that they could no longer use their bows and arrows and bought their manioc flour from Liverville. On the farm he said it took one hundred and twenty-six natives to do the work of twenty-five white men. He agreed with my own contention that the African was losing his own arts and not learning those of the white man and was, in fact, going backward. He said that in the last few years wages had been raised by the government three times but they spent no more on food. The family allowance they received was spent on beer and women. The beer was seventeen francs a bottle and a woman — by an arrangement with her husband, who got the money — three francs more. To compare the difference between work done with and without supervision he said that ten boys with a white man cut a hundred fence poles a day as opposed to twenty on their own. Again the "no professional conscience." I quoted the Dalgleish report where it was stated that one white man did the work of three Africans. But of course there is the point of view that the white man is a fool to work so hard. His African clerk drew three thousand francs per month, only a thousand less than many workmen in Belgium, and he had just spent two thousand five hundred francs on a suit of clothes which he had kept for six weeks and then sold for two hundred and fifty francs. He said the drivers cut the material off the seats of trucks that cost thirty thousand francs to make haversacks.

We visited the head clerk's house, a nice little brick villa, but it was very untidy and badly kept though his wife was literate.

There were swallows' nests on Delbeke's stoep which he said were often torn down by owls in the night. I had never heard of this before though in the Transvaal I had had weavers' nests torn to pieces by hawks.

He had a lot of poultry which he caponised by a hormone tablet inserted under the skin just behind the comb. He made a small slit with a razor blade, pushed in the tablet (kaponetten — Bayer) and fastened the wound, after having wiped it over with alcohol, with an ordinary office stapling machine. He said the change began almost at once. The birds stopped crowing and fighting and within a fortnight the flesh became more tender and they fattened fast. The head and neck must not be cooked or used for food as it could produce impotence in man.

The roads on the ranch were very good and required one man to every two miles to keep them in order, and as they had several hundred miles of road this was a big item of expense.

Monsieur Delbeke was a widower with grown-up children in Belgium. His wife had died only a year or so ago and had lived in the Congo with him most of their married life, so he felt her loss very much. Such men are remarkable, spending their lives in the wilds, devoting themselves to their jobs till finally they are forced by age, or illness, to return to a homeland which has become alien to them, and to a life which has lost its meaning. There are ranches in the United States, in Africa and Rhodesia and stations in Australia which are just as isolated, but there the men who run them are at home. They are born in the country and expect to die in it, which must make a big difference.

The country was attractive, open rolling down country spotted with bush and large trees. In the bottoms were patches of forest and these were being destroyed by chopping and fire as tsetse breeding grounds. I was bitten for the first time here by apparently the only fly in the area. The natives saw it at once, as they are terrified of them, having at last realised that they are responsible for sleeping sickness, and nearly knocked me down as they hit it.

There were some thick patches of forest full of wild pig and bush cow. The lions appear to eat the pigs which are very verminous and the leopards to live on the monkeys and baboons, though they did attack the stock in the beginning and still take an occasional calf.

We were taken to see the finest dance I have seen in Africa. It had been laid on for us, with a hundred and fifty-six dancers, more, I was told, than had performed for the Governor-General himself. By great good fortune they were in a dancing mood. We dined a little late and then drove towards the village where Africans from many miles around had assembled. This dance was called that of the Men of Mungonge, but to me it was a snake dance, completely un-African, and derivative of the East. It had to do with the initiation of the boys and took place on the edge of the village by the light of three enormous fires. No women or children were allowed to watch and any woman who appeared was chased into the forest. The others remained shut in their huts.

The procedure was more or less as follows: The selected boys, in chains, kneel in the bare ground beyond the fires. The witch doctor goes up to them, asks their names, gives them the new one that will be used while they are undergoing initiation and shouts it aloud towards the darkness of the forest.

A dozen naked dancers, painted with white stripes and wearing feather headdresses, now dance in and out among the kneeling boys and jump over them. The fetishist strikes the ground in front of the boys with an axe. As he does so from the distant forest come wild, eerie cries. Three new dancers with arrows through their cheeks dance about the boys to distract them. The drums beat more wildly and four long white ghostly snakes creep out from the darkness of the forest. They are composed of men, naked but for tiny loincloths, their bodies striped like zebras with white. On their heads they wear large fan-shaped openwork headdresses made of thin peeled wands. They advance crawling on their hands and knees, continually bowing and raising their heads which gives the impression of an undulating and writhing serpent. As they reach the kneeling boys they break their formation and run, leaping and dancing over them, even flinging themselves backwards over their prostrate bodies, and finally drag them off and beat them. They were not actually very rough but the tradition of brutality must have been very strong because some of the young men were terrified and ran to us, cowering like frightened dogs, almost under our chairs. In actual practice the dance ended, I assume, with the victims being circumcised and held in some secret grove till their initiation was complete, usually, in the good old days, a matter of several years.

No women were ever allowed to see this dance. It was, the men said, "too beautiful for women." When it was over the men went to the water where they washed off their paint and burnt their headdresses which the women must never be allowed to see.

We stayed about a couple of hours but the dancing went on till dawn. It is impossible to get Africans to stop dancing once they start. Some dances go on for days.

I was told that the women had dances of their own which the men could not see. Too good for the men, I supposed.

This Bapende dance we had seen was easily the best I have ever seen in Africa, because it had both story and design, build-up, a plot with a climax, and would make a wonderful ballet.

Next day we drove back to Kikwit, with African cyclists precipitating themselves into the bush whenever we came near them. There was plenty of room but they never heard us till we were almost on them. Then they gave a terrified look over their shoulders and shot off the road and fell into the grass. This had been the general procedure right through Africa, in fact on the whole trip only one Gold Coast cyclist pulled to the side and went on pedalling calmly. This custom is due to two things, I think, first their slow reflex — they do not hear the car coming — secondly their refusal to use brakes. I imagine that they have all tried them once, put them on too hard, shot over the handlebars and then never used them again. The roads right through the Congo were bordered with lemon grass to prevent erosion, and every curve had narrow islands of grass planted in its centre to control the traffic.

When we said goodbye, almost the very last remark to me by our hosts was, in reply to my question: What about the water at Leo? Can we drink it? — "Oh yes, Monsieur Cloete, it is quite safe they say, but the functionary in charge of the waterworks is a friend of mine and he drinks only wine or bottled water. Of course he prefers wine." This solved the problem. We said, "So do we," and we could use soda water to clean our teeth.

● *The Congo*

24

The Great River...Leopoldville...Brazzaville...
Cockatville...Bumba

● As soon as we reached Léopoldville, which seemed like our home town now, we checked in and set off for Brazzaville where we were going to spend one night.

We were met by Monsieur Maillard of the Information Service who took us to our hotel — a modern one right in the town. We dined with him and his wife at their house — a nice villa with a garden full of flowers. His wife was young, pretty, dark, vivacious, with a nice, partly wild cat called Minou. We talked cats, we talked Africa.

The French have even less colour feeling than the Belgians. Poor whites sink into the black mass and are assimilated by it. If they fail to keep their heads above water they are not repatriated. There is no check whatsoever, as far as I could tell, on miscegenation. Only the Portuguese seem to go further in this direction and encourage the production of mulattoes. How good or bad this policy is only time will show. Certainly it would appear that where there is no prejudice against them the mulattoes adapt readily to a Western way of life. If the African, as some people think, is an inferior race, the white cross should produce good results when the male is of a good type. My own view is that neither race, black or white, is superior; they are merely different. In tropical Africa the African is the superior because he can live and any living man is superior to a corpse. In a Western culture the white man is superior because of inherited and acquired characteristics which are, chiefly, a drive that makes him work beyond ordinary necessity, and his different concept of time.

Here in French Equatorial Africa the natives are citizens of France and very proud of it. As long as they behave this seems to work out nicely and when they cease to behave they become black again. On the whole, as far as one could tell driving about the native towns of Poto Poto and Bas Congo, everyone seemed happy enough and in no way resentful of the white man. This is something one feels, there is no other evidence. There is much less done for the African on this side of the river but he has political rights which he may prefer to benevolent dictatorship.

In the morning we visited a wood carver who was producing heads and masks for sale. Decorative enough, skilful enough, but not real works of art, without the integrity of the older works created by craftsmen whose work had been stimulated by veneration and fear. These things were made for money. But we saw one man who worked in ivory and cattle horns who was a real artist and produced most realistic and beautiful catfish which seemed to be actually swimming, and whose fins and long whiskers were removable for packing — an ingenious idea of his own.

The roads round Brazza were very poor, but the shops beautifully modern with very good and artistic window displays. Many buildings were lovely, the modern blended into the old colonial architecture, tied into it by the magnificent trees that lined the streets and filled the compounds. Bougainvillaea poured over the walls in opulent purple and dark red swathes, creating an atmosphere of peace and beauty. There was no mad building going on as in Leo, no rush, the atmosphere was one of peace, almost of decadence.

French Africa is poor, but whether this is due to lack of development, or simply because there is nothing to develop, I do not know. On one side of the Congo is a thriving modern city and on the other an almost static society. On the one side Belgian efficiency and on the other French laissez-faire. But there was beauty here. The most beautiful modern cathedral I have ever seen was just being completed. The style was Gothic, if there can be Gothic without pillars. The arches rose straight up from ground level.

Our visit was now over. We drove back to the dock, crossed the river again and returned to the Regina where we found our cat and fed her.

Next morning I had an appointment with the Governor-General at 8 A.M. so we went to bed early. Monsieur Petillion had a wonderful gift for conversation — a rare combination of intellectualism and executive capacity. He wore light-coloured trousers and a white uniform jacket, open at the neck, with gold buttons, epaulettes and medal ribbons. His office, most comfortably furnished, was air-conditioned. The windows looked out on to the garden with the Congo River flowing beyond it. Over the river was France, and the Africans who were now citizens of that once great republic. Over there was communism. Not much as yet, but beginning. To the east, thousands of miles away, was Kenya and the Mau Mau. Uganda, the Sudan, Egypt.

Just now things are going well in the Belgian Congo. But its troubles will come as the number of Evolvés of Evolvants increases.

"Ah, monsieur," the Governor-General said, "there are great anti-colonial factions in the world. UNO, America, India, can see no good in what we do. Even some people in England, but as you have seen, we have done a lot and continue to do more and more. But the more industrial schools and hospitals, the more evolution there is, the quicker will the African demand the right to self-government. We forge weapons against ourselves. And what those others, who criticise us, forget is that one does not destroy the mysticism of thousands of years in a generation."

Which was the best, I wondered. French freedom or Belgian social services? The next ten years would be, according to the Governor, the most difficult. Perhaps he is right. But I do not see why the difficulties should end there, though they may change in form. One thing he was clear about — there would be no political representation for white men in the colony till the black men were able to participate in government. He said things are going well, but perhaps not quite so well as they appear on the surface. The African here, as elsewhere, remains at once too eager and too recalcitrant; eager for the outward semblance of civilisation, and recalcitrant as far as its inner meaning and ethics are concerned.

Everything the Governor-General said was optimistic — the ten-year plan. The North was developed and going well. He was about to concentrate on the South; to move his best men, to attack the great rolling plains we had crossed and see what would grow there. Something would grow. But certainly, something. Optimism is necessary in Africa — optimism, patience and a belief in God. Beyond this, energy, stamina and the ability to resist heat, disease and the terrible lassitude which destroys the very fibres, physical and moral, of the Western man.

The conversation ended when I said: "Your Excellency, what would happen if the white man left the Congo? How long would it last?"

"A few years," he said, "because we have built well. The buildings will stand."

"And then?" I said.

"Then, monsieur, the forest will return."

This is the classic reply all over the continent. There is no other answer.

In the evening I went to a party given at the Sabena Guest House for some visiting French journalists. We dined in the garden decorated with coloured fairy lights strung between the big silk-cotton trees. I met some friends I had made on my first visit to Léopold-ville and listened to some interesting conversation. Suicide, which was once unheard of among men, is becoming more common. A functionary with twenty-five years' experience called it "the suicide of despair."

His theory, which corresponded to my own, was that the African had the greatest difficulty once he was separated from his tribe. He is like a bee alone. He exists, but only with the greatest difficulty. This suicide story I have heard before. In Nigeria, the Gold Coast, and Liberia where soldiers had been killing themselves for no reason — or perhaps for the reason he gave, of spiritual despair.

It would sometimes seem that the African remains much nearer to the past, which he is losing, than to the future which he is failing to reach. Perhaps subconsciously he realises this. Perhaps because with him when thought, hope and wish merge into one emotion he is unable to bear disappointment, and is seldom spurred by failure, as is the Western man, to renewed and greater effort. But perhaps, above all, he is bored. He now has the white man's toys — the bicycles, the sewing machines, the clothes, the dark glasses and hats, the gramo-phones, all of which he coveted but which do not compensate him for his losses — the wars of the old days, the capture of women and slaves, the great hunts with rings of flames, the ritual murders, the dances and cannibal feasts. Perhaps, after all, a past of ten thousand years cannot be uprooted by a few years of superficial Western in-struction. Perhaps we have not touched Africa at all, the real Africa. It is this thought that lies at the back of every white man's mind — missionary or civil servant. Perhaps they have given their lives for nothing. Perhaps we work upon water which, whatever we do, re-mains the same. Boil it into steam or freeze it into blocks, it even-tually regains its original form. This is what would happen in Africa if the white man left the country. War — a hundred wars at once. The destruction of the so-called evolved or civilised blacks by the peasant farmers and a slipping back into the great African sleep from which we have attempted to arouse the continent.

Why has Africa, south of the desert, remained static — a Stone and early Iron Age culture — for so many thousand years, and north of the forests frozen into a state of primitive feudalism? Why, when Timbuctoo was once one of the great cultural centres of the world? Why, when once civilisations came here from the North or the East? Civilisations that built Zimbabwe, that made the bronzes of Ife, the brasses of Benin, that mined the gold of the Zambezi basin and the tin of the Rooiberg range of the Transvaal. Why is nothing left but a few ruins, a few artifacts? No memories, no folklore. As these men passed, so could we pass. Moving like a ripple over the great lake of the African soul, disturbing the reeds on its fringe for a moment, hushing the shore birds for an instant, and then nothing — nothing more at all.

There were at this dinner people from all over the North — from Dakar, Casablanca, from Morocco, Tunisia, and their story was much the same.

There is little doubt that in the Bush the Africans are quite ready to retain the white administration which, despite its many defects, is not corrupt. The peasant farmers know this and appreciate it. But they can be influenced by the rabble rouser who talks of nationalism, who says: "We can do what the white man does. Why not be administered by one of your own people?"

And as more and more become literate they are affected by what they read in the local African press. Africans see the white man's riches — his houses, his motorcars, his radios, his imported food. They are told that these all spring from their labour. That they are exploited. They think they too should have these things. They do not think of the vast capital required for the enterprises which produce such things. Of the cost of the education of the men who run them, of the losses and failures on the way, of the sacrifices made by those who are prepared to risk their lives and health away from their native lands.

Next day, at Cockatville, we were met by Monsieur Bernier, the manager of the local H.C.B. factory, who drove us to the rest house where we washed and had a welcome drink of cold beer. Cock is low-lying, right on the equator, and humid. The air had a thick, degenerate quality; if that of New York in the fall can be compared to champagne, this stuff was like warm stout. It was not meant for breathing. There are now 1200 white people here. There were only 500 a few years ago but the town has grown in importance as a river post. Actually, it is built on an island with only one road, a raised causeway, leading out of it.

We were taken to visit the botanical garden, once the most important experimental station in the Congo, and saw rubber and cocoa growing again, and coffee, for the first time, with its white, fragrant jasminelike flowers — there were a few left — and the berries that stuck like green oval marbles to the grey bark. There were red and pink frangipani with enormous blooms and *Petrea volubilis* climb-ing on the pergolas. We saw pinky-mauve orchids in clusters, one of the parents of the hybrids in common use at home. We were shown a sensitive bush — a legume with pink fluffy ball-like flowers which, in its early growing stages, collapses if touched, a protection against being grazed off by buffalo and other game. There were standard bougainvillaeas eight feet high with stems thicker than my arm, a blaze of red and purple, and I found, duly labelled, two flowering shrubs that I had seen before, *Rubiaceae stenocarpa*, the cream poin-settia-like plant we found first at Badageri in Nigeria and later saw everywhere else, the white variant of Ashanti blood, and the brilliant red-orange starlike flower which we had seen near Liverville whose Latin name was *R. mussaenda elegans*.

At 2 p.m. Monsieur Bernier drove us to the boat — the *General Olsen* — built in Antwerp in 1948, the best and most modern of the river fleet, diesel-driven and equipped with radar, which has been added since an accident occurred some years ago when a ship ran into a half sunken tree and almost foundered. The first river steamer on the Congo was brought over from the Mississippi in sections and the model, except for the paddle wheels in the stern, has changed very little. The older boats are still stern-wheelers, burning wood fuel which is picked up each night.

Bernier stopped with us some time talking. He told me of the reluctance of the African women to go to hospital till almost dead and how most of such deliveries were made by Caesarian operations because the women had been so torn about and damaged before they came; of how compulsory vaccination was resented, and the way they infected their wounds with medicines of their own and returned to complain of what had been done to them in hospital. There was a fifty per cent loss before one year old of children delivered in the Bush by native methods as opposed to five per cent when born in hospital.

Before going to Cockatville I had been told that the women there were vicious and sterile. Sterile they seemed to be, because I never saw so few children or so few pregnant women in Africa before. Beau-tiful too, I had been told, and I did see two or three who had more looks than usual and a greater appearance of refinement. I had also been told that many liked to be the mistresses of white men from whom they learned sexual evolutions which made them more attrac-tive as marriage partners to their own men. It is interesting how each race picks up the vices rather than the virtues of the other.

Our cabin-de-luxe was large — it had two beds with mosquito nets, plenty of room to move about, an electric fan and a private bathroom.

When Monsieur Bernier left us we slept till dinner. This was the first real rest for some weeks; since Accra in fact. Next day we were able to appreciate the Congo. Its immensity, the swiftness of its current, the shot-olive brown and grey of its surface, the forests that came to its very edge — to resist it for a while and then to be destroyed. On the edge of the river there is an endless war between the land and the water. Chunks are torn out and become islands, or float away to be broken up in the rapids and sent in fragments to the sea. Some islands grow in size, others diminish. The river's course changes continually, and the ship's path is made by buoys of floating oil drums against which the water ripples, and by white-painted road signs attached to the forest trees. For the Congo is a road. It and its tributaries are the main arteries of traffic of the colony. The Congo, in the old West Coast slaving days, was known as the Zaire. When discovered it was believed to be the Nile and in no way associated with the Zaire.

The boat continues sliding endlessly through this enormous conservatory of palms and trees, of forest giants. Sometimes the trunk of a great tree is reflected which, as the wake catches it, changes shape and writhes like an enormous distorted snake behind us. And there are birds. Pied white eagles, hornbills, ibis that rise screaming from a tree as we pass; a flight of finches, and red-breasted kingfishers shaped like bee-eaters that fly high in the sky.

Sometimes, when near the shore, the forest smells sweet, almost sickly, from the perfume of some hidden flower. Sometimes it stinks of putrescence from another.

Evening comes and the sun goes down, a scarlet ball in the misty sky, like a winter sun in New York. We are going due east. The red sun casts a scarlet bar along the river right up to our stern. On each side of us the forest darkens from green to olive, from olive to sepia, from sepia to indigo, touched with the mauve and pink of sunset.

Flicking lights, a village, the ship hoots, lets out a cry like an animal in the night and slows up. It is quite dark except for the searchlight, and the ship's lights, the little fires, and the flicking of lanterns carried by the people of the village. Boys jump off the ship with lines. The lines are made fast from the bow and the stern to two big mangoes. More people come, torches begin to flash, canoes creep in between the ship and the shore. A market springs up. Where there was nothing when we came, there are now two hundred people. Buying and selling at little market stalls set on the earth beside a stable lantern. Passengers, black and white, go down the gangplank. More canoes come, more people. The canoes are tied with lianas to paddles driven into the marshy ground. With the increased illumination huts become visible in the background. The people shout and talk — the beach hums. There is a chorus of tree frogs, disturbed by the light and noise. This could be the background of a ballet, with drums and dancing. The second movement could be the witch doctors' assistants driving off the women, children, and seizing the boys to be circumcised — followed by the Bapende snake dance. The finale being a silent village, the boys coming back a year later, with a broken pot put down beside a hut to show that one of the boys had died of the hardships he had endured, and end up with the weeping mother alone upon the stage.

Next morning we saw a monkey swimming the river. The second that day, the captain said. Its little head was no bigger than a cricket ball in the water. This is a drama of the forest — a small monkey swimming the great river. There are two white egrets on a fallen tree, and a new kind of kingfisher — gray with a red-brown tail. Swallows skim the water. A big fish rises, jumps with a splash . . . pursued by a crocodile.

There were some interesting people on board. We were the only tourists, the others were government servants, the employees of great companies, some with their wives and children. There were four bearded priests in rather soiled white who drank beer and wine, played cards and acted in a very human and friendly manner. They were not cultured gentlemen like most of our parsons, but big-boned peasants who had given up their lives to Africa. There was nothing unctuous about them, a hush did not fall on the saloon when they came in nor did the conversation change in tone. They knew the world and life, and though they hoped for the best they did not invariably expect it. I am not a Roman Catholic but felt that such men do more good than most Church of England or Nonconformist missionaries and parsons, both in Africa and out of it. There was a man who was going to a mine up country where there were gorillas. He had seen an African who had had his calf torn out and the fingers of his right hand bitten off, and he had also seen a gorilla killed near the mine which weighed four hundred kilos. I exchanged recipes with one charming lady, for malaria. I told her about paludrine. She said her Russian nurse had taught her to use the gall of a carp.

There were often some very impressive flies in the saloon, like giant horseflies, which I was told were elephant flies. The killing and hunting of them provided one of the passengers with occupation right through the voyage. I caught a very fine moth with red underwings that were five inches across, under a glass. At night when the decks were lit up masses of insects came out of the forest to visit us; most of them were cicadas — cri-cris — some of them were pale green and quite large. They had wide-set eyes and intelligent bulldog-like faces. I caught one for Tiny but I have never been able to get her really interested in insects. She remains a city girl.

There was an old planter who said cocoanuts should be watered with salt water. I said that this explained why, in the West Indies, they said they would only grow within the sound of the sea — where they must get some salt on the trade winds from over the ocean.

One evening we watched one of the crew delousing another African's head with his fingers and a sheath knife. When he caught one he squeezed it against the blade and put it into the palm of his hand. He must have been paid by the head because his client counted them when he had done.

We saw quite a variety of kingfishers. There was a small grey one with a red tail, a grey and white one, a beautiful dark purple one with a canary-yellow beak and primaries of electric blue, and the more common ultramarine birds with orange chests. There were egrets on fallen trees, eagles with white heads and chests, which had nests as big as tables on some of the higher forest trees.

I heard a great deal of talk about the American penetration. Since the East was lost to them, the general impression seemed to be that they were intent on exploiting Africa. The Germans, too, were back in strength.

At last we saw the smokestacks of the H.C.B. factory at Bumba ahead of us. An hour later we had arrived. We were met by Monsieur Maisse, the manager, and driven out to the plantation at Alberta.

After lunch we drove out to see some native villages with Monsieur Cambier, who had retired to live in Belgium but who could not stand it and had come back. His wife had remained in Europe because she was frightened of the storms in the Congo; with good reason, having had her stove struck while she was cooking in the kitchen. Monsieur Cambier was a real colonial, having been born in the Congo and gone about with his father as a boy. He said when he was about eleven they had come across a hut in which he had seen human legs, arms and hams being smoked over slow fire. Among the Maniema it was the custom to place the bodies they were going to eat in water and consume them raw when putrid, in imitation of the crocodile, a habit which, it was said, gave the emanations of their bodies a very evil smell.

We talked about crocodiles and again I got the length of the biggest as seven metres, and was told that they smashed canoes with their tails. We were shown a company village of small brick houses that once held a hundred people but which had been deserted because the crocs had taken two children and it was believed to be bewitched. This is how, in Africa, great capital expenses can be lost: good houses abandoned for superstitious reasons. I saw a plant that was very like a chick pea whose leaves when mixed with pili-pili they used to attract and catch fish. It apparently knocked them out so that they could be taken by hand.

The Maisses had a very nice garden which ran down to the Congo riverbank. There were masses of flowers including the Sceptre of Solomon; some of it was in seed and the head resembled a pineapple. They had a tall hedge of mixed red and yellow crotons, and both pink and white Honolulu creeper growing over an arbour. At dinner the coffee was home grown and the green beans were boiled before being roasted to remove most of the caffeine, which appeared as an oily green scum on the water.

Our hosts had a charming little blond daughter of five named Françoise, who seemed very healthy in spite of the climate. But they were always nervous about her going too near the river because of the danger of drowning and the crocodiles. She spent her time teaching Tiny French wrongly, pointing to a picture of a cat and saying *lapin* or a dog and calling it *chat*.

We were taken to see the company's agricultural training school for African assistant planters at Yaeseke. These were boys hand picked for character and intelligence. It was a two-year course and while learning they were paid 750 francs a month, out of which they bought some of their clothes and food, but were still able to save 5000 francs a year. When they were qualified they received 1500 francs the first year and 1750 francs the second, which rose when they became full-fledged assistant managers to 2300 francs on a three-year contract, and finally went up to a possible 5000, with a commensurate pension at the end of their service. Each boy cost 300,000 francs to train. The company's aim was to substitute as many Africans for white men as they could. It was estimated that a white man cost a minimum of 400,000 francs a year in salary, fares to Europe, housing and medical attention, to maintain.

This particular place was a bad area for dengue fever or filaria. This is a worm that lives in the blood and sometimes appears in the corner of the eye, the only place from which it can be extracted. Our host's wife — he was the superintendent of the school — had had one and he had taken it out before it crawled away. I checked once more on the size of the crocs and got the figure of twenty-three feet, which still seemed to me excessive, though I suppose possible. I was told of full-grown chimpanzees weighing one hundred and sixty-five pounds, as much as a man. Of African children being very spoilt, which I knew, and that with the elimination of the witch doctors they were brought up without discipline or fear, the two being certainly related whatever the modern school of educationalists may say. I saw a copy of *La Voix du Congo* edited and very well written entirely by Africans, with an article on corruption. The French was much better than the English in the West Coast publications.

The native housing here was very good, the cheapest type cost 15,000 francs to build and that of a clerk 60,000 francs. The simplest form consisted of a single room built of Kimberley bricks — big sun-dried rectangular blocks of mud set on a concrete base with burnt-brick corners and an iron roof. The more expensive was a regular small villa of burnt brick.

Our guest-house home was set in a kind of park surrounded by widely spaced oil palms among which the local black cattle and some goats grazed on the short grass. Everything had been done to ensure our comfort. The houseboys were excellent and spoke good French though, like most Congolese except the really evolved, they used *tu*, the second person singular, which at first was disconcerting.

An amazing thing was the almost total agreement about the character and capacity of the African that I found everywhere among men of all classes who had spent their lives among them — government and company servants, and even missionaries. Each noted exceptions but, by and large, talking to one man one was talking to them all. Most of these men liked Africans and were trying to push them forward. They recognised their good qualities. Their capacity for happiness, their endurance, their immense charm and, once one gets used to it, their good looks. But almost all acknowledged their inability to fully understand them.

One great difficulty is that of language. How many men in all Africa speak a native language perfectly and associate with Africans in their native life in such a way as to understand their fables, taboos, customs and habits? A few thousand at most.

Missionaries are probably the best linguists but I should not include them as their attitude is not sympathetic enough to induce the confidences that would illuminate the African psyche. How then can people, with whom we cannot communicate, be understood? Or how can they understand Western thought patterns? Communication is now added to the factors of colour, economics, education and home environment. The nearer one got to the bottom of the question the more difficult it became. Time is the answer. But how much? How long is there?

25

● LEAVING ALBERTA early we stopped at Bumba to buy cigarettes at a big general store on the beach. We were served by a very attractive blond French girl, with long hair. She told us of the drama which had occurred in the night. A lighter, filled with bricks urgently needed for building, had come loose from its moorings and had drifted down the river. Several boats had gone in search of it. "Ah, ça c'est l'Afrique, monsieur," she said laughing. Laughter is the white man's only protection against ulcers. To do the best he can and when things go wrong to say: That's Africa, and laugh.

Yaligamba our next stop, the H.C.B. experimental station, was about forty-six miles away. It was a pleasant drive through country that had been completely deforested. The only trees we saw were very poor stuff. For once the forest has gone and the grass comes in, the seedling trees have no chance and deterioration sets in fast. The villages were set back from the road as they have to be by law to avoid accidents to children, poultry and livestock. There was some culture — rice and groundnuts — and we saw small government-built silos to store reserves of food and seed. If this was not done the natives would eat or sell the lot and then starve. We passed some chiefs in Western dress with caps made of monkey skins riding on bicycles to some kind of official meeting. We were met by Mr. S. de Blanck.

He was one of the most interesting men we met on our trip. Slight, suave, middle aged, beautifully dressed, he spent part of his time collecting seeds which might be of value in such places as the Amazon and the East Indies. He was a man of immense culture and erudition, the third generation on the Congo, and as much at home in Paris or London as in the tropical forests. His wife lived in England since she did not care for travel or hot climates, but his house here was large and elegant, and he was a superb host. There were purple bougainvillaea and blue plumbago in a vase in our suite, a tin of cigarettes, matches, a new packet of Gillette razor blades and a Pear's soap cake in the bathroom — in fact everything was de luxe, including the conversation.

After lunch we went down to the laboratories to see the experiments being conducted by his staff of young scientists. There was a pathologist who dealt with plant diseases, a pedologist who conducted soil tests and surveys, and an agronomist. We were given short explanations by each — a sort of digest for unscientific children. The oil palm has diseases of various kinds. Some were obvious, such as the fronds being yellow instead of green — this was due to a soil deficiency, but most of the diseases were fungi. We saw cultures and affected leaves. From selections and checks in the seed bed it was believed that seedlings with the most leaves proved the most productive. It had been found that the roots of the oil palm at a distance of 4.9 feet from the bole grew upwards towards the light, and that it was here the fertilizer should be placed.

Leaves were being analysed for mineral trace elements and soil samples were being checked. All the routine tests were done by African chemists whose work compared favourably with that of Europeans in Belgium.

I was told, much to my surprise, that the soil of the Congo was not fertile. That what I had seen that seemed to represent the ultimate in fertility and fecundity was an illusion. Owing to the conditions of heat and moisture, there was an immensely quick turnover. Life and death, growth and putrescence merged into one rapid process but there were few reserves in the soil. I was shown big maps where tests had been made — this was now done before any new planting took place — and there were big patches where nothing would grow without artificials. There was plenty of iron in the soil which was more or less useless but gave the ground its red colour. There were, however, great shortages of both potash and phosphorous.

The Congo basin had once been a great lake which had smashed its way out to the sea where the rapids begin at Léopoldville. I was told that no European figures were any use here, the best soil in the Congo being worse than the worst in Belgium.

We went through a plantation where there was a cover crop of a kind of velvet bean, rather like the kudzu vine called *Pueraria javanica*. It grew luxuriantly, smothered weeds and fixed nitrogen in the soil. I was told the cattle would not eat it but I think they might have liked it dried into hay or made into silage.

There were masses of birds. We were awakened by drums and a

charming bird which seemed to say: "This is how to speak distinctly," over and over again.

We visited the mission where an albino girl was taking care of a number of orphans, including two very pretty little mulattoes. Both the fathers and the nuns seemed very cheerful. They said a knowledge of chemistry was one of the best antidotes against witchcraft because the boys learnt to perform what appeared to be miracles themselves. The girls slept in dormitories — their beds were planks eighteen inches wide. Rather like the bed boards once used in the British Army.

There seems to be no doubt that the felling of the forest reduces the rainfall. I was told that one could actually watch the storms going round the denuded section.

There was a swimming bath for the white officials but there was some difficulty in keeping it full since the African ladies kept baling the water out to drink and cook with. It was easier than pumping it from their well. I heard a story about a man who went away for a couple of days and came back to find a party in progress in his house with the African guests wearing all his and his wife's clothes.

We lunched with the manager, Monsieur Drousie, and he took us round the plantation which is one of the biggest in the world: over 17,000 acres are already under cultivation, 1400 of which have cocoa growing under the shade of the palms. A total of 37,000 acres under oil palm is the ultimate target.

We saw land being cleared by bulldozers. It had been cut over by hand and the rubbish and fallen trees were pushed into lines to make room for the lines of young palms. This reduced costs and saved humus, burning being the alternative. In a year or so everything but the biggest trees would have rotted. They had 260 miles of road on the plantation, dividing the different blocks, all in very good order, and employed 2600 men.

There was a mill which dealt with the rice they bought from the natives, and lines of nice brick cottages. We saw everything from virgin forest to young first-year palms and old established blocks of trees. I again heard of village pumps being broken up to obtain ammunition for guns, of cassias planted for shade being killed because it was too much trouble to sweep up the leaves when they fell.

I was told of a young planter just out from Europe who was lost in the forest. Word was sent out by planton, plantation messengers, on bicycles, and within an hour the talking drums of every village and isolated hut beat out their message to send searches till he was found.

Mr. de Blanck now drove us to the river where Mr. Lancaster, another Englishman in charge of the plantation of Mokaria, would meet us. De Blanck crossed the river with us in a small dugout, pirogue with a single paddler.

When our new host came we said goodbye to our old one with much regret. A parting present from him was a new cake of Pear's soap. I had told him I had not had any since I was a boy.

On the drive to Mokaria we saw a veritable mirage of butterflies. It was almost impossible to see the road through the fluttering of their wings. They were brown, but reflected the sunlight so that the whole road shimmered in a haze of butterflies and heat.

Our gear we dumped at the guest house and went on to the Lancasters for lunch. He had served in India and some of his tiger and leopard skins carpeted the floor. His wife, a very attractive sparkling brunette, had been born in India.

At the office we met an agronomist and discussed the native rotation of rice, manioc, and banana which needed a seven- to twelve-year period of rest. This was becoming impossible owing to the increase of population. I was shown buildings made of a mixture which was three parts earth, two parts sand and one part cement, on a concrete foundation, which seemed very serviceable and were cheap to erect.

Here are some stories I heard, some gossip, some ideas. In putting up a new eight-foot chimney that weighed six tons, one of the boys turning the windlass got tired and just let go. An accident was prevented only by a white foreman jamming the wheel with a crowbar. White women have to pay twenty francs to get an African nursing sister to come and baby-sit if they go out. One woman came back and found the nurse in bed with her house boy for which she said she got another, supplementary, twenty francs. One of the boys wanted to get rid of his aging wife because now he got only fifty francs for her instead of a hundred when he hired her out for the night. There were, on an average, four cases of rape here a year, something very unusual in Africa. Accidents were caused by tree cutters dropping three trees at once by cutting two of them half through and causing the third to bring the others down. Finding a house which had been forgotten when a new road was being cut. In six years the forest had covered it completely. Three stages of psychosis brought on by loneliness. First, the man talks to himself. Next, he answers himself. In the third stage he employs two voices and develops two personalities. These are materials from which the cakes of fiction can be baked.

We visited the hospital which was run by a Spanish doctor. Among the population worm infection is one hundred per cent and V.D. thirty. People came to the hospital too late and then when they died there it was said that the white man had killed them. If they died in the Bush no one was concerned and the witch doctor got no blame. I saw a dying baby — her little bullet head lolling as her mother held her. The doctor said she had been given an enema of pili-pili (red pepper) which is effective in small doses, but they do not measure and it was much too strong for a small child.

The Mokaria plantation was rubber and cocoa, which interested me very much after my glimpse of Firestone where I had not had time to go into the details of tapping. The panels are cut at a rate of about three quarters of an inch a month with a small gouging chisel, and kept open from the first light to about 10 A.M. when the heat coagulates the latex. A good tree runs about ninety drops a minute, forty drops is considered fair. The plantation is carried by the good trees. The latex oozes out as soon as the cells below the upper bark are cut or broken. If the cut is too deep the tree is injured, so the work is very skilled. Most trees are grafted but the graft does not always take, or even produce as much as the mother tree, and is more susceptible to wind damage, so a new system for the selection of clones (pedigreed trees), known as the testatex system, has been evolved.

In the first and second year all sickly seedlings are pulled up. This is an application of the survival of the fittest theory. At the end of the second year each little tree is scratched four inches above ground level with a three-pronged knife. Those whose latex reaches ground level are good and are then transplanted.

The trees are bled alternately on one side and then the other. It takes seven years to work round the tree completely. They are rested at regular intervals and each tree is numbered. The collectors add a few drops of a solution of ammonia to the cups to prevent coagulation. This process is reversed in the factory, where formic acid is put into the coagulating tanks to make the latex stick to the plates, where it builds up into sheets rather less than a yard square. These are floated in running water down to the rollers where they are squeezed and then go to the drying sheds to be smoked. This process cures them like hams, or any other organic matter, and the smoke covers them with a protective film. They are then compressed into solid sixty-kilo bales for export. Before leaving they are powdered with talc to prevent them sticking together in the hold of the ship, which occurred on one occasion. I cannot imagine a more difficult problem than removing hundreds of tons of rubber, which has been fused into a solid mass, from the hold of a cargo vessel.

Cocoa was the next item of interest. Cocoa is, I think, the most beautiful crop in the world. The tree itself, really a very big shrub, has an attractive shape — pretty leaves, the young growths that tip each branch being pinkish bronze in colour. The fruit grows amusingly on the main trunk and older wood. Green at first, it turns citron-yellow when ripe. It is nice to handle and easy to reap, and, above all, cocoa is a shade crop. Best of all was to see it growing in the giant primary forest where only the undergrowth and smaller trees had been removed to make room for it. This was, to me, the finest compromise of the ancient, secret Africa with the new. It was like being in a church.

The nursery where the seedlings were grown was almost a grotto, protected by great screens of woven leaves. Here, in the dark warm womb of the forest, there were forty thousand seedlings, each in its little basket pot waiting to be planted. I thought of the miserable seedlings that I had seen in the full sunlight in the Liberian nursery. The sun, to the cocoa tree, is an enemy.

Now we went to the factory where the fruit was cured. The beans or berries were put into boxes in steps where, covered with sacks, they fermented. The smell was strong, like that of beer — one could have become drunk on it. As it matured, the cocoa descended step by step, getting hotter and hotter like a compost heap. By the time it reached the bottom one could hardly touch it. It was now spread on a wire drying frame — a kind of wide moving belt which climbed slowly up the automatic drying tower where the moisture was removed. Once dry, it was ready for export to the chocolate factories of Europe and America. The installation — a very good one — was German. And it had been put up by a German engineer, with local African help, in four months. Mr. Lancaster said they would sooner have had English machinery but England could not supply them in time and had declined to erect the plant themselves.

I learnt more about cocoa, *Theobroma*, the drink of the gods. Montezuma was said to have drunk fifty cups of it a day and called it chocolatl. The best seed came from Venezuela. What we saw here had come from there via the Portuguese island colony of San Tomé on the west coast.

Cocoa is subject to several diseases, chiefly fungus infections. In fact I touched one seedling that looked sick and it came up in my hand, the whole stem just below ground level having rotted off.

We now went to visit the sawmill where a new bandsaw was being installed and watched the timber being cut into planks and balks. It was odd to see mahogany used as scantling for the roof, and big planks of furniture woods set across streams as bridges.

After breakfast we left for Elizabetha. For the first hour or so we passed through a highly populated area where one village seemed to run into the next. Being Christmas week, and Sunday, the road teemed with people. They swarmed like ants carrying food home to their nest. Palm wine in great round glass bottles, manioc in baskets, chickens, alive, hanging head downwards from the handlebars of bicycles. This was a rich part of the country and harvest time. Cotton bolls were lying out on tables made of saplings to dry. There was cotton packed into openwork baskets that would weigh about two hundred and twenty pounds ready to be shipped to the Co-op and stacks of rice in bags. In front of almost every house was a twenty-foot tower with a ladder leading to the top where the rice heads were being cleaned and given a rough winnowing by allowing them to fall. Below the towers the grain lay in golden heaps.

It was, of course, the women who were carrying things. The men were resting or riding out to visit their friends. We saw a number of them wearing scarlet felt hats. They are the fashion in these parts and in the dark green of the forest give a Corot-like impression with that little touch of orange scarlet which so often distinguishes his pictures and those of his imitators. We saw the usual wild red canna which seems to have more or less naturalised itself all over West and Central Africa. It was burnt and salt was extracted from its ash, and the round seeds made into necklaces.

At Yasaka the H.C.B. motor launch, or Pac-a-pac, with a white man and his wife arrived at the dock to pick us up, and to collect a native clerk and his wife and baby and a bale of green football jerseys for the local team. We passed native fishermen who had lines out, tied to anchored palm branch floats which, stripped of their foliage, looked like miniature canoes. The fishermen waited among the trees and bush that lined the bank. Presumably when the fish bite, the arc of the float is pulled down into the water. Till then the fishermen can rest.

After fifteen minutes on this river we came out into the swift waters of the Congo and went upstream. The forest came right down to the water, dipping its branches into it. Trees had fallen in and were being washed away, trees that had stuck in shallow banks were catching reeds and papyrus and building up new islands.

The surface of the river was dotted with the white thistledown seeds of the silk-cotton trees. So it was to be a white Christmas after all. The seed heads looked like snow on the water, and later we saw the great trees standing out in the dark forest, covered with burst snowy pods. How so small and fragile a seed can produce so great a tree is one of the miracles of God.

And so to Elizabetha and the rest house where lunch, five days' rest and Christmas awaited us. This was the prettiest rest house we had been in. It was surrounded by trees — traveller's palms, guavas, wild almonds, cassias, mangoes and coffee bushes. In the living room by the writing desk mangoes hung in a cluster that I could touch by reaching out my hand. Two hundred feet below us the Congo flowed, leaden by day and silver in the moonlight. It was full moon. Canoes floated by like straws, floated as they had done for hundreds, perhaps thousands of years, propelled by long-handled, spear-shaped paddles, driven by black arms. Women climbed down the steep banks for water as they had always done. Sometimes one is taken by a crocodile in the less disturbed parts of the river. Till relatively recent times some of the tribes here were cannibals and the Arab slave traders from the East Coast menaced the more peaceful clans. This was the very heart of Africa, almost its centre, quiet enough now, but its civilisation no more than a veneer.

As we had driven here from Mokaria, we had seen few smiles and no one had waved. There was a feeling of sullenness, dislike and apathy. It was my idea that these people, like most Africans, want the benefits the white man brings but resent his presence. Now they are trapped by their own new needs. They must buy and sell. They can no longer live by the river and the forest. The time to stop the white man was in the eighties and nineties, when it would have been easy. The African is now involved in the great industrial machine which we describe as Western culture. He cannot get on without his contacts with the outer world. If the white man withdraws the African would continue to exist, but the last, the least evolved, would be first, would be the survivors. Millions would perish of starvation and in the tribal wars that would at once ensue. Without European technicians, without trade with Europe and America, every vestige of civilisation would drop like a garment to the ground. The machines would be eaten up with rust, the houses be swallowed by the forest and the roads go back to jungle paths. Without the European the African is lost. Like children, Africans resent their failures and blame their parents and their teachers; like children they try to run away from home but have nowhere else to go. Like children, they have an Oedipus complex and hate their father.

In a copy of a magazine written entirely by Africans there was an article denouncing a professor in South Africa for suggesting that birth-control clinics for Africans should be set up in the Union to prevent overpopulation. The author wrote as if contraception were a new and wicked idea specially invented by the white man to thwart the Africans' passion for begetting children. He had obviously never heard of Malthus, had no idea of the overpopulation of the world or its contracting ability to produce food. He did not realise that even today South Africa, a so-called agricultural and farming country, does not always produce enough mealies, the staple food of the African, to feed its people, but has to import vast quantities from the New World. I do not attack the author. The piece was well written in beautiful French. It was, within the framework of his knowledge, perfectly logical, given a Roman Catholic training, and a hatred of Dr. Malan and all his works, which is typical of all black Africa. The trouble was that the frame was too small, the picture only postcard size.

It is here, on the wider concepts of government, sociology and economics, that the African fails almost a hundred per cent.

To the bush African, the peasant, the white man is irrelevant. To the partially educated working African he is the inexplicable hub round which his work revolves. To the educated and near educated African he is a liar and a cheat, and is hated. He, the African, has done all that he believes to be required of him. He has his diploma, he drives a car and lives in a properly furnished house. But there is still something missing, some quality the white man has which he has not. Something, in fact, that the white man, out of fear of competition, has held back. That this something may be twenty-five hundred years of climbing from a state of barbarism into his present position is beyond the African's understanding.

Supposing, however, that the African is brilliant — a success in all fields, a scholar, a sportsman and a gentleman — he is accepted everywhere in Europe, then he returns to Africa and is rejected by the white man, sometimes even the same white man who in England he thought to be his friend. Now a dangerous man has been created. We have taught him all we know. He understands the white man's ways, his habits, his methods of thought and action, and he turns against him.

I have met Africans, a very few of them, to whom none of these things have happened, who had no chips on their shoulders, who were in every way educated and civilised. Black Western men with whom one could be glad to claim friendship — but how many are there? A thousand, ten thousand, a hundred thousand — out of Africa's hundred and fifty millions? They are neither trusted nor liked by their own people.

It is often said that we do not want black Europeans, that the African must retain his own culture. Personally I have failed to find a culture in any way comparable to a modern technological civilisation. There are only primitive music, primitive dancing, primitive carving and arts and crafts of various simple kinds. The most advanced work we have seen are things which they have now forgotten how to make, such as the bronzes of Ife, and the brass work and wood carving of Benin, though the kente cloths of Ashanti which are beautiful and of the highest quality, are still woven. Apart from them, there is very little.

If we do not want black Europeans, if that is not what we are trying to make, what *do* we want? If the African does not want to be civilised, Europeanised, what is he striving for? Why does he demand a European education?

Africans can be divided into many classes. Fully evolved and educated Africans, like my friends, who are happy, as happy probably as white men — it is only Africans who think all white men are happy. A great number of them have become integrated in European society and have preferred to remain in London or Paris. Then there are Africans who have high academic qualifications but who have failed to adjust themselves. They tend to become leaders of anti-white political parties. Then there are a great number of more or less educated men, varying from those who have failed to qualify, or to complete their work at schools and universities, to those who can only read, write, and do simple sums. There are, in addition, African expatriates, in Europe and America who actively attack all Europeans in Africa, but who would never return to their native land to live and help educate their people. Many of them are subsidized by unsuspecting tribesmen who believe them to be working for some patriotic or religious purpose.

This enormously vocal minority are the Voice of Africa as the European and the American hear it, as UNO hears it. They probably represent much less than one per cent of the population. They are interested primarily in themselves, their own enrichment and aggran-

Monuments of the Asafo (note little dog dying between lion's feet)

Methodist ladies dancing at Abori

King in palanquin, his "soul" sitting in front of him

Chiefs' umbrellas and drums (note human skulls wrapped in white cloths·
on two left-hand drums)

Fishing canoes at
Senya Beraku

Woman chewing newly severed goat's leg, Odumase millet festival

Old castle

Christiansburg Castle

The Right Honorable Kwame Nkrumah, Prime Minister of the Gold Coast

Witch doctor assistants in circumcision dance

Drummer
in hysteria

Bapende chief

Bapende hairdos

Basenji
hunting dog
wearing
wooden bell

Dancers with arrow-pierced faces

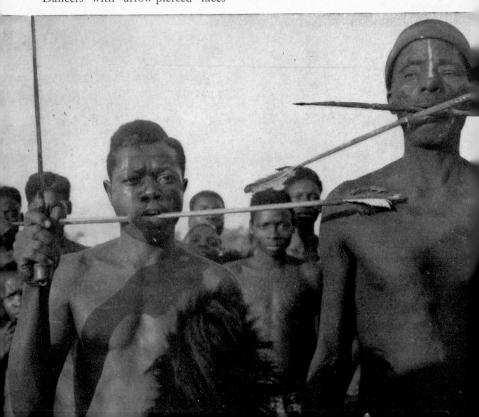

disement. No one despises the bush African man as much as these so-called educated men. No one deals with them more ruthlessly, if they are given positions of authority. In fact, the one thing the African has to fear is the African.

After lunch we drove thirty miles into the bush to see some Topeke girls dance. The tom-toms began to beat, and the dancers, nine girls varying in age from ten to fifteen, marched towards us. They were painted in white, yellow and red. The two oldest girls had what looked like high-necked Victorian blouses painted over their naked bodies. They wore glasses and had hats made of red parrot feathers stuck vertically into their hair. Round their waists they wore the thick girdles of scarlet washerlike beads that we had seen from Kano to Lagos. Below them came a six-inch skirt material with a small oblong flap in front, fully nine inches long. The older girls wore a string of bells and large seed pods round their wrists, and all had a small sporran of beadwork over which hung a series of nut shells strung on strings, whose purpose was to jingle up and down with a pleasant sound when the young ladies jerked the lower portions of their bellies to the rapid beating of the drums. In their hands, which they held in front of them as they danced, was a small peeled stick that they used at intervals to wipe the sweat from their faces. Between their legs was a narrow cloth fastened to their girdles. Their thighs and buttocks were decorated with circular tattoos — dark indigo dapplings, like those on the quarters of a grey horse. The steps they made were rather like those of a child of three when it hears music. One of the older girls carried a knife and I have the impression that we were witnessing the much expurgated edition of a female circumcision dance. The highlight of the performance was when the girls came forward, in turn, to within two feet of us, turned about and, without moving any other part of their bodies, vibrated their buttocks, sending their little skirts flying, in a movement so rapid that it suggested the vibrations of a humming bird's wings. The dance appeared to serve no purpose save that of proving the abdominal dexterity of the young ladies who performed it. As a further sign of evolution, one of the girls with glasses had at least fifty safety pins dangling in a fringe from her sporran. Two of the girls were quite pretty and beautifully formed. Their breasts looked strange, as do those of many African tribes, to the European, as they had no areolas.

The whole village, three or four hundred people, including children, watched the performance. Some of the older men had amazing cicatrices on the face, even down the nose, and round the lips. The scar tissue was raised from the surface of the skin in a decorative arrangement of symmetrical warts, pimples. The pain they must have suffered was unbelievable and, probably, to a European insupportable. I was told that these dances had been far more erotic at one time, every motion of the sexual act being simulated till a state of orgiastic frenzy was attained. The missionaries have stopped all this.

We visited the hospital next day. It had three hundred beds and last year treated eight thousand hospital cases. The two white doctors and fifteen dispensers handled three hundred and fifty thousand cases in all. A truck goes round to dispensaries each day to bring in those requiring treatment at the main centre, and a doctor visits each bush dispensary once a week.

There is very little tapeworm, since there is practically no meat. The worms that infest them come from drinking dirty water and walking about with bare feet (guinea worm). At one time they were given sandals but in wet weather, when the infection is most likely, they carried them in their hands so as not to damage the soles. Shoes were valuable. If they got worms the white man would cure them. In earlier times, the African expected to be paid for operative treatment. They had submitted their bodies to this form of white man's amusement and expected a cash return.

I had an interesting talk with the doctor who has been eight years in the Congo, about some of the differences between the white man and the black. A much thicker skin which does not join as well as a white man's but tends to curl up in ridges leaving the wound open. Skin grafts are only about fifty per cent successful. The big bones and muscles appear to be more elastic and break less easily. The nerve centres are much less sensitive. An ulcer can be lanced without the patient batting an eyelid. There appear to be differences in the digestive tract. The skin has from five to six times as many sweat glands as a white man's. They do not suffer from stomach ulcers or appendicitis; cancer is very rare. The hair, both of the head and body, is of a different texture. The heel bones project. Actually the differences have not been sufficiently studied, but some believe that the brain and nervous system are as different as the body and its organs from those of the white man. This would suggest that the African's development will follow different lines even if he becomes Westernised. The doctor considered that the tribal African was satisfied with eating, breeding, fighting and dancing, but that now, already, some of the more evolved had grown psychologically and had developed a super ego, a moral sense and susceptibilities absent from their fathers and even from themselves when younger. Then we spoke of native medicines and there is no question that they have some remedies which we have not got, and have cured cases that the white doctors have given up. This is the field in which some foundation should finance research. There is no doubt that they have herbs that contain substances which, if analysed, could be of the greatest value to medicine. And he told me of herbs which, if placed on the breast of an old woman long past child-bearing, will cause her to give milk by stimulating the mammary glands. Here was something the fashionable beautician would give a lot to know.

The natives of this area were very backward before the coming of the white man. Cannibals who had not yet reached the stage of becoming cultivators of the soil, they were harvesters — living on the oil of the palm, of fish out of the river, and men if they could catch them. Now, with some persuasion, they grow rice, bananas and small quantities of manioc.

In the afternoon I went to the factory, one of the largest of its kind in the world. There are 174 miles of railway line on the plantation that brings in 400 tons of fruit a day. In a good month, 6000 tons of oil are extracted. The palms are of the highest quality, yielding over 4 tons the acre and the soil is excellent.

Certain peculiarly African factors exist. When we went round, the feed of one palm kernel pipe was choked. The attendant was sitting down looking at it and doing nothing. He became active only when the manager appeared. White supervision remains essential. Supervision which must struggle against apathy, against a kind of amorphous, passive resistance that finally gets the white man down and necessitates the long European leave he receives every second year — this, more than illness or the climate. Was I on the Congo, or back in Lagos where I had been told the same thing? It's not the climate, it is the African.

26

● THE DAY WAS SILENT, oppressive, a storm was coming. One could feel it though the sky was clear. We went to look at the river. It flowed in a leaden flood, unchanging, suddenly menacing. We saw a swirl in the water, then another. Crocodiles. Four of them. They were rare here but must have been disturbed and were on the move. They were in keeping with the general feeling of the place today. Even the trees seemed to be waiting for something. Then the sky darkened to purple, to black. We had dinner. Before it was finished, the storm broke. There was a roar of wind, thunder and the smell of rain, and it grew cold. A tornado was sweeping towards us. But suddenly it changed its course. There was a peculiar smell in the air, of rain, of wet humus and rotting vegetation, ozone and sulphur. The brimstone of the Bible.

I had seen many storms, but never one like this. I had been nearly struck by lightning, and never smelt this smell. Africa in one of her most terrible manifestations had stretched out her hand towards us, and then had drawn it back. We turned in but we both had the feeling of having been near something that was paranormal, of an impact that we should never forget.

Next day was Christmas Eve. In the afternoon we went to a children's party given by the manager's wife, Madame Fauconnier. There were twenty children, most of them very young. They were presented to Father Christmas, who came trudging up the path from the river below the house with a long stick in his hand. He was followed by three boys with the gifts in baskets. Father Christmas had a ledger in which were entered the crimes committed by every child. These were all recapitulated before the child received its present.

We dined with the Fauconniers, a party of twelve. On the table there was a small imitation Christmas tree decorated with glass balls, stars and lighted candles. Soup, fish, turkey, caviar and a big cream cake. Then songs were sung, and red and white wine, and champagne, was drunk.

Next day we left for Stanleyville. The drive was long and dull. We saw masses of butterflies; one big patch of bright blue ones sitting on the road looked like a bed of flowers. We even had to stop once to scrape butterflies out of the radiator.

Rooms had been reserved for us in the Sabena Guest House at the airport. There was an interesting cat here, a tabby with ear tufts almost like a lynx, part wild, but very friendly. Its coat was dotted rather than spotted in the usual tabby manner. On the veranda after dinner we watched a wagtail catching moths by artificial light.

We called on the governor of the province, a very capable man, who told us about the okapi-capturing station in which he was interested. We talked of the natives. Their idea of land here is much the same as it is on the West Coast. It belongs first to their god, then to the tribe, to their dead ancestors and their unborn children. Wild trees belong to the tribe but planted oil palms to the descendants of those who planted them, wherever they are situated. The African, he said, is most communalistic and unselfish in his own tribe but most individualistic away from it. This was dangerous because they were individualistic before being, in the full sense, individuals. He said that it was no use being sentimental about people who were without sentiment and he thought European law not applicable to the African mentality. He said he thought they ought to do what Napoleon had done in France when he made his famous code. The laws of all tribes should be collected and a committee of chiefs and notables on the one side and administrators and lawyers on the other should synthesise them into a legal system which followed the native tradition. The Governor passed me on to one of his senior officers, Monsieur Siquet, who showed me around.

New buildings were going up on every street. Stan, like Leo, resembled a builder's yard — there was dust everywhere. It rose in clouds as trucks, vans and heavy equipment roared through it. Heaps of material were stacked at every corner. Outside the town native cities were going up fast. I was taken into some of the houses. They were cooler than any I have ever been in. The Belgians seem to have evolved the best form of tropical architecture in the world, based on the simple fact, which every schoolboy knows and every architect seems to have forgotten, that hot air rises. To enable it to rise they have a double roof with a vent in the middle, open sides under the eaves, and other ventilators at ground level where air can get in.

We were taken out of town to see some of the new villagisation schemes. This is the first and most important move in civilising the bush people. Permanent homes and permanent agriculture, as opposed to the shifting, land-wasting methods of the past. The lands are planted, rotated and rested under the direction of white agricultural officers and the surplus products marketed through co-operatives which are being established wherever possible. The main crops here were manioc and banana. But something new was being put into practice when we arrived. A hundred talapia had just been liberated into the communal fish pond. These fish feed on manioc leaves and the record return under test has been nine tons of fish per hectare, or approximately four and a half tons to the acre per year. The talapia is an excellent table fish and we ate a lot of it at one time or another.

We then visited an Arabised village. These people were the descendants of Africans who had been employed as raiders by the Arab slavers and had absorbed some of their culture and their blood. This was the stamping ground of such famous raiders as Tipoo Tib. It was difficult to think of this as a country which, fifty years ago, was a veritable hell, where Stanley, when he was here in 1878, lost two hundred and thirty-six men of the three hundred and forty-seven who had accompanied him.

Beyond the Arab town were the falls where the Wagenia fishermen set their traps — big baskets that came to a narrow funnel end in the rushing waters. They are fastened by lianas to clumsy frameworks of trees set among the rocks. The force of the water drives the fish into the traps and holds them there till they are released. I was told there were fierce fights over the catch sometimes. I watched a girl get a small fish out of a trap. She put it into her mouth to hold it. She held its head in her teeth and its wriggling tail banged up and down on her chin. These people are considered remarkable inasmuch as none of their girls has yet been tempted to become a white man's housekeeper, though they are very pretty and have had many propositions made to them. There are great flat rocks on the river's edge in which there are holes containing round stones like cannon balls, which in the floods revolve round and round, making the holes still rounder and deeper as they bore their way into the rocky beds.

The women were washing on the edge of the river and great outcrops were bright with their multi-coloured *pagnes* laid out to dry in the sun. I watched one woman holding a naked child of ten over her knees and giving it an enema. This interested me, for I had always imagined this to be a relatively modern technique. She had a gourd with a nozzle into which she poured some medicine, probably a solution of pili-pili, and then, lowering her head to its opening, blew into it to force the liquid into the child's bowels.

We visited the new dam at the falls, an immense project with huge curved slabs of steel fitting into grooves in concrete pillars that could be raised or lowered according to the strength of the river.

We dined with Monsieur and Madame Siquet. Both were charming. And they confirmed the story that Africans believed that white people ate Africans — not only ate, but canned them. Africans were sure of this because they had seen a brand of corned beef with the picture of a Negro's head on it. Monsieur Siquet told me about some Africans who had been taken on a tour in Europe. He did not think the intellectuals got much from it, but one member of the party was a master carpenter who employed thirty men in his shop. He was so impressed by what he had seen that he ordered a complete set of machinery — saws, mortising machines, planes, the works in fact — and threw out all his workmen when he got back. He had too much trouble with them, he said. With these machines he could get as much work done alone as he had done with his workmen, and have no headaches. This was interesting coming from an African employer dealing with Africans.

Monsieur Siquet said that he told his young officers that there were two keys to any act they did not understand in the native. Either witchcraft or envy would explain them. He is right, they do. And some of the clever ones, the evolved ones, use witchcraft to exploit their envy.

The next day was New Year's Eve. We went to the dinner party given by the hotel. At midnight songs were sung — "Auld Lang Syne" and "Tipperary," both in French.

Next morning we left at eight-thirty for Usumbura. There were only four people on the plane — this was hangover day. A holiday, January the first, 1954. We were out of the Congo now and the Ruanda Urundi.

We met a functionary, Monsieur Fogenne, who drove us into the mountains to see some native lands. The slopes were very steep but were being contoured and the natives had mixed crops, chiefly bananas, manioc, groundnuts and small plantations of coffee trees. We passed the site of the new multi-racial university which was being bulldozed, and then went down to the lake. Tanganyika, the biggest crevasse in the world, 1437 metres deep with an area of 32,000 square kilometres. It was like a sea and is sometimes very rough. There are both hippos and crocs in it which sometimes come quite close to the sandy shore.

Next day we went to see a villagisation scheme which was most interesting on the lower Ruwizi. The lots were ten acres in extent and divided into eight fields of seventy-five square yards. No. 1 was wood plot for burning (grevilea and gum), No. 2, reserve, No. 3, cotton, No. 4, cotton, No. 5, manioc and maize, No. 6, manioc alone, No. 7, grass fallow, No. 8, house and yard. On these little farms they were able to clear 12,000 francs per annum. A big irrigation project was being developed for fishponds and rice. There were acres of bananas and we saw some of the big-horned Ruanda cattle for which this area is famous.

Until water had been brought here by diverting a river, this immense area had been useless.

I learnt a great deal about local African customs. There are normally no villages in these parts, merely huts surrounded by fences of ficus hidden in the depths of banana plantations that are like small forests through which paths are tunnelled. This was a land of fear. Fear of the slavers. Fear of the sorcerers who, according to Pierre Ryckmans, once governor, killed thousands of people every year. Even today superstition is very strong. They refuse to eat mutton, believing it brings leprosy. They have died after walking over a bewitched powder. They live by rote, by custom. Any innovation breaks the chain, creates the abnormal and is punished. The trials were by ordeal, as in West Africa. The only natural deaths were from wounds, starvation, smallpox or age. Any other death was due to bewitchment of some kind, by some person, who would be discovered by the sorcerer. Strangers were killed on sight. But where a man was known to have been murdered, vendettas began which lasted generations. There was even a class of gangsters — hired killers — who committed murders for their clients. The witch doctors got poisons from the coast so that there could be no local antidote. Criminals were beaten with banana stems, then tied with the green bark which bit into them as it dried, and tortured, with much ingenuity, by the women till they died. I was told that administrators must know the language. This was more important than knowing the law. Ancestors are important, but their powers weaken with the memory of the survivors, four generations being the maximum length of time that anyone is remembered or feared. Chiefs

can succeed in two ways only — by being either very just or terribly
tyrannical. The people here are divided into classes — the Batutsi or
nobles, tall men of Nilotic origin and the Bahutu or common people,
who look like most ordinary Africans. They do the work of the
fields and herd their master's cattle. And finally the Batwa — the
pygmies who are hunters and potters. The Batutsi are also called
Watutsi or Watussi and are sometimes seven feet tall and famous
for their high jumping, dancing and sacred, big-horned Ankoli cattle.

We took our meals at the Pourquoi Pas, a small restaurant in the
town, and met a most interesting man, a Monsieur X, to whom I
had, at the instigation of the restaurant proprietor, introduced myself.
"There's a man who knows the Congo, monsieur," he said. And he
did. He was a scientist in the employ of the government who, because I was a stranger, was prepared to let his hair down. The subject
was the same. Africa. The African.

"Ah," he said. "The African. In dealing with natives one must
not go fast, one must listen to all the evidence carefully, weigh it up,
then decide and never change."

He had been here fifteen years and knew both the North and the
West. He said that in his work, a matter of carrying out tests — as
a biologist — he found Africans as good or better than Europeans.
Routine work of this nature does not bore the African. He can be
trusted with slides and report malaria if that is what he is looking
for. But if he found something else with it, sleeping sickness or
syphilis, he would ignore them. He had not been told to look for
them. Then he told me of an African bishop in this area, a man
who had translated African poems and folklore into French, who
had told him that they would always need men like himself. Technicians and scientists, but not the others.

"Missionaries?" I said.

"The missionaries were good at first. They are now not over-
respected. They are interested only in numbers. A man is not
converted because he wears a medallion on a string round his neck.
The Protestants are the best."

This interested me because this is a predominantly Catholic
country with probably ninety-nine per cent of the education in the
hands of the Roman Catholic Church. The Protestant religion was
alien here, so it had to make a better showing. In Rhodesia, which
was predominantly Protestant, the boys from the Catholic missions
were the most highly regarded for the same reason. Each religion
sent its best men into these areas.

"Altruism?"

"No. That the African does not understand. For nothing he gives nothing. The African," he said, "has a personal not a social approach."

This corresponded with my idea — *men not parties*. Party leaders becoming chiefs in the eyes of their followers, and the party itself a kind of tribe within a tribe or race.

He told me he had lived with the pygmies for months during an official investigation of the forests and had had several pygmy wives. It had been hard, he said, to come back after one had lived like an animal for so long. He told me of secret ceremonies where a virgin is raped by a young man to excite the elders. Of how, before marriage, an old woman beats a girl, telling her with each stroke what she can and cannot do with her husband. In this way they remember.

He told me of clearings in the forest, esube, that may even be made by the buffaloes and elephants for their own delectation. Of a sacred clearing he had heard but had not been able to reach because of the rain, caused, his natives said, by the Bonema, the sacred snake identified with the rainbow because its head and tail were buried in the ground. No white man had ever reached this place. They were always stopped by rain. He told me of a chief who had given him a small blue feather which gave him almost unlimited power when he showed it. Of native medicines, one which would produce an abortion; of a contraceptive that was poured into the body of a woman before her period, which caused the ova to be passed, whether it was fertilised or not; of a herb which he said had cured gonorrhoea in two days. He told me that whenever a snake was killed the head was taken to the witch doctor, who pounded it up, mixed it with herbs and stored it away. When anyone was bitten this mixture was moistened, heated, put on the wound and effected a cure. The "langue véhiculaire," such as Ki Swahili, was of no value since it was native neither to the African nor the white man. It was merely a compromise. No one, he maintained, really understood the African mind.

We talked about the family allowance which might be necessary in the towns, but was absurd in the Bush where the children often did not even belong to the father, but to the mother or the eldest maternal uncle, where wives and children were an asset and not a liability, something which the law makers of Belgium, who had never been to Africa, could not appreciate. He told me about the waste of wild game where, by native law and custom, the chief had to be given the quarters, the "droit de cuissage," and if there was more than he could use it was simply allowed to rot.

Then we got on to the Ruanda Urundi. It was vastly overstocked with cattle which even in a famine could not be killed. The cattle belonged to the king who divided them among subordinate chiefs, who went on dividing them, right down the line to the single individual, to whom his cow was the ultimate reality. It made him valid, and gave him the position of a man and not a slave. Without stock he had no rights and no protection. He said that in the old days the Africans were better off and better dressed, though they had less money. Now they spent too much on beer and women. On show girls and cocktails, like white men, I thought. He said some cows were good milkers, giving up to 12 quarts off grass alone. He had spent six months studying the cattle question, mainly to discover the importance of urine in the native culture. They wash their calabashes in it and even drink some. By doing this, he said, you become part of the cow. The difference between urine and milk is that the cow voids it, whereas milk is extracted from her. Without the formality of first taking urine, drinking milk is a form of stealing. But by this rite you become part of the cow and are entitled to her produce, which, since you are now identified with her, is your own.

Going home, the swallows were feeding on insects attracted by the electric light on the veranda of the Grand Hotel. One pair was building its nest by artificial light in a corner. The geckos profited by the artificial light too, here as elsewhere. Living by day behind the lamp brackets they come out to feed on the insects that are attracted to the lights at night. I saw a quite small one rush out like a bulldog and seize a moth as big as itself, which struggled so hard that they fell to the ground together, where the fight continued and the moth was killed and eaten.

This was our last night. We were called at four-thirty and went down to get some coffee in the restaurant and say goodbye to our friend, "the square cat of Usumbura," as we called him — a very fat cat, black and white Persian, almost square, in fact, with a passion for guava jelly which I used to give him on bread for breakfast. He waddled after us to the airport bus, his tail erect and vibrating.

It was the end of the holidays and children whose parents lived here were going back to school at Costermansville, which is now called Bukavu. We were the only adults. The plane was sitting, waiting like a ghostly night bird, on the runway when we reached the airport.

27

● THERE WERE TWO well-dressed mulatto children returning with
the other white children to school. In the Congo mulatto counts as
white, if acknowledged by the father. That is to say if the child is
the result of an established ménage. If he is an accidental deriving
from a white N.C.O. or artisan and a native prostitute, he remains
with the tribe and is treated as a native. There seems to be no
particular tragedy in the lives of these mulattoes provided there are
enough of them to form a social grade of their own, and I feel that
in tropical Africa they certainly have a place since they will live here
for the whole of their lives, thus forming a link between the white
men who leave the country when their service is over, to live in
Belgium on their pensions, and the pure Africans.

The air trip took thirty minutes over eroded hills, mountains and
streams. The children all lit cigarettes in a very grown-up manner
once they were airborne and away from their parents. Our hotel
room overlooked Lake Kivu, and the view of the distant mountains
was wonderful.

At breakfast we had a big dish of the strawberries and cream for
which Costermansville is famous. When we had finished, I called
up Dr. D'Hooghe and Monsieur Vin, whom we had met at the
Congo exhibition in Bulawayo in July, and made appointments to
see them. Then we went for a walk. The town consisted of one
very long street that runs along a peninsula, that juts into Lake Kivu.
There were yellow cassia trees in full cascading flower and a really
large potato tree different from any I had seen before with unser-
rated leaves. High above us two cranes circled, calling loudly. We
had coffee in a restaurant on the sidewalk. Africans were coming in
from the country with loads of potatoes, onions, leeks, cabbages,
cauliflowers, lettuces, carrots, beetroot and strawberries.

I checked up on our living expenses since our exchange facilities
were limited. The room was 450 francs per day, breakfast 40 francs

each, lunch 60 francs and dinner 80 francs — a total of, say, 1000 francs per day allowing for tea, wine, cigarettes and incidentals.

The hotel was the finest in the Congo, very well run, comfortable and luxurious, and the restaurant attached to it was rather like a night club, with good food and wine, though, in spite of their being so easy to get, few vegetables were served. Everything seemed to be imported by air from Belgium.

We took a taxi to Dr. D'Hooghe's house which was almost on the *Pointe*. Our hosts were charming; both talked perfect English. The other guests were a Swiss businessman and the Procureur du Roi, who had been twenty years in the Congo. Conversation at dinner was most interesting because these men were colonial experts who had dealt with Africans all their adult lives. Here are some of the opinions I heard stated. A necessity for collective group responsibility. Chiefs must have power. (Power was being removed from the chiefs in the West Coast. Collective responsibility would have made the whole Kikuyu nation responsible for the Mau Mau and might have nipped the movement in the bud.)

The most basic question came up. The civilisation of the women, with the corollary that a civilised man must come from a civilised home. It is the key to all African progress.

The African does not understand supply and demand and expects the same price when there is a glut as he got for his produce in a scarcity, and will let fruit or vegetables rot rather than sell them for what they will fetch on the open market.

The backwardness of the African before the coming of the white man was put down to life being both too easy and too hard. Normal life was very simple. There were the fruits and animals of the forests and the fish in the rivers to be had without much trouble. There was no cold winter to combat, no need to store up reserves of food. There were no starving wolves or bears. The lions and leopards could live on game and interfered very little with mankind. On the other hand the storms, floods and droughts, when they came, were so terrible that nothing could be done against them. They were the work of malignant gods who had to be placated. In addition, any initiative or inventiveness was at once put down, since any change in a way of life which functioned more or less satisfactorily might offend the gods and cause disaster. So the most progressive individuals were killed, or driven out of the tribe where, being alone, they perished miserably.

How right or wrong these opinions were remains to be seen. But it was remarkable how, right through the continent, they remained consistent, with very little divergence, between country and country. None was given lightly and all by men of considerable experience. It is difficult to see how people who have never lived in Africa can have sounder views or more practical opinions. Certainly there are generalisations but they are drawn from a thousand particularisations by a multitude of men over a whole subcontinent. Nor are these people anti-African. On the contrary they like the Africans and have devoted their lives to administering and developing the country for their benefit.

Of course there is exploitation. Exploitation is another word for profit, but if there were no profit there would be no development. And immense sums are spent on native housing, schooling and medical attention.

The following day we drove out to look at a settler's farm which had been taken over by the government. It seemed very small to me — only sixty acres, but it appears that one hundred is the largest concession ever given to a white man for farming and five hundred for ranching. There was quite a good house on the place and plantations of quinine and coffee. There was also a grapevine in a big conservatory. This was the only one here, I was told. This was my first close-up of cinchona — quinine. It looked rather like privet and was planted close together in lines, alternate trees being thinned and the bark removed for sale till the optimum spacing was arrived at. The coffee looked sick — probably because it was unshaded by larger trees.

Coming back we went into some native lands. Acres and acres of plantains whose stems were black, beautifully marbled and striated with white that shone as if polished. There were no villages here but hidden in the banana woods were the tiny huts of the owners. They had a fixed bamboo screen on the right of the door reaching halfway across the floor. Behind this partition was a raised clay bed. Opposite to it a storage shelf. On the other open side of the entrance was a second bed. This was the man's bed and the screen arrangement was to make the entrance easier to defend. These plantains were used chiefly for pombe — beer — which some of them distill illegally into alcohol.

A point not generally realised when looking at these African huts is that the native does not regard a house as a white man does. He does not become attached to it or regard it as a permanent structure. It is simply a nest, like that of a bird, in which they sleep at night or huddle out of the wet in the rains.

Expedition followed expedition with Monsieur Vin and other officials. We went to a *fête hippique* and saw a nice exhibition of *haute école* by a retired French cavalry officer. The show was followed by a dance by the local tribe and some bastardised pygmies. The master of ceremonies was a very big African in a lounge suit made of shot grey and purple taffeta.

African dancing is, on the whole, I think, overrated. It consists mostly of leaping, stamping and clapping hands and thighs and is, to the Western eye, without system or art. Some of the individual steps are remarkable and if they were welded into a whole ballet by someone like Katherine Dunham a splendid effect could be achieved. But here, in the daylight, on the green grass of a showground, it was without emotional effect, as far as I was concerned. In the forest, at night by the light of great fires and the moon, it is quite different.

We went on a picnic up into the gorilla mountains. The gorillas are not to be found near the roads, but we were in the bamboo whose young shoots form part of their diet. It grows at an altitude of two to three thousand metres. After that one gets into the giant heaths and then the bare rock and lichens. There were fine tree ferns, feathery maidenhair, much coarser in texture and taller than that of the Cape, blueberries very like those found in Switzerland, and Spanish moss bearded the trees to which orchids clung in cushioned growths. Much of the bamboo had green cushions of moss growing on the joints. Some of the old stems were greenish white like long, thin, weathered bones, and creaked as they rubbed together in the wind.

Our next trip was with Monsieur Vautier, a district head, with whom we were to visit a villagisation scheme at Luberizi. We went over the escarpment round a series of hairpin bends which followed the contour of the mountains back to the head of each of the innumerable valleys in our path. There were ten roadblocks on this narrow winding stretch of road. At each there was a small hut with guards who beat on a signal drum (a 45-gallon oil drum) when a car was coming. When the next roadblock heard it they held up all cars till the road was clear. It was a remarkable system without which there would have been innumerable accidents. Another plan in the Congo is to open a road on alternate days to traffic going in opposite directions. In fact it seemed to me that the Belgians had an answer to most problems. There was more planning and less trusting to luck or expediency than I had found elsewhere.

After lunch we went to look at the African Co-op. The crops here were cotton and manioc, and so successful had it been that they had bought their own heavy equipment. Apart from a white treasurer it was an entirely African run and owned concern.

They had experimented with groundnuts, but rats had eaten the whole crop of several acres till they had been exterminated by the use of Warfarin, the new rat poison which works on the blood and does not affect any other animal. They were now attempting to poison the hundreds of bats which got into the roofs of the houses and made them impossible to live in. I looked at a soil survey of the district which showed that only twenty per cent was good agricultural land and the rest was marginal or useless. These surveys are typical of Belgian thoroughness. We visited some new dams on a marsh land where rice and fish were to alternate. The fish, talapia, would fertilise the soil for the rice and the rice residues would nourish the fish. It sounded a wonderful rotation. There is some salt here, leached out of the soil, which elephants and hippos sometimes come to lick. We saw two giant white herons near the water, and both grey and yellow wagtails.

We visited some villages that had been reorganised. The huts were built on a concrete platform which sloped away from the walls and had a foundation course of burnt brick above ground level. They had communal wash places for laundry, piped stand taps for the people, and cattle troughs for watering the stock. I was told, among other things, that literates here charge the bush natives as much as a hundred francs for writing a letter for them. We saw some magnificent Ankoli cattle with horns six feet long and seven to eight inches in diameter at the base. They were humpless, but a cross with the Zebu cattle of the coastal area must have entered into the ancestry of the Afrikander of South Africa.

We now climbed up the mountains to a group of eight dairy farms which were going to be increased to make a settlement of fifteen.

Much of the native land was overgrazed and the country overpopulated. The people could not be moved since these mountain tribes die in the lower malarial areas. But they had been forced from grazing into agriculture by the government as the only answer to the problem. They drink milk and make butter, which they do not eat but use as beauty aids mixed with castor oil which they extract from the shrubs that they plant near their houses. The mixture gives the girls a nice bronze polish and they seem to like the smell. The virgins wear their hair in a cockscomb hairdo. It is shaved on the sides of the head and left in the middle, and the married women shave it front and back and wear it in a high band from ear to ear. The children were carried in the arms or piggy-back, or sometimes on top of a load. We passed a string of women heavily laden with bamboo for fuel coming down from the mountains. The huts were primitive. A frame of bamboo and twigs plastered with cow dung. The bamboo is quickly attacked by borers and in one settler's barn all the poles and rafters were surrounded by little heaps of white dust, the residue of the insects' work.

We passed a stone monument with a copper plaque to commemorate the death of Lieutenant Tondeur, a Belgian officer, and nine Askaris killed and eaten by the Bashi in 1902.

In the evening we met Dr. D'Hooghe who took us to call on the Monseigneur, a charming old man who entertained us with communion wine and biscuits. He was under no illusions about the African or his converts. He said the difficulties really started when the African troops were taken abroad; that is to say, after the war. This coincided with the general opinion in West Africa and with what I was later to hear in Kenya where many Mau Mau and city gangsters were former Askaris. He told us of a UNO commission which in 1949 visited the Congo to investigate African feelings about franchise. The commission consisted of one Chinese, one Guatemalan, one New Zealand Labour Party man and one Frenchman.

This was to be a big day, almost our last, and as soon as we had swallowed our coffee and rolls we set off for the INEAK research station, where we saw coffee growing under the shade of big red flowering kaffirbooms. We saw pyrethrum growing for the first time. This was a disappointment. I had thought of fields of big pink and dark red flowers, like the garden varieties, but instead they were rather miserable little white marguerites growing untidily on low grey-green bushy plants. Both this crop and quinine are losing value owing to the new synthetic insecticides and anti-malarial medicines, which is serious for the Congo since they are the two best crops for the high ground. The Belgians still believe in quinine, as they say no one knows the after effects of such drugs as paludrine, which they maintain may produce impotence. One would perhaps be more prepared to believe this if they did not have such a surplus acreage under this crop to dispose of.

We visited a tung-oil nursery and watched a tree being budded like a rose. We saw a small plantation of red quinine that is used

in the manufacture of drinks like Dubonnet. Then we went into
the coffee plantations which were shaded by *Erythrina* in full red
flower and saw two white sports. In another section a leguminous
tree like a mimosa, called *Leucaena globa*, was being used. It is
good stock feed and so serves a double purpose. The silk-oak —
Grevillea robusta — is another favourite shade tree. The old-fashioned pruning of coffee has given way to the simpler form of a
multiple stemmed bush, instead of a thick single central trunk. The
young branches were weighed down with green berries dotted all
along their length. This change in pruning was brought about because it was much simpler and could be done by Africans. *Coffea
rustica* is indigenous to the Congo. *Coffea arabica* came originally
from tropical Africa. We were shown some tea trees. They belong
to the camellia family and have large white flowers which are followed by big capsules, each containing from one to five seeds. The
parent trees are not cut down but in the plantations the bush is
held to waist height. We saw cuttings of both tea and coffee under
glass, in hotbeds, which were nearly a hundred per cent successful.
I was shown how to make temporary flowerpots out of banana bark.
A most practical idea, as the potted cuttings could be planted out
without being disturbed. A section of banana stem was cut off about
one foot long and embedded into the ground. This was the form,
round which the pot was to be made. A strip of banana bark was
then torn off a nearby tree, placed over it and trimmed off at ground
level. A second strip was now placed over the form at right angles
to the first piece. This was not trimmed. It was turned upwards and
bound top and bottom with a strip of thin bark which was then
squared off. The pot, now complete, was removed from the stump
and ready for use.

We were shown some experiments in distilling perfume from
roses, and various essential oils, including menthol, which came
from one of the blue gums. We saw musk, wormwood that is used
for absinthe and looked rather like the foliage of Eschscholtzia, a
stramonium related to our stinkblaar, coriander that looked a bit
like parsley, patchouli — another big herbaceous plant — and various other plots where plants were being tested out, that might replace at least some of the quinine and pyrethrum acreage. But the
best bet seemed to be pastures and dairy cattle.

We talked with the director about Lake Kivu which was curious
in having no crocodiles, and about the production of fish — *Talapia
nilotica* — that were caught at night by fishermen in canoes with

nets and flares. During the day the fish stayed very deep but came up when it was dark to feed on algae and plankton. The fishermen tapped the sides of their dugouts to attract the fish by the vibrations, exactly like the fishermen in the Bahamas. And why not, since some of the slaves there were certainly brought from the Congo basin?

Lake Kivu was the original source of the Nile till its northern exit was blocked by a flow of lava. The water then backed up and deepened till it found its way south into Lake Tanganyika. We were shown some new native houses which had been built of concrete on the design of their own huts, but which they refused to use, and others, in wood, of a design suggested by UNO which they did not like either, as they had windows. We were shown a tiny pilot tea-curing plant. Tea grew well here but the factory was the problem. The settlers would not grow tea till there was a factory, and money could not be found for the factory till there was tea to process. The idea now was that the government should put the factory up. In the meantime there was no tea growing except on the station where they were trying several kinds.

The buildings here, like everything else in the Congo, were very good, built of stone, artistically designed and with wonderful gardens where great bushes of purple bougainvillaea grew out of a flaming sea of orange cannas in not a riot, but a madness of tropical colour.

We now moved on to the Mushweshwe government farm where they had some tame buffalo. A big bull, five years old, in a loose-box which the manager entered — which is more than could be done with many domestic bulls. He told me that they took blood samples from him without difficulty. He could not be let out, for no fence would hold him. He escaped one night and the staff were awakened by the crash of the big wooden gate to the stable yard that he had worked through as if it were paper. There were two buffalo heifers, unbelievably ugly, and about two years old, also in boxes. One was tame and licked my hand. The other, of exactly the same age, was very savage and charged as soon as we looked at her. We were told that it was entirely a question of the age at which they were taken, and there seems very little doubt that buffaloes would have been domesticated by any other race than the African. The Governor of Portuguese East had told me he was attempting the experiment and I wondered how it was going. Till I saw these animals, I had had very little confidence in it. There were also three elands. They were very quiet and affectionate. They have been tamed by a number of people and run with their cattle. The cows have even been milked. Being immune to trips one would imagine that more could be done in this direction than has so far been accomplished. There was also a charming, very tame white-moustached young wild pig called Oscar, who whimpered like a dog when we left him. They had some very nice Nandi cows from Kenya which gave up to nine quarts of milk on kikuyu pasture. An interesting thing about these animals is that the bulls have to run with the cows continuously as they remain in season for only half an hour, which renders controlled serving impossible. They had had some lava rats which they thought might be used for fur breeding but in the manager's absence the African farm labourers had eaten them.

After leaving here we picnicked by a hot spring which contained lime and deposited it over the rocks. We saw a herd of big-horned cattle against the skyline. Their horns formed complete semicircles and were most dramatic.

We now reached the farm at Lugware where settlers from Europe were trained and acclimatised in a course that lasted a year. They were hand picked and had to be farmers' sons or have farm experience in Belgium. The government advanced them capital on generous terms but supervised all expenditure.

On our way home we visited the kraal of a notable. His compound was enclosed by a ten-foot reed fence arranged like very narrow X's with crossbars lashed to the top and bottom. It was held up by tall wild fig tree cuttings, and poles. The compound was interesting because it was multiple. Inside, each led into the other through narrow openings. There was no design or order, the compounds just went on and on, reed walled, each more or less a circular or elliptical courtyard connecting with another. There were huts and small shelters in each. The chief's hut was very fine, much bigger and better constructed than the others, but the whole place had an Arabised, Northern feeling, and was obviously designed for defence. The people here are particularly fond of beans and grow forty varieties on which they overeat themselves till they become ill. Monsieur Gillon told me of the trouble he had had in trying to get them to grow a new variety of manioc which gave much bigger returns than the one they had. It took years, and even now many of them stuck to the old kind whose roots were not much bigger than a small beetroot. He had issued citrus trees to all the villages but, with one or two exceptions, they had all been allowed to die.

The last expedition was to the market at Kabare. We watched

one woman having wire bangles put on her ankles. She knelt with her back to the stallkeeper, who slipped them over her heel, using a big sail needle as a shoe horn. These anklets were light, made of galvanised wire. Then I heard a goat bleating piteously. I went to see what was happening. I found a young black goat being held down on its back while a butcher split open its brisket. Its golden eyes were dilated, its mouth wide open. I asked the district officer who was with us if this sort of thing was allowed. It cannot be stopped, he said. It is the custom. Tiny went off and threw up behind some blue gums. I turned away. The goat continued to cry. To them an animal is an animal, the functionary said.

In Africa an animal is an animal, I thought. And a man, if he does not belong to one's own tribe, is an animal.

28

The Forest ... Costermansville (Bukavu) ... Kisenyi ...
Park Albert ... Butembo ... Mambasa

● THIS WAS THE END of the Congo. What we were now going
to do was tourism pure and simple. I reorganised my impressions,
the cumulative feelings acquired so far on our journey. Everywhere
there had been a feeling of uncertainty, not of fear because neither
here nor in West Africa is there a real settler problem, but of worry
over this period of transition. The infant they had nourished was
being weaned too fast. Too much was being expected of it. Everyone was in one way astonished at the material progress that had
been made, particularly in the Congo, and disappointed in individual
Africans. The only optimism I had found was among teachers in
West Africa who were delighted with the results their students had
obtained in competitive examinations. They did not seem to look
beyond that.

There is little trouble here, because there is no land problem.
There are only twelve million natives in a country ten times as large
as Britain. There are only eighty thousand white people, including
women and children. The number of settlers is negligible, possibly
three or four thousand. The colony is run by the administrators, a
hand picked lot comparable to the old Indian Civil Service, the great
companies, which exercise a well-organised, far-seeing kind of benevolent local dictatorship and are linked to administration by the missionaries to whom almost all native education is entrusted. The
country could carry on forever with these three separate but related
organisations — the government, the companies and the church.
The rest — the traders, the settlers, the small businessmen — are
merely additions. And this form would seem to be the general pattern of the future in Central Africa. It certainly works. The Africans
increase and profit by it, and enough money is made to permit great
development projects, including such things as native co-operatives
handling their products, acting as intermediaries between the peasant
and the company that purchases their products. White labour is so

expensive that the black is trained to the highest possible level. But in spite of this there have been some troubles and there is danger from the activities of such fanatical anti-white religious sects as the Kitwala, an offshoot of the Watch Tower movement in Rhodesia, which is in some curious way related to the Jehovah's Witnesses of America.

Lack of legitimate grievance is not enough to prevent sedition, particularly when it has outside backing. There are three great dangers to which the white man, who does not know Africa, is exposed when he tries to understand it. To judge the African by the exceptions, men like Félix Eboué, who came from the West Indies and who are as numerous as men like Einstein or Churchill are among white men. To accept well-dressed African students whom they meet in London or New York at face value. There are numbers of first class educated Africans, but few of them are inclined to politics, since to succeed in this career extremism is essential. And finally, to confuse the African with the American or West Indian Negro, who has lived for two centuries or more in a non-African environment, and about seventy per cent of whom are believed by most authorities to have at least some white blood.

When thinking of Africa, it is the illiterate mass of peasant farmers who should be considered — their progress, their comfort, their happiness.

With eight days of driving, covering some two-thousand-odd kilometres, we expected to be in Entebbe ready for the last lap of the trip — Nairobi and Kenya.

Our driver was Baron Alec Jolly, a Belgian cavalry officer of British descent, whose mother was English. He had been born in Cape Town, spoke English to perfection and was one of the nicest men I have met. He had been in the Resistance and a prisoner of the Nazis from whom he had escaped. He was without affection for the Germans. A rolling stone, who had done everything from driving one of the enormous refrigerator trucks that bring meat from Kenya to the Congo to farming and running a garage.

We left early and drove along the west bank of Lake Kivu. A wonderful mountain drive of hairpin bends, of roads carved out of the face of gigantic cliffs, with the lake like a small sea on our right. It looked like a Japanese print with tree-clad islands floating in the early morning mist and great mountains rising up mysteriously behind them. We stopped for lunch at a small hotel at Kalehe and then went on past beautiful houses belonging to rich settlers, many of whom spent half their time in Europe. Some of these men are nobles who look down on everyone whether they are Flemings or French-speaking Walloons, who do not get on particularly well together either. It is interesting in these days when colour prejudice is so much in the news to find minor racial and linguistic differences among white people a bar to full understanding.

Some of the gardens were magnificent, the wild tree ferns and palms blending into lawns decorated with ornamental exotic trees and shrubs. Hills ran like ribs from the backbone of the mountain, launched themselves as peninsulas into the water and sank under it to reappear again as islands. Kivu was a fairyland, one of the most exotic playgrounds in the world.

The road now ran across the lava block, which had cut off part of the lake, and into the native village of Sake which was built on the ashes of the ancient flow. It was hideous and looked as if it had been constructed on a black industrial slag heap. Now we came to the newer lava flows. Here one could see the whole evolution of the world in an area of a few miles. The oldest flow of 1912 was covered with bush, small trees and grass. The lava cracks and crevasses were beginning to collapse as they were filled in with decaying vegetable matter, leaves and rotten branches. The roots cracked them, the coarse grass clothed them, and it must have been paradise for game because the ground was so rough that it was almost impossible to get through it.

The next piece was the flow of 1938 where the lava was clearly visible. There were lichens, tufts of grass and a few small shrubs. Then we saw the last flow — that of '48 — where the lava was completely bare and looked like black dough that had been rolled into every kind of convolution, or like the waves of a flattened oily sea frozen into stillness, or boiling molasses suddenly stilled and waiting for time and weather to change its form. There was no beauty here but I received a great emotional impact at finding myself so near to the beginning of things — igneous rock, the lichens and ferns that duplicated the earliest green things in our world, the beginnings of the forest. Here one could feel the hand of God closing, contracting. The finger of God pointing to ultimate unknowable truths. The pulse of God, which is man's own pulse, when it is tuned to cosmic reality.

The volcanoes were about to erupt again, and have done so since we left. But owing to the mist we scarcely saw them — only once as a red glow reflected in the night sky above the crater.

We drove through native lands of high fertility. The bananas and kaffir corn were growing splendidly. Near the road there was a lovely pale *eau de nil* green lake in the crater of an extinct volcano. The women here carried their children in a cow skin, which still had the hair on it, in a kind of sling on their flanks. We saw one who was left-handed. Her child was on her right hand side and the right breast more developed and longer than the left, which was usually the longest.

We met Monsieur de Castellaire, the uncrowned king of Goma and local representative of the settlers, for a drink. We had an introduction to him and Tiny had met him at Bukavu. A handsome man in his late forties, very much a man of the world, with many interests in the Congo and elsewhere. He employed a great deal of labour. He said he had had ten thousand men through his hands in one way and another and only found ten who were absolutely reliable, none of whom could read or write. This was illuminating and even if exaggerated could not be dismissed as fantasy.

We spent the night in Kisenyi. In the morning we were woken by the wild, mad laughter of the ibis which had been roosting in the blue gums near the rest house. This is a wild and splendid noise.

We now visited the mission at Nyondo. It was like all missions, wonderfully sited at the top of a hill with a view over half the world. Owing to the rain the road was so slippery that we climbed the last few hundred yards on foot. We passed a beautiful, slim girl. She stood at least six feet in her sandalled feet. A Watussi princess, we were told, and certainly she looked it. She was very pale-coloured with a proud, aristocratic fine-featured face. The married women who had children wore a band of dry millet husk round their foreheads that looked like a flat golden fillet. We met an old priest who had been in the Congo for forty-seven years. A wonderful old man. And some young African priests. It was Sunday and the faithful were being summoned to morning service by a battery of drums. A great improvement on bells, I thought. The congregation was a mixed lot of pure Watussi, local natives and a mixture between the two.

Water was so scarce that it and pombe were of equal value. The elephant and buffalo drank with the cattle in amity when the rain filled the pans.

We drove on through wonderful scenery, past little toy volcanoes between which there were native lands and plantations. We saw one covey of crested guinea fowl whose feathers were almost blue, a most beautiful variety, that I had not seen before or since. We finally entered the Parc National Albert, after passing through a shooting reserve.

Then we went through some thick forest-clad mountain passes where the trees were covered with heavy green moss, and little kloofs that were a solid mass of tree ferns, some of them twenty feet high. After this the country opened out into rolling, very dry and dusty bush veld and at last we reached the Ruindi camp, and taking an African ranger as guide set off to see what we could find.

We saw giant waterbuck which had white quarters instead of the half-moon of the South African variety, and both kob and topi. We passed buffaloes, elephants, baboons and monkeys as we drove down to Lake Edward where we saw one of the sights of our lives. The grass was short, green as a lawn, but broken here and there by big tussocks of elephant grass. Hippos quite near the shore were blowing and making a noise like cattle lowing, to which, I suppose, they owe the name of sea cow. Round them, in the water, were Egyptian, dwarf and spurwing geese, two kinds of duck, coot and several big white pelicans painted pinkish by the failing sun. Swallows skimmed the surface and a bright blue kingfisher dived and came up with a fish. There were herons, white ibis, and spoonbills standing in the water. A great marabou stork, his head sunk into his shoulders, marched along at the water's edge. Black plovers ran over the short grass, waders of four or five kinds, including a jack snipe, paddled in the shallows. One even stood on long stilt legs on a half-sunken hippo's head. I could have stayed for hours. The scene had a strange combined quality of peace and beauty. It joined onto my picture of the creation and the melted world of lava. This was when God began to make the living things. The birds should come first. It is difficult to explain even to oneself why one is deeply moved. Or why only such beauty can move one — a scene, a picture, a child, a woman. When, for one instant, one feels oneself one with the whole . . . with life. No longer alone and irrelevant.

Coming back we saw the tall white dung-encrusted trees, where the pelicans roosted. They were tinged red in the sunset. All along the dusty roads partridges, having their evening dust bath, rose from under our wheels. When we got in it was almost dark and five big buffalo bulls were grazing within a hundred yards of the camp, like oxen.

As soon as dawn broke next morning we went off again in a new direction. We saw hippos a mile from water, and returning to it, and others lying in small shallow pools where their exposed backs looked like great pink, rounded, water worn rocks. The hippo paths were interesting. They were very narrow, with a sort of central keel scuffed up in the middle. The hippo sign resembled that of an elephant but the balls were smaller and wetter. Cranes flew over us, their heads and legs extended. We saw more waterbuck, warthog, baboons, topis, two kinds of monkey, a mongoose and a leopard coming down from a big tree. The guide spotted it. Actually there was nothing for him to see but the tail, which hung down like a snake from a single, not very thick limb of a flat-topped thorn about twenty feet from the ground. Leopards sleep in this position by engaging their dewclaws in the bark. When it heard us it stood up, turned round, came down to the fork of the tree, stood there a second and then dropped into the thick patch of bush that surrounded the trunk. We saw a number of elephants, some very close by. One bull had immense, thin tusks, so long that they dragged on the ground. We watched another pull up tussocks of grass, bang them against his chest to knock off the earth, and eat them. In all we saw about twenty elephants. We also just got a glimpse of a lion and saw a dead hippo in the river which the vultures had begun to eat. The elephants seemed to like a low bush that grew in big patches. But the whole area, like all elephant country, was unbelievably untidy, with trees broken down, bush torn up and big patches reduced to bare tramped earth, with dry dung in the standing places where they slept.

We now set off for Butembo and climbed the great escarpment of Kabisha that closed the Reserve, and got into bamboos once more. We passed wattle and quinine plantations on roads lined with *Podocarpus* (yellow woods), and stopped for a drink at a small hotel called the Trois Canards where the landlady, a charming woman, was lamenting the death of her chimp. "He died in bed, monsieur, like a little child." This evidently consoled her. She showed us his cot in her room. She said the leopards took dogs from the farms about here and that ten buffalo had been killed recently as they had been doing damage to the crops. They had been driven up out of the Reserve by the drought. She evidently liked animals as there were three donkeys, chickens, ducks, pigeons and several cats and dogs.

In the morning we reached Beni about eleven and had tea at the Ruwenzori Hotel. This was by way of being a pub of some pretensions and comfort. Women passed us with loads on their backs, and headstraps, which they supported with their hands interlaced behind them. Some had babies perched on top of the loads and a series of three, who came in single file, had short-handled hoes balanced on their heads with the blade to the rear, that made them look as if they were crested, like cockatoos.

We now entered the forest, which closed over us, coming down like a wall on either side of the road. There were clearings where bananas and manioc grew, and native huts with roofs of ruffled, curling leaves held down by long withies put on from the outside.

We were now on the main road leading from Stanleyville to the east and reached Mambasa for tea. It is a tiny forest centre, with a permanent white population of under ten people. The hotel had the usual central dining-sitting-room-and-bar, but here it was combined with a small bookshop. The pavilions were covered, even over the roof, with purple bougainvillaea and yellow allamanda which I had not even realised was a climber. We had a bathroom and lavatory, with no water, till a string of boys came with tins which they carried up a ladder and emptied into a little reservoir above our heads. What went up had to come down. But it had to get up first.

In the lounge we met a very nice young man, an instructor in physical training from Léopoldville who was delighted when we told him we had seen his installations under the grandstand at the sports ground. He told me he had eaten meals with fathers and uncles of his pupils who had been cannibals, and they had told him how good human meat was.

We had been going to see Putnam, the American who had tamed the pygmies and cashed in on them, but he had just died in the hotel here, or rather — since he appeared to have gone more or less native, and become as allergic to houses as his own pygmies — in the vine-covered arbour outside it, surrounded by his retainers. He was believed to have had several pygmy wives but how true this was I do not know. I was interested, though, to find the number of men right through Africa who asked me if I had ever slept with a native woman. The idea had no appeal for me as the charm of the black woman — sex without involvment — is the very opposite of my taste. But for those who wanted it that way nothing could surpass the African.

Next morning we crossed the Epulu River and drove into Putnam's camp, a few hundred yards off the main road. The track or drive went through a village of pygmies and pigmoid bastards. There was a big green caravan parked near the house. A white woman's naked foot and leg were visible through the door, but there was no reply when we spoke. Feeling we were not very welcome, we turned about and drove on past the okapi station to Captain de Medina's camp.

It was a collection of thatched bush houses, sheds, and huts with a big cleared space in front of it. At the back and sides the great forest hemmed it in. Captain de Medina and his brown, grown-up son greeted us on a stoep where buffalo, bongo, waterbuck and other skulls were piled up in a heap. Above them a pangolin skin was nailed to the wall. Dogs ran out, a big tame sheep came up to have his head rubbed. African carpenters were making tall, very narrow crates for the export of okapi by air. With animals it is essential to pack them tightly with a minimum of moving room so that they cannot injure themselves.

And so we began one of the most interesting days of my life, for this man de Medina was a notable character. A thick-set Portuguese of immense vitality and charm. Once a professional meat hunter on contract, he was an accomplished naturalist, and for a time director of the zoo at Léopoldville. He was now in charge of the okapi-capturing station in the Ituri forest. He had been presented to the King in Belgium.

De Medina said he would show us the okapi after lunch, and the tame elephants when they came in in the evening. Then he talked about gorillas. He had shot a number of them when collecting young ones for the zoos. He said they were easy to kill. Some he had shot at close range with a .38 pistol. But he said it was a hair-raising experience. "Une chasse très palpitante," he called it. He said the teeth of the natives who accompanied him — all skilled hunters — chattered with fear when facing gorillas. When one came upon them, the old gorilla came forward beating his chest. Then he dropped down and advanced sideways throwing up sticks, stones and earth, scooping them up with both palms. Then he rose to his full height and screamed. A terrifying sound. Often the oldest son, also a nearly full-grown male, would attack when the father was dead. To obtain a young one the hunter had to kill the mother too. This seemed like murder, so de Medina evolved a new plan of bolting them with dogs and catching the young with nets, in which they became entangled. Never have I been more impressed by anyone. De Medina acted while he talked. He was both the gorilla and the hunter. He crouched on the ground with his knuckles on the floor. He scooped up imaginary soil as he shuffled forward. He raised himself and drummed his chest. He screamed. He was the young gorilla rushing forward to help his father. He was the hunter waiting with his rifle at the ready. He raised it. He fired. Then he was the gorilla. He was hit, he screamed, he clapped his hand to his chest. He fell. In that small open-sided room we had seen a drama of the forest enacted.

He showed us photos of gorillas, of skinned gorillas — a solid mass of tendon, ligament and muscle. We saw pictures of natives who had been wounded by them, their faces torn apart by a light glancing slap. Subali, the gorilla in the Bronx Zoo, had been taken by de Medina; so had four others which had died after they had left his care. The young were raised by native women who nursed them like babies. He said he had shot chimpanzees that weighed one hundred and seventy-five pounds and were 5¼ feet high. He said a chimp in the zoo had pulled off a man's fingers so that the tendons were left exposed, stretched like the strings of a violin. He said the natives used to eat gorillas — catching them with nets — and that they considered them the next best meat to man — particularly the hand grilled over the embers, which he had eaten. This was supposed to be the best part of a man, too, with the fat bubbling out of the burst, swollen skin.

Then he described the method he had evolved for capturing okapi. Plenty had been caught before he took over but most of them had died, either through being damaged when captured or afterwards, through a misunderstanding of their psychology. This is where de Medina was so outstanding. He knew what animals were thinking. A path used by the okapi was found — it had to be within 800 feet of the main road. Game pits, 6½ feet long, 3¼ feet wide and 6½ feet deep were dug along it. The bottom of each pit was lined with a deep layer of leaves so that the okapi would not injure themselves in falling. As soon as one was taken a high fence of green branches was put round the trap, which was left open at the end which the okapi was facing. Here a small circular bush kraal, ten metres in diameter, was constructed and earth carefully shovelled into the pit to make a ramp for the okapi to climb, which it did as soon as it was able to look out over the edge of the pitfall. This was the critical moment. The danger being that, terrified, it would fling itself at the barrier in an effort to jump or smash through it. Here Captain de Medina's ingenuity was fully revealed. Round the kraal at intervals of one metre he had men stationed. They had to stand absolutely still. De Medina stood as if frozen, in front of us, to show what he meant. The okapi dashed to the edge of the kraal, saw a man and stopped. It made two or three more dashes. Each time it saw a man. After a few more halfhearted attempts, it settled down. The moment of hysteria, which was the danger, had passed. In the kraal there was a bucket of water and some of the leaves that are its favourite food. It is important that the kraal should not be so solid that the okapi cannot see the men because it might try to jump if it did not know they were there. Nor must it be open enough for it to try to force its way through. Now a long passage of branches lashed with tie-tie (lianas) is made to the main road, only two hundred yards away. It has to be narrow, only 2 inches wider than the okapi, so that it cannot turn. Where the race ends a cut is made into the forest so that a truck can back right up, and a ramp built leading into it. The interior of the truck is garnished with leaves and branches. The last portion of the race, 23 feet from the ramp, is closed off. The okapi goes down the race, finds the block and pauses. The block is removed. It sees in front of it a dark leafy tunnel that must lead to escape, to safety. It runs straight into the truck and the back is fastened.

At the other end, at the acclimatisation station, it comes out in the same way — through a tunnel of leaves into one of the big yards where it will live. While the okapi is in the first kraal, waiting for the long runway to be built, guards are left both day and night to protect it from leopards, to which, enclosed like this, it would have proved an easy prey.

De Medina explained all this with gestures and diagrams drawn on a piece of squared paper. His success has been almost one hundred per cent. Twelve have been caught in the last four months and four have been born in captivity in the last year. He was particularly proud of one cow, heavy with calf, captured on July 16, which dropped a healthy heifer on the twentieth — four days later — and raised it. This I agreed with him was almost tops in animal capture and handling. He said he had been sure she would abort or let the calf die. They keep one bull to six cows on the station, and sell only bulls. The gestation period is about four hundred and twenty-six days. He told me the okapi mother hides her calf and leaves it to go and feed when it is small. The okapi can call if in pain or frightened, and the bulls call in the night. The mother washes the calf continually, and will pull down small branches for it to nibble with its prehensile tongue.

Now it was time for lunch and we all sat down. We had "Primus" beer and an excellent meal. Tiny reached for the pickles, of which she is inordinately fond. Among the other condiments on the table was an enormous round carton, as big as a chocolate box, of quinine tablets from which everyone helped themselves. During lunch a tame grey parrot walked about the floor, picking up fallen matchsticks and breaking them. De Medina said that this showed he wanted peanuts, which were given to him. He was accompanied by half a dozen pigeons which tried to steal his nuts. Some fat puppies also staggered in and were carried out again. And the tame sheep stood waiting for titbits.

When we had had coffee, we went and looked at the animals in his compound. There were green parrots with brown speckles. Some big chestnut-brown Gambia forest rats, quite the most beautiful rats I have ever seen. A pangolin — a sort of armadillo — with its baby on its back. A poto, with its baby. A tree hyrax. A green forest iguana. A colobus monkey. A baby baboon, and four completely adorable little chimps that leapt into one's arms and wanted to be held like babies. One rather older than the rest wanted to get loose, and showed me how to slip its collar over its head. It goes like this, it seemed to be saying, and demonstrated the first part of the process. I went over and petted it and fed it some fruit. It showed me again and then, when I refused to help, it went into a tantrum, had what, in a woman, would be hysterics. It screamed, it tore its hair, it lay on its back and drummed its heels on the ground and then, finally, with a desperate effort — since I was such a fool — it liberated itself and ran to one of the boys in the yard who brought it back. I would certainly like to have a chimp. They are so human. And their humanity is their doom. These babies were all on the way to America to be used experimentally, injected, operated on, shot up into the stratosphere. But they become dangerous as they get older so that in the end they must be put into a zoo or destroyed. I think most wild animals are safe enough if their owner never leaves them and if they see no strangers. But this is impossible, so they have to go. And I think it is better to put them down than imprison them. My friend Cleland Scott, for instance, who raised many lions gave one to the London Zoo. It knew him well but when he visited it a year later, it bit him. A reporter then said this showed that wild animals were not to be trusted. Surely it showed that wild animals should not be betrayed! One is always reading that it is sentimental to attribute human feelings to animals but my idea is that the whole things is in reverse — that it is we who have animal feelings. Most animals show all the emotions — fear, love, hate, anticipation, pleasure, and show them in very much the same way as human beings. Anyone who has had a lot to do with animals knows this — everyone, I am inclined to think, except the scientists who study them so objectively that they really do not understand them at all. Anyway, a film of this chimp's tantrum would be of great psychological interest, and probably cure any child or woman of similar habits.

It was now time to go and see the okapi. The entrance to the acclimatisation station was through a gate decorated with red and white poles topped by buffalo skulls. Once inside there were camps of about half an acre in extent fenced with high posts lashed and woven together, and entered by a stile of steps so that no gate could be left open and an okapi, worth about six thousand dollars, escape. There must have been a dozen or more okapi, several with calves, and a bull, rather bigger and darker than the cows, that was used for stud. We went into the enclosures. They seemed very tame and made no attempt to run away. But they are difficult to keep in captivity if certain precautions are not taken. They always sleep in one place (in the forest they sleep in forms) and their dung must be removed at once since they are very clean and lick themselves all over if fouled, with the result that they reinfect themselves with worms from their own excrement. De Medina profited by this habit of cleanliness to dose them. He would mix sulpha drugs and cod-liver oil with Vaseline on a stick and gently push it through the bars, from where they could not see him, onto their coats. They would then discover the mess, lick themselves with their long black tongues and swallow the medicine.

We were shown one okapi cow with only one ear and leopard scars on her back. When attacked they gallop through the forest and try to scrape the leopard off against the branches. They appear to have no other means of defence though I imagine they would have a powerful kick. The okapi is a most curious animal, a kind of forest giraffe with a sepia, almost plum-coloured, coat that is striped like a zebra on the hind quarters.

The bushmen working on the station had killed and eaten a recently captured okapi. They saw no particular harm in this because, from their point of view, it was a more or less common animal and keeping them was just another form of white man's madness. I was told that they killed sleeping elephants by severing their trunks, or cutting the femoral artery of a hind leg. They also use poisoned arrows like the bushmen of the South. When he hunted meat for the army, de Medina said it was first boiled and then smoked.

We saw a young lion in a cage that was going to Belgium next weekend, and two big chimps with long, very heavy chains fastened to their necks. Their drinking vessels were empty and one of the attendant boys had to be called to fill them. From the way they drank, they had not had water for some time.

We now went to see the elephants. They were kept by the Service des Eaux et Fôrets, 2nd Escadron de Chasseurs Cornacs, and were just coming in from grazing in the forest when we arrived. We did not see the biggest, for they were not safe with strangers, but none were really very large though some had long thin tusks that almost reached the ground. It is evident that in captivity the elephant does not grow out fully. Something must be missing in the diet. Minerals, perhaps, or some psychic factor in their life, which is why, to my mind, the longevity figures of tame elephants cannot be true for wild animals free to travel in search of what they need.

Each elephant had an African on its back and they were driven down to bathe in the river. When they had done they returned, and one of them picked up the francs that were thrown down in front of him and gave them to his mahout. They were then all given a few handfuls of salt and some bananas. The white officer in charge said that in the morning he had bought 440 pounds of bananas for them, but that now not 22 pounds were left. The men, or their wives, had stolen the rest. He told me discipline was very hard to maintain since only these men could handle the animals, and so they were indispensable and knew it. At one time very young elephants were captured by the mothers being shot, but a new technique has been evolved, and weaned animals are taken by stampede of the herd with shots and pursuit by mounted men. The bewildered babies who lag are roped with very thick, soft ropes by catchers on foot, who snub them onto trees. Monitor elephants are then brought up and they conduct the newly captured animals back to camp where they are slowly tamed and trained. Elephants have to be sung to. We heard the singing — a monotonous chant. This was one of the few things the Indian mahouts, who were brought over to train the Africans in the care and handling of elephants, managed to teach them. Today, with tractors, elephants are of no great economic value. But the capture and training continues in a small way, more as a curiosity than anything else — as a proof that African elephants can be tamed.

We now went back to camp where we watched the baby chimps

being put to bed in little boxes lined with big green banana leaves. Dinner was excellent with good wine and very tender Kenya beef. De Medina passed Tiny the pickles, which amused me. He was certainly a close observer. We were told about the African peacocks, worth a fabulous amount, and shown some of their blue feathers. This is, I think, the turaco. We saw the pangolins fed with chunks of ants' nest from which they extracted the insects. Our host said red and grey parrots cost one thousand francs here and that a wife could be bought with one red tail feather, which only chiefs were allowed to wear.

At last it was time to go. We were told if we ran into elephants or hippos on the road not to sound the horn. We should stop and put out our lights. They would smell the petrol and move on. We might see okapi, de Medina said. He then told us how to shoot leopards at night — not that we were going to. If surprised on the road, they run in front of the car and then jump off the road sideways into the bush. When they do this, stop the car and put the spotlight on the place where they jumped and they will be found sitting, watching the car. He had shot many that way.

We said good night again, and drove back to Mambasa. All we saw was a tiny buck with her fawn. They looked like long-legged rats. They were called boloko, we were told. And so ended a wonderful day.

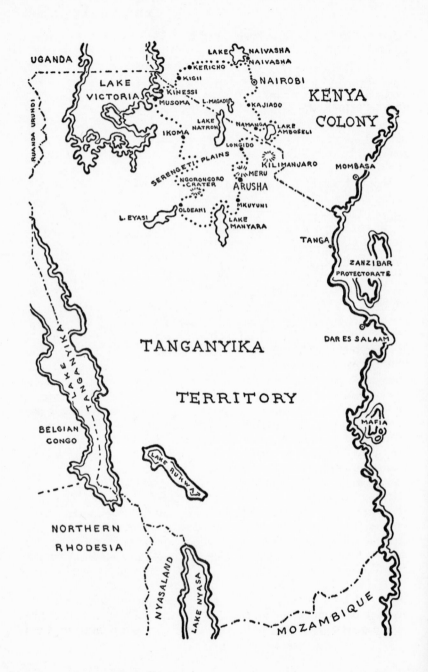

29

The Shadow of the Panga...Mambasa...Mutinanga...
Fort Portal...Entebbe...Nairobi

● I HAD TRIED on several occasions to discuss the old Congo Free
State — the days of the couchou — but got no takers. Long ago as a
child I remembered reading H. de Vere Stacpoole's *Pools of Silence*
about the Belgian atrocities of those now forgotten days, and since
then had read other books on the subject showing how whole areas
had been depopulated, how defaulting chiefs had been decorated with
the entrails of the dead — those who had been eaten by cánnibal Askaris when they did not bring in the required amount of rubber. Stories
of women ravished, of officers afraid of their men, and of the African's
terrible oppression of Africans when given positions of authority in
this era. Casement, the British consul, was responsible for some of
these reports, others came from the Germans who wished to replace
the Belgians. There is no doubt that many stories were exaggerated
but had a basis of truth. My old friend Peter Rainier, the engineer
and author, told me of what he had seen himself in the early nineteen
hundreds when he crossed the Congo on foot, and the evidence is supported by many photographs. Actually most of the crimes were not
committed by Belgians, but by the dregs of Europe — adventurers
recruited for service in what was then the world's most unhealthy and
dangerous area, in the very heart of dark and cannibal Africa.

And today, what was once the worst and most brutally administered
territory under white authority is now perhaps the best. Certainly
nowhere else is the African better taken care of, or his future more
secure. But here in the forest by the Ituri and Semeliki Rivers one
felt the ancient pulse of Africa. Could it be tamed? We were on our
way to Kenya now where a key might be found in the Mau Mau outbreak.

We left early and passed several families of pygmies on the road,
who had been hunting in the night. They were all but naked; the
women had nothing on but bunches of leaves before and behind, like
the pagans of Jos. This must have been what Adam and Eve wore,

not one fig leaf but a bundle slipped onto a string round the waist. They carried long hunting nets rolled over their shoulders and the men had bows. One man had a live monkey trussed up that he carried by the tail.

We passed one albino woman with black tattooing on her face, but saw little else of interest till we stopped at Fort Bodo. It had been built by Stanley, but nothing remained of it except a circular earthwork.

From here we went on to Mbao where the pygmies were assembled to dance for us. This was a rather sophisticated affair and was paid for with several kilos of salt, about three hundred francs, thrown like pennies into the dancing crowd, and some fifty blue paper packages of cheap cigarettes. But beneath all this organisation for the tourist, one could detect some of the old flavour of the forest and, in its almost pure form, the ancient pygmy odour. They smelt stronger than any people I have smelt before, and entirely different. It was a very strong, musky, rather monkey-house smell, due no doubt to their diet, which I did not find unpleasant. Tiny liked the pygmies because, for the first time in her life, she towered by several inches over the crowd that surrounded her. I do not think the pygmies washed much and I saw a woman, naked but for her leaves, take an open knife from round her waist and scrape the dust and sweat from her sagging breasts with it.

There were some bigger men among the pygmies, more or less pure Negroes, but the majority were under five feet high and the women not much over four feet. The dance music came from a big drum, some smaller drums and Pan-like bamboo pipes. One man had a frill of long blue feathers round his head that came from the wild African peacock de Medina had talked about. Many of the men carried bows, about three feet long, that were covered with monkey fur. The arrows were made of reeds tipped with iron. Some were painted with poison and they were fletched with some kind of rather stiff leaf which did not reach to the notch. A few of the girls had their buttocks very prettily dappled with circular dappled-horse-like tattooed designs. The dancing was not complex. They all went round and round the drums, stamping and jiggling. But it seemed to give them great pleasure and the dance would go on for hours after we had left.

We set off for Mutwanga on the first contrefort of the Mountains of the Moon. The hotel was most beautifully situated at the foot of the mountain. A troutless trout stream ran bubbling along below our window. When I enquired about trout I was told that they had wanted to put them into it but that nothing exotic was allowed into the National Park. They were not even allowed to have donkeys to take older visitors on picnics in the mountains. The proprietress said she had gone into it with the functionary in charge and the reason he gave for his decision was that the droppings of the donkeys might affect the local flora.

The effects are sometimes interesting when reasonable regulations are carried to their quite illogical conclusions by the little men who enforce them.

Soon after leaving the hotel, the country changed. There were big patches of heavy bush and groups of wild teak trees and euphorbias. We saw one elephant with her calf, then twenty together some distance away. Then we saw a remarkable sight. Hundreds of massed swallows, looking like a swarm of bees as they darted and circled among a big swarm of smallish locusts that were flying across the road. We saw Lake George in the distance, and more elephants before we passed into Uganda via a tin shed where our papers were looked at by an Indian British customs official.

In Fort Portal we stopped at a garage for gas and found three wrecked cars in the yard. I was told by the proprietor that he had put in twenty claims for major accidents in the last three months and he had three more wrecks to collect over the weekend.

Next day we stopped at Katwe to go into the newly opened Queen Elizabeth Park. Katwe is a miserable dusty town that has developed round the salt industry. The salt comes from the bottom of an old volcano which must be a veritable hell of heat to work in. The rest camp is built on a peninsula that juts into the lake and from the stoep we watched elephants bathing below us and saw plenty of hippos and flamingoes. On the drive in we had passed close to a herd of waterbuck who never even looked up.

The central buildings and pavilions are made of thick palm stems set vertically and jointed with cement. The roofs were papyrus. It was altogether a very pretty group of buildings and wonderfully situated. We picnicked by the roadside and then drove on to the Lake Victoria Hotel where rooms had been booked for us. This was a magnificent place with bungalow annexes, and we spent a happy five days resting. We had now seen all the African lakes except Rudolf and Nyasa. The second day we were here Ernest Hemingway arrived, somewhat battered by his double airplane crash, and I introduced myself to him. We had some drinks and dined together several times.

Since leaving Costermansville we had crossed the equator three times and when we left for Nairobi we would cross it yet again, which would make a total of eight times on the trip. I put our names in the book and we were asked to Government House where we met Sir Andrew and Lady Cohen. Lady Cohen was a very handsome brunette who had, I think, been at Oxford and Sir Andrew had the reputation of being a very capable and most liberal man. Since I left he has become seriously involved in one of those typically African political affairs where the removal of the Kabaka produced such strikes, boycotts and outbreaks of violence that the police have been doubled and radio cars and a 999 dialling system installed. Once again the strong meat of education has produced a dangerous form of political indisposition.

We now flew to Nairobi, a short, but for me disastrous flight — for while over the Great African Rift the plane soared and bobbed like a leaf in the wind and I all but died. I got out of the plane in a trance and thanked God that John Lambert of the South African Tourist Bureau was there to meet us and take charge, while I continued to expire on a chair in the waiting room. On the next seat was a good-looking woman of fifty-five or so, very smartly dressed in a grey tailored suit with a neat brown belt round her waist and a holster with a pistol in it. John in the uniform of the K.P.R. with a webbing belt and holstered .45 had not surprised me. But the lady in grey did. On the way to the New Stanley Hotel we passed a truck containing Kikuyu, accompanied by armed guards, who had been picked up and were going to be screened. There were roadblocks and barbed-wire entanglements everywhere. We were in a new world. The world of emergency — a euphemism for war.

We saw African police and Askaris, very smart in their navy blue jerseys with leather shoulder pads and khaki shorts, carrying service rifles. We saw jeeps and Land Rovers with white troops in them; we saw radio cars. The atmosphere was that of London in the early days of the war — an alertness, a feeling of waiting for something, of controlled anxiety.

Not everyone was armed, but enough were to make the fact that many people went armed apparent. In the coffee room of the New Stanley, young men came in to meet girls and pushed their sten guns under their chairs. Some of the girls had guns. You wondered about them. About their future in Kenya, about that of the little canary-headed children as you watched them running about between the tables. There were a lot of children. They could not be left at home. Not in the emergency.

Another thing that struck us almost at once was the happiness of the Africans in the streets. They chattered like birds, smiling at each other, nodding their heads and talking. The Indians seemed happy too. And why not? The brown man at last had got the white man where he wanted him. Not on the run, but jittery. Nervous. It was showing in the women and children. The children could not even play in the suburban gardens of their homes. Some women were becoming ill. Illness was an escape mechanism for those who dared not be afraid. But this was true only of some of them. The rest were facing it. Many had fought off attacks with amazing courage. But the difficulty was the enemy. Who was the enemy? How many Mau Mau did we see in the streets of Nairobi? (This was before Operation Anvil when thousands were picked up). How could you tell? Today a boy was a trusted servant, a friend. Tomorrow, because he had taken the oath, he was an enemy. A betrayer who would throw a plate of hot soup in your face to give the gang a chance to rush you before you could use the pistol in your lap.

One friend told us that only a week ago a boy he had had twenty years came to him and said: "Bwana, you must pay me off. I must go."

He said: "Aren't you happy with me? Have you any complaints?"

"Bwana," he said, "I am happy but I have been made to take the oath and now I must kill you or be killed."

Another woman, going to her linen cupboard, found under some sheets that she seldom used two simis — native swords — sharpened to razor edge. Her servants were just waiting for the high sign to kill her.

Another woman, whose ayah had been arrested by the police, was told that her only regret was that she had been picked up before she had had time to kill the children. And she had been in the family seventeen years, had been her mother's maid, had come to her at her marriage, and brought the children up.

At a girls' school near Nairobi the children have Mau Mau drill each week. When the alarm is given they hide under the beds. The prefects stand by the doors of the dormitories with a pound bag of pepper and hockey sticks, while the mistresses patrol the passages and guard the stairs with pistols.

These are all personal experiences. They are what we saw, or heard from friends at first hand, and since leaving, our friend Mrs. Leakey and her husband, who asked us to stay with them, have been killed.

This is the emergency that was declared in 1951. How long does an emergency last? And how did we get this far? Why was not more done when it began? Who is to blame and what happens next?

These are the questions. That's all you can get at first. Just questions. No answers, or at least so many answers that they are not answers. So many solutions, from "kill the damn lot" to straight-out appeasement, that there are no solutions.

But slowly the picture begins to emerge. It is multi-faced, cut like a terrible bloody jewel. That of the settler whose whole life is tied up in Kenya. That of the Mau Mau — the leaders, the gangsters — the willing and the unwilling. That of the loyal Kikuyu. That of the missionaries. That of the Indians who think they could fill the vacuum left by the white man, of the Indians who feel the white man essential to the prosperity of the colony. That of the Indians in India who support self-determination wherever it may be. That of the Communists. That of the British Labour Party who, in some curious way, identify themselves with African labour. (Unfortunately Kenya has always been regarded as a gentleman's colony and as such stands very low in the esteem of the British public. Today nothing is more despicable than a gentleman.)

One thing alone is certain. Almost the whole of black Africa is watching Kenya with interest and approval. I have heard sympathy expressed for the Mau Mau from the Cape of Good Hope to the Gold Coast.

What is the Mau Mau? What is its cause, its origin? It is not a question of land, or not entirely a question of land. There is a land shortage. But the Kikuyu have increased so much in numbers since the British took over the country that this was inevitable. There seems anyway no particular reason for every African to have a farm. Not every American has one, nor has every European. The land they have is some of the best I have seen in Africa and, with proper methods, could produce double the food it does, and there are thousands of acres of bracken which they have not cleared.

But land has been the basis of the agitators' argument. The white man has stolen your land. The white man wants you to terrace your land, not for your own good, but so that when you have finished he can take it over. Nairobi is going to be declared a city which will mean further thefts of land. The white highlands are Kikuyu territory. (This is a lie. The Masai grazed the white highlands and killed any Kikuyu who ventured onto them. In the open the Kikuyu are no match for the Masai. Only in forest country could they hold their own, for in the bush the long spears of the Masai were useless.)

What happens in Kenya affects the whole continent, for what happens here today may happen elsewhere tomorrow. The Mau Mau movement is in fact a revolution, a war against the white man, and the Africans and Asiatics who support Western civilisation. Some of the people who have done the most for the Africans have been killed, just as those Africans who were most friendly with the white man have been destroyed. This is war against the West, against Christianity, against progress. The first aim of the terrorists has been to bind the Kikuyu people, willing or unwilling, by unbreakable oaths to this terrible society, and to smash by threats, arson, mutilation and murder the bridge of understanding that was being built between the races, and, with it, the possibility of a multi-racial society living in association with each other to the mutual profit and happiness of all. This was, and is still, the only hope for Africa although the revolt has set it back.

It is perhaps an illusion to think of Africa as a black giant awakening and throwing off his chains. The black giant has been disturbed in his ten-thousand-year sleep and is annoyed. He wants to be left alone. He wants to go back, and the Mau Mau revolt is an expression of this desire. It is the sum of every African grievance, real or imagined, coordinated by clever agitators and canalized into its present form. These anti-white, anti-progressive, anti-Western feelings are more or less general among all Africans. That the Kikuyu have been the first to resort to organised violence and terrorism to attain their ends is due to this tribe's peculiar political talents — their intelligence and gift for intrigue. They are a people who have shown considerable ability in working with the white man as clerks, drivers, mechanics and servants. They are certainly the most highly developed of Kenya's forty-odd tribes. But even among themselves political tension has rarely been absent. Oratory and forensic skill are much admired and political associations have continually been formed, and dissolved, only to reappear under new names.

The most important of these societies was the rabidly nationalistic Kikuyu Central Association that was started in 1922 and proscribed in 1940. It is here that the figure of Jomo Kenyatta first begins to become significant.

In his book *Facing Mount Kenya* he says: "Thaai — peace, greetings — to the members of the KCA [Kenya Central Association], my comrades in arms of the past, present and future," and it was he who, under the auspices of the KCA, was responsible for the formation of the Independence Schools Association which refused to co-operate with the Education Department, chiefly on the female circumcision question and, breaking away from all authority, proceeded to issue its own completely valueless certificates of competence. It was these schools which have fostered the belief that the white highlands were once Kikuyu land, a belief which is now probably held by most of the younger members of the tribe. It was in these schools that parodies of Christian hymns were sung and the name of Jomo substituted for that of Jesus Christ.

Kenyatta was born in 1898 and educated at the Church of Scotland Mission School. At one time he was employed by the Nairobi Municipality. Joining the Kenya Central Association, he became its president. In 1928 he published a Kikuyu newspaper and the following year he went to England with the intention of engaging in politics. In 1930 he returned to Kenya but left again almost at once for England and the Continent. He studied at the London School of Economics, married an Englishwoman and had a child by her. He spent some time, two years it is believed, in Russia, and finally returned to Kenya in 1946, where he again entered politics and became president of the Kenya African Union which had originally been set up in 1944 under the title of the Kenya African Study Union.

Facing Mount Kenya received some attention as being the first book written by an African anthropologist about Africans. In it he describes the tribal life of the Kikuyu before the coming of the white man with such skill that even circumcision becomes a kind of *fête champêtre*, a sort of coming-out party. Before the white man came everything was lovely in Africa. He ignores the true state of the Kikuyu at that time, which was one of perpetual war with the Masai and Arab slavers, and of terror of their leaders — the Elders — who ruled them with an iron hand.

Of the origin of the tribe itself very little is known save that they came from the north or east some five hundred years ago and settled in the vicinity of Mount Kenya, where they expanded, obtaining forest land from the Dorobo by means of gifts of cattle, goats and women. There was a supreme council in each area whose members were all experts in witchcraft and used some of the most deadly poisons known between the coast and the lakes to dispose of any troublesome or unwanted members of the tribe.

Witchcraft, and the administration of oaths, some seventy in number, have always been an essential part of the Kikuyu culture, and the significance of these ceremonies is deeply embedded in the subconscious of the tribe. This has been seized upon by the originators of the Mau Mau, whose aim is to unite and discipline the whole people, welding them into a striking force which they can use to satisfy their own political ambitions.

The oaths sworn, despite the fact that they cut across all tribal usage by being administered at night, by force and to women, are unbreakable and their bestiality and horror such that, according to competent psychologists who have examined captured gangsters, many of those who have taken them are destroyed as men. There is no doubt in my own mind that the pattern is not African in origin. Features of the old oaths have been used to give them validity, but onto them have been grafted European Black Mass ceremonials. A knowledge of psychology is apparent in the administration of oaths to women, giving them an importance in tribal affairs they have never had before, and in the administration of the oaths during the hours of darkness, thus adding the terrors of the night to the already obscene rituals.

The initiates are summoned by messengers who invite them to a tea or drink party at some appointed place. From here they are led in pairs to the oath hut where they are made to strip their clothes, watches and everything else of European origin. Surrounded by guards whose simis glisten in the dim light of a lantern, a rukwaro — a loop of grass and twigs — is placed over their heads. Smaller loops are placed on their wrists. A goat screams as it is slowly killed and its blood mixed with earth and placed in a hollowed-out banana flower. This is circulated seven times over the initiates' heads by the oath administrator. There are further ceremonies such as crawling through an arch decorated with sheep's eyeballs, each pierced by seven thorns from the kei apple tree, and over a banana leaf trough filled with blood. In others the eyes of a human victim are pricked seven times and the brain of a dead man is bitten and eaten seven times. Seven is the mystic number which reappears in all later oaths where human blood is drawn and drunk. Worse follows, but here the details are so revolting as to be unprintable in their bestial sexuality. The object of all this is to render the circumstances unforgettable while the initiate swears not to reveal the secrets of the society, not to sell Kikuyu land, to follow their great leader Kenyatta, to pay the fees, to bring in the head of an enemy, to steal from Europeans, to help drive the Europeans from the country, to worship no leader but Jomo, to burn European crops and kill their cattle, to steal firearms, to kill even a father or a brother if so ordered and, when killing, to cut off heads, extract the eyeballs and drink the liquid from them.

These men, these leaders and organisers, cannot be described as savages since they read and write, wear European clothes and drive cars. Many are mission trained. They telephone, write letters to each other, and use rubber stamps. Some at least have been to Europe, have lived among white people and been accepted by them. And then comes this reversion, not to barbarism but to something much worse.

Most of the Mau Mau are literate, most are well dressed. Those that I came in contact with in a small engagement, where I accompanied the police, were clean, neat and some had quite new clothes. They were recruits being called up for service in the Aberdares. Twenty were killed, among them a young woman. In a captured picture, which I was not allowed to have since it was still secret, a group of gangsters were posed like a baseball team and seemed very pleased with themselves as they stood and sat (the front row sitting) against a background of forest, holding their pangas, simis and rifles in their hands. They had their girl friends with them. The snap was good, clear and sharp in every detail. The man who took it, one of themselves, was a good photographer with a good camera. Not a savage. A man of some education who understood focusing and exposures.

What are the bright spots in the emergency? The loyal Kikuyu who have sacrificed everything and risked everything in resisting the Mau Mau. Thousands have been killed — men, women and children. Burnt in huts whose doors were wired up. Split open when pregnant, their babies chopped in half. But still the resistance goes on by Christians and old-fashioned tribal pagans, many of whom, in spite of torture, having refused to take the Mau Mau oath, have been slowly killed. I have details of the massacres, pictures of dead black girls (and white ones), and children. I have copies of the oaths in their full and awful obscenity. I know the story. I have tried to tell it. To tell of a life among enemies, where even among Africans there is no trust left, where a loyal chief's sister has betrayed him to the killers; where among white men every African may be an assassin, even men they have known all their lives and regarded as their friends.

What is the answer? What is the future, not only of Kenya, but of Africa? I do not know. Only that this thing will never be forgotten. It is an idea. An evil idea. But it is exciting, for people who pine for war; who, though they have few spears left today, still long to wash them in the blood of their enemies. The shadow of the Panga — the Hammer and Sickle of the African — means the end of the boredom.

30

Safariland...Nairobi...Arusha...Banagi

● To THE WORLD in general Kenya is known for its big game, its safaris, the fast and immoral life of its inhabitants and the brutality of its settlers. Now this banner of inaccuracy is blazoned with the scandal of Mau Mau, the unnecessary rebellion.

Poor Africa, in the hands of master minds which conceived a groundnut scheme in a place where groundnuts will not grow, and an egg scheme in a colony where only the hardiest native hen will live. Minds which refuse to face the fact that Africa is still a savage land whose soil is not susceptible to modern Western agricultural methods, and whose people are not yet equipped to rule themselves on democratic parliamentary lines. Minds which, stumbling in a miasma of appeasement, offer amnesty to murderers, a weak device lacking in both morality and justice.

The settlers — some four thousand in number — are, on the whole, serious, hard-working men who have given their lives and their fortunes to Kenya. Who, in fact, have made the colony. In the early days there were some bad hats with more money than brains, and a sufficiently aristocratic background to make their scandalous doings good copy for the yellow press and supply sexy plots to the more romantic novelists. If Lord *this* runs off with Lady *that* against a background of snow-clad mountains on the equator, to the accompanying beat of tom-toms and the screams of dying elephants, it is news, whereas if Mr. Smith of Surbiton commits adultery with Mrs. Jones among the aspidistras, it is not news. It is very easy to criticise distant places sitting in an armchair at home, but in Africa the ratio of balancing, psychological factors is changed. The scale of measurement is not the same when a man carries his life in his hands every hour of the day and night. When the invisible mosquito is more dangerous and harder to deal with than the lion. When every time he leaves his homestead he has some anxiety about what will happen in his absence. If a man should be judged by his peers, then colonials should be judged by colonials, or by men who at least understand the life of the frontier.

So much for the settlers of Kenya, who are no better and no worse than people anywhere else. A hard-working lot of men, many of whom believe themselves to have been betrayed by the British Government's criminal ineptitude in handling the emergency.

As to the game, it is still there, though its numbers are vastly reduced by hunting, poaching and the increase of the native population which is continually encroaching upon its range. Game must quite rightly give way to men. But big game remains big business in Kenya. Twelve hundred safaris leave Nairobi each year for trips into the bush that last from a week to several months. There are twenty-three accredited white hunters and ten learners, and the cost of a safari is £200 per week, which includes everything except licences, liquor and cigarettes. All my life, since my father told me my first African hunting story, a safari had been my ambition. Had I been born earlier I should have wanted to be an ivory hunter or transport rider. Freddy Selous, the son of the great hunter, was my best friend at school, and the wild had always called me. It took me cattle ranching in the Transvaal after the First World War. I had done some hunting but no big stuff and now I had the chance and the means, but the desire to kill had gone.

But if the desire to kill had gone, if the home in which to hang the trophies had gone, the wild animals still remained. I wanted to see them, and a white hunter, Stanley Laurence Brown, who found himself free between two safaris, said he could take us out. The expense was, of course, a major consideration, but I knew if I did not go now I would never go. So I justified the whole affair by writing it off as an anniversary present to my wife, to whom, naturally, I grudge nothing. There was a slight disagreement when she said she would sooner have a new mink coat. But I pointed out that one could always get a mink coat and we might never get a chance like this again. I also said that minks got moth in them and that since we intended to live more or less in the tropics furs were useless. She said furs were never useless and it only showed how naïve men were to associate valuable furs with warmth. After all, a horse blanket would keep a woman warm. But had I ever seen one at the Stork Club? I said no, but that after all it was my anniversary too (why had I never thought of this before?) and we went. And, once it was over, she enjoyed it. Actually "safari" really means journey; its association with hunting is more or less fortuitous since on all journeys in Africa hunting was necessary to feed the carriers.

On the way to Amboseli we saw gerenuk, a rare, long-necked, grace-ful, giraffe-like gazelle, and oryx, that look rather like donkeys with long straight horns, soon after we left the main road. We drove across the lake which was white, and dry as a desert, towards a splendid mirage of a vast tree-fringed sea and a great castle. The castle was, of course, a rock outcrop some miles away.

All the rest huts were occupied, so, leaving the boys to put up the tents, we handed over the rifles to the warden who locked them in a steel and concrete safe as a precaution against a Mau Mau raid, and drove off to see what we could find in the way of game. We saw some impala, several giraffe, herds of Grant's and Thompson's gazelles. The Granties are almost white, and the Tommies marked like South African springbok with a dark brown streak along the flank. There were plenty of zebras and wildebeeste. In the night we heard leopards and hyenas and when we left to look for game again in the early morning, the snow-capped crest of Mount Kenya — the mountain that Hemingway and Jomo Kenyatta share between them — was visible, rosy in the equatorial dawn. We saw several hyenas coming back to cover and a lot of baboons systematically working their way across a clearing in search of insects. There must have been at least a hundred of all ages. One mother, instead of having her baby on her belly or back, was carrying it under one arm and running on three legs. We saw more giraffe, one with twin calves, several pairs of tiny dik-dik and bat-eared foxes that charmed us as they stared and then darted into their earths. We saw some buffalo in a swamp, only their heads showing, several elephants and five rhinos. Two single ones and a group of three, consisting of the parents and an adolescent child, about the size of a Hereford bull. We saw vultures, saddle-bill storks, blue jays, shiny starlings, Egyptian and spurwinged geese, kingfishers, ground hornbills, white cattle egrets and the little red-billed creeping rhenoster birds that climb about the necks of the giraffes and over other game like nuthatches on the trunk of a tree. Farmers hate them as, having eaten the ticks, they enlarge the wounds and eat the bloody flesh at its edges. Some people even believe that they do not eat all the ticks but leave some to keep the wound open.

Dust devils whirled across the dry bed of the lake. Giant yellow fever trees that had been pushed over in the wet season by the ele-phants had come up with great circles of earth, that looked like mud walls, sticking to their roots. One small wood might have been shelled. Every tree in it was snapped off. Elephants are dirty and untidy feeders but continue to bring one's heart into one's mouth every time one sees one. One can never tire of wild elephants. It is easy to see how elephant hunting could have got hold of a man in the old days when they could be hunted in the open on horseback, and a fortune made on a single safari — three or four thousand pounds, when pounds were pounds. On this side of Africa, ivory was an integral part of the slave trade, the captured slaves being forced to carry the tusks to the coast by the Arab slavers.

After lunch we picked up our armoury and set off for Arusha. The road was good and the country, after we crossed the Tanganyika border, rather like parts of Natal and the Cape. Many of the farmers here are Afrikaners — Boers who came long ago and settled in country which resembled their old homes. We passed some Masai with their long, shining spears, their ochre-red cotton cloths draped over their nakedness, their copper double bell-shaped earrings dangling on extended lobes right down to their shoulders. An interesting and dying race. Only fifty thousand remain. A withering remnant of a once magnificent tribe who prefer death to civilisation. Not that they suffer hardship, they are well off. They have immense herds of cattle but they pine away without their raids and forays. They are dying of boredom and of syphilis. Because their women are failing to breed, they are bastardising themselves with their enemies — the despised Kikuyu. Even their sport of killing lions with spears, as a proof of manhood, has been checked because too many of them get killed. Killed — what is that to a Masai moran, a warrior? Unless there is danger of death there is no possibility of a full life. The Masai are a Nilotic people — tall, slim, handsome and so highly strung that, when excited, they tremble and may even fall down. They kill no game since they eat no meat, but live among it, pasturing their herds in friendship with beasts of the plains. They live on milk and the fresh blood that they draw from the veins of their cattle.

As we approached Arusha there were more native huts and small fields. There were hollow beehive logs hung in the trees. Great bunches of corncobs hung in others, tied so closely together that they looked like giant pineapples.

We spent the night in the Safari Hotel and pushed on in the morning towards Makuyuni, where we made a camp in the forest. This was one of our hunter's favourite places — he often used it. The ground below the great trees was swept clean. Their giant buttresses rose out of the clearing, which was like an enormous room whose walls were the forest. Lianas hung down like ropes. One got the usual underwater feeling, and a sense of mystery that it is impossible to escape in the high forest. A sense of age, peace and isolation.

Here we were met by John Glen, the game ranger. A very fine-looking young man suffering from a broken heart. The fourth, or was it fifth, girl to whom he had been engaged had just jilted him. He was, however, very philosophical and wanted beer. We had no beer. So we went to lunch with him in his mountain hide-out — a very nice house built on a site that would have made an eagle's eyrie — and drank his beer.

At the local Indian duka we bought batteries for our flashlight, cigarettes, marshmallows and a big jack fruit — the first I had ever eaten. It was quite good and a taste for them would be easy to acquire. This is one of the world's heaviest fruits and may weigh ten or more pounds.

Next morning we set out for Lake Manyara. We drove through the forest, over two drifts and out onto the plain that ran up to the wall of the rift of this gigantic split in the earth's surface. We had come down into it from Nairobi and were now reaching its edge again. The lake shimmered on our left. And in the far distance the thing we had really come to see.

Flamingoes by the thousand, the hundred thousand, the million I should think. They lined the lake for miles, standing shoulder to shoulder forming a border two hundred yards thick. A pink frill like a lace edge to the white water. Something dainty and feminine in the starkness of the bush.

The tsetses came in dozens. Their bite felt like a hot match head being pushed into the skin. They had to be squashed to kill them. I let them bite and then took them between my fingers. Tiny slapped hysterically and then gave up and, in spite of the heat, put on her coat and a scarf and a rug over her legs.

As we drove across the short-cropped grass, a red jeep and a truck, that we had seen the previous afternoon, passed us loaded with fresh meat. They must have been shooting all night by spotlight. The jeep's windscreen was down and we found where they had made a camp. They tried to avoid us but we had no difficulty in seeing the amount of skinned meat they had with them. A great deal of poaching goes on. Some farmers make biltong for sale and shoot game to feed their boys in quantities which far exceed their licenses. The sequel to this was a wounded buffalo that I spotted going into the bush near where we were going to have our picnic lunch. Tiny might easily have gone into the trees and been charged if we had not seen it. Stan and his gunbearer got out of the car and went after it. We saw them disappear and then heard two shots. Then there was one more shot. It exploded dully, heavily. There was an instant's silence and then, like the crack of a whip, came the echo from the hills. Then the buffalo gave a bellow, smothered deep in his chest, and groaned.

"Come on up," Stan said.

We went.

It was an enormous old, almost hairless bull, with its great horns splintered and worn down around the curve. Flies were on its eyes already. Stan found the bullet wound that had crippled it. There was the rake of a lion's claws over its quarters and it had been torn by a hyena in the scrotum. But even in death it was menacing. Less an animal than a Thing. Hideous. Bulk personified. A kind of devil.

It was dark when we got back to camp. It had been a wonderful day. Next day we climbed the escarpment and looked down on Lake Manyara. It looked like a mirror fallen on the green carpet of the bush below us. We went through patches of whistling thorn, curious small trees with enormous white thorns whose bases are greatly enlarged by some parasite. These goitres are pierced by holes, made either by the ants which swarm on them or by the escaping insect which inhabited them. The cold wind whistles through the holes giving them their name. They seem only to grow at high levels and on the black cotton soil that we call turf in South Africa. A very rich, heavy clay which cracks into crevasses when dry and becomes glutinous and impassable in the rains. We now came to heavy mountain forest where the trees wore blankets of green moss as they had in the Congo, so thick that in some places it had smothered them. Beards of Spanish moss waved in the wind. Then the country opened up. The kikuyu grass was very green. There were patches of white belladonna lilies among the trees and small clumps of lion's-claw bush. There were giant lobelia and bamboo thickets.

We were now almost on the top of Ngorongoro though we did not know it till Stan stopped the car and led us to what we thought was just a grass-clad shoulder of the mountain. To our astonishment we found a sheer drop of a thousand feet below us and there, spread out, was the immense tapestry of the crater floor — a design of toy trees, lakes, patches of bush and animals that appeared to be no bigger than pinheads. With the glasses we could see many more, but it gave one a strange feeling, for the glasses cut away the little foreground there was — the yard or so in front of us — and we were projected right into space, balanced above the vast nothingness below. The far side of the crater was fourteen miles away and it is, I believe, the largest extinct volcano crater in the world.

Having stared our fill, we drove on and began to drop down towards the Serengetti plains. The sky became threatening, there was some thunder and a shower of icy rain which made the black lava of the road as slippery as Vaseline. Masai herders stood, spear in hand, impassively watching their immense herds grazing on the short khaki-coloured grass. They stood immovable, red figures grasping their spears, or sitting with the spears driven point upwards into the ground beside them. What was in their minds? It is useless for anyone to tell me that there is any resemblance in their mental processes to my own. Could I stand for hours on one leg, spear in hand, watching the cattle that were an extension of my own personality; dreaming of lions I had hunted, men I had killed, wars and raids that I or my fathers had been engaged in? Could I live at all without a knowledge of the past, of cause and effect, without a sense of time which is really the film on which historical events are portrayed in my mind? Without history there would, at most, be "long ago" which would mean the times of which my father spoke. The savage floats like a log on the sea of time. The tides move him back and forth, storms drive him here and there but the sea about him remains the same — unchanging. The events he participates in, the sights he sees are the same as those that all his race, from the dawn of time, have seen.

Watching the Masai spearmen grazing their herds, we were peeping through a pinhole into the past. This has always moved me. It is why I love the continuity of the wilds, or even such segments of it as are left in more civilised places. A man rowing or sailing a boat, a skein of flying wild fowl, a heron flapping solemnly over a marsh, a solitary horseman on a plain. These things are as they have always been, or have been for many hundreds of years. They can be accepted, admired, thought about — but there is no puzzle in them. Here the pages can be turned back and there is a kaleidoscopic variety in the pattern, but no change in the contents.

The rain stopped suddenly. The sun pierced the leaden clouds and struck a slanting golden blow at the mountaintop on our left. And there in this great beam, playing like motes of dust in a splash of sunlight in a room, were a great flock of storks riding the air currents of the storm. White against the grey sky, they flashed into gold- and black-tipped silver in the sun. Up and round, swirling in some joyous aerial dance, these great European birds seemed to be celebrating their arrival at the equator.

To the Masai these were known birds — they came each year. They marched over the dry grass following the locust swarms. But they knew nothing of them nesting in Germany and Holland on the borders of the North Sea, nothing of their flight, of the way they were caught and banded, nothing of the baby-bringing story that went from Europe to America and is believed there — where there are no storks — by city children who have seen no bird bigger than a gull upon a refuse dump.

This was the point that was being driven deeper and deeper into my mind. It had nothing to do with black inferiority or white superiority. It was the difference in background, outlook and tradition which separated us. Ours were based on Jewish religion, Greek art and Roman law — all meaningless in Africa. We were trying to impose our ideas onto people who did not really want them. The difference was not so much a question of colour as of culture, and heredity.

At this time of year — the end of the dry season — the Serengetti plains are a desert, a dead land of dry pans, dusty grass and leafless trees. But we saw a giraffe and plenty of Tommies. They must be able to go without water for a long time as they looked well, or they may obtain moisture by digging up bulbs or tubers. They ran and jumped just for the hell of it. Those on the right would pass in front of the car, crossing the track in great leaps. Then a herd on the left would race past us and cross over to the right. The last buck who had been dawdling would suddenly put on a burst of speed and gallop to the front, passing all the others, just to show them, and us, what he could do. The young buck had a trick of pronking like the springbok of the South, making a series of stiff-legged jumps, bouncing over the veld like a ball.

We passed another herd of Masai cattle in very poor condition and when I asked about water Stan said they could go up to ten days without it. They certainly looked as if they had. Another curious habit of East African cattle is the way they graze in tight groups, almost shoulder to shoulder. Even the mixed calf and sheep herds do this. Whether they are trained to do it or whether it is an inherited characteristic I have not yet been able to discover. The cause is obviously protective. In this formation there are no strays drifting about on their own to be picked up by a lion or leopard.

We camped in the open without tents near a few trees which gave us wood for our cooking fire. The night was beautiful and bright with stars. The African sky a clear luminous indigo above us.

In the grey of the dawn I noticed vultures perched on the trees that dotted the plain. As the sun rose and the day warmed up they flew off, seeking the kills of the night. There were four kinds of vulture — a big black king vulture that I knew, some griffon vultures, another kind that was almost white, and a small one that I think was the Egyptian vulture.

We were now having trouble with the following wind which blew our own dust along rather faster than we could travel, so that we could neither breathe nor see. At intervals we stopped the car and turned to face the wind, with the engine still running to cool it off. In a following wind the fan fails to function. There is no cool air to circulate. Usually the plains are traversed in the opposite direction, from Banagi to Arusha, for this reason.

But at last the country became less desolate. We saw four cheetahs stalking a herd of Tommies. The buck thought they were safe, relying on their speed to escape if the cheetahs came too close. But the buck were wrong. When they run, cheetahs overhaul them easily. Then we saw two rhino on the horizon and went to have a look at them. A mother, and a child as big as a tank. Then lions — one very fine big maneless lion, with a suit that seemed too big for him, padding open-mouthed across the plain towards water. We called him "the thirsty lion" and liked him better than any of the others we saw later. We prefer the maneless ones as they look more like big cats. A mane always seems untidy to me, though this is heresy in the hunters' world.

Then we saw a herd of buffalo — there were big pans of water, a chain of them — and wildebeeste and zebra in herds that must have been thousands strong. An Egyptian goose, followed by a string of babies in single file, crossed the track and brought us to a standstill. There were more lions. A married couple asleep under separate trees within a few yards of each other. It was remarkable how close we could go to them in the safari car. They did no more than look at us and then went on washing like great cats, licking their paws and wiping their faces. We went to within ten yards of them. They do not seem to associate men with cars as long as one does not talk. But before approaching them, as a precaution, Stan had loaded a heavy rifle and put it beside him.

The next thing of interest we saw was an impala whose horns had been cut off. Stan said it must have been raised as a pet by the Masai, who had done this so that they would recognise it among the others when it grew up. The Masai are only man killers. They leave wild animals, except lions, alone.

We saw some great bustards. This is, I think the same bird that was only exterminated in England in the eighties. The cocks displayed like turkeys, their whiskered heads sunk into white chests that were blown up like balloons.

The country became more broken with hills and trees. There were great numbers of zebras and it was interesting to see how their light and dark stripes broke them up in the bush, making them almost invisible until they moved. The stallions were slightly bigger than the mares and more brightly coloured. The foals were more muddy, their stripes less clearly defined. Then we saw the ranger's house at Banagi. The miracle of the Serengetti plains was behind us.

31

Lion and Warthog

● THE RANGER was away chasing poachers but Mr. A. C. Brooks, a young Canadian who was doing research on a grant, was acting for him and gave us tea. The ranger had a fine collection of Masai spears. The blade is long and sword-shaped, rather than leaf-shaped like most spears. The weapon is made entirely of iron, the blade and shaft two separate pieces joined by a short piece of hardwood in the middle. Brooks showed me how to tell the genuine from the Birmingham copies imported to sell to tourists. If one looks along the blade of a hand-made spear, it is wavy, never quite true, whereas the machine-made article shows no variation.

After tea we paid our park entrance and left for Ikoma, twenty or so miles away. The first part of the drive was through a patch of old twisted thorn trees forty feet high with trunks two feet in diameter. Still leafless, they were a blaze of sweet white honey-scented flowers, tiny, and buzzing with a myriad bees. They were giants of their kind, very old, for they grow only an inch in five years. It gave one the feeling of being in a cathedral perfumed with incense as one passed between the ancient twisted columns.

The bush now got heavier and there were more topis, a beautiful purple-bronze colour with bright chestnut legs. When they ran they dodged to the left and right as if pursued and evading a charge. Stan shot one for meat. That night we ate the liver and very good it was. But I still had the same feeling of depression that I had felt when it went down. Something alive had ceased to be alive. Something beautiful was no longer beautiful. The buck that had been standing under a tree, his coat shining, iridescent, bronze as a pigeon's breast in the sunshine, was now just meat. My feelings were completely illogical, as much part of a personal transition as that through which the African is passing. A few years ago I was a hunter and a killer. Even now, with hounds, I would hunt anything, I am sure. The music of the hounds, their barking when they brought something to bay, would strike some atavistic chord in my nature and I would be changed. A great deal of amusement can be obtained by being one's own guinea pig, by examining one's loves and hates, greeds and lusts, to seek for the truth and chase it back to its origins in a prehuman past. To see the checks and balances, where reflection and taboo have put a bit into the mouth of the libido and the id.

We saw more impala. They had the best heads I have ever seen. This area must suit them. More giraffe, zebras, a family of six-banded mongooses, more topi and my first kongoni which is the East African hartebeeste. Then we came out of the tsetse bush and into overgrazed native-inhabited country. We crossed a little water-less river and arrived at Ikoma, a crumbling German fort, a remnant of their East African empire, that crowned the hill above us.

We made our camp on the flat at its foot, among some big blue gums and ornamental sisal that the German officers must have planted, and where no doubt they dreamed of *der tag* when they would open up the rest of Africa as if it were an oyster. In Africa a blue gum often survives the dreamer who planted it. All over the country I have come across solitary gums marking the site of some dead white man's homestead, the only thing that has survived the savage teeth of time. The storms, the heat, the forest fires, the ter-mites — all conspire to destroy what man has made in Africa.

Having set up our camp we left it in charge of the head boy and set off for Nairobi to pick up Stan's new lady clients. They were the survivors of the American All-Girl Safari — some of the jetsam that still bobbed on the waters of adventure. This must have been quite an affair. The girls, who varied in age from thirty to seventy, appear to have pursued the wild game and the more accommodating hunters with the utmost energy. The veld rang with the sound of shots, cries of triumph and the sobs of those who never meant to hurt the poor thing, and yells of fury from those who missed the poor thing. There were quarrels between those who wanted to take pictures and those who wanted to shoot. Quarrels about the white hunters and neo-roustabouts who accompanied the deadly lovercade. There seems to have been a great deal of hard liquor about and quite a lot of hard feeling in a good-natured female-doggy sort of way, and considerable danger from trigger-happy man-hungry female Tarzans, unaccustomed to firearms, who were at the same time somewhat high and in the heart of darkest Africa.

The two girls we were going to meet were, according to Stan, the pick of the basket, both in their thirties and attractive. If they agreed, we were going to return with them and a second white hunter for another fortnight in the bush. I wanted to do this partly because I had not seen enough, and partly because I wanted to see a real safari in action. I was interested in the psychology of the hunters. What exactly did one get out of a safari? In many ways no more than could be got out of any camping trip anywhere off the beaten track in Africa or America. The main difference was the expense, which proved that you were well off, and the trophies, which proved you had really been there, and which could only be duplicated by other people who had been there too. Then for killers — and there are plenty of them — there were lots of things to be killed. Among the killers there are the men who have been crossed in love. They take it out on the animals. The lady killers are harder to understand but I'm inclined to think it must be an answer to some of their frustrations. Maybe it's their husbands they kill symbolically, or other girls. I have a prejudice against lady hunters, though our two were pretty. It is a good thing for a woman to understand and be able to use firearms, but hunting is something else. It is probably a great pity that women should be becoming tough. They are not supposed to have the hunter and warrior instinct that is born into boys. Though on the other hand, among some races, such as the American Indian, some African tribes, Arabs and Abyssinians, it was the women who tortured the prisoners with the greatest ingenuity. So perhaps ladies have a certain latent sadism.

Other safari types are the photographers and animal lovers, naturalists; hunters, who want to do just one safari and collect a reasonable number of good heads; killers, who want to kill everything on their licence; specialists, who will hunt for weeks or months for a record; escapists, who want to get out of it all in a big and expensive way; drunks, who like to do it in the bush; nympho and other maniacs; and tourists, who do it because it is one of the things to do and something to talk about when it is done. It is the white hunter's highly paid business to stand up and deliver all that is required of him by his clients. To play cards with the card player, to drink with the lush, to agree with the prohibitionists. He must be all things to all men, organise the safari in all its details, see that his client, no matter how stupid, does not get himself into trouble or danger. He has to be a first-class shot, to know a great deal about the habits of game — where they are to be found, and the portions of their anatomy that are the most vulnerable. (He is not, as a rule, a good naturalist or botanist. The names of birds or trees or the breeding habits of game do not really interest him.) He has to be a good mechanic, a bit of a doctor and a taxidermist, and to combine all the best-known qualities of the lion, the dove, the bull, the parrot and the serpent. If the client wounds a buffalo or lion he has to go in after him and get him. Dangerous game cannot be left wounded. It is this which to my mind makes the hunting part of a safari something of a farce. The hunt is organised by the white hunter. The game is found by him, the client is manoeuvred into position by him and should the game be wounded and not killed it is the white hunter who must take its charge. The client need have no veld craft, need know nothing beyond how to point a rifle and pull the trigger. Many a den contains trophies shot by a man who could not go out on his own and find and kill, much less skin and cook, a little steenbuck.

Spiritually the white hunter is the final product of a long professional line which began when the first Stone Age hunter clubbed his animal to death. Both the hunters and the game are doomed. The world has now no place for gentlemen adventurers, explorers, hunters, buccaneers, privateersmen, pirates, highwaymen, or leaders of irregular cavalry. The white hunter is a romantic hangover from a brighter, more colourful and adventurous world. He is the cowboy of African veld.

Our route back to Nairobi took us past some gold mines to Musembo on the edge of Lake Victoria. To cross Mara Bay we got up in the dark and proceeded on board the ferry. There we waited with a crowd of cheerful Africans and Indians of all ages and sexes till the sun rose. Then we set off like a Noah's Ark across the waters. The sun came up like a red ball through the mist. Our engine turned over. Africans shouted. Africans pushed. We were fully waterborne, functioning, afloat.

While the car was being landed we watched some African men washing in the lake. They cleaned their backs by lying down in the shallows and rubbing themselves in the sand — a very practical idea. Washing water remains a great health problem in most of Africa owing to bilharzia, and, like malaria, venereal disease and malnutrition, is another cause of African inefficiency.

We spent the night at the big and country-club-like Tea Hotel at Kericho. Kericho is the centre of the East African tea industry and the tea gardens were spread over the rolling country all round us in a monotonous green carpet of waist-high shrubs. We arrived in time for tea and got into conversation with some friends of Stan's. It was only after twenty minutes or so that I noticed that one of the boys was still industriously using a carpet sweeper on the same piece of grey wall-to-wall carpet just behind our chairs that he had started working on as soon as we came in. I believe that almost every word that is spoken in Kenya is listened to by someone and the information passed on to the Mau Mau. Kericho was about to be proclaimed a dangerous area, and on the previous night a farm less than five miles away had been burnt to the ground. After dinner Stan ran into a drunk in the bar who insisted that they were related. Stan said they were not. He'd never seen him before. "That doesn't matter," the lush said, "We're related all right, old boy. You see I've slept with your sister." Stan had no sister. But his almost brother-in-law insisted on the relationship and tried to borrow a fiver.

Before leaving Kericho we had a curious experience — an old Kikuyu woman turned to glare at us, her lips writhing back like those of a snarling leopard. Her eyes blazed with hatred. This was a Kikuyu grandmother — a Mau Mau if ever I saw one — and it was her like who would prevent the cult from dying out even when it was defeated in the field. What point of contact was there between her heart and mind and that of any white administration however competent and well-meaning?

Later in the day in Nairobi we met Stan and his two other clients, Mrs. Lou Schilling and Mrs. Peaches (very aptly named) Guererro. Both ex "All-Girl Safari" girls. Both home-town Honolulu girls. Both delightfully American from the tips of their red-lacquered toes to the tops of their permanents. It was like being back in the good old USA again to listen to them. To drink martinis, not as dry or as cold as they should be of course, but still martinis, and smoke Chesterfields in their company. The world was suddenly brighter, more vivacious. Wisecracks snapped like whips. They said sure, certainly we could go with them. Thank you, we said. We would be no nuisance as we were not hunting. Not hunting? Whatever are you doing then? They seemed surprised. I could feel my masculine stock falling. Just sort of messing about, I said. This, of course, sounded silly. One does not mess about at two hundred pounds a week. A man should want to kill things. I explained that once I had liked killing things — when I was younger, I added lamely. They looked sympathetic. Evidently I was impotent, I could see them thinking. At least I would not bother them that way, and we became all girls together, dominated by the virility of our white hunter.

We met two or three more ex-All Girls. One reminded me very much of my mother, with beautiful white hair which had been blued to a kind of lobelia colour. My mother had had an unfortunate accident of this nature once when she thought she would fix her own hair. We had created quite a sensation when we went to the Berkeley Grill. Another looked like a dried-up governess with tight lips. She was strung with cameras and a light metre even in the hours of darkness. The third was younger — a hot-looking little piece. This made five we had seen, including what I now called "our two." What common denominator had this group? All were Americans, none were virgins, all must be well off. All must be escaping from something since they were progressing towards nothing. All were probably bored and in search of adventure, of something new. Nairobi was agog with stories of white hunters pursued and pursuing, of one lady who had shot a buffalo and then, finding that she could not have the head prepared by the time she was ready to go back to America, had bought another mounted head from the taxidermist. After all, a buffalo was a buffalo, and they all looked the same, didn't they? There was no answer to this from the sporting fraternity. They were speechless. There was the tale of a cuddly blonde of forty who had taken an intimate picture of a naked Masai who was sitting by the roadside. He got up, looked at her and spat.

Our arrangements were now made. Another white hunter, David Lunan, and his car were engaged and off we went back to our camp at Ikoma. An incident of some interest took place at Musembo, where the ladies had to go through some formalities about their game licences. The African clerk pushed the papers back across the counter and said he was busy doing the accounts. He would see to them when he was finished. After half an hour there was no sign of his finishing, so Stan took them to the district officer who dealt with them at once. Nothing more than an official stamp and an entry was necessary. But here in Tanganyika, a country which was being run entirely for Africans, the clerk enjoyed using his petty power to hold up a white man quite unnecessarily. He would, of course, have held up an African in the same way and for the same reason, to show his power and if possible to obtain a bribe.

As we got near Ikoma we saw two magnificent buffalo bulls. One of them, Stan said, must have forty-eight-inch horns, almost a record. Of course, though they hunted them for several days, they never saw them again.

A routine now developed. We each went out with our own white hunter. The girls returned every evening, jubilant with their trophies. They really liked shooting and their shooting was improving every day. They shot two buffaloes, one roan, four zebras, impala, oribi, topi, wildebeeste, kongoni, Tommie, Grantie — in fact everything there was to shoot. The camp was festooned with strips of drying meat and filled with hungry native ladies who were prepared to exchange black flesh for red with the safari boys. Under one tree the skinner squatted, unceasingly practising his art. Vultures circled the camp or sat patiently waiting on the trees. Kites swooped down, swift as swallows, to snatch up any fragment that fell from the cook house — another rather bigger tree. At night hyenas came quite close. As soon as it was dark one heard their moaning scream and sometimes their insane laughter.

Owing to the drought there was very little water. The river was quite dry. There were not even any pools, and we had to dig for water in the sandy bed of the stream. These miniature wells were soon filled with muddy water which we used for washing. Drinking water we had brought with us in two big drums. But owing to these drought conditions we were attacked by moths as soon as we settled down to drink anything. They were mad with thirst and precipitated themselves into our glasses. After the first day or two most of this insect life had been destroyed with Flit, but while it lasted Tiny, though she displayed her usual courage, was far from happy. Perhaps being small herself, she realises how potentially dangerous small things are.

We saw some fascinating sights. Thirty-four giraffe in one herd evidently drifting to new feeding grounds. A very dark giraffe bull lying down. He got up on his knees first and then raised his hindquarters. Another time we saw eighty-six young, almost full-grown ostriches walking in extended order across the veld. They were accompanied by a full-grown cock and hen who occupied the extreme flanks. This must have been a collection of seven or eight clutches of chicks in charge of a couple of child lovers. Some lionesses do this too, and take charge of cubs in a kind of kindergarten school. We still have a great deal to learn about the way birds and animals communicate. The Kenya ostrich is an immense bird standing, I should think, fully a foot higher than the South African variety. Many wildebeeste had young calves. They were a pale chestnut colour. So were the young topis — both must darken with age. We saw a white-tailed jackal that I had never seen before, and two large red monkeys with long white tails which they dragged behind them like thick white cotton ropes. We saw vervet monkeys in a thicket of prickly pear and were puzzled at the way they could eat the fruit and run about among the thorns without being hurt. We saw a zebra that was separated from its own herd screaming through the bush till it found it again. We saw a lame zebra and knew he would not last long. Nothing lives in Africa if it is damaged. We saw herds of eland galloping through the bush, some even jumped over each other. They are very fast for short distances but, if fat, can be run down with a good horse. They are easily tamed and remain docile when adult.

One night we had a storm. The ground trembled as the lightning struck and the thunder rumbled. The river came down in spate. Now we had plenty of water but it was dirtier than ever. The black cotton soil was difficult to get through in the hunting car even with the extra-low gear. And out on the plain there were hyenas lying half in and half out of every pan enjoying a bath. We chased one to see what speed he could make. At twenty-six miles an hour he was not at all out and still loping, with that rather dragging gait that is typical of all hyenas. They always run as if they were a little lame in one hind leg. He kept looking back over his shoulder at us with what Tiny called his big round eyes. She liked hyenas and wanted a pet one. Later we shot two of them. They take a lot of killing and tend to tear out their own entrails when wounded. Their teeth are unbelievable, more powerful than those of a lion. They can crush the largest bone. I wanted to solve the problem of their sex organs which have always been much disputed by hunters — the older ones claiming them to be hermaphrodites. Actually the sex organs are hidden in the interior of a kind of bag that is situated very far forward on the belly, almost up to the last ribs. On each side of this sunken, grey, hairless purse there are two large teats about as thick as a man's little finger and an inch and a half long. Both specimens were exactly the same and David said they are all like that. The first we thought was a male, though we did not open him up to prove it. The second was certainly a bitch as she was in pup. Leaving her on the veld we went off to see what would happen.

Within five minutes the vultures began to come. First they circled, then they landed and with open wings, throwing their bodies back to break their impetus. Then hyenas drifted up from all directions. I imagine they knew what a shot meant or had seen the vultures coming down, or both. They slunk in like wolves, saw the body was one of their own kind and drifted off again. All except one. This one stood over the body smelling it and then charged the vultures as they thickened and crowded about him. He kept jumping over the dead hyena which I am sure was his mate until finally, seeing he could do

Topeke girls dancing

Pretty girl,
Congo

Wagenia fish traps

Women bringing bamboo
fuel from the mountains

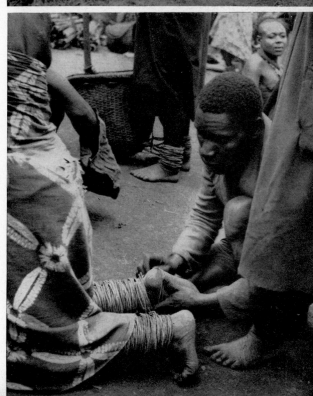

Adjusting new anklets
at market, Kabare

Tamed elephants
bathing and
drinking

Okapi

Pygmy chief wearing blue feathers of the wild African peacock

Pygmy
drummer

Pygmies dancing

Warthog

Lion

Lion with kill

Giraffes

nothing and, overwhelmed by the vultures which returned as soon as he had cleared them away, he moved off a few yards and lay watching them attack the body. Some marabou storks now arrived. In all there must have been forty or fifty birds round the corpse. The vultures did not eat it with enthusiasm but were attacking its under-parts. When we left they were still quarrelling round it, hissing, click-ing their beaks and beating at each other with their great wings. The hyenas would probably return as soon as the meat began to putrefy, if there was any left by then, and would crack the bones for their marrow.

There does not seem to be any great mystery about how the vul-tures know so quickly when something is dead or sick. Every acre of the upper air in the wilder parts of Africa is patrolled by birds, circling endlessly, out of our sight, but where everything that happens below them can be seen. They not only watch the ground but the other circling birds. As soon as one comes down the others nearest to it follow it to the ground. This goes on, rather like the ripples caused by a stone thrown into a pool, and before long a hundred or more vultures from as much as fifty miles away may be assembled round a dead or dying beast.

Hyenas are believed to have killed women and children, and have bitten the faces off sleeping men. When hungry they will form packs of a hundred or more and attack living and injured game. They appear to have no natural enemies. They live on sick or wounded animals and follow the lions, eating what they leave of their kills in the company of other carrion eaters — jackals, vultures, marabous, kites and crows. And finally the old lion who has fed them for so long falls victim to his guests. It is strange to picture the scene. The old lion — thin, lame, his teeth gone or going — surrounded by hyenas, rushing at them, killing one or two with a tearing slap of his great claws. But the rushes get weaker. The hyenas become bolder and more numerous. They close in. There is a final scurry and the king of beasts goes down under the scavengers.

We shot a warthog for bait and after splitting him open dragged him round the camp to see what he would bring. He brought a leopard which ate half a topi that was hanging in a tree, and hyenas that finished up the warthog — his hide, his bones, even his skull had disappeared by the morning — and the noises they made while they did it were unbelievable. They moaned, laughed, screamed, like a dog that has been run over, like a woman; they lowed like cows. No wonder there are so many natives who believe in lycanthropy with these strange body-eating, spotted beasts.

We saw plenty of waterbuck, a bigger variety than that of the Transvaal, with white quarters instead of a half-moon. And in a patch of heavy bush, standing under an immense thorn tree we came across an old buffalo bull that must have been both deaf and blind.

We had seen about all we could here and the girls had got the heads they wanted so we decided to move to Clyne's Camp in a restricted area where no cat (that is to say lion, leopard, cheetah or lynx) or buffalo could be shot. But we wanted to bait for lion, not to shoot one. Clyne's Camp was about forty miles over a rough trail which Brooks had blazed in the Canadian woodsman's manner. He had given us a rough map; we were to turn off where there was a saucepan hanging from a tree. We found it easily. It was pierced like a sieve with .22 shots. If it hadn't been the Africans would have stolen it. This had been a hunting base from which Clyne, who had been dead for years, used to take his clients out to shoot buffalo, rhino and lion in those unrestricted days. He had had everything laid on — electricity, a kitchen garden and all amenities.

There were plenty of rhinos about. We ran into three almost at once. A pair with a big calf. All three charged us. We were in an open clearing and Stan simply accelerated and swerved out of their way. It was most interesting to watch. It would have been less so if they had caught us in the cul-de-sac that we got stuck in soon after we left them.

After this little adventure we shot a kongoni, and putting a wire hawser round its horns dragged it back to the plain below our camp. Here it was gutted. Then one of the boys climbed a tree with one end of the hawser which was put over a branch and fastened on to the car again and the buck dragged up. The boy now made it fast with a rope through the tendons of the hocks and the hawser was cast loose. It hung with its forelegs about five feet from the ground. Having done this we drove off to camp and had an excellent supper of guinea fowl stew, made by Stan in a pressure cooker. We had not brought a tent, just a fly which was fastened up between two trees, and our beds and mosquito nets. During the night we heard lions several times and as soon as it was light saw two of them lying by the bait. When we drove down they retreated into the bush. The bait was stripped of meat, almost up to the middle of the back. The tree was scarred with claw marks and the grass below it torn up by the jumps they had made. There was also quite a lot of lion mane about, rather like sheeps' wool in a pasture, where they had fought, and there were some deep spoor marks showing how they had chased each other. At one time there must have been half a dozen lions round the bait.

Lions will drive crows and vultures away from their kill because they foul it. Jackals they do not seem to bother about, but they will not allow hyenas near them. When baiting for leopards the tree should be smeared with guts, and guts dragged about in the vicinity and round its base. No branches must be cut and the bait should be hung in a fork nine or ten feet from the ground. The hide is carefully constructed by clearing out the middle of a thick patch of bush as if it were a little room, and cutting a window into it that faces the dead buck.

We found a giraffe skull complete with its vestigial horn butts and enormous leg bones, four feet long, that weighed, even when white and dry, at least twenty pounds.

We noticed some other things. Kongoni, when they canter, have all their feet off the ground at the same time. Roan antelopes look like donkeys with their big ears carried sideways. Kongoni horns grow out from the head parallel to the ground and their ears before turning upwards. Ostriches, when worried by flies, wipe their backs with their wings, alternately using right and left, as they walk along. Hyenas come to a kill with their tails up. Eland, like the wildebeeste, often run with zebras, counting on their hearing to give them warning of danger. Warthog families run in single file with their little tails erect. They live in holes made by ant bears (aardvark) or jackals, and enter them bottom first, turning at full gallop and backing into them. Their lower tusks are sharp as razors, being continually stropped against the upper and much heavier teeth. When there are leopards about at night the bush buck bark like dogs, and the monkeys make little croaking froglike noises.

Because this was our last day I tried to impress it on my mind. I did not want to forget. We sat under a thorn tree scarified by lions. In the heat of the day the wildebeeste bulls snorted at us as they stood alone under the trees. A bat-eared fox popped up to stare at the car with insatiable curiosity. The hyenas lay like dogs in the sun. A vulture swung down in spiral flight. The plains game looked up as a lion stalked over the yellow grass half a mile away. They knew he was full fed. A blue jay flashed in the sun. In the vlei the ibis gave their clattering cry. Everything was as it had always been, unchanged for ten thousand years. In the time of the Pharoahs of Egypt, of Christ, of Julius Caesar and Ghengis Khan. Was this its charm, its mystery?

32

The Little Battle...Nairobi...Thika

● BECAUSE Sir Evelyn and Lady Baring were friends of my cousin's at the Cape, we were asked to spend a night at Government House. Owing to the emergency the front drive was permanently closed; there was a great deal of barbed wire about and a strong Askari guard. Some men were even distributed about the garden in the evening, lying on the lawn in a prone position with fixed bayonets. Several members of the staff had recently been found to be Mau Mau and all indoor servants, instead of going barefoot, wore boots so that their approach could be heard. There was a notice on the wall saying that in the event of an alarm visitors were requested to assemble in Lady Baring's sitting room on the ground floor. There was actually very little danger of the Governor being attacked. The Mau Mau are too well run and organised to go that far. The Mau Mau have done nothing really to alienate public opinion at home or abroad. So little in fact that they have almost succeeded, in some places, in putting over the idea that Mau Mau does not really exist and is an invention of the brutal settlers to justify their sadistic practices. Thirty-odd white people, most of them women, children and men over fifty years of age, have been killed under particularly revolting circumstances. This has been enough to make every farmer nervous and drive some of the more timid out of the country, but not enough to arouse British opinion, which has, by adverse propaganda, been persuaded that these gangsters are fighting for their freedom. In a war of nerves and propaganda the Mau Mau have had a success. No wide publicity has been given to the fact that they have murdered two thousand of their own tribesmen, and the outside world either has not heard of these atrocities or does not believe them. Nothing was made of the mutilated livestock, hundreds of which were slashed to death or left with amputated legs waiting for a bullet to end their suffering. Knowing the sentimentality of their own race, the British should have plastered every paper with these pictures, since the human atrocity pictures of disembowelled women, babies cut in half, men sliced like cheese with pangas or decapitated with their eyes gouged out and brains removed, are considered too frightful to be shown.

But there has been little interruption of business life. The roads have not been sniped, surely the most obvious method if the attack was to be pushed home. There has been very little arson or destruction to immovable property other than Government schools and the huts of those of their own people who refused to collaborate. This, at least, is my own impression.

And into this amazing muddle Sir Evelyn Baring, a man who is by nature a peaceful diplomat, and a sick man at that, found himself precipitated by one of the worst pieces of luck imaginable. Several deputations have gone to Government House to ask him to resign, one while we were there, and I met some members of it on their return. Nowhere did I hear a word against the Governor. Everyone liked him but this was not the job for a man who has spent his service on the secretariat side and had never been in direct contact with the African. The whole situation had been wished onto Sir Evelyn, who anyway had his hands tied by the British colonial policy of handing over the mass to the tender mercies of the few. But no action was taken until it was too late, and then too little action. Why, for instance, was Operation Anvil — the clean-up of Nairobi — delayed for nearly two years, when everyone knew from the beginning, and told us, that the heart of Mau Mau was in the city? Why, only in the last few months, has land belonging to terrorists been sequestrated, and then only that of a few leaders? Why, among people who understood collective responsibility, has the whole Kikuyu tribe not been made responsible? Why have loyal African chiefs and white policemen and soldiers been penalised and murderers allowed to escape the price of their crime on a technicality? A great deal of this was in my mind but of course I could not mention it. One cannot cross-examine one's host even if he is not a governor. The dinner conversation consisted of the usual banalities — the weather, flowers in the garden, tennis, wild life, and some remarks about India from a guest who was a friend of Lord Halifax's. He had just returned from India and had told him that politically India was far more advanced than he had suspected and administratively far less competent than he had hoped. This is going to be the great problem of all self-governing countries — the big gap between theoretical politics, the organisation of parties and the rest of the

democratic superstructure, and the actual administration of a territory on the local authority level. Another thing Lord Halifax had
said was that there was no one to replace Nehru. I said there was
no one to replace Nkrumah in the Gold Coast. There was other talk.
Someone said that sixty-seven per cent of the six hundred elephants
shot in Uganda by the elephant-control people had old bullets
embedded in their flesh. Sir Evelyn, speaking of Jomo Kenyatta,
mentioned his magnetic eyes — they show even in photographs —
and said he was not a pure Kikuyu.

In the morning we were woken by the Lincoln bombers going
over to drop high explosives in the Aberdares where the Mau Mau
were hiding. A very expensive and not very rewarding operation
from what I heard, and had guessed before I heard.

I went to see the police dogs training centre. The dogs were first
class, both in controlled attack and identification. Unfortunately,
identification by a dog is not accepted as evidence in a court of law.
More use could probably be made of dogs in the forest and on guard
posts. The difficulty lies not in the dogs but in finding good handlers
to work them. We heard about the V.C. dog, a bull terrier, who had
caught fifty criminals and been wounded several times.

We obtained an appointment with Mr. L. B. Leakey, the curator
of one of the best small museums I have ever seen, and he told us
some of the beads we had bought in Kumasi dated from about 850
B.C., and showed us specimens similar to them in the museum collection. Mr. Leakey is a well-known archaeologist, and an expert in
Kikuyu law and custom, speaking the language as fluently as he
does English. He acted as one of the interpreters in the Kenyatta
trial and is, on the whole, sympathetic to the African point of view.
We later met his sister-in-law who asked us to go and visit her in
the country. Since then her home has been attacked, she has been
killed and her husband buried alive in a ritual sacrifice. So though
in one way the Mau Mau have done very little, in another that little
touches one at every point.

We also met Dr. Christopher Wilson, another expert who has
been in East Africa since 1911 and who gave me a copy of his new
book, *Kenya Warning.* I already had his other one, *Before the Dawn
in Kenya,* which described East Africa before the white man came
and completely refutes Jomo Kenyatta's *Facing Mount Kenya.*

I saw quite a lot of Hemingway, who had come into the New
Stanley Hotel from Entebbe while we were away. He was in a pretty
poor shape — lucky to be alive, I thought, but able to drink gin and

grenadine and read his obituaries in all languages that had been sent to him by his agent. One of the few men to learn of his own greatness before he died — a kind of preview into the post-Hemingway world when the man became a legend. It gave one an odd feeling which called for more gin and grenadine for all of us. Sid Perelman of *The New Yorker* was here too, and our friendship was really begun and alcoholically cemented by Ernest's bedside in a premature wake in which the body presided as the host.

We dined several times at the Muthiaga Club with Lord Delamere and other friends and while we were sitting there someone came in and said that the caddy master, who had been missing for some days, had been found murdered in a bunker.

I now got the opportunity to go out with the police in the Fort Hall and Thika area where a very distinguished young district officer, Candler by name, had just been ambushed and killed. His head had been cut off. This horrible detail had been kept from his wife but a London newspaper got hold of the news and published it. She was left with two young children.

My rendezvous was at the Blue Posts Hotel at Thika, at 8.00 A.M. I left our hotel at 6.30 in a taxi I had ordered the night before from the Overland Taxi Company who were known to be reliable. It was considered inadvisable to pick up a taxi in the streets of Nairobi since many drivers were gangsters and taxis had been often used in attacks. And when one did use a taxi one told the hotel clerk where one was going before leaving, as a precaution. I carried no weapons except a hippo sjambok that had been given me in the Congo.

The road between Nairobi and Thika was excellent, but as one got further away from the town there was less traffic and the sisal plantations were in a poor state of cultivation, in flower, and very dirty. Outside Thika was a wired-in roadblock held by several turbaned Indian soldiers with a mounted machine gun. The Blue Posts was once a popular country hotel but was now almost deserted because this was one of the worst areas in the country.

While I was having a cup of coffee a very good-looking young police officer came in to look for me. We met the local superintendent — a very soldierly type of Irish police officer who had served in the near and far East. My young friend's jeep flew a blue and white flag captured from the Mau Mau. He carried a Patchett gun with a short fixed bayonet, and had an Askari driver and two armed Askaris in the back seat. We set off in convoy. He took the lead. I came a hundred yards or so behind with the superintendent. I sat in a position of safety between him and the driver. I was told if we were fired at to jump out and take cover. There were two African police-men armed with .303 service rifles behind me. I felt odd going into what might be action unarmed, and a civilian.

The superintendent also had a Patchett gun, a nice little automatic weapon that I had never seen before, at full cock on his knee and never took his eye off the country in front of us. There were beautiful places for an ambush all round us most of the time. In some places we had to almost stop to make hairpin bends round high red banks. A nice bomb could have been dropped into the car quite easily by someone lying above us just extending his hand. Further on in the reserve some men were cutting back the grass and bush from the road to clear it for a distance of about fifty yards. But this was after Candler had been killed. The stable door was being locked when one of the best horses was stolen.

A hundred yards ahead of us was the leading jeep with its little blue and white captured battle flag flying gaily. The bright sunlight sharpened the glittering bayonet on the young officer's weapon.

The country was beautiful hill country with rich, red cultivated lands. There were patches of wattle, little dry rustling mealie fields, isolated native huts and small herds of cattle. And Kikuyu men and women looked at us with hatred as we passed. This was the reserve, enemy country, but the enemy was undeclared, the war was un-declared. It was only an emergency. To kill a man here before he attacked you was murder.

We passed a scene of tragedy where a loyalist post had been overrun and the garrison massacred. The ruined buildings with their charred rafters stood stark against the sky.

We stopped at a police post. It was surrounded by a deep, moatlike trench filled with sharpened stakes. More stakes defended the base of the barbed wire that surrounded the compound in which the garrison and their women and children lived. Inside there were built-up earth ramparts and it resembled the pictures of forts I had seen as a child. The *chevaux de frise*, the barbed-wire entanglements, the watch tower, the sentries patrolling went back to the old Colonial days, to the Foreign Legion.

While we were here we got news over the radio of an action taking place a few miles away. The inspector listened to the news and gave instructions. He turned to me and said: "You're certainly lucky. You might have come out every day for months and not run into anything in daylight."

We moved up to the scene of action. Some police were deployed. I was told the home guard were out. There were a few scattered shots. One bullet passed fairly near us, cracking like a whip in the air. Everything was going according to plan and we went on, continuing our tour.

We were now in the prohibited area, the mile-wide strip surrounding the Aberdares, in which any African could be shot on sight. Before us was an enormous, impenetrable mountain area of great trees, bamboos, forest, deep dongas, caves, ridges and cliffs — much of it primeval and not even explored. The forest bled out in little wooded ridges, in patches of bush. The valleys of this rolling country all ran inwards like the spokes of a wheel to the nave of the forest. As far as I could see, a gang or food party should be able to get through the prohibited zone without too much difficulty. There were strong police posts with watch towers every thousand yards around the perimeter, but I felt that any competent Brownie could have crept by them if she had a little luck. We entered a post. It had a garrison of forty or so, with two white officers and some white, red-beret'd forest fighting troops who went out on patrol at night. I climbed the watch tower and stood by the sentry. He had no field glasses. They had been asked for but had never been issued. I asked if any of the front — for that is what it is — was wired. No wire. Surely, with a million pounds a month being spent the forest could have been wired off? Or if that was too expensive, the bottoms could have been wired off, forcing the gangsters up to the hilltops which could have been cleared. I stood on the tower. I was looking at the stronghold of the hard-core Mau Mau. The few thousand who were making mockery of the might of what had once been an empire. They were entirely dependent on food from the outside, but very little serious effort seemed to have been made to cut their communications. Even roads had not been effectively blocked. The bombing of this immense area with high explosive was an expensive farce. A non-lethal gas, such as tear gas, would probably have been much better. Howitzers firing into the forest would probably have been cheaper, more effective, and much more demoralising since the enemy would never have known when to expect a shot. Area after area could have come under fire, with tremendous psychological effect. Green English lads are useless for this work, particularly if they are fighting with kid gloves. Special commandos with high rates of pay should have been raised to go into the forest and get the Mau Mau in their lairs.

We now returned to the site of the little battle. Twenty men and one girl had been killed and some prisoners taken. They were recruits who had been called up and were being led into the forest by a gang of four hundred Mau Mau who had spread out over the country on a recruiting mission. We went up to the road to where the carrying parties were bringing in the dead. Each body was tied to a narrow stretcher made of bush saplings tied together with strips of bark. As they were brought in they were dumped along the roadside. It had taken some time to collect them, for the running fight had covered quite a lot of territory, most of it broken country with scattered huts, patches of trees and old mealie lands. The wounds were terrible, most of them having been inflicted by home guard shotguns at close range. The dead were all boys of from eighteen to twenty. The girl who was probably a guide, carrier, or prostitute, seemed younger, and there was an older man who must have been in some earlier fight with the loyalists since he had a deep, recent panga wound on his thigh that was beginning to granulate nicely.

I was interested in my own reaction to the bodies. It was thirty years since I had been on a battlefield. I had no feeling at all except some interest in the fact that the clothes of the dead were so good, and that the boys were all in such good condition. These were not starving vagrants driven to revolt by despair. They were boys who, a few days ago, had had jobs in garages, shops and houses. Boys who had been to school.

The home guard were jubilant. There were about a dozen of them grouped here about the dead. They were armed with single barrel shotguns, whose butts were painted red for identification, and pangas; and an older man, wearing a Burberry, carried a bow and arrows. They were dressed in ordinary old clothes but wore pale Cambridge blue ribbons round their hats and left arms. These home guard colours are changed at intervals for security reasons.

It was now that I fully realised that this was a civil war. These were Kikuyu killing Kikuyu. They had to kill or be killed. And the home guard and loyalists numbered only about five per cent of the million who compose the tribe. They live in a state of perpetual danger and though they are gathered into armed posts with their women and children, they are sometimes rushed, the gate always being the weak point.

No weapon of precision had been taken in this little run-in but a bugle was captured. Bugles have great significance among the Mau Mau. They blow them when they attack and they are rallying points like the colours of a regiment. They have been stolen at various times from the army and the police.

The bodies were to be left a while so that they could be seen. A team of fingerprint experts was sent for, and told to hurry before rigor mortis set in. It was a strange scene. The white and black uniformed police, the jeeps, the home guard in ragged civilian clothes ornamented with ribbons, the tumbled, crumpled dead — their blood black on their black skins, their wounds already buzzing with flies. Beside us was the smouldering hut from which some of them had been flushed. There was not a cloud in the sky, its emptiness was broken only by a vulture in hopeful circling flight.

Our next call was on the local district officer, where I met two loyal chiefs — very fine men, who carried their lives in their hands. Both had been attacked at various times and both had killed Mau Mau. One of them, Chief Paulo, spoke very good English and was going to be moved to take on a job as district officer in a few days time. The other, a cheerful fat man who never let go of his shotgun, spoke no English but replied through his friend. What did they think of the oaths? Could a man be cleansed? No, they said. The oaths were unforgettable. What about the negotiations by General China, the gangster leader, through whom the government was trying to persuade the gangsters to surrender? A mistake, they both thought. A sign of weakness. They said the gangsters were too gently handled, and too much time was wasted on legal procedure when they had been caught redhanded. We shook hands and I wished them luck. Men like this are bright spots in Africa. The rare black stars to which we must hitch the wagon of all hope and progress.

I was now taken to see some articles that had been recently taken from the Mau Mau. Homemade rifles, penicillin, a small bag of graphite, an old Mills bomb, pistol and rifle ammunition, an old and useless automatic, several pangas and simis, and two strangling ropes that looked rather like army pull-throughs. This would seem to be an Indian contribution to murder, being the weapon of the Thugs, and un-African. The homemade guns are useless as weapons, consisting of galvanised water-pipe barrel fastened to a wooden stock. The striker is made of an ordinary door bolt fastened to a short piece of heavy elastic, which is tied to a curved spring. It is fired by pulling the elastic and letting it snap back. Such a weapon is probably much more dangerous to the firer than to the target. So the captures of homemade weapons reported in the press can be discounted. They are useless and only serve the purpose of deceit and camouflage; if a gang carrying guns is seen at night no one can tell how many weapons are effective and how many are homemade. In the confusion of an attack the real weapons can be evacuated while the police chase these symbolic ones.

I saw a nice looking, well-dressed Kikuyu girl of twenty or so who had been picked up carrying ammunition, for which there is the death penalty. I got a glimpse of some gangsters in confinement waiting for transfer. They were dangerous, fanatical-looking men, their hair was long, in plaited ringlets, and they wore unkempt beards. On the way home we stopped in to see some prisoners who had been taken that morning. One was slightly wounded in the leg. Their eyes were like stones, they were quite unafraid, they answered no questions. They knew nothing could be done to them, no third degree. I was told that within seventy-two hours the police would get a telegram from an Indian advocate asking on what charge so-and-so, son of so-and-so, was being held. I asked how they found out.

The police said, "That's what we should like to know."

It was interesting to note that on our return journey, the Africans who had been so sullen when we were outward bound were now most respectful and stood on the side of the road with their hands raised in greeting. They had heard about the action. They knew twenty of their people were dead. We were worthy of respect. This is the tragedy of Africa. Respect and fear walk hand in hand.

I was told, as an example of the increased expense the emergency is causing, that this Thika area, before the emergency, was policed by one white man and fourteen native police. It now had seventy white men and five hundred natives, apart from home guards and regular troops, and still was one of the worst areas, with almost daily incidents. There had been sixteen murders and seven ambushes within half a mile of where we stood.

There was not, it appeared, a hundred per cent co-operation from some of the sisal planters and farmers who were doing so well that they did not wish to disturb their labour by the close examination of their lines. But this lack of co-operation was typical of the emergency. The army and police did not get on. The regular police and temporary police did not get on. The settlers were divided. There was no over-all authority, no over-all plan. A million pounds a month was being spent and people who were profiting by it were in no hurry for the end. There were ex-officers who enjoyed being in uniform again, and Kikuyu home guards who were taking this chance to bump off some of their enemies.

Everyone — Police, C.I.D., Intelligence and Public Relations — was most helpful, giving me all the information I wanted. Police atrocity pictures and copies of the oaths and descriptions of the oath-taking ceremonies. These facts were all published as an appendix to the *White Paper* prepared by the members of Parliament who had just visited Kenya, but were withdrawn in England as being too obscene. Too obscene for whom? How are members of the House to know what is going on if they are not allowed to know what is going on? One copy was, I believe, lodged in the House of Commons Library, together with a photograph album prepared by the police of a record of the various incidents. Till these matters, obscene or not, are made public there can be no understanding of what is going on in Africa, or of the African in his present stage of development. Some people imagine that Jomo went wrong because he was disappointed in the way he was received on his return. But his actions were always subversive. And his claim to being a civilised man is scarcely upheld by his organisation of the Mau Mau. No one has done more to set back the cause of the African or to discredit the claim of the educated African to civilisation than Kenyatta. When I pointed this out at a Rotarian lunch at which I was the guest, I caused something of a sensation. I said everyone should read the oaths, including the wives of the Rotarians. I have always assumed women to be human beings and capable of facing facts. Facts that have caused the deaths of some of them. I also said they were unduly optimistic about the emergency being under control or nearly over and now, a year later as I write, Michael Blundell acknowledges that things are very little better and that it will be years before the affair is concluded. Years I consider an understatement. Generations is nearer to it. Mau Mau has gone into history. The oath has been taken by women for their unborn children. Gangs have been found committing murders, whose oldest member was only fourteen. The police have found older men instructing children in the use of the panga on a human body. Children are engaged in espionage, running ammunition, food and medical supplies to the gangsters. In addition, the Mau Mau have had certain successes. They have not been beaten in spite of the forces deployed against them. Since the rebellion began they have gained increased representation in legislature and wages have gone up ten shillings a month. General China, a notorious murderer, has been given his life and allowed to treat with his brother gangster generals. The police have been censured for corruption and the ill-treatment of Mau Mau prisoners. One British officer has been condemned to five years' imprisonment for acts of brutality in action. There is no doubt of his technical guilt, but to the Mau Mau this is a victory. They can be as brutal as they like but the white man cannot retaliate. Considering the atrocities they have witnessed, the forces of the Crown and the settlers have shown remarkable moderation. The government has forcibly evacuated several white men from their farms, a notable triumph for the Mau Mau, attributed to the ritual murder of Mr. Leakey since the order immediately followed the atrocity. And now, the greatest triumph of all — since it is an acknowledgment of impotence — amnesty to any murderer who surrenders coming in with one of the leaflets dropped into the forest by the planes that once attacked him. The good treatment given to the detained Mau Mau and their dependents, in terms of food, housing and services, are all regarded by the Mau Mau adherents as signs of British weakness, and completely misunderstood by the loyalists who have seen their women and children butchered by these gangsters who, when captured, are given every legal facility and allowed to profit by every technical loophole.

There are certain parallels between the situation and the techniques used in the Spanish civil war and what is happening in Kenya today. The Spanish civil war jeopardised the free world's Mediterranean bases. The Kikuyu civil war and rebellion, which are part of the general African unrest, jeopardise African bases and sources of raw material which would be vital if a war with the Far East should ever develop. Everywhere on the continent disorder is being deliberately created and the law challenged. If the police and military fail to establish order their power is lost. If the rebels negotiate they have won a victory. They cease to be rebels and eventually take over. This is what happened on the West Coast. This is the game that is being played on the East, with the Mau Mau as deluded pawns in a much bigger scheme.

If, on the other hand, the military put down the rebellion a storm of propaganda is let loose by their agents and accomplices all over the world. The police and troops are accused of every possible atrocity. The rebels become martyrs struggling for freedom against a tyrant. The government is represented as holding its power by force alone, in spite of the fact that the whole agitation comes from a mere handful of self-seeking rabble rousers who in no way represent the mass of the people. This pattern is consistent everywhere in Africa. And only the most naïve can fail to see in it the hand of those who want world revolution, but who realise that its prelude must be a state of public disorder, a breakdown of services and utilities, a weakening of the government and such lack of confidence that a single incident is sufficient to cause bloodshed and riot. Africa is ripe for trouble. All the factors are present — thousands of half-educated detribalised Africans in a state of transition, hundreds of educated Africans intent on seizing power, the support of Communists, leftists and liberals all over the world, and above all, nervous and inept governments who are probably more responsible for revolutions than any agitator because of their failure to grasp the nettle of sedition as soon as it shows above ground. A hundred executions three years ago would have saved more than eight thousand African (loyalist and Mau Mau) lives. But of course such brutality cannot be permitted, so women and children continue to be butchered and murderers go free in the name of justice and democracy.

33

The African Giant...Nairobi...Lusaka...
Johannesburg...Cape Town

● THE FLIGHT BACK was uneventful, we came down at Lusaka and spent a few days in Johannesburg, and then caught the Blue Train back to Cape Town. Nothing remained but to try to put in as few words as possible some generalisations about a hundred-odd million people. There appeared to be some which were quite uncontroversial. Such as the development of Africa being dependent primarily on the white man, and secondly on the social development and education of the African woman as well as the man. This, when by and large the educated African was trying to get rid of the white man, the women were resisting education, and the men wanting it for the wrong reason.

The bright spots were the few really civilised Africans, both men and women, whom I had met, and the resistance to Mau Mau by those Kikuyu who preferred death to joining such a society, and the attitude of the Moslems in Northern Nigeria who did not demand freedom at once, knowing it would mean anarchy.

But something had gone wrong in the white approach. Few educated Africans were prepared to work with their hands, few understood anything about the spiritual aspects of civilisation and saw only its material advantages. Many used their knowledge to defraud their simpler compatriots, most were purely tribal in outlook and hated all other Africans. The Belgians put it best when they talked about a lack of professional conscience, of doing a job well for its own sake, among the Africans.

The African giant was said to be throwing off his chains. He was flexing his muscles. There was talk of a Pan-African movement, of Africa for the Africans. There were powerful influences at work, catalyzers which crystallized every passion; sticks stirring a continent so that its millions ran like ants about a broken nest. And the nest of African habit and custom had been disturbed, the pattern of ten thousand years shattered in this period of transition.

I searched but could find no giant. He was big alright. A hundred millions big, but each part was against every other part. His hands were at his own throat, his feet tripped each other up whenever he took a step, his internal organs were out of order, his brain deranged, fevered by a dream. His ears could not understand the thousand languages of his tongue. But his blood pounded in his veins as the tom-toms throbbed, the adrenalin loosed into its stream envenomed him. Hatred enveloped him like a cloak. Hatred of the white man who had betrayed him, who had led him like a bride to the door of a church called civilisation, and then abandoned him. He was having difficulty in going forward so he wanted to go back into the security of the ancient tribal womb where everything was unchanging and changeless, where time flowed past him like a river, where thought was unnecessary because there were precedents and rules for every event. Kenya was the place where the poison in his blood had come to a head and burst like a boil. But all over Africa there was sympathy for the Mau Mau. Most Africans wanted them to win because they did not know what Mau Mau was, did not realise that they had slashed and tortured to death almost two thousand of their Kikuyu brothers. But one does not read of this in the African press.

Africa is a three-ring circus where Nkrumah, the Black Leopard of the West, restlessly paces his dark forest, where Kenyatta, the Hyena of the East, is caged, and Strydom stands at bay in the South, like an Afrikander Bull with lowered horns pawing the dusty veld about his belly. All Africa lies within this ideological triangle, all Africa is dominated by these men, and the principles they represent. In the middle lies the Belgian Congo whose top spins so fast under the whip of progress that its future is a blur. And Huggins' Rhodesia, which seems almost stable. On the periphery are the Portuguese colonies of the East and West where progress, moving at a more leisurely pace, has not yet muddied the waters of racial understanding.

But everywhere there is a feeling of unease, of tension. There are no simple solutions but there are facts, trends and questions. There are generalisations and common denominators. One can generalise about the Africans as one can about Americans. Americans are efficient, progressive, they like football games, baseball, ice cream, chicken, films, television, they have a high divorce rate, they carry heavy life insurance, they buy things on time, they have more motor-cars per head than any other people. These are generalisations . . .

A generalisation consists of a series of particularisations fused by a single mind into a kind of composite whole. Perhaps the thing that surprised me most was that the generalisations about Africans made by the British, American, Belgian and French people whom I met resembled each other so closely that they might have come from a single man. They were drawn from all classes. From governor-generals to district officers, from archbishops to missionaries, from the managing directors of great companies to isolated planters.

They had asked me what I was doing. I had replied that I was getting material for a book about Africa. One governor had said: "Write the truth. No one has done it yet." I said: "Why not?" He said: "Who could? No government official can because his files are secret. No company servant can because it would get him into trouble and might endanger his pension. No missionary because he is unwilling to acknowledge that he may have wasted his life. No settler, because his experience is too limited and localised."

What is the truth? Have I told it? I have described what I saw and heard. What I felt — which was a profound sadness. The overall picture seemed dark, like a night sky illuminated here and there by stars of faith, honour and incorruptibility. I met Africans I should be proud to call my friends. I met others, highly educated men, who were pretentious fools. I moved for months in a world of paradox — of devotion and corruption, of beauty and horror. I saw unbelievable slums in Lagos, Accra and Ibadan. All African-owned and African-administered. I saw splendid buildings, universities and assembly halls. I saw tattooed savages and black university graduates in this incredible transitional turmoil. The young men are stuffed full of education and rarin' to go. Go where? Only to the top.

I got a picture but it was not the picture I wanted. I had hoped, when the African was on his own, when nothing held him back, he would be capable of great things. I ignored Liberia, Haiti, Abyssinia. Things must be better now. These people had had a better chance. But I found that often the better the chance the greater the resentment. I had thought that the white man was the black man's problem. I was wrong. The African's problem is to get on without him.

I had received a shock at the high percentage of literates, and more than literates, in Port Harcourt jail. In the Congo I had seen pregnant evolved African women who were suffering from morning sickness, and been told of a man who had committed suicide because his wife had been unfaithful to him. Something new in African custom. From all the evidence it would appear that the African psyche is taking on a new pattern and that these people are going to be plagued by the white man's psychoses without his background, heredity or possibility of rationalisation.

We have in Africa something unprecedented in the history of the world — the most advanced technical processes co-existing with the most primitive practices. We have black races which hate each other and whose only common bond is their dislike of the white man. If the white problem was solved they would turn upon each other.

In West and Central Africa the white man owns no land and cannot settle. The few thousand farmers of the Congo Highlands scarcely count in this immense black sea. Only Kenya, Rhodesia and South Africa are affected by the problem of permanent white settlement, and the only hope for these countries is some kind of symbiotic association, more or less satisfactory to all races, evolved slowly, by trial and error. Any idea of holding the African down permanently is absurd. Equally absurd is the idea of a general African franchise which would destroy the whites. The ratio of white to non-white is 1 to 4 in South Africa, 1 to 12 in Southern Rhodesia, 1 to 100 in Portuguese East Africa, 1 to 170 in Kenya, and 1 to 200 in the Congo.

Officials in the Gold Coast see education for adults (male and female) as well as children, essential if the Gold Coast is to be saved from ultimate dictatorship and chaos. The transition is actually a race between the educators and the demagogues. That is to say, the Gold Coast can be saved from a dictatorship only if an informed public opinion can be developed. So far, so good. Nkrumah in partnership with Sir Charles Arden-Clarke has succeeded. Both are exceptional men with exceptional qualities. But suppose Nkrumah were to die, or to be overthrown. And the Gold Coast is the pattern, or one of the patterns, of the African future.

Developed Africa is modern, as modern as America, and it is impossible to imagine the state of New York being administered by Harlem, though the American Negro is vastly superior to and more sophisticated than his African cousin.

Then there is the question of the Asiatic, the Indian who, however much one may like individuals, is a poor citizen, evading his public duties while he demands his civic rights. In Kenya the response of the Indian to the rebellion has been very bad; and the amount of income tax paid by them is minuscule when their numbers and wealth are considered. They are a people with dual allegiance who send their money out of the country and stand in the way of African progress by occupying the middle rungs of the ladder which he must climb. There is some reason to believe that Indian Communists are behind much of the racial trouble in Africa. And certainly the Indian press and the pronouncements of Pandit Nehru encourage Africans in their belief that immediate autonomy is both practical and possible.

In general the black man is not being exploited. His wages, when related to his output, are very high. Everywhere, even in South Africa, the white man's aim is to better the African's conditions and help him to raise himself. It is obvious to most Europeans living in Africa that all races must live together and progress together. If the African, instead of complaining about the colour bar, began to work hard, educate himself and do a good job, it would be impossible for anyone to hold him back. But there is little evidence of this at present. The principle of socio-economics has not yet been grasped by the African, who prefers his dream of such alibis as colour and discrimination to the work that would eventually disprove them. Even today, everywhere, the rewards are there, the positions for Africans available. All that is missing are the Africans who are ready to make the sacrifices which have to be made by anyone, whatever their colour, to achieve success.

What is the African to do? Co-operate with the white man and accept a Western standard of culture? Revolt against it? Or relapse into apathy? Will he compromise to get the white capital and white technicians he must have to develop his country? What happens to his personality when he must copy the customs and the manners of people whom he hates? Can he be at one and the same time a civilised urban man and a native leading his traditional life in a kraal? These are the problems which up to the present he has failed to understand. He blames the white man for his failures, and gives him no credit or thanks for his successes. His aim is to get as much as possible for as little as possible. He believes in honesty for others. He does not know, or refuses to believe in the horrors which existed in Africa before the white man came This should have been taught to him in the schools but it has not been done. If he is any good at all he is told he is wonderful. And in his own framework, in the context of Africa, he is, but very few Africans could compete on an equal basis with white men in Europe or America.

Is the African capable of directing his own affairs if he is given time to assimilate the incredibly rich cake of a technological civilisation?

I saw African typists, laboratory workers; Africans handling cranes and heavy machinery, working in machine shops — it seemed to me they were capable of doing almost any job provided they had some white direction and assistance. But they were also, I felt, incapable of doing any job for long without it, particularly when it came to management, direction or finance. The remarkable thing was how much, not how little, they could do, what marvels they had achieved in so short a time. But they do not see it this way. They know so much more than they did that they think they know it all, and are not ready to wait and learn the rest.

But let us have no illusions. The black man hates the white. Above all he hates him for being white, because this is something he can never be. Then he hates him for his deception, for making him think that the only difference between a savage and a civilised human being was a university degree. I believe that there are more white men ready to compromise and meet black men on an equal basis than there are Africans ready to meet white men. One reason being that no African political leader can get anywhere except on an anti-white platform and no black man is trusted by his people if he is friendly to white men. It is easy to see the African's point of view. His life has been disturbed. Like an ant carrying its eggs to safety he has tried to rescue its essentials, and then, distracted by some new bauble, dropped them to chase a glittering shadow. He sees the white man's things. His houses, his cars, radios, refrigerators and wireless sets, his clothes and comfort — and wants them. He has no idea how the white man got them. What technical skill and organisation lie behind them, or what the white man has given up to attain them.

The two facts that stand out are colour and education. These are the differences between the haves and the have-nots, as he sees it. Colour he cannot change; but he can learn. This is the white man's secret which he is fool enough to teach the African, provided he gives lip service to Christianity and democracy.

He has worked hard. He has shown that he is as well educated as the white man. He has insisted on passing the same examinations, getting the same degrees, just to prove this, and then found that there is something still missing. What is the gimmick, the trick, the secret ingredient? Education had seemed to him to be a kind of fetish. A diploma, something one held in one's hand, which made everything go well. The sweat of learning was like the years spent in the Poro Bush under the witch doctors, which qualified a young man for full tribal manhood. The diploma was a talisman, like those his parents had bought from the ju-ju man to keep him safe from evil spirits when he was a child, and it had failed him. Why had it failed? Because he had regarded it as an end, not as a tool with which to carve out a career. He had spent years making the chisel and now was confronted by the block of wood that he must carve. Academic education is not civilisation. It gives the knowledge but not the drive. It does not supply the devil that sits on every white man's shoulder. Nor that most vital thing — the white man's concept of *TIME*.

The African is one with time. For him it is not subdivided into days, hours, minutes, seconds. He is not continually looking forward to this or that event. To a raise in salary, to the next holiday, the new fur coat or motorcar. He is not continually regretting the past, the opportunity that was not taken. He lives in the present, in the *now* which escapes all white men except the peasants who live close to the soil. The white man exists in the present only when he is playing games, hunting, fishing or watching a spectacle — only then is there no future, no past, only then is he submerged in the present. And these interests are the vestigial remains of his ancient barbarian pursuits, of war, of hunting, of watching the tribal dances and participating in tribal ceremonies.

The minds of men are mainly the products of their cultures, so that studies of cultures become in effect studies of psychology. And until the African's early life and background can be changed he will remain unaltered. How this can be changed is a problem few men, black or white, are prepared to face. To understand him at all, this background must be taken into account. His animistic explanations of phenomena are so final that he has no urge to speculate. He accepts and fears. His world is largely malevolent. Evil forces surround him and must be placated. The good things that happen are disregarded and forgotten, the bad remembered. But nothing is ever his own fault. All misfortune is the result of outside forces, of witchcraft, of the evil eye.

He is unable to sustain anxiety for long. It must at once be allayed by some ritual process. If this is impossible he often reacts with hysterical violence. He has no clear distinction between thought and behaviour patterns. In some languages to think, to hope, and to wish, are all expressed by one word. He sees himself as a cog in the great tribal wheel. He cannot see himself as an individual — alone. Moral, courteous and well-behaved in his own tribe, conditioned by fear to its laws and taboos, he is without consideration for the outsider. As far as he is concerned the alien has no rights. He is the most communalistic of men within his tribe, and the most individualistic away from it. Detribalised, he is a lone wolf owing no allegiance, acknowledging no sanctions. Because he is unable to criticise himself, he has incredible self-confidence. The intellectual African believes that he has nothing more to learn, and is, for instance, ready to accept a ministerial post. If things go well, he believes himself omnipotent, if the bubble of his self-confidence is pricked, he dissolves into impotence. He has been overcome by some greater force. He seeks an outside reason. Today he blames the white man.

The African child plays with no blocks or Meccano sets. He sees no reason why a square peg cannot be fitted into a round hole, or why a clockwork motorcar should not be impelled by spirits. He has a curious capacity for disassociation, for living two lives alternately, or even simultaneously. All Africans expose one face to white men or their educated compatriots, and another to the village.

Western civilisation has been imposed upon a tribal background which has been unchanged for a thousand years, which had rules of conduct for every event, rituals to cover every disaster. The European is accustomed to change. But change breaks up the system of tribe and clan, divides men by the measure of their acceptance of change, education and civilisation. Divides them even more utterly from their own women.

The African woman is against Westernisation. She dislikes innovations, especially those which take her man away from her and cause him to live a life of dissipation and disgrace. Change that teaches him to think more of his wife than of his mother and sisters, which she considers absurd, and makes him, when he returns, look down on his relatives and call them polygamists and kaffirs. As for the girls who go to town — they all go wrong, and are ruined, refusing to work in the fields or respect the tribal law.

She has some justification for her beliefs. Transition often tends to ruin the African as much morally as it benefits him materially, by crushing out his native culture and reducing him to the lowest level of white civilisation.

Love with the African is not a matter of sex as it is with the Western man. His strongest link is with his mother, his eldest sister, who probably carried him when he was a child, and other men of his age group, with whom he is tied by the rites of circumcision. With a woman the ties are with her mother, her elder brother, her children, and the other women of her own age.

The frenzies of sex which so revolted the early missionaries should not be confused with the orgies of the Romans. They are above all religious, dedicated to fertility and not to licentious pleasure.

There can be no analysis of the African character, but there are certain common denominators that are true of almost all tribes. The past is much nearer to him than the future. His unconscious is much nearer

to the surface. His dreams are more real, his desires more ephemeral
— whims assume unbelievable urgency, and long-range plans are forgotten before they are half accomplished. Without much sense of
the future, which is synonymous with hope, he is most susceptible to
fear. Fear of enemies, of gods, of devils, of spells and witchcraft. To
cure this his environment must be changed by the education of the
woman who brings up and forms the next generation. But the woman
wants no change, and the man feels that if the woman is educated she
will no longer work in the fields, and if he wants to eat he will have
to work himself — a very strong incentive to bar female education.

In the mind of the African there exists a curious area where propa-
gation — the fertility of man, beast and field — is mixed up with the
blood of sacrifice, ritual murder, cannibalism, and the gods and the
spirits of his ancestors, any of which, unless propitiated, will destroy
him. The fields, by not bearing crops, the women by leaving him
childless, the gods by sending misfortune upon him, and his ancestors
by haunting him if they do not receive continual gifts. And since
blood is the very source of life, blood is the best offering. That of
white cocks, of black goats and cattle, in sacrifice, but best of all, the
blood of men. To human blood every god of sea or river, of field or
forest, must respond.

It is this concept, this atavistic belief (and the African is probably
in a state of psychological atavism) which causes ritual murders all
over the continent. Christianity is nowhere powerful enough to
arrest completely such occurrences, even among its converts.

The Christian African prays. He goes on praying and nothing
happens. He does not exactly abandon the Christian God, but he
decides to supplement Him with other, older, tribal forces. It is in this
way that these old customs bcome grafted onto the Christian religion.
It is a particularly easy transition because the Old Testament, which
naturally has a greater appeal to the African than the New, is filled
with stories of blood and sacrifice.

The African has two excuses for his lack of progress — the colour
bar and his geographic isolation. The colour bar has an aspect that
is seldom understood by the African. It is also a social and economic
bar, and as such exists among all races. Racial, social and economic
classes practise a kind of natural segregation all over the world. Nor
does the African realise that in the West all kinds of manual work
are done by white people who are literate and that there are slums
and hardship in Europe. The African, once he can read and write,
will seldom pick up anything dirtier than a fountain pen or heavier

than a pencil. He is evolved, an intellectual, and therefore free of toil.

There is a story about Albert Schweitzer. He asked an African to help him carry in a piece of wood for the hospital he was building. The man said: "I do not carry wood. I am an intellectual." Schweitzer replied: "How lucky you are. I had always hoped to become one."

If the African is slighted in any way he thinks it is because he is black. Not because he is drunk, or a fool, or making a nuisance of himself. The white man is supposed to love every black man. The African cannot see that not every white man loves all other white men. Or that he himself is utterly contemptuous of other Africans who are less well educated than he is.

The isolation excuse is also overemphasised. The West Coast has been in touch with Europe for four hundred years. The North has been in touch with Europe and the Levant through the great caravan routes across the Sahara for a thousand years. In the East there has been a trade with Arabia, Persia, India and China for two thousand years or more, and what civilisation did they acquire?

The African has domesticated no animals, has developed no agricultural crops. Every beast he possesses, every vegetable he eats, except for the fruits of the indigenous West African oil palm, has come from Asia or Arabia on the east, or the Americas on the west.

Why, in so vast a continent, are there no records? No monuments? There are the bronze heads of Ife, the terra cottas of the Nigerian Plateau, the great ruins of Zimbabwe, but they exist in a vacuum without even a myth or folk tale to explain them. There was a civilisation in Benin of a high order. In the fifteenth century the Portuguese had a mission there. Benin was Christian. What was left of its Christianity when it was taken in 1897? Slaves found crucified. Of all they had learnt, only this form of torture remained. There are stories of great empires. There are works of art that can have been produced only by such states. But everything is lost — has been forgotten. Conquerors have come and gone. Africa has swallowed them.

There is even a theory that Africa, far from being on the upgrade, is a continent where deterioration has already set in. But we know nothing. In Africa there are only theories, only ideas, only speculations.

The Roman Catholic missions are the most reliable, seem to be doing the best job. Their missionaries are more realistic, give more, expect less, and concentrate much attention on manual training. The Roman Catholic Church is the one by which our ancestors were reclaimed from barbarism. The holy figures of Our Lord, of the Virgin Mary, and the Saints fill the blank in the African mind which would have been filled by their own idols and make the transition easier. The distinctive raiments of the priests replace the terrifying masks and garments of their witch doctors.

I found that when I got into territory which had been German the old men who remembered them regretted their going. They were hard but just, and above all, they were quick. The African likes quick justice. He wants things done with so that he can forget about them. I had been wrong again. My concept of justice is British. That it is better for ten to go free than for one innocent man to suffer. The African does not think this way. If an innocent man suffers for a crime it simply means that he has been bewitched, or has an inferior talisman, one which he got cheap from a poor witch doctor. He does not believe in sworn evidence. The Bible on which he swears is, to him, just a white man's ju-ju. He would not lie if one of his own sacred objects was brought in, but that is against our law.

Most Africans, regrettably enough in their present state of development, understand only force. His passion for education is his belief that this is the strongest force of all. If force is not used it is due to weakness, not to mercy. Nor has he gratitude in the sense that we know it. There can be no gratitude without altruism, and this concept is completely foreign to the African.

Nor does cruelty mean anything to him. His tortures were unbelievable — impalement on sharp stakes and amputations were everyday occurrences before the white man came to stop them. And these people, with these memories, are expected to become democrats overnight.

Another factor that has been almost completely ignored is that, in my opinion, the African is bored to death. His more erotic dances have been checked, his sacrificial orgies, his wars, and his raids have become crimes. Singing hymns will not make up for them. Mother Hubbards and khaki pants will not replace his barbaric finery. Human life to him has no great value, particularly the life of a stranger. Kill a stranger and you have a nice trophy, a conversation piece in the head, and a body which, according to those who have eaten human flesh, is the best kind of meat.

The ritual murders of Basutoland are not decreasing. On the contrary, the pressure of transition is so great that stronger and stronger medicine horns are needed to combat it. Strong medicine needs human blood and fat. Human brains and blood, mixed with earth and excrement, are eaten when some Mau Mau oaths are taken. Other ceremonies include copulating with a menstruating prostitute and a sheep. Again, the men who do this are literate, well dressed, able to communicate with each other by letter and telephone. Men who can repair precision arms, use cameras, drive cars, who can, in fact, perform all the acts of civilised men. These oaths were designed by Jomo Kenyatta, who took ancient Kikuyu rituals and blended them with the Black Mass whose details were available to him when he was a student in England. Mau Mau is a religion with a hideous parody of the Apostle's Creed, affirming faith in Almighty God with Jomo Kenyatta taking the place of Jesus Christ.

Such things may strike anyone who does not know Africa as unbelievable, but they are true.

What then are the answers? They are simple. Education and religion. But how many white men are educated? How many are Christian? Is not every white boy coming from a Christian home faced with the problem of how to live according to his ethics in a world of competitive business? Most of us effect some kind of compromise. A lot give up their ideals, a few abandon the world and take to a religious life, some break down under the strain. Yet the African, with a much more limited background, is faced with the same problems.

The African has an immense capacity for faith. It is his faith that kills him if he believes he has been bewitched. It is the same faith which makes him face death as a martyr, like the Kikuyus who have died rather than take the Mau Mau oaths.

The danger comes from those Africans who have been to mission schools and left them neither Christian nor educated. They have learnt a little of our religion, enough to make them despise their own pagan gods, but not enough to worship ours. They have had enough schooling to enable them to understand propaganda, but not enough to be able to refute it.

It is possible that, unknowingly, the missionaries with their schools and teaching have done as much to create unrest as the Marxists. The missions ploughed and harrowed the land. The Communists sowed the seed and may reap the crop. The missions wanted boys to read the Bible, to sing hymns, to wear clothes, and never thought further ahead. It did not occur to them that women would prostitute themselves to buy the clothes or that the boys would read red propaganda. It was the missions that broke down the old order by ridicule, by education, by injunction. The missionaries that created new groupings that were out of their tribal context, new collective habits. Every revolutionary leader has been to a mission school. So, of course, have all other leaders, but what can they promise? How can heaven in the distant future compare with freedom now?

It has probably been a great mistake to send Africans to Europe and America to continue their studies. In our great cities they met Communists who infected them with their ideology, negrophilists who flattered them, negrophobes who insulted them. Only the very strongest could escape confusion and further psychological fragmentation, and as though the transition period was not enough to cause unease among the Africans, there are other influences at work fomenting trouble and hoping to profit by it. Educated Africans who want the jobs the white men have but which they are at present incapable of filling. Indians who would like to step into the vacuum left by the white man in trade and finance. Anti-colonial interests in UNO, in the United States, in the Church, and the British Labour Party, all of which, though they may mean well, are unaware of the chaos that would ensue were their hopes fulfilled. And finally there are the trained Communist agitators — white, African and Indian — whose aim is to create trouble in Africa, because Africa is of primary importance as a base, and a source of supply in the event of another war. There is evidence of Africans travelling to the USSR via Addis Ababa. Communists come down the West Coast from British and French Territories. They slip across the Sudan border into the Congo, they infiltrate up the river and its tributaries from Matadi. They come down the East Coast in dhows or into the northern territories with Somali traders.

The Communist game, in a big but very quiet way, is being played in Africa, and is being assisted by liberal anti-Colonial elements which open a propaganda wedge for their ideology by their support of every so-called freedom movement. There is little actual communism yet, only unrest which may lead to the chaos which precedes communism.

Can anyone imagine that if the white man was driven out of Africa it would remain a political vacuum? Do they think the millions of the Far East will not pour in, that technicians from behind the Iron Curtain will not replace those who have left? The future of Africa must be bound to the West if it is not to pass into the hands of the Communist East.

Here is the picture as I see it. The short-term progress of Africa, and the African, depends on white leadership, administration and tuition. Given this, the African is capable of varying degrees of self-government, as the Gold Coast, the pilot plant of self-government may prove. But in the long run Africa's future is entirely dependent on the education of its women. It is the women who hold the future of the continent in their pink henna'd palms. Without a civilised hearth, a *foyer* as the Belgians say, there can be no civilisation.

Corruption must be checked. Isolated kraals reorganised into villages. Witchcraft replaced by Christianity. Education rationalised. The land redistributed into economic units and a system of agriculture, suited to the country, developed. But there is no single solution in Africa. The continent is still in flux. The white man is the first stabilising influence it has ever felt and, at the moment, it resists stabilisation. How is it possible to legislate for countries which contain both highly industrialised modern cities and forest-dwelling pygmies; or for tribes, some of whose members are so advanced that they hold European and American degrees, while others lead the lives of savages, naked, in a Stone Age culture? A country where vast tracts are still covered by unexplored forests, or abandoned to the wild beasts that have inhabited them since the beginning of time?

It is difficult to believe that the opinions of so many men, of so many different types, who have spent their lives in Africa, should all be wrong, or that their critics, most of whom do not know Africa, should all be right. The answer is not immediate freedom, which could mean black tyranny and tribal wars. It is in improved agriculture, villagisation and the redistribution of land. The establishment of settled urban native householders. The creation of an African middle class. The establishment of industries and co-operatives. The educational emphasis to be put on production and efficiency rather than on academic honours. The training of women to be housewives. The encouragement of monogamy and contraception in the urban areas. Adult education by means of films. The development of savings accounts as a basis for the establishment of small businesses. Assistance in such social amenities as dramatic societies, libraries, bands, dance groups, sports of all kinds. Shows of everything — handicrafts, babies, agriculture, again with the emphasis on Africa. The development of African culture by the use of Western techniques. Even religion must be reconsidered. Even the possibility of reconciling polygamy with Christianity.

Nothing is simpler than to suggest these programmes. In principle everyone concerned agrees with most of them. In practice the powers which direct such affairs from a distance of several thousand miles would agree to none of them. They are too simple. They have, in addition, the defect of having been thought up by men on the spot and not by the experts at home.

The scientific investigations into racial differences have shown that the white races on the whole are superior to the black, but that this is probably due to better environment. But till this is rectified, white superiority must continue.

Human beings are born into two worlds. One — of things, events and phenomena, governed by principles of physical causation; and one — of human relationships, governed by cultural and ethical principles which are local and arbitrary. It is this first world that the African fails to appreciate. To him it is a magic world in which he can live in the womb of his tribe. He never has to clear his mind of its ambivalence, or think on personal lines. Never to pinpoint his ego on the map of fact. Where there is no choice there is no conflict. And now, suddenly, he finds himself in an Aladdin's cave of material and intellectual riches. He does not know what he wants — everything, nothing, something.

A civil servant on the West Coast told me that it was not in intelligence that the Africans were inferior to us, but in moral and social qualities, in political and financial integrity. They are afraid to be unpopular. They place too much value on the esteem of their countrymen and too little on principles.

But there can be no status quo. Africa cannot stand still. It must go forward or regress. And in the minds of some Africans there remains the possibility that a life bounded by tradition, in which every man, woman and child plays a well-known part, is the best. That perhaps the African is nearer to the earth and the ultimate truths which the modern Western man refuses to accept, and that the African is happier in his strange no-man's land, "'twixt sleep and wakening where fact and fancy meet," than the white man.

It seems certain that the African cannot make a success within the Western framework without applying the Western concept of time. But are we absolutely convinced of the success of our own experiment? Our science whose ultimate achievement seems to be bombs of greater destructive powers? Of populations which appear to suffer from increasing neuroses? Of publishers who find endless sales for books explaining how a man should make love to his wife?

There is no doubt that ritual murder continues in Africa, that there are still slaves.

But how many of us are free? And how many hundreds of thousands of lives do we sacrifice to the god of speed on the highways of our land? One more world war and our complex civilisation may go down and the African, nearer to the earth in his plains and forests, may survive.

The danger to the African is that he falls between two stools. That he loses his past without gaining the future. That, grasping the glittering bauble of materialism, he loses his greatest talent — that of living, of survival. His resistance to the white man may be due to an instinctive knowledge that he is being led astray.

I have tried to paint a picture of the Africa that lies beneath the decoration of civilisation which has been thrown over it like a cloak. I have seen no reason to go into the details of administration, of imports and exports, that can be found in every Blue Book and Government Report. My story is of the things that I have seen and been told. Everywhere, across the continent from the Atlantic to the Indian Ocean, across vast territories administered by the British, the French and the Belgians, through the free Republic of Liberia, from the glaring desert fringe to the dark forests, the story was the same, the picture the same, the voices the same. Monotonous disillusion varied only by a spiritual optimism whose basis was faith, the fetish of white fingers crossed in hope.

This is Africa today, the continent on which hundreds of millions have been spent and are invested, where thousands of lives have been lost in exploration, war, development and research; where a vast superstructure has been built upon the flimsy foundation of what may only be a wish-fulfilment dream. A great deal, an unimaginable amount has been done for the African. But how much of it does he want?

APPENDIX
AND
INDEX

Appendix — Tribal Oaths of Mau Mau

● Much has been written from time to time about the significance of Tribal Oaths. There are some seventy in number. They play a large part in the life of the Kikuyu, still held, as he is, in the grip of pagan superstition and ideologies. The originators of the Mau Mau movement chose the more powerful features of these many oaths to ensure that the Mau Mau version would be supremely powerful — as it has since proved to be, despite the fact that in *three* ways it transgresses Kikuyu custom, which prohibits the administering of oaths by night, by force and to women.

The original aim of Mau Mau, as expressed in the words of the oath, was secretly to unite, discipline and foster political consciousness among the Kikuyu, with the ultimate object of satisfying the political aspirations of its leaders (Jomo Kenyatta and his followers), if necessary by force. The original oath was:

(a) If I ever reveal the secrets of the organisation, may this oath kill me.

(b) If I ever sell or dispose of any Kikuyu land to a foreigner, may this oath kill me.

(c) If I ever fail to follow our great leader, Jomo Kenyatta, may this oath kill me.

(d) If I ever inform against any member of this organisation or against any member who steals from the European, may this oath kill me.

(e) If I ever fail to pay the fees of this organisation, may this oath kill me.

As the Mau Mau campaign gained strength and the advocates of violence came to the fore, the terms of the original oath were amended to include, *inter alia*, the following new clauses:

(a) If I am sent to bring in the head of an enemy and I fail to do so, may this oath kill me.

(b) If I fail to steal anything I can from the European, may this oath kill me.

(c) If I know of any enemy to our organisation and I fail to report him to my leader, may this oath kill me.

(d) If I ever receive any money from a European as a bribe for information, may this oath kill me.

(e) If I am ever sent by a leader to do something big for the House of Kikuyu, and I refuse, may this oath kill me.

(f) If I refuse to help in driving the Europeans from this Country, may this oath kill me.

(g) If I worship any leader but Jomo, may this oath kill me.

With the introduction of these new terms there came an increase in acts of violence by Mau Mau.

The oath so described is the general, or third-grade oath from which no Kikuyu, man, woman or young person, is exempt, and which may be taken again and again by the same person. Its effect has been to create a mass of violent-minded, often bewildered people, chained by superstition and fear to the commands of their unscrupulous leaders. In the early days the ritual was primitive but not bestial, its symbolism alone being sufficiently powerful to bind the initiates to the terms of the ghastly oath. In more recent times bestial practices and numerous stages of ceremonial have embellished the ritual in certain areas, particularly Meru.

With the launching of the violent campaign came the need for leaders of *gangs*, committees and other Mau Mau organisations. To them was administered a stronger, or second-grade oath in the following terms:

(a) If I fail to lead the children of Mumbi in proper manner, may I die.

(b) If I fail to support the Independent School Movement, may I die.

(c) If I betray the leaders of the Kenya African Movement, may I die.

(d) If I fail to support this organisation until the day of independence, may I die.

(e) I must sacrifice my blood and the blood of Kikuyu for freedom.

There is a third, or first-grade oath taken only by political agitators; the terms are political and vary from time to time to accord with circumstances. It is significant that no instances have come to light of its being administered since the declaration of the state of emergency when the principal political agitators were arrested and detained on account of their complicity in the Mau Mau Movement.

Apart from these three basic oaths, two new versions have been devised to meet the needs of the Terrorist campaign. (1) called *githaka* or Forest Oath is administered by Forest Gang leaders to followers, (2) *Batuni* or Platoon Oath, the most recent innovation, is gradually being administered to all Mau Mau soldiers and recruits. By taking this oath a man becomes a full-blooded Terrorist. The following are some of the common terms of this *Batuni* oath:

(a) To burn European crops and kill European cattle.
(b) to steal Firearms.
(c) if ordered to kill — to do so; no matter who is to be the victim, even one's father or brother.
(d) when killing — to cut off the head and extract the eyeballs and drink the liquid from them.
(e) particularly to kill Europeans.

It will be seen from the foregoing that the terms of the Mau Mau oaths have become increasingly more violent and bloodthirsty, envisaging even the killing of father by son and brother by brother. It is not surprising therefore that with this increased emphasis on brutality and murder an increase in bestiality has invaded the ritual thus forcing the initiates to reach the necessary pitch of bloodlust and degradation. This all leads to driving the Kikuyu to become primitive beasts who will ultimately massacre all Europeans in Kenya. That this object is being attained is obvious from some of the things the Terrorists have already done; i.e., Lari massacres, decapitation and mutilation of all victims, torture before murder, drinking of human blood. (Ex-Chief Luka's child was cut in half, its blood drunk, the two halves flung at the mother, who was then killed.) Pregnant women split open along the stomach. Victims held down and heads slowly sawn off with pangas. Maiming of cattle in every sort of horrible way. Ear cropping their own people who refuse to take oaths for future identification.

During the last few years the young children have been indoctrinated with a hatred of Europeans and a fanatical admiration of Jomo Kenyatta. This had been done through the Kikuyu Independent Schools (Government sponsored). These young men are the backbone of the Mau Mau. They owe no allegiance to either Christian or pagan ethics and care nothing for tribal law. That is our problem now — how to lead them back to sanity and prevent them from contaminating other tribes.

Index

Date Due

FE 12 '60		
MR 28 '60		
JUL 12 1962		
	PRINTED IN U. S. A.	

ED ON